the
seed
hunter

The Beginning of Life

Mark De'Lisser
author of *Ashes to the Breeze* (Cogito Publishing, 2025)

Everything it could ever possibly be,
abundant potentiality,
is already held safely within the seed.

A knowledge beyond knowing,
life sleeps the soundest sleep,
patiently waiting until the conditions are right for growing.

Dreaming of the day it is sown,
and with faith we wait for the seed to wake and grow.

Showering the soil with whispered prayers,
wondering what's happening below.

The seed is sacred.
The beginning of life,
a gift from the Earth offered back to the Earth,
and so continues the cyclical dance of death and rebirth.

The seed sings the song of creation,
ancestral wisdom passed down from generation to generation,
our most precious heirloom.
A wish for the future,
a promise from the past.

The seed is sacred.
It must travel through the dark to get to the light.
It must first struggle,
it must fight,
ever knowing that freedom awaits on the other side.

The seed is sacred.
We must treat it so.
Plant your intention,
watch it grow.

MITCH McCULLOCH

Discover the world's most
unusual heirloom plants

the
seed
hunter

contents

Part 2. Plant Guide

the rare &
the unusual

Humans have a tendency to collect things. As a child I collected football stickers and Pokémon cards, and later, when I started working as a chef, I began acquiring exciting and unusual recipes that I could try out on anyone who was willing to eat my food. Now I track down rare and unusual fruit and vegetable seeds to grow in my garden. These crops are so fascinating that I want to share some of my discoveries with the world.

I was a chef in London for several years, but after moving out of the Big Smoke and starting my own garden in Friston, Suffolk, I began to research heritage vegetables. I was excited by their stories, and I knew that growing them would allow me to experiment with new flavours, colours, and textures in the kitchen. At the same time, to gain a deeper understanding of farming and to explore the food-production system, I began working at Maple Farm in Kelsale, a Soil Association-certified organic farm that specializes in growing ancient grains, producing truly free-range chicken eggs, and maintaining a large market garden to supply its farm shop. My time there was fun and inspiring. Every day I was given different tasks, and I found myself being exposed to life at the heart of a well-run farm.

After starting to document my garden antics on Instagram, I quickly built up an engaged audience. I delved deeper into the world of seeds, connecting with growers across the globe, and through the power of the internet I discovered thousands of like-minded people. Most were more than happy to share their knowledge and swap seeds. This inclusivity and community were pleasantly surprising after the big egos of commercial kitchens and the live-fast ethos of city life.

Early in 2022 I moved to the south coast of England to build a showcase garden within Four Acre Farm in Ringwood. Having come up with the nickname 'The Seed Hunter' when I started my seed quest, I thought hard about how to get more people interested in growing and eating heirloom crops. I knew people would be interested in finding out about my discoveries and their history, so when my agent, Stuart Cooper, suggested making a guide to some of the world's rarest and oldest heirloom seeds, I was sold.

Seeds are the basis of all life. They represent past, present, and future, and without viable seeds we are unable to produce food for ourselves. It may be hard to imagine that something so small can tell tales, but every single one has a story and many have shaped human cultures on almost every continent. My passion for collecting and growing heirloom seeds isn't just about tracking down the most flavoursome varieties; I'm also on a mission to trace these plants back to their origins and unearth the stories behind them.

I never thought I'd write a book, but here it is. I hope you find it inspiring.

Part 1.

grow
guide

What to Grow

One of the most thrilling aspects when starting out with a garden is deciding what to grow. Before jumping straight into selecting plants, however, it's worth bearing in mind a few pivotal points.

Geographical location and local climate are completely out of your hands, but they should be key factors when you select and plant out your crops. Choose the varieties carefully; for example, if you live in a cold climate, the thick-stemmed tomato 'Sweet Siberian' is quick to mature and capable of setting fruit in low temperatures, and 'Bleu de Solaise' is a vigorous, extremely cold-resistant leek that becomes sweeter after a few frosts, when the foliage also turns a wonderful purply blue.

Try to make informed decisions like these about which varieties will perform best in your area. This will ensure that your garden is as abundant and productive as possible.

The polytunnels help me grow tender crops, such as tomatoes, peppers, and melons, that taste disappointing from the supermarket but are sensational when grown at home.

Climate

The geographical location of your growing space might come with other factors to consider. It might be an exposed site that is susceptible to strong winds, or low-lying land that has a tendency to flood. Instead of looking at these "challenges" as a hindrance, think about how you can use them to your advantage.

If wind is a problem, try growing dwarf bush beans instead of trailing varieties that require support from structures that may be damaged by wind. If soggy soil is bogging you down, celery and celeriac are fantastic options, since they grow naturally in wet soil.

The orientation of the garden will also play its part. For instance, if you have a shady patch that receives only three or four hours of sunlight a day, research and grow crops that will perform better in these conditions, rather than chancing it with sun-loving crops that won't produce very well. By working in partnership with the land and not against it, you will achieve much better harvests.

Size

Whether you already have a working garden or are starting out, the size of the plot will play a large part in dictating what you can grow. Planting a mix of food crops will not only provide you with an abundance of flavours and ingredients to work with in the kitchen, but also make your garden resilient to pests, diseases, and extreme weather. My advice to any new grower is to plant a little of everything, rather than lots of the same crop.

If you are short of space, work out what particular crops are of greatest

importance to you or excite you the most, and grow those. It's worth bearing in mind that certain crops, such as brassicas and squash, require a long growing period and/or take up a lot of room. You may love both, but when space is short, it pays to choose crops that will give you the best bang for your buck in terms of growing space. Supermarket tomatoes, cucumbers, and aubergines, for example, are notoriously bland and cost a pretty penny, so by growing these yourself you will have a far more economically fruitful garden than if you were to fill your patch with cabbages, which are abundant and therefore cheap in the shops.

Budget

Seeds, compost, and equipment (such as polytunnels) can quickly add up and become a financial burden. If you're sticking to a budget, you will need to prioritize, and that includes choosing what to grow as well as what to buy.

Melons, aubergines, chillies, and other warmth-loving crops perform better when grown undercover, so if your budget doesn't allow for a greenhouse or polytunnel, consider growing crops that do not require so much protection from the elements.

When working to a budget, the main things to consider are good-quality

My garden at Four Acre Farm in Hampshire is 196m² (2,110ft²), the average size of a UK back garden. I built it to demonstrate what's achievable on a domestic scale, with the emphasis on growing heritage food crops, but also considering soil regeneration and habitats for wildlife.

A garden can be a rich mix of
habitats to encourage biodiversity
as well as productivity.

compost (see page 20) and a reputable source of seeds (see page 350). By choosing to grow from seed you will naturally save money compared to buying plug plants from the garden centre or nursery. It's good to remember that any money spent in the garden is an investment in your well-being, and the harvest at the end is your reward for tending the land.

Purpose

Having said all that, arguably the most important thing to consider when starting a garden is what you want to achieve. For me, it's creating an alluring, immersive area planted with rare and exciting food crops, with copious flowers to add beauty and make a more well-rounded ecosystem.

Creating habitats is at the forefront in my garden. The small wildlife pond attracts many insects and amphibians, while log stacks inoculated with native culinary mushrooms provide a much-needed – but often overlooked – habitat for many creatures, including wood-boring beetles and centipedes, while providing me with fresh and tasty mushroom harvests.

However, perhaps you're a real garlic connoisseur with limited space, in which case your priority might be to grow as many different garlic varieties as physically possible. Maybe you want to grow vegetables competitively and make room for enormous squashes or outrageously long beans. Or perhaps you have a family and want to create a garden that can also be used by children and pets. Ultimately, your garden is an extension of yourself, and the most important thing is to grow plants that excite you and create a place that you want to spend time in, a place that will fill you with happiness and satisfaction, one that reflects you and the world you were born into – the world that inspired you to start a garden in the first place.

Approach your garden as a philosophy rather than a set of recipes. In the kitchen, the recipe is only a guideline, and to take a meal to the next level you must feel and taste your way to perfection, do what comes naturally, experiment, be creative, and learn from your mistakes. The same goes for your garden.

The most surprising part of the garden can be productive. Log-grown mushrooms (below left) are just as important in my garden as a show-worthy harvest of garlic bulbs (below).

Tools & Equipment

Tools

Garden centres are full to the rafters with a ludicrous number of gizmos and gimmicks, most of which are completely unnecessary. When it comes to tools, it's surprising how little you actually need to maintain a garden.

The essential gardener's toolkit contains a dibber, a rake, a spade, a hoe, a hand trowel, and a hand fork. Rather than the usual iron or steel, I prefer copper-headed tools. These beauties don't just look good but actually bring remarkable benefits. Iron is corrosive and oxidizes in the presence of water and oxygen to form rust, whereas copper will never rust but instead forms a beautiful green patina. This patina does not flake away as rust does, meaning that copper tools last considerably longer than their iron and steel counterparts. A small amount of tin is added to copper during the smithing process to create bronze, making the tools even stronger and tougher.

The advantages of hardwearing, long-lasting copper tools don't end there. Not only do they stay sharper for longer than iron tools, but also they enrich the soil with trace elements. On top of that, because copper isn't magnetic, when you use it in the garden it won't disturb the soil's magnetic field. This is particularly interesting because humans and other mammals naturally have iron in their blood, creating an independent magnetic field. Slugs and snails, on the other hand, have copper-based blood, meaning they don't have an independent magnetic field and are naturally more sensitive to the Earth's magnetic force. When you use iron or steel tools in the soil you leave behind a signature in the magnetic field, and when a slug slithers around during the night it is naturally attracted to this disturbance – which is, of course, right where the unsuspecting gardener has just planted out their crops. By using copper tools we leave no magnetic residue in the soil, making the growing area less attractive to slugs and snails.

Support structures

Structures and supports are necessary if you grow trailing or vining crops, such as tomatoes and beans. I like to use hazel poles, rather than the more ubiquitous bamboo, for my garden supports. Hazel is very sturdy and can withstand the harsh winds on my exposed site, as well as the weight of heavy cropping from rampant runner beans. I believe that the garden should be aesthetically pleasing, and I find the naturally knobbly hazel much easier on the eye than bamboo. Tomatoes, cucumbers, melons, and other vining plants are usually trained up a line of garden twine. This is an effective and

> **"**
> **It's surprising how little you actually need to maintain a garden.**

The wonkiness of hazel sticks is a more natural sight than bamboo canes in the garden, and they offer more grip for climbing beans, too.

organized way to grow and maintain such plants, but most garden twine is very thin and tends to cut into the stems as they become laden with fruit. To avoid this, I use thick baling twine, which gives more support, stretches less, and has a greater surface area, thus cutting into the stems much less. The downside of baling twine is that it is made from plastic, but that does mean it can be used season after season and is perfect for burying under your crops when planting, since it doesn't rot and break away halfway through the season.

Netting and other equipment

It is vital to cover crops with horticultural fleece and/or netting if you wish to extend the growing season and protect them from pests. It is well worth investing in good-quality fine horticultural mesh to avoid the heartbreak of discovering that your cabbages have fallen victim to a catastrophic munching session by caterpillars. Covering crops with horticultural fleece to keep them snug during the cold months will extend the growing period and give you earlier harvests.

If you use them extensively, both materials will need to be supported by metal row covers, but proprietary ones are often flimsy and/or expensive. I have found 20 x 3mm (³/₄ x ¹/₈in) flat mild-steel rods a cheap and long-lasting alternative.

Permanent structures

Polytunnels and greenhouses are not essential to growing your own food, but they do give growers in a temperate climate the opportunity to push the boundaries of what they can cultivate. Sun-loving crops, such as peppers, melons, aubergines, tomatoes, and cucumbers, often perform better undercover, and I rarely grow any of these outside.

Baling twine is perfect for setting up strong, long-lasting lines for vining crops to climb. Bury it under the roots as you plant the seedlings out, and secure it to a point high up in the greenhouse or polytunnel.

There are some disadvantages to growing in a polytunnel and greenhouse, however. The initial cost of the structure can be high, assembly can be tricky and time-consuming, and on exposed or windy sites you will need to dig extra foundations to ensure the structure is safely secured into the ground. In the summer these structures can become outrageously hot, limiting the time that you can spend working in them during the day and necessitating a solid watering routine to ensure good plant growth.

But don't let this put you off. Even something as simple as a polytunnel will unlock a new world of plant possibilities, give you a protected area to work in when the weather's bad, and allow you to overwinter certain crops, such as salad.

Having a dedicated propagation station is the best way to remain organized and on top of seed-sowing throughout the year. If you have the space and funds for it, a potting shed is triply useful, providing a protected place to work, bringing in light from its full glass front for numerous seeds to germinate and grow on, and providing room to store tools, compost, row covers, spare pots and seed trays, and so on. My sunny, south-facing potting shed is my favourite place to spend time in. I find it particularly cosy in late winter and early spring, when I'm shut inside with a nice cup of tea, catching up with seed-sowing. If you don't have room or budget for a full-size shed, you could set up something as simple as a makeshift potting bench and cold frame in a corner of the patch, or a small section of a greenhouse.

> **66**
> **My sunny potting shed is my favourite place to spend time in.**

Steel rods bent into arches are a simple, cost-effective support for netting or fleece.

Soil

The "no dig" method

I choose to grow using the "no dig" method, inspired by the work of the horticulturist and writer Charles Dowding. I believe a lot of my success in the garden is down to the fact that I've followed his method closely.

To put it simply, no-dig is a gardening approach based on pre-industrial farming techniques and permaculture principles that leave the soil undisturbed. With the no-dig method, instead of digging to aerate the soil or mix in compost, you feed it from above with a layer of organic mulch applied annually.

By not disturbing the soil, we avoid harming or interfering with the soil food web, a complex community of living organisms – bacteria, nematodes, fungi, insects, worms, and so on – that are responsible for building soil structure, cycling nutrients, storing carbon, and much more. For years the importance of the soil food web and the part it plays in making plants healthier and more nutrient-dense has flown under the radar.

By switching to a no-dig system, every gardener can play their part in restoring one of the world's most precious but overlooked and neglected resources: soil. But there are many other benefits to the no-dig method:

- **Less watering** The mulch retains moisture in the soil by protecting from wind, sun, and heat, and reducing evaporation. This is especially helpful in dry and/or hot climates.
- **Bigger yields** An ongoing trial set up by Dowding has proved over ten years that no-dig beds yield considerably more kitchen-ready produce than dug beds.
- **Fewer weeds** When you dig, you bring to the surface weed seeds that have been lying dormant underground. The light triggers germination, resulting in more weeds than before.
- **Better structure** You can walk over a no-dig bed without running the risk of compacting the soil. Soil that is regularly dug is susceptible to compaction from foot traffic because its structure has been impaired over the years.
- **Less labour** No back-breaking work digging the plot over every year.

Getting started with no-dig couldn't be simpler. If you're already growing and are digging your plot as a matter of course, all you need to do is stop digging and start mulching with a high-quality organic material (see pages 20–22). An annual mulch of 10–15cm (4–6in) will give your plot all the power it needs to grow for the whole season.

If you're starting from scratch on an old flower bed, weedy pasture, or lawn, begin by removing shrubs, brambles, and broadleaf perennials (such as docks) with a trowel, ensuring you remove as much of the taproot as possible.

Cut back the area with a mower, then cover it completely with cardboard that has had any tape, labels, or staples removed, ensuring you overlap the sections by 25–30cm (10–12in). I like to give it a quick splash with the watering can to weigh it down and keep it in place; this also kick-starts the biodegrading process.

Now add an extra-thick (30–35cm/ 12–14in) layer of compost on top of the cardboard. It should be this deep when you start a new no-dig bed; you can reduce

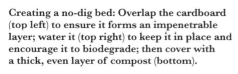

Creating a no-dig bed: Overlap the cardboard (top left) to ensure it forms an impenetrable layer; water it (top right) to keep it in place and encourage it to biodegrade; then cover with a thick, even layer of compost (bottom).

it to an annual mulch of 10–15cm (4–6in) afterwards. Spread out this extra-thick layer with a rake, breaking up any lumps, then walk all over the bed, treading the compost down on to the cardboard to ensure that it has good contact with the soil and to help to kill off the weeds below.

The cardboard and mulch act as a weed barrier, depriving the remaining plants below of light. Over the next few weeks the grass and plants below will die off and worms will eat their way through the cardboard, leaving you with a deep, weed-free no-dig bed.

To plant, just dib a hole in the compost and pop in a seedling. You may want to keep an eye on the watering in newly made beds for a couple of weeks, until the plants' roots have managed to get down below the soil surface.

Rich, well-rotted compost – and lots of it – is the key to a low-input, productive garden.

Compost

Compost is king. A good source of this beautiful multi-tasking substance is the key to gardening success, and sowing seeds is no exception.

It can be expensive and difficult to get hold of a large amount of compost, however. I've had the privilege of looking under the microscope at various types, from homemade to various brands of bagged compost and assorted manures. The results were truly eye-opening.

My investigations showed that there's nothing your soil will enjoy more than homemade compost (see panel opposite). It's naturally rich in microbial life that is specific to your area – and, of course, it's entirely free. Next, the local organic horse manure was buzzing with microbes and fungi, promising great things for any crops

A rough guide to composting using a static heap

Concocting your own compost is fun and rewarding. The bigger the heap the better the compost, and in my experience using either four wooden pallets to form a box-shaped heap or galvanized-metal mesh to make a large circular bin is the easiest and most cost-efficient way of creating a neat, well-sized heap.

There is a great deal of mystery and lore behind composting, but in essence the key is to have the correct ratio of nitrogen (green material) to carbon (brown material; see below), as well as the appropriate amount of moisture, warmth, and airflow.

The correct carbon-to-nitrogen ratio is essential for speedy and thorough decomposition, and I've found a 50/50 mix works a treat. Woody material contains lignin, which takes a long time to break down. It provides support and structure for the heap, creating little chambers and air pockets to ensure there's good ventilation for the microbes breaking down the compost. Green waste decomposes far more quickly. A heap with too much carbon will lose heat and compost slowly, while one with too much green material will become sloppy and smelly.

A compost heap can be positioned under a lean-to roof or left out in the open. It should be moist but not soaking, so to protect it from rain, make a roof from cardboard weighed down with bricks or stones. The cardboard can be composted once it's served its purpose.

People often wonder if it's OK to compost blighted or diseased plants and foliage. I always do, because the composting process kills the nasties.

One of the keys to having a crumbly, evenly decomposed compost is to turn the heap about halfway through the process to mix things up. If you have the space, it's ideal to turn the whole heap into a second bin or bay to continue decomposing, freeing up the original bin to be refilled with new material. Otherwise, just give it a good mix-up with a garden fork or pitchfork.

Compost breaks down faster during the warmer months, and your heap may become dormant in the depths of winter. On average, compost should be ready in 3–6 months. A surefire sign that it is ready for use is when worms begin to appear in it.

Nitrogen
Coffee grounds
Grass clippings
Kitchen scraps
Seaweed
Flowers
Weeds
Green foliage and plant material

Carbon
Dried leaves
Twigs, sticks, and woody stems
Cardboard and paper
Woodchips
Straw and hay
Nut shells
Sawdust
Wood ash

grown in it. The local council's compost, made from green waste in windrows, was void of biology and hardly broken down at all, and it was a similar story for most well-known bagged composts available in garden centres, most of which had very little biology. This is because mass-produced composts are sterilized during the process, and/or not composted enough, and/or composted in anaerobic conditions.

Over the past few years there has been a huge spike in gardening, and that – coupled with the move away from peat-based products for environmental reasons – means compost is in huge demand. This has resulted in standards dropping and many companies calling products "compost" when they are in fact not composted enough, or something completely different, such as digest, a by-product of the biofuel industry.

For sowing seeds, it's best to use a specially formulated seed compost, since it will contain the correct balance of nutrients to aid germination, early growth, and root development. Contrary to what many gardeners believe, seedlings enjoy growing in regular "full-fat" (nutrient-rich) compost. I use an exceptionally high-quality, peat-free seed-sowing compost that is made using worms to recycle organic green waste into a very fine, rich substance, bursting with beneficial microbes and nutrients. Although it's expensive, I think the results are worth it. Before sowing, I sieve the compost through a 6mm ($^{1}/_{4}$in) screen to remove large lumps (which can cause poor germination and inhibit root growth) and create a fine consistency. I then mix in a handful of perlite, a lightweight, granular material that aids germination by improving aeration and drainage and providing insulation.

If you do want to add homemade compost to your seedling mix, ensure the compost has gone through a thorough, prolonged hot composting process to kill off any lurking weed seeds and some harmful micro-organisms. There's nothing worse than sowing a tray of seeds only to discover more weeds than vegetable seedlings. A tumbler (a compost bin with a sealed chamber that you can spin easily) becomes intensely hot and breaks the material down much faster than a standard compost heap or bin, so it's perfect for killing off stowaway weed seeds.

Manure

Even though well-rotted horse manure is one of the best and cheapest sources of organic matter, it has its drawbacks. A nasty, persistent weedkiller called aminopyralid that is sprayed on paddocks can remain dormant in manure for many years. Aminopyralid is lethal for tomatoes, potatoes, and legumes (peas and beans), causing their growing tips to curl and become distorted. It's not known quite how long it persists in manure, but some people have experienced plant deformation from manure five years old or more.

A simple way to test for aminopyralid is to germinate some beans in the manure, let them grow, and check for distortion; make sure you do this in samples from various parts of the heap, for an accurate test. If you suspect that you have manure contaminated with aminopyralid, I urge you to report it to your local council.

Another thing to consider when using horse manure is dewormer residue, although this is usually more of a problem in fresh manure, since the heat created by decomposing compost speeds up the breakdown of these chemicals. A thorough hot composting over several months will rid the manure of any residue.

But don't let these chemicals scare you away from using horse manure. It's an incredible source of compost that's rich in biology and usually cheap and local – just approach with caution. I was really keen to use manure in my no-dig garden, and after some research I found a local lad whose family has a stable in the New Forest. All the grazing and feed is totally organic and the horses are bedded down on larch sawdust cut and milled in the area. I ran tests for aminopyralid by germinating a bean and potting up a tomato into the compost, but there were no ill effects and I have had wonderful success with it.

Elsewhere in the garden

For paths I use woodchips, which are a great mulch for walkways that are heavily used. The downside is that, especially when they are fresh, there are often large chunks that provide hiding places for slugs. Woodchips can also blow around in the wind and get dragged across beds by birds.

I have no woodchip paths in the polytunnel and main growing areas of the garden, opting instead for large areas of compost. The lack of paths allows me the freedom to plant crops where I want and to find natural desire lines leading through the growing beds. Having bigger beds means fewer rules when it comes to planting, and maximizes space and productivity.

Give young seedlings the best chance by sieving the compost to remove lumps.

Planning the Growing Year

A garden is a living organism that never switches off. It's easy to get side-tracked, pottering around the patch loving life and forgetting to think about seed-sowing dates. Although most late sowings will catch up and still give you a good crop, the key to having a garden full of produce almost all year round is a certain amount of planning. To give you an insight into how my potting bench looks throughout the year, here's a month-by-month guide. Remember that the timings given here are those I follow in my northern hemisphere garden in the south of England; you may need to alter them for your growing location.

> ## 66
> ## The key to having a garden full of produce almost all year round is planning.

January

The start of the year is usually the best time for gardeners to sail away on their holidays, since there is very little growing action. I sow chillies and peppers in January in a heated propagator, and grow them on in small pots on a south-facing windowsill. Onions can also be sown in seed modules or trays and kept indoors until they have germinated, then transferred to an unheated greenhouse, a polytunnel, or a cold frame to grow on.

February

The days are lengthening, but there can still be a bitter chill in the air. However, that doesn't stop things from hotting up in the garden.

This month you can sow broad beans, spinach, peas for salad shoots, Welsh onions, cauliflowers, fennel, early cabbages, turnips, and radishes, along with some herbs, such as parsley. Having a hotbed made from fresh manure inside a greenhouse or polytunnel will allow you to germinate many of these crops in the garden, without filling up your home with seed trays.

From mid-February onwards, it's time to think about sowing tomatoes and aubergines with the assistance of a heat mat, airing cupboard, or warm windowsill, along with chillies and peppers if you didn't do so in January. Aubergines and chillies can take a while to get going, so early sowing will encourage the plants to flower more quickly and produce more fruit before the season ends.

Spring-sowing varieties of garlic should be sown in situ now. In mild areas carrots can be sown direct in polytunnels or greenhouses for an extra-early crop.

March

Depending on your location and climate, ground temperatures could really be on the rise in March. However, freezing conditions can still be expected.

All the seeds that can be sown in February can still be sown now. You can also make first sowings of summer salads, such as lettuce and chicory, along with leeks, Welsh onions, beetroot, parsnips, carrots, and turnips. A welcome sense of satisfaction hits, knowing that if you sow peas and mangetout now, it won't be long before you're enjoying these garden delights. From mid-March onwards you can sow celery and celeriac, and towards the end of the month the first early potatoes are finding their feet in the soil. If you want to get ahead, sow melons and watermelons in late March, provided you have room to grow them indoors.

Slugs can be a real problem at this time of the year. Be cautious when planting out seedlings, since they can be savaged overnight. It may be beneficial to grow plants on until they're larger and more resilient. Rodents are also destructive now, so provide protection (see page 50).

April Spring is usually underway by now, but the risk of frost hasn't passed. It's the last chance to sow celery and celeriac, while the warmer weather from the middle of the month onwards means you can sow basil, Brussels sprouts, cucumbers, summer and winter squash, corn, and melons. Second early and maincrop potatoes can go into the ground, while carrots, early and autumn brassicas, broad beans, spinach, Welsh onions, and spring radishes can all be sown now.

May As the days become longer, the soil begins to warm up and plants burst into action – including weeds. May is a busy month for gardeners. It's time to plant out summer crops, such as tomatoes, while the seed-sowing action continues to ramp up. Common, runner, and soy beans will need to be sown, along with rutabaga and brassicas to overwinter, such as purple sprouting broccoli. Keep sowing lettuce and basil. By the end of May, ideally all cucumbers, melons, squash, corn, and potatoes should have been sown.

June It's halfway through the year and there's still time to sow most of the summer crops, although the bell for "last orders" is about to be rung. After the summer solstice (the longest day), our attention moves towards preparing for autumn and winter crops.

July The summer is in full swing and it's time to start thinking ahead and planning cool-weather crops. Sow cabbage early in the month, and then, in the middle of the month, turn your attention to hardy salad greens, such as winter lettuce and chicory. Chinese cabbage and pak choi can be sown towards the end of the month, which is also the last chance to sow root crops, such as carrots, beetroot, turnips, winter radishes, and rutabaga.

August This is the perfect time to soak up the sights and sounds of the vegetable patch at its peak – a time when the garden is abundant with fabulous flavours. It's time to dip into the seed stash to search for packets filled with the seeds of leafy greens, such as spinach.

September By now seed-sowing is beginning to slow. The start of the month is the last chance to sow Welsh onions and cold-hardy lettuce, as well as spring cabbages.

October I'm a late October baby, so this is my favourite month, and I have vivid memories of the change in seasons. Towards the end of October, I direct-sow home-saved garlic cloves from the best-performing bulbs of the crop, and top all the beds with their annual mulch of compost.

November In mild regions, late sowings of broad beans can be made now, for overwintering. If you haven't already done so, now's the time to plant out garlic, which requires a long period of cold if it is to form good bulbs the following year.

December This is the only month when I don't sow seeds. However, there is a tradition in the UK that if you sow onion seeds on Boxing Day (26 December), you will have good luck and a fruitful harvest. The tradition stems from contestants cultivating onions for competitions, with such varieties as 'Kelsae' (see page 95) being popular choices among the giant-vegetable-growing faithful.

The seed-sower's calendar

Use this at-a-glance guide to remind you what to sow, plant out, and harvest when. Fuller information for each crop is given under the main entry. The months given here apply to the northern hemisphere.

January

Sow Onions • Peppers • Shallots

Plant out None

Harvest Broccoli • Brussels sprouts • Cabbage (winter) • Chicory • Collard greens • Kale • Leeks • Lettuce • Parsley • Parsnip • Radish • Rutabaga • Spinach

February

Sow Aubergine • Beetroot • Broad beans • Broccoli (standard/raab) • Cabbage (summer) • Cauliflower (summer) • Fennel • Garlic • Lettuce • Onions • Parsley • Peas • Peppers • Radish (spring) • Shallots (including sets) • Spinach • Tomato • Turnip • Wasabi • Welsh onion

Plant out None

Harvest Broccoli • Brussels sprouts • Cabbage (spring/winter) • Chicory • Collard greens • Kale • Leeks • Lettuce • Parsley • Parsnip • Radish • Rutabaga • Spinach

March

Sow Aubergine • Beetroot • Broad beans • Broccoli (all types) • Cabbage (summer) • Carrot (early) • Cauliflower (summer) • Celeriac • Celery • Chicory • Collard greens • Corn • Fennel • Garlic • Kale • Leeks • Lettuce • Melon • Parsley • Parsnip • Peas • Potatoes (first early) • Radish (spring) • Shallots (sets) • Spinach • Tomato • Turnip • Wasabi • Watermelon • Welsh onion

Plant out Broad beans • Broccoli (standard/raab) • Cauliflower (summer) • Fennel • Onions • Peas • Radish (spring) • Shallots • Spinach • Wasabi

Harvest Broccoli • Cabbage (spring) • Cauliflower • Kale • Leeks • Lettuce • Parsley • Parsnip • Rutabaga • Spinach • Radish • Wasabi

April

Sow Basil • Beetroot • Broad beans • Broccoli (all types) • Brussels sprouts • Cabbage (summer/autumn) • Carrot (early) • Celeriac • Celery • Collard greens • Corn • Cucumber • Kale • Leeks • Lettuce • Melon • Parsley • Parsnip • Peas • Potatoes (second early and maincrop) • Radish (spring) • Spinach • Summer squash • Tomato • Watermelon • Welsh onion • Winter squash

Plant out Aubergine • Beetroot • Broccoli (all types) • Cabbage (summer) • Cauliflower (summer) • Fennel • Lettuce • Peas • Radish (spring) • Turnip • Wasabi

Harvest Broad beans • Broccoli • Leeks • Cabbage (spring) • Cauliflower • Kale • Lettuce • Parsley • Radish • Spinach • Wasabi

May

Sow Basil • Beans • Broad beans • Broccoli (sprouting) • Brussels sprouts • Cabbage (autumn/winter) • Cauliflower (autumn) • Collard greens • Corn • Cucumber • Kale • Lemongrass • Lettuce • Melon • Parsley • Parsnip • Peas • Potatoes (maincrop) • Radish (spring) • Rutabaga • Summer squash • Welsh onion • Winter squash

Plant out Aubergine • Beans • Beetroot • Broad beans • Broccoli (all types) • Cabbage (summer/autumn) • Celeriac • Celery • Collard greens • Corn • Fennel • Kale • Lettuce • Peas • Radish (spring) • Summer squash • Tomato • Turnip • Wasabi • Watermelon • Welsh onion

Harvest Broad beans • Broccoli • Cabbage (spring) • Cauliflower • Garlic • Lettuce • Kale • Parsley • Peas • Radish • Turnip • Wasabi

June

Sow Basil • Beans • Broccoli (sprouting) • Cabbage (winter) • Carrot (standard) • Cauliflower (autumn) • Chicory • Collard greens • Kale • Lettuce • Parsley • Parsnip • Rutabaga • Summer squash • Welsh onion

Plant out Aubergine • Basil • Beans • Beetroot • Broccoli (sprouting) • Brussels sprouts • Cabbage (autumn) • Cauliflower (autumn) • Celeriac • Celery • Collard greens • Corn • Cucumber • Fennel • Kale • Leeks • Lemongrass • Lettuce • Melon • Parsley • Peas • Peppers • Radish (spring) • Summer squash • Tomato • Watermelon • Welsh onion • Winter squash

Harvest Basil • Beans • Beetroot • Broad beans • Broccoli • Carrot • Cauliflower • Collard greens • Fennel • Garlic • Kale • Lettuce • Parsley • Peas • Potatoes (first early) • Radish • Summer squash • Turnip

July

Sow Beetroot • Broccoli (standard/raab) • Cabbage (spring) • Carrot (late) • Cauliflower (winter) • Chicory • Chinese cabbage • Collard greens • Fennel • Kale • Lettuce • Pak choi • Radish (winter) • Rutabaga • Turnip • Welsh onion

Plant out Basil • Beans • Broccoli (sprouting) • Brussels sprouts • Cauliflower (autumn/winter) • Collard greens • Fennel • Kale • Leeks • Lemongrass • Lettuce • Parsley • Peppers • Rutabaga • Summer squash • Tomato • Welsh onion • Winter squash

Harvest Aubergine • Basil • Beans • Broad beans • Broccoli • Carrot • Cauliflower • Celery • Collard greens • Cucumber • Fennel • Garlic • Kale • Lettuce • Onions • Parsley • Potatoes • Peas • Peppers • Radish • Shallots • Summer squash • Tomato • Turnip • Watermelon • Welsh onion

August

Sow Broccoli (standard/raab) • Cabbage (spring) • Chicory • Chinese cabbage • Lettuce • Pak choi • Radish (winter/spring) • Spinach • Welsh onion

Plant out Beans • Broccoli (standard/raab) • Cauliflower (winter) • Chicory • Chinese cabbage • Collard greens • Fennel • Kale • Lemongrass • Lettuce • Parsley • Peppers • Radish (winter) • Rutabaga • Welsh onion • Winter squash

Harvest Aubergine • Basil • Beans • Broccoli • Cabbage (summer) • Carrot • Cauliflower • Celery • Collard greens • Corn • Cucumber • Fennel • Kale • Leeks • Lemongrass • Lettuce • Melon • Onions • Parsley • Peas • Peppers • Potatoes (second early/maincrop) • Radish • Shallots • Summer squash • Tomato • Turnip • Watermelon • Welsh onion

September

Sow Cabbage (spring) • Lettuce • Pak choi • Radish (winter) • Welsh onion

Plant out Broccoli (standard/raab) • Cabbage (spring) • Chicory • Chinese cabbage • Collard greens • Kale • Lettuce • Parsley • Radish (winter/spring) • Spinach • Turnip • Welsh onion

Harvest Aubergine • Basil • Beans • Broccoli • Cabbage (summer) • Carrot • Cauliflower • Celery • Chicory • Collard greens • Corn • Cucumber • Fennel • Kale • Leeks • Lemongrass • Lettuce • Melon • Onions • Parsley • Peppers • Potatoes (maincrop) • Radish • Rutabaga • Shallots • Spinach • Summer squash • Tomato • Turnip • Watermelon • Welsh onion • Winter squash

October

Sow Garlic

Plant out Lettuce • Pak choi • Radish (winter) • Turnip • Wasabi

Harvest Aubergine • Cabbage (autumn) • Cauliflower • Basil • Beans • Broccoli • Brussels sprouts • Carrot • Celeriac • Celery • Chicory • Chinese cabbage • Collard greens • Cucumber • Fennel • Kale • Leeks • Lemongrass • Lettuce • Melon • Parsley • Parsnip • Peppers • Potatoes (maincrop) • Radish • Rutabaga • Shallots • Spinach • Summer squash • Tomato • Turnip • Wasabi • Welsh onion • Winter squash

November

Sow Broad beans • Garlic • Shallots (sets)

Plant out Turnip • Wasabi

Harvest Basil • Beans • Broccoli • Brussels sprouts • Cabbage (autumn/winter) • Carrot • Celeriac • Celery • Chicory • Collard greens • Kale • Leeks • Lemongrass • Lettuce • Pak choi • Parsley • Parsnip • Peppers • Radish • Rutabaga • Shallots • Spinach • Summer squash • Tomato • Turnip • Wasabi • Welsh onion • Winter squash

December

Sow seed Garlic • Shallots

Plant out Broad beans • Wasabi

Harvest Broccoli • Brussels sprouts • Cabbage (winter) • Chicory • Collard greens • Kale • Leeks • Lettuce • Parsley • Parsnip • Radish • Rutabaga • Spinach • Turnip • Wasabi

The "second spring"

As the summer kicks into full swing, with its many jobs, don't lose focus on sowing if you want a year-long supply of produce. This latter half of summer is called the "second spring", when the potting bench fills up again with seedlings. Kale, winter lettuce, beetroot, fennel, turnips, Welsh onions, spring cabbages, and chicory, among others, should be the focus now.

Seed-sowing & Seedling Care

There's something magical about raising plants from seed. The anticipation of welcoming plants into the world, mixed with a slight anxiety about whether the tender young seedlings will survive their journey to fully grown plants, is a potent combination. I find it utterly mesmerizing even just to hold the seeds in my hand and get to know how the different types look.

Setting yourself up for success

Obtaining good-quality seed from a reputable supplier is paramount, since old or incorrectly stored seeds will not germinate well. If possible, find a local supplier, so that the seeds are adapted to growing in your environment. To assist you in your quest for seeds, I've put together a directory of seed-savers, keepers, and suppliers of heritage produce; see the back of the book (page 350) for the QR code.

It may sound obvious, but remember to label sowings as you go. It's easy to lose track of what you've planted, and it's hard

to distinguish between young seedlings. Plants have different germination and cultivation requirements, so it really does pay to be organized.

Sowing seeds

The first thing to consider is whether you should sow seeds direct into the ground outdoors, or into trays or pots indoors. Seeds sown direct into the garden are more at risk from pests, such as rodents and slugs, as well as fluctuating weather and soil temperature, which can delay or even stop germination. To give my crops a greater chance of success, I sow most seed indoors (in the potting shed or greenhouse, or on a bright, warm windowsill in the house), then plant out the young seedlings once the time is right. This also allows me to choose the strongest and healthiest plants to grow on. There are some exceptions to this rule, however (see Direct sowing, page 32).

Broadcast-sowing under cover

A quick and effective way to sow many small seeds is to broadcast (scatter) them into a seed tray. Fill the clean tray with seed compost (see page 22) and water lightly. Scatter the seeds evenly and thinly over the compost and pat them down gently. Some people cover the seeds with a very fine layer of compost. However, I usually leave the seeds on the surface or sometimes cover them with a fine layer of vermiculite – a lightweight, naturally occurring mineral that keeps seeds moist during germination but drains quickly. It

For controlled sowing, tip seeds into the palm of your hand, rather than sowing directly from the packet. These parsnip seeds are fairly large and easy to sow individually.

also holds on to plant nutrients, such as potassium, magnesium, and calcium, releasing them slowly back to the plants. Bear in mind that there are some crops, such as celery and celeriac, that need light to germinate, so it's essential to leave their seeds uncovered.

Water the seeds carefully using a fine rose on your watering can. It's beneficial to cover the seed tray or pot with a cloche or glass cover to stop the compost from drying out.

An alternative method when using seed trays is to sow seed in rows. Make little trenches in the compost using the wrong end of a pencil, and scatter the seeds thinly along each row. Sowing seed in rows is great if you're short of space and want to grow different types of seed in the same container, because you can keep the crops separate, but do label the rows so that you can keep track of what you're growing.

Sowing in pots and seed cells

Starting plants off in seed cells, or modules, is a super-effective way of sowing individual seeds or just a few seeds per cell. Seed cells are basically seed trays that are divided into compartments. The advantage is that the plants don't have to compete with many others for nutrients, and don't need pricking out (see page 31), which is good for those that dislike root disturbance.

Crops that have bigger seeds, such as peas, beans, cucumbers, and squash, are best sown individually in the cells. Some root, bulb, and stem vegetables, such as beetroot, leeks, radishes, and onions, can be multi-sown, two or more in a single cell (see panel on page 30). After germinating, the seedlings can be planted out and grown together as a group.

You can grow different crops in the same seed tray – just be sure to label them carefully.

29

Crops suitable for multi-sowing	Seeds per cell
Beetroot	4
Bulb onion	4
Leek	4 or 5
Peas	2
Radish	4 or 5
Spinach	3
Turnip	4 or 5
Welsh onion	6–8

Germination

Once the seeds are sown, it's important to keep them in a warm place so they can germinate. The temperature required depends on the plant; peas can germinate in soil temperatures as low as 4°C (39°F), while at the other end of the scale, melons require a minimum of 18°C (64°F) and ideally around 27°C (81°F). The panel on page 32 gives the minimum and optimum soil temperatures for germinating many of the crops discussed in this book.

A greenhouse might seem the best place for seeds to germinate. However, low temperatures at night can easily cause seeds or seedlings to rot, while a roaring-hot greenhouse with no ventilation will quickly cook your seeds. Bear in mind that the temperature outside does not always reflect the temperature of the compost in seed trays or pots. On a cold, sunny day the greenhouse can get much warmer than you would expect, and overnight the soil can be much colder than the air temperature would suggest.

Providing additional heat indoors
Poor germination because of cold is usually a problem only in the winter and early spring. During these cold months, I sow sun-loving crops indoors, placing the seed trays or pots either on a heat mat or in a polytunnel on top of a "hotbed" (thick layers of fresh horse manure), to maintain a constant temperature that will coax the seeds into life. A warm airing cupboard is the ideal place to get free heat; just keep a close eye on the trays, removing them to a light place as soon as the shoots emerge, to avoid legginess.

Providing protection outdoors
Once outside temperatures are high enough, a polytunnel, greenhouse, or shed is perfect for germination. Be aware that rodents love to nibble on freshly sown seed, especially those of cucumbers, squash, beans, and peas. Covering the soil with a clear cloche weighted down

with a stone is a simple and effective way of keeping them out. Early spring sowings are usually more at risk of being eaten by rodents than later ones, since the natural forage is scarcer for wildlife early in the year.

Although plants don't require light to germinate (except for celery and celeriac), I keep my trays of germinating seed on a bright windowsill, since darkness can result in spindly, lanky seedlings. I've lost count of the number of times I've left seeds to germinate on the back shelf of the shed, only to discover a tray full of leggy seedlings that are good only for the compost heap.

Pricking out

Seeds that have been sown en masse into a tray or pots will soon become crowded and must be rehoused into individual containers. Once the seedlings have germinated and are big enough to handle, the strongest ones can be moved into

individual cells or pots, where they can grow on without competition from their neighbours. Known as "pricking out", this process is best carried out when the seedlings are fairly small and haven't developed much of a root system. Prick out seedlings when they have two strong seed leaves (the first pair to show), rather than waiting for the "true" leaves to appear, as is often recommended.

> **66**
> **Seeds sown en masse will soon become crowded and must be rehoused.**

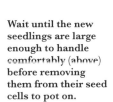

Wait until the new seedlings are large enough to handle comfortably (above) before removing them from their seed cells to pot on.

The potting shed (right) is the perfect place for starting off warmth-loving plants, such as these peppers, while it is still too cold outside.

	Minimum soil temperature	Optimum soil temperature
SUN-LOVING CROPS		
Aubergine	16°C (61°F)	24–32°C (75–90°F)
Celery, celeriac	10°C (32°F)	15–20°C (59–68°F)
Common, runner, and soybeans	8°C (46°F)	16–32°C (61–90°F)
Corn	16°C (61°F)	16–34°C (61–93°F)
Cucumber	16°C (61°F)	16–35°C (61–95°F)
Melon	18°C (64°F)	24–32°C (75–90°F)
Peppers/chillies	16°C (61°F)	21–34°C (70–93°F)
Summer/winter squash	16°C (61°F)	16–32°C (61–90°F)
Tomato	10°C (50°F)	16–32°C (61–90°F)
Watermelon	18°C (64°F)	22–32°C (72–90°F)
COLD-TOLERANT CROPS		
Beetroot	4°C (39°F)	10–30°C (50–86°F)
Brassicas (e.g. cabbage)	4°C (39°F)	6–30°C (43–86°F)
Broad beans	5°C (41°F)	8–15°C (46–59°F)
Carrot	4°C (39°F)	8–30°C (46–86°F)
Garlic	0°C (32°F)	0–10°C (32–50°F)
Lettuce	2°C (36°F)	4–24°C (39–75°F)
Onion, leek	2°C (36°F)	10–32°C (50–90°F)
Parsnip	2°C (36°F)	10–20°C (50–68°F)
Peas	4°C (39°F)	4–24°C (39–75°F)

Potting on

Most plants are happy to remain in seed cells for up to a month before they start running out of space and food. At this stage, they can be planted out into the garden (see page 34) or potted on into bigger pots. Potting on is the process of transferring a plant into a bigger container, and it's a great way to keep plants growing while you wait for space to become available in the garden, or for the frosts to finish, or to bulk up such plants as tomatoes, squash, corn, and cucumbers, which are best planted out short and stocky.

Direct sowing

Carrots and parsnips grow best if sown directly into their final growing location, since they don't respond well to being transplanted. To do this, create a shallow trench in the soil using a dibber, then scatter seeds thinly in the trench, backfill with soil, and water well. Similarly, potatoes and other tubers are also best sown (planted) directly, as is garlic, and many people choose to sow beans, peas, and corn directly into the garden.

Stratification

Stratification is a process by which seeds are treated to simulate the natural conditions they would experience in the soil over winter, and which initiate the germination process. Some seeds, such as wasabi, will not germinate without this artificial "cold snap". To stratify seeds, put them in the fridge in the autumn and leave them for three months, before sowing as normal.

Store seeds in their packets in an airtight, rodent-proof container such as a tin with a tightly fitting lid (top).

Seeds sown individually in seed cells (above) can be pricked out and handled very easily. Just squeeze the underside of each cell to free the seedling and its root ball.

Seed-sowing tips

Different seeds have specific germination requirements. For the best germination, sow each variety according to its preferences, using the seed packet for guidance.

Soak the seeds of peas and beans in lukewarm water for three or four hours before sowing. This will rehydrate them and kick-start their life cycle. The soaked legumes can then be sown in seed cells as normal.

Be sure to fill seed cells completely by pushing compost into each one. The more compost you can squeeze in, the longer the plants can stay in the cells.

Always sow at the correct depth. Small seeds are best sown on top of the compost; cover with a thin layer of compost or vermiculite or leave them uncovered, and place a cloche or glass cover over the container to stop the compost from drying out. Medium-sized seeds may be planted to a depth of about 5mm ($\frac{1}{4}$in); alternatively, sow them on top of the compost and cover with a fine layer of compost or vermiculite. Large seeds are best planted deeply, pushed into the compost to a depth of about 2.5cm (1in).

Don't rush to sow. It can be a good idea to get ahead with some slower-growing crops, such as aubergines and peppers/chillies, but many other heat-loving crops will grow rapidly once established.

Sow more than you need. It's always good to have a few spares to replace crops that are lost or damaged. Spares also make great gifts for friends and family, and they're a useful addition to the compost heap if all else fails.

Plan to succession-sow. Sowing a few seeds of the same crop every couple of weeks will stagger harvests, help you to avoid gluts, and keep the garden producing to its full potential. When one plant is harvested, another will take its place straight away.

Never let your seed-sowing compost dry out fully, since it will become hydrophobic (water-repelling) and difficult to rehydrate. It's vital to monitor the moisture level of seeds and seedlings regularly.

Aftercare

Compost, heat, light, and moisture all play their part in growing healthy seedlings. At this tender stage, it's crucial to keep a close eye on your seedlings and manipulate their environment to optimize their chance of flourishing and becoming strong, productive crops.

Once the seeds have germinated, they need light, air, and water. Early sowings of sun-loving seedlings can tolerate cooler conditions at this stage, and a sunny windowsill indoors is the ideal home for them until they can be moved outside later in the year.

If young seedlings do not get enough sunlight they quickly grow tall, fragile, and spindly as they search for light instead of focusing on root production. Keep them in a well-lit area or use grow lights. Proper ventilation is also critical, so keep your seedlings in a well-ventilated spot, but out of the way of cold draughts. If you are using a cloche, ensure good airflow by leaving the lid ajar.

It's essential to water all seedlings carefully. Overwatering will cause the plants to damp off and die, but if they dry out, they will fry in the sun. Keeping an eye on the weather will help you to determine how often to water young seedlings. On hot, sunny days, they may require watering twice a day, while in cold, cloudy weather they may require only a splash of water every three or four days. It's best to water seedlings in the morning, to give the plants and soil a chance to dry out before evening and reduce the risk of fungal diseases.

A dibber is the perfect tool for making a planting hole. Rotate it in the ground to make an opening just larger than the root ball.

Preparing the ground

If you use the no-dig method, preparing your growing beds for planting out will be quick, easy, and painless. Because the beds are mulched annually, in the autumn, often all that is required is a quick rake to even out the soil surface and break up any clumps of compost.

Planting out

Planting out is one of the many joys of being a gardener. Every time I pop a plant in and wish it on its way with good intentions, I can't help letting my mind wander to the day when I'll be back to harvest the fruits of my labours or see the plant bloom with a beautiful blossom.

Most crops can be planted out when they are still relatively small. Smaller plants

A healthy growth
of white roots
at the bottom
of the pot is the
sign that these
multi-sown leeks
are ready to be
planted out.

by covering newly planted seedlings with a layer of horticultural fleece.

I use three tools for planting out: a copper trowel, a small copper dibber, and a long-handled wooden dibber. The quickest and most efficient way of planting – and the one that disturbs the soil as little as possible – is to use a dibber to create a hole that is slightly deeper and wider than the seedling's root ball. This way you can plant a vast number of seedlings in no time at all. I find the small copper-headed dibber great when I'm working close to the ground and planting out crops that have been grown in seed cells, while the longer one, with its thicker tip, is useful for dibbing out rows for carrots and making bigger holes for brassicas and similar crops, as well as regular holes for plug plants straight from a seed cell. The long-handled dibber is also brilliant for making many planting holes over a large area without having to kneel on the soil.

The trowel allows me to make small holes for planting out potatoes and bigger seedlings without disturbing the soil too much. For seed potatoes, make a small slit in the soil by pushing the trowel back and forth until the space is big enough for you to slip the potato in. It can then be covered over and mulched or earthed up when the foliage first appears.

You will make life easier for yourself later if you take this opportunity to tie up tomatoes, cucumbers, and other plants that require support. Tie a loop knot in one end of a length of baling twine and place the loop into the bottom of the planting hole, then plant the seedling on top of the knot, burying the string as you backfill the hole. This doesn't damage the plant's roots, and as they grow they will anchor the string. Tie a simple knot to the struts running along the top of the greenhouse or polytunnel so that the string can be easily removed if the plants need fleecing against a late frost. (If there are no struts inside your polytunnel, run galvanized-

Using a fine rose on the watering can will soak the soil without disturbing it or battering the delicate seedlings.

have a tendency to establish themselves more quickly than bigger plants, and this short turnaround will keep the potting bench and seed trays free for more seed-sowing action.

It's traditional to "harden off" seedlings, slowly acclimatizing them to living outside by moving them outside during the day for a week or two before transplanting them. This is certainly useful if you're raising seeds in a warm house and transplanting them into a cold vegetable patch. It may be because I raise many of my early sowings in the potting shed, where the night-time temperature is not very different from outside, but I've found the process can be skipped entirely

steel wires between the hoops at each end and tie your strings to these.)

If possible, plant out your seedlings on a cloudy day, but don't delay getting them into the ground. This is also a convenient time to hand-pick any weeds, and I often carry my dibber and trowel in a bucket that I can also use for weeds.

Spacing is a minefield. The distances between plants specified on seed packets can be misleading, and because I want to grow as much as possible, I tend to plant my crops as close together as is feasible. It should go without saying that you must take care to give the crops space to grow and flourish, but planting crops tightly comes with various benefits. Those that are grown to be picked as a cut-and-come-again harvest, such as lettuce, form small, compact heads from which the outer leaves are picked regularly, meaning they can be planted close together. Not only will you maximize your growing space, but also plants really enjoy growing together, forming a type of companionship (see also page 40).

Watering

Remember to water new plantings in thoroughly and keep an eye on moisture over the next few days, until the roots have had time to establish.

There are many ways of watering, from automated sprinklers and drip lines (perforated hoses) to a hosepipe or good

Watering tips

Use a rain gauge to take away some of the guesswork involved in deciding when to water outdoor plants.

Podding crops, such as beans and peas, and fruiting crops, such as tomatoes and cucumbers, require watering when the flowers start to appear, to help the plant set pods and fruit.

Always water at the base of the plant, not over the foliage. Wet foliage is susceptible to blight (see page 51) and other airborne pathogens. Watering at the base also ensures that the water reaches the roots. Water needs a moment to soak into the soil, and applying it gradually using a rose attachment so that the water penetrates the soil fully will help to stop water run-off.

Keep an eye on the soil moisture in polytunnels and greenhouses, since high temperatures can cause the soil to dry out quickly.

Water in the morning. This allows time for the surface of the soil and the foliage to dry out before nightfall, reducing the risk of slug damage and airborne pathogens.

If in doubt, water deeply but less often.

Test the soil for moisture by poking your finger in fully. If the tip of your finger feels dry, it's time to water.

Plants growing in exposed or windy sites may require frequent watering, since wind causes moisture to be lost from both leaves and soil.

Rainwater is always best. Water harvested from the roof of a house, garage, or shed and stored in a water butt or tank is naturally rich in minerals and (usually) warmer than mains water, so it will give your plants less of a shock.

66
Take care to give the crops space to grow and flourish.

old-fashioned watering can. I tend to use a watering can or hosepipe with a rose attachment. Watering plants individually in this way offers a brilliant opportunity to inspect your plants and see how they are performing; with an automated system you lose this connection and may not know if the job is being done correctly.

It's important to consider various factors when deciding how often to water your plants. More often than not, too much water will cause more damage than too little, so it's critical to find a balance. All plants need an adequate supply of water, but this varies according to type, life-cycle stage, soil, situation (undercover or outdoors, in pots or in the ground), and of course the local climate, to name a few. Water new plantings thoroughly to help the roots adjust to their new surroundings and make sure that they make good contact with the soil. In hot and sunny weather, particularly, keep a close eye on newly planted crops for the first couple of weeks and water every other day until the roots have established, a process that usually takes about 7–10 days.

The thick layer of mulch on top of a no-dig bed retains moisture in the soil. In my garden, below the mulch there is a sandy gravel soil that was abused for years by ploughing and heavy machinery. I'm fortunate not to have compaction, since the land was subsoiled (loosened and broken up) before I made the patch. Needless to say, the sandy soil is very free draining, and despite the mulch I have to water the entire garden twice or three times a week during hot spells.

Every garden and every growing season is different, and your watering routine should reflect that. Sandy soil will dry out more quickly than heavy clay. Raised beds also need watering more often; because they are above the ground and usually filled with free-draining compost, when the temperature rises sharply on hot days, moisture will evaporate from them much more quickly than from the soil below ground level.

Water plants that are growing in pots or containers very carefully. The potting mix in containers can dry out quickly and can require daily watering at the height of summer. For this reason I tend to grow very little in pots. One crop that I do house in containers is peppers (both sweet and hot). I grow them in heavy-duty square black plastic 11 litre (3 gallon) pots that I line up along the paths in my polytunnel, to make the most of the space. I monitor them closely by lifting the pot and feeling its weight; if the pot is light, it requires watering. Always give pots a thorough soak, since dry soil in pots can become hydrophobic and difficult to rehydrate.

Feeding

If you want to give your soil and crops a boost, include a weekly feed in your watering routine. I use a number of natural, nutrient-rich liquid feeds, many

Dried seaweed can be added to the annual mulch for a no-dig bed. It provides important nutrients and is a great alternative to synthetic fertilizers.

Seaweed is a renewable resource that can be foraged – in moderation – if you live near the sea.

of them homemade, such as comfrey tea or compost slurry from my own heap. Everything I use is natural – there are no artificial nasties in my garden.

My favourite liquid feed is seaweed extract, which acts as a broad-spectrum fertilizer that boosts the plants' growth both above and below ground. It contains complex carbohydrates and an abundance of vital minerals in a highly bioavailable form (meaning the plants can access and absorb them easily), providing all plants with the valuable nutrients they need to grow and thrive and increasing the production of chlorophyll, the chemical that allows them to make their own food using sunlight – a process known as photosynthesis.

I feed my plants weekly or biweekly by diluting seaweed feed in a watering can. To ensure the feed travels deep down into the soil rather than running off the top, soak the soil with water before feeding.

Living so close to the coast, I often forage for seaweed on the beach. I use it to make my own seaweed feed by fermenting it with water and molasses sugar in a large water butt for several months. If you wish to do the same, check the local laws for foraging and remove only seaweed that has been washed up, leaving any that is still growing. I do also buy seaweed extract, though, since there are some wonderful products on the market and my plants love it.

66
Every garden and every growing season is different, and your watering routine should reflect that.

Companion Planting

Gardening offers the opportunity to increase biodiversity, and by growing different plants together we create a naturally balanced landscape that brings numerous benefits. A biodiverse garden is a healthy and productive garden.

A good example of this is companion planting, where particular plants are grown alongside crops to protect or enhance them. Some companion plants draw up nutrients from the depths of the soil, while others release them via their roots to nourish their neighbours; some are fragrant and confuse hungry pests; and some attract beneficial insects, such as ladybirds, lacewings, and hoverflies, which will chow down on aphids. Companion planting helps to break up monocultures – the same type of plant grown en masse – and therefore makes the life of pests and diseases much more difficult.

Growing small numbers of different crops and pollinator-friendly flowers together reduces the risk of disease and pest infestation.

There are some obvious combinations to steer clear of. Over-vigorous plants, such as mint, will run riot and quickly smother the plot. Beware of planting tall plants alongside short ones, in case you shade your valuable crop (although this can be beneficial for low-growing plants, such as lettuce, that appreciate shade from hot sun to delay bolting – flowering and running to seed). Moisture-loving crops, such as celery, that are natives of boggy land will not make a good companion for tomatoes, which are notorious for performing poorly when they have wet feet. There are conflicting opinions, particularly regarding what *not* to plant together, but I believe that, broadly speaking, all plants enjoy growing alongside friends.

The technique of companion planting has been used by Indigenous farmers and horticulturists for millennia. One of the most famous examples is the "Three Sisters" method developed in North America by the Indigenous Iroquois, who grew squash, beans, and corn in close proximity (see pages 154, 174, 322, and 338). The plants nurtured one another and formed a symbiotic relationship that helped them to thrive, just as in a family.

More recently, growers have come to believe that crops that are a good match in a culinary sense will also cohabit happily in the veg patch. Basil and tomatoes are a good example. Not only do both love the same warm, sunny, well-drained growing location, but also basil's aromatic foliage repels aphids and other tomato pests, while the herb's roots produce substances known

Marigolds produce a strong scent that deters aphids and other flying pests.

understood, and it's a very exciting field for research. The intertwined complexity of life will forever amaze me, and it can be used to the grower's advantage.

Leguminous crops (beans and peas) help to make nitrogen – which is essential for good leafy growth – more available in the soil. This is called nitrogen-fixing and it is in fact another form of companionship or symbiosis, this time between a bacterium and a plant. The group of bacteria known as *Rhizobium*, which are already present in the soil, colonize the legume's root system, causing it to produce nodules to house the bacteria. The bacteria then fix (absorb) nitrogen, which is in turn absorbed by the plant. When clearing legumes from the patch, always cut the plants at the base and leave the roots in the ground, so that these nitrogen-fixing bacterium allies stay in the soil.

A brilliant use of companion planting is a logistical one: to make more of your growing space by interplanting and intersowing. At any time, you can pop in plants or seeds between rows of existing crops to form a growing overlap. For example, if you sow a row of carrots between lettuces, the salad leaves can be harvested while the carrot seeds are germinating. Once the carrots have germinated and grown on for a few weeks, the lettuce – which has now begun to stop producing – can be removed, making way for the carrots. Or, sticking with lettuces, you could grow Welsh onions among your salads: when lettuce is grown in rows there is always a small patch of soil left outside the circumference of the lettuce, and these little spots are perfect for multi-sown Welsh onions. The compact onions grow straight and tall, so they won't shade the lettuce, but they do make perfect use of the tiny patches of vacant soil.

Perhaps the best-known approaches to companion planting involve flowers. I grow a vast number of flowering plants that not only add beauty but also attract beneficial

as exudates that are believed to improve the flavour of the tomato's fruit. The tomato plants also provide dappled shade for the basil plants, protecting their delicate leaves from harsh weather.

Another common companion planting is carrots with alliums, such as leeks and onions. The strong scent the alliums emit is believed to deter carrot root fly, while the fragrance emitted by the carrots is said to deter onion fly.

Companionship is happening all over the garden all the time. There are countless unsung heroes, such as the underground mycelium (fungal) network and trillions of microscopic bacteria, some of which are responsible for decomposition, while others form symbiotic relationships with plants. These networks and collaborations are only just starting to be

Even a small
part of the garden
devoted to native
plants and flowers
will reap huge
benefits in terms of
pollinating insects.

insects, which help with pollination and control pests. The aim is to create a garden brimming with different fruit, vegetable, herb, and flower species that will entice a wide variety of wildlife. Here are some of my favourite flower companions:

Calendula (*Calendula officinalis*)

Many gardeners will know this plant already as a great source of pollen that attracts beneficial insects. It's a biodiversity magnet and there are many cultivars in a host of colours. My favourite is 'Indian Prince', which is deep orange with a rich crimson centre.

Growing hint

When deadheading (removing spent flowers), keep the withered blooms to dry and store for use in teas.

Catnip (*Nepeta grandiflora*)

This is the stuff your kitty goes silly for! Despite being famous for its effects on felines, it doesn't just attract cats. The flowers of this aromatic long-season perennial provide nectar and pollen for bees and many other pollinating insects from late spring through to the end of summer.

Growing hints

Buy catmint as a pot plant at any time of the year, although spring and autumn are ideal times to plant it in the garden. It's notorious for sprawling, and as the summer goes on the plant can almost develop a bald spot in the middle. To avoid this, give it the good old Chelsea chop (see panel opposite).

Cornflower (*Centaurea cyanus*)

This proper old-school wildflower is super easy to grow, being unfussy about soil type and very drought-resistant. One of my favourite things about cornflowers is that they grow tall, to 75cm (30in) or more. The long, narrow, hairy stems and fringed flowers make it an excellent cut flower.

The most popular is the vivid sapphire-blue variety. This year I've interplanted it with a striking orange calendula. The colour contrast is stunning, and the bees and butterflies just can't keep away. I use cornflowers as a border plant at the perimeter of the patch, rather than planting them among my vegetables.

Growing hints

Cornflower can be sown directly on top of freshly raked compost or soil. Mixing them with other seeds, such as poppies, borage, and chamomile, and sowing in this fashion is a great way to create a mini wildflower meadow.

Calendula (above) is a glorious ray of sunshine in the veg patch and a magnet for many different insects.

Cornflowers (opposite) have a light, almost feathery presence and attract pollinating insects.

Marigolds (*Tagetes* spp.)

Marigolds are many growers' go-to companion flowers, particularly with lettuce and tomatoes. Their roots release pheromones that deter cutworms, so interplanting them with lettuce is a great way to deter those pesky pests. Planted alongside tomatoes, marigolds provide a double benefit, deterring pests (such as aphids and blackfly) with the strong odour of their leaves and flowers, and attracting beneficial pollinating and predatory insects. It can be a pain to find ants farming aphids on your tomatoes, but marigolds are great for attracting ladybirds and guess what the favourite meal of ladybirds and their larvae is? Aphids.

I recommend growing dwarf varieties, since they don't take up valuable cropping space and can be popped in at the corners of beds. They also fit perfectly underneath cucumbers and tomatoes growing up string or canes.

Growing hint

When the plant reaches four branches high, pinch out the stem to encourage bushiness and more blooms.

Nasturtium (*Tropaeolum majus*)

These vigorous, vine-like, low-growing plants are one of the most effective traps

The "Chelsea chop"

This pruning method allows you to limit the size and control the flowering season of many herbaceous plants, and is particularly useful on plants that tend to sprawl. It gets its name because it is usually carried out at the end of May, and gardeners have traditionally used the RHS Chelsea Flower Show (which is held at that time) as a reminder to do it. The Chelsea chop keeps the plant compact, while delaying flowering for better blooms later in the season. Simply cut back the stems by between a third and half, using clean secateurs.

for cabbage white caterpillars. Anyone who has grown brassicas of any kind will know that if you don't cover these crops, you spend all summer picking off caterpillars. But peppery nasturtium leaves are a delicacy for the caterpillars, so growing them among or next to brassicas is a great form of natural pest control. The humble cabbage white butterfly gets a lot of flak, but it's an important part of the balance of nature, and growing decoy plants is the perfect way to give it a safe place to breed. As with marigolds, I advise growing dwarf nasturtiums in the veg patch, since the larger varieties can smother a whole bed in just a few weeks.

Growing hint

Nasturtiums don't respond well to being transplanted, so it's a good idea to sow seeds directly in their final planting position. Dib a hole slightly wider than the seed and about 5cm (2in) deep.

There are many other flowers that are popular with the insect community, but when selecting companion flowers I look for species that provide food or other useful properties for humans as well. Multi-use crops like this are a great way to create a fully edible landscape where every plant plays its part and has its uses. I do get a lot of joy from purely ornamental plants as well – the key is having a diverse mixture of crops and flowers growing together in harmony.

Weed, Pest, & Disease Control

A patch plagued with weeds, pests, or an outbreak of disease is the stuff of most gardeners' nightmares. But I believe that Mother Nature has the answers – after all, she created the problems – and I have never used any synthetic weedkiller, slug pellet, plant food, insecticide, or fungicide. For me, one of the main driving forces behind growing my own veg is the ability to produce fresh, chemical-free food, so it would seem counter-intuitive to buy a "magic" bottle full of suspicious-sounding ingredients that claim to work wonders for plants or kill off pesky insects. Instead, I use a holistic and regenerative approach, with an emphasis on working with nature rather than against it.

Weeding

There's no doubt that no-dig gardening results in fewer weeds, but every garden is different and comes with its own problems. Weeding is best done little and often, so whether I'm planting, watering, pinching out side shoots (shoots that form in the joint where a leaf or stem meets the main stem), or harvesting crops, I always have a weed bucket to hand. It acts as a constant reminder to pluck out any weeds that have sprouted since my last visit. Weeding as you go saves time and stops a build-up of weeds, allowing you to focus on the fun stuff, such as sowing seeds and harvesting the bounty. The key is to monitor the types of weed you have and handle them accordingly.

Weeding tips

Remove broadleaf weeds, such as docks and dandelions, with a trowel, digging out as much of the taproot as possible.

Hand-pull weeds after watering; they will pop out easily in freshly watered no-dig beds.

Hoe when the sun is shining, so that the cut weeds shrivel before they have a chance to re-establish their roots.

Grass and clover are best pulled out by hand; their tough, fibrous roots will resprout if left in the ground.

Maintain the edges of grassy or weedy areas by mowing or trimming to prevent creeping weeds from infiltrating the veg patch.

Keep up with the deadheading, since allowing flowers to dry out on the plant will spread seed. This can be a nice way to self-seed a flower garden or border, but in the vegetable garden I reduce weed pressure as much as possible. Any weeds that run to seed can be deadheaded if you don't have time to pull them out by hand.

Thoroughly hot-compost material that contains lots of seeds. A temperature of 54–60°C (130–140°F) for seven days will kill most seeds. Used correctly, a compost tumbler (see page 22) will become hot enough to kill off weed seeds effectively.

Remain vigilant, since the early detection of vigorous perennial weeds (those that survive from year to year), such as bindweed, is crucial for effective control. Hand-pulling is the most effective method of controlling a small or medium-sized infestation of bindweed.

Bare ground is very welcoming to weeds, so grow more plants and flowers or put in cover crops or green manure (plants that manage soil erosion, weeds, and soil quality).

To kill off a large patch of weedy pasture, cover it with a double layer of tarpaulin or a thick black plastic sheet that doesn't let light through, and weight it down so that it can't blow away. The weeds underneath will be starved of light and die, leaving bare soil within 6–8 weeks.

Mulch, don't dig. Adding a layer of compost or woodchips to beds or paths suppresses weed growth by blocking sunlight and smothering the seeds, while not digging prevents the seeds stored in the soil from being brought up to the surface, where they could germinate.

Stay well away from weedkillers and other chemical weed-control products. Most contain poisons that are harmful to humans and to the life in the soil.

A hoe (opposite and above) will allow you to loosen weeds easily without disturbing your valuable crops.

Pests and diseases

Pests and diseases plague all gardens at some point. For me, controlling them is about mitigating the risk to my crops while creating an ecologically balanced, diverse, integrated system. There is a wide range of techniques for managing pests while building and preserving the health and productivity of the garden ecosystem. A healthy plant is a more resilient one, less susceptible to whatever the world throws at it. The best way to approach pest control is in a holistic, ecologically conscious way, by creating and maintaining a balanced, healthy garden ecosystem.

Observation

Paying attention to plant health, pest populations, and the ecosystem dynamic will help you to identify and detect any problems before they become too bad. Early intervention includes manually removing pests or infected leaves before they have a chance to cause much damage.

Biodiversity

Natural diversity maintains a healthy balance within the ecosystem, reducing the risk of pest or disease outbreaks, and one of the best ways to achieve this is by creating habitats. Wildlife ponds, log stacks, insect hotels, hedgerows, ponds, birdhouses, and pollinator-friendly plants all contribute a mosaic of habitats that attract beneficial creatures. After all, every pest is itself food for something else. The aim is to create a balanced ecosystem where insects, birds, amphibians, and other creatures play a role in controlling pests. Ladybirds, lacewings, spiders, beetles, toads, and hedgehogs are just some of the many pest-munching predators that can keep unwanted populations in check.

Companion planting

This is an easy way to reduce damage from pests and increase overall productivity. It involves growing different types of plant together that have a mutually beneficial relationship. Some companion plants have natural pest-repelling properties, while others attract beneficial insects that prey on pests. See also page 40.

Protection

Protecting crops with physical barriers, such as netting or mesh, is sometimes the only way to keep vulnerable plants safe from caterpillar infestation, birds' persistent beaks, or troublesome carrot root flies. Never overlook these simple methods.

Soil health

Healthy soil is the foundation of a thriving garden. If you focus your attention on feeding, building, and maintaining healthy soil, your plants will be less susceptible to pest attack or outbreaks of disease. Using the no-dig technique, mulching with different materials (such as compost, manure, and seaweed), and planting cover crops or green manure are perfect ways of keeping your soil and plants in top shape.

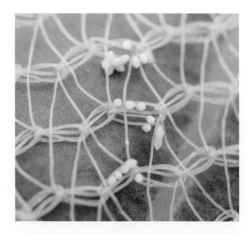

If the netting is too close to the plant the cabbage white butterfly will still be able to lay its eggs, so be sure to leave a gap.

Common pests

Allium leaf miner
The larvae of this fly prey on alliums in the spring and autumn. White dots appear on the foliage as the adults feed, then the larvae burrow into the stems and bulbs, causing disease and rot. Protect with horticultural mesh.

Aphids
Aphids come in many different colours and can cause catastrophic damage, stunting seedlings and transmitting viruses that cause leaves to deform or turn yellow through lack of chlorophyll (chlorosis). However, they are a vital food source for countless insects and birds, so attracting predators is the best approach. If plants are particularly young and vulnerable, or if there is a large infestation (which can happen early in the year, when some predators are still hibernating), take more action by picking off the aphids by hand, gently tapping or shaking the plant, spraying with water to dislodge them, or mixing garlic and chilli in water to make an unpleasant spray that will kill the aphids. Remove and compost virus-infected plants.

Birds
Our feathered friends can peck at brassicas, pea shoots, and other treats. The most effective way to stop this is to cover crops with horticultural mesh. Be sure to weigh down the netting carefully, so that birds can't find their way under and become trapped inside.

Blackfly
See Aphids.

Butterflies
The simplest way to protect your crops from egg-laying butterflies is to use fine horticultural mesh over vulnerable plants, such as cauliflower, broccoli, and cabbage. Keep watch as the plants grow, however, since butterflies can still lay eggs on leaves that touch the mesh. Remove caterpillars by hand as soon as you notice them. If all your vulnerable crops are tucked up under mesh, consider planting decoy crops of nasturtium to lure away cabbage whites (see page 45).

Cabbage root fly
The larvae of these grey-black flies feed on the roots of brassicas in the spring and summer. Signs that you may have an infestation are poor growth and yellowing and wilting foliage. Take pre-emptive action by netting your plants with fine horticultural mesh.

Carrot root fly
These tiny black flies produce larvae that burrow into and feed on the roots of carrots, parsnips, and celery from late spring until mid-autumn. The foliage fades and discolours, turning yellow or scarlet, and you will find tunnels in the roots. Protect your crops with fine horticultural mesh.

Celery fly
The larvae of these flies feed on the foliage of celery and celeriac and are active for a long time, from mid-spring until early winter. Squiggly white lines appear on the foliage, which then dries out. Protect your crops with fine horticultural mesh.

Cutworms
This is a generic name for moth caterpillars that live in the soil and feed on plants. They are most problematic in the spring and summer, when you may notice missing, decapitated, or half-cut stems with wilted foliage. Use trimmed-down toilet-roll tubes as protective collars around the stems of young plants. You can also lure the cutworms out by watering an area generously, covering with light-blocking polythene or tarpaulin, and leaving it for a day, after which the larvae should have worked their way to the surface. They can then be easily spotted, collected, and disposed of.

Flea beetle
These small black, brown, or bronze beetles jump like fleas and are most active in spring and summer. They are easily spotted jumping off plants when disturbed, and you will also see round, unappetizing holes in the leaves. To prevent them, net your plants with fine horticultural mesh.

Leaf miner
This is a generic term for insect larvae that feed on leaves. They are most active in the spring and summer, and their tunnels on the surface of the leaf

Blackfly are attracted to juicy new growth.

are plain to see. Use horticultural mesh to protect your plants, or lure the larvae elsewhere using companion planting (see page 40).

Leatherjackets

The maggot-like larvae of crane flies or daddy-long-legs that live in the soil, leatherjackets are most active in the spring. Plants will rapidly collapse and die as their main stems are severed at ground level. Use trimmed toilet-roll tubes as protective collars around the stems of young plants. You can also lure the leatherjackets out by watering an area generously, covering with light-blocking polythene or tarpaulin, and leaving it for a day, after which the larvae should have worked their way to the surface. They can then be easily spotted, collected, and disposed of.

Onion fly

The larvae of this fly feed on the roots, bulbs, and stems of allium crops, and are a problem in the summer, when you may notice wilting leaves and soft, decaying bulbs. Net your plants with fine horticultural mesh.

Pea and bean weevil

Although these small light brown beetles cut alarming notches out of the leaves in the spring, the damage is usually not catastrophic and the plants should still crop well. Protect by fleecing any overwintering crops.

A crop of corn destroyed by rats.

Pea moth

These brown moths lay eggs on peas and the emerging caterpillars burrow into and feast on the seeds inside the pods, so that often the damage is noticed only once the peas are shelled. They are most active in early and midsummer, so later sowings and those being grown for dried peas are most at risk. Use netting if pest pressure is high.

Rodents

Rodents can devour trays of freshly sown seed overnight, or snap tender seedlings in search of the seeds below. They will gnaw on squash to get at the sweet seeds inside, strip corn to the cob, and steal tomatoes for moisture in hot summers. Without the help of a clowder of cats, controlling rodents can be a challenge. Many natural growers claim that strong-smelling garlic spray is effective; otherwise, your best bet is to protect newly sown seed using physical barriers or by keeping them in places where rodents can't reach, and to watch your crops as they ripen so that you get to them first.

Slugs and snails

These land-based molluscs can wreak havoc on young seedlings. They hide in the wooden sides of raised beds, under pots and logs, and among woodchips. Starve them of habitat close to growing areas by keeping borders and grass edges short. In wet years pressure from slugs and snails can be torrid and intervention necessary, so head out into the garden at dusk, armed with a torch, and search them out. I often chop them in half and throw them on the compost heap, or leave them somewhere the birds will find them; if you choose to relocate them, bear in mind that you will be transporting an imbalance from one ecosystem to another. Beetles, centipedes, ducks, hedgehogs, toads, and slow worms are just a selection of slug-scoffing sidekicks that can help to keep populations under control.

Spider mite

These tiny mites cover plants in a thin, cobwebby silk. They can be a problem in the summer, particularly in dry conditions, so keep crops in polytunnels

and greenhouses well watered to increase the humidity. Remove and compost infested plants as soon as you notice the damage.

Stem and bulb nematodes

This microscopic, worm-like soil-borne pest is one of very few nematodes that feed on parts of the plant above the soil. The stems of infected plants may swell, rot, crack, and die, and leaves may brown and shrivel, but for a positive identification it is often necessary to carry out a laboratory test. The best protection is to encourage healthy soil (see page 18).

Swede midge

The larvae of this small fly prey on the growing tips of brassicas in late spring and early summer, causing distorted, brown, or shrivelled foliage. Brassicas that produce heads (such as cabbages) may appear misshapen. Net your plants with fine horticultural mesh.

Thrips

Minute but highly active insects, thrips can cause a lot of damage in the summer. Foliage yellows, the growing tips may become distorted, and growth becomes stunted. Maintain good housekeeping with regular pruning and wash the insects off if you see them. Dispose of any badly infested crops.

Whitefly

See Aphids.

Wireworm

Wireworms can run rampant, burrowing into potatoes and other root crops, but are easily trapped with decoys. Before planting potatoes, cut large pieces of old potato and set them on the soil surface. Check them for wireworms every few days, and if you spot any, remove and destroy the bait. Repeat until pressure eases before planting.

Woodlice

These crustaceans are often more beneficial than not. They can attack root crops or seedlings, however, so maintain good housekeeping and remove dead or decaying leaves.

Common diseases

Blackleg
Most likely when cool, wet conditions are followed by warm weather, blackleg kills and stunts potato plants. Healthy stems wither and wilt, leaves turn yellow, black patches appear, and often the stem will be rotten to the core. Plant potatoes in a free-draining spot and maintain good housekeeping to ensure good airflow around the foliage.

Blight
Potatoes (especially maincrop) and tomatoes are at risk of blight in damp conditions. If you spot it on potatoes, cut off all the foliage and leave the tubers to sit in the ground for a few days before lifting. With tomatoes, watch out for rotting foliage and remove the affected plants; those growing outside without protection are most at risk. Blight is preventable to a certain extent by maintaining good housekeeping, allowing free airflow through the plants and any support structures, and removing suckers and side shoots from tomatoes. Contrary to what many people suggest, blight-infected vegetation doesn't have to be burned or isolated, and can be thrown on the compost heap.

Blossom end rot
Look out for rotten, dark brown patches at the base of the fruit. Blossom end rot affects tomatoes and is caused by calcium deficiency, which is often a result of inadequate water, because plants absorb calcium through their roots. The simple remedy is to water more regularly.

Canker
This destructive tomato disease can enter the plant via open wounds in the stem, stalk, or fruit, or from infected seeds. It particularly likes warm, humid conditions. Foliage may be yellow or brown and dry, stems can be brown and form long cankers, and fruit may have white spots. Prevention is key, so keep the foliage as dry as possible when watering and prune regularly to ensure good airflow.

Celery leaf spot
A fungal disease that affects the foliage of celery and celeriac, celery leaf spot often occurs during prolonged hot, dry spells. Small bright yellow spots appear on the leaves, later fading to a rusty brown. Keep the plants well watered in hot weather, and do not allow the soil to dry out.

Chocolate spot
This fungal disease most often affects broad beans, and can be a problem in the spring. Red or rusty brown spots appear on the foliage and, under the right conditions, can quickly cover the leaves, causing them to shrivel and wilt. Maintain good housekeeping by pruning to encourage good airflow.

Club root
A soil-dwelling disease that causes poor root formation in brassicas, resulting in stunted growth, club root can remain in the soil for 15 years. Affected plants will have a swollen root system with few or no fibrous roots. Avoid growing brassicas in affected areas for 5–7 years.

Grey mould
This fungal disease blights the flowers, stems, leaves, and fruit of many plants, taking the form of grey, fuzzy mould and causing the plants to shrivel and die. Reduce the humidity inside polytunnels and greenhouses, encourage good airflow, and remove dead or decaying leaves regularly.

Mildew
A powdery white mould that quickly spreads over leaves, mildew is most problematic in the spring and autumn. Foliage is covered in a thin, white powdery substance that spreads quickly. Mildew occurs naturally as plants begin to weaken, so trim, prune, and remove infected leaves to slow the spread.

Mosaic virus
This is the name given to several viruses that cause foliage to take on a mottled, lumpy, almost variegated appearance. Leaves may be puckered, shrivelled, and curled. It is often spread by aphids and other insects, so keep on top of these pests to prevent the spread of the

virus. Remove and compost any infected plants.

Onion neck rot
This fungal disease causes stored bulbs to rot and spoil. Decay begins in the neck after harvest and spreads into the bulbs. The only way of preventing it is to cure and store your bulbs correctly.

Onion white rot
A destructive soil-borne fungal disease that can contaminate soil for several years, onion white rot causes yellow, wilted foliage, poor root development, and visible mould and rot around the root plate and bulb. It is most commonly found in early and midsummer. Avoid using contaminated onion sets, and if white rot is present in your soil, avoid growing alliums in the area for several years.

Root rot
This is a soil-borne disease that causes roots to rot. You will notice a rapid decline in growth, and wilted, browning leaves. To avoid it, grow plants in a free-draining location and add horticultural grit to heavy soils.

Rust
Rust is usually a problem only in excessively moist conditions, but if you notice the tell-tale red or yellow streaks on the leaves, remove and destroy the infected foliage. Ensure all plants have adequate space around them to allow good airflow.

Scab
Scabby potatoes are the result of a soil-borne disease, and although they may look unsightly, they are perfectly edible when peeled.

Harvesting & Storage

Harvesting is the most rewarding part of growing food, but it's not just a question of sallying forth with a picturesque basket over your arm. It is crucial to know when fruit and vegetables are fully ripe and time your picking accordingly. Harvesting in the correct way will promote further growth and keep many plants producing in abundance for longer.

Knowing how to harvest and when each different crop is at its peak of flavour and texture is like a sixth sense, and it will come with time. To get you started, each entry in this book includes specific information that will help you to harvest your crops successfully.

Harvesting also brings you into close proximity with your plants, so take the opportunity to check their overall health and remove any dead or dying foliage. Carrying two buckets when doing the harvesting rounds will remind you to weed and maintain your crops; use one bucket for your bounty and the other for weeds and foliage destined for the compost heap.

Manicuring

If I intend to use my produce straight away, I do most of the cleaning and trimming at the patch, best described as "manicuring". It's surprising how much foliage and soil a small harvest can accumulate; maybe it's the chef in me, but I'm not a fan of soil in the kitchen or a fully loaded compost bucket on the work surface.

There's something delightful about turning a harvest into kitchen-ready produce in the very garden it has grown in. It's a peaceful time to think back to the day the seed was sown, to the weeks that followed of nurturing the plant, right up to the moment of perfection when you cut it off the stalk or lifted it out of the ground. Humans have evolved over hundreds of thousands of years to produce a burst of the brain chemical dopamine when we harvest fresh food straight from the earth, causing us to enter a state of mild euphoria. No wonder you feel so good after snipping a couple of juicy melons from the vine!

Manicuring veg in the patch makes life much easier back in the kitchen. It's very convenient to have direct access to the compost heap for the unwanted scraps,

Harvest with a properly sharp knife or secateurs, to cause as little damage to the plant as possible.

and to wash soil-covered crops using a bucket of water that can then be poured straight back on to the garden. However, it's best done if you intend to eat the produce within a few days; crops that are being harvested for storage may not benefit from being so squeaky clean. Check the individual entries for details.

Storing your bounty

Growing enough food to feast on throughout the year was one of my main goals when I started cultivating crops. Home-grown produce can be stored for much longer than supermarket veg, and growing from seed allows you to choose long-storing varieties.

How you store your bounty will depend on the crop. Garlic, onions, and shallots can be plaited and hung up in the warmth of the house, where they not only look fantastic, but also can be positioned conveniently close to the kitchen work surface. Roots and tuberous crops, such as carrots, celeriac, and potatoes, prefer to be kept in sacks in a cool, dark place. Beans, peas, and other legumes must be carefully dried, shelled, and jarred, while gluts of softer vegetables and fruit can be turned into ferments and preserves. Every crop is different, and throughout the book I provide storage information and ideas for dealing with gluts.

Look out for long-storing varieties and aim to grow an assortment of different types of the same crop. I like to grow many different types of onion, for example, with varying storing abilities. 'Walla Walla' is a large, sweet, crunchy one that's best eaten straight out of the ground, while 'Jaune Paille des Vertus' is one of the tastiest storing onions and can last for a year; its flavour, much like that of a fine bottle of wine, improves as it matures, becoming well rounded and much sweeter.

> **"**
> **Knowing how to harvest is like a sixth sense, and it will come with time.**

Seed-saving

Without the incredible work of seed-keepers, seed-savers, and plant-breeders, we wouldn't have the heirloom (historic) varieties we do today. Saving your own seed creates a closed-loop system, shortening the supply chain, and over time your plants will adapt and acclimatize to their growing locations, building up immunity and resistance to local pests and weather patterns.

Seed-saving may seem like a piece of cake, but in fact it could be a book in itself. When growing plants for seed to save, there are many extra factors to consider, from cross-pollination (breeding with other varieties) to growing enough of the same variety to maintain a diverse gene pool.

But don't let this put you off. As gardeners we are guardians of the land, and by saving seed we can take responsibility for maintaining a tiny piece of biodiversity handed down by our ancestors, in our very own gardens. Small-scale growers have been saving seed for decades and are responsible for many of the marvellous veggies we enjoy today;

in fact, it was only in the last century that the "professionals" took over. In no time at all you'll be cultivating top-notch home-saved seed that will grow true to its parent year by year, adapting and improving to its situation with each generation and becoming more resilient and productive, with better germination rates and healthier plants.

According to the United Nations Food and Agriculture Organization, during the twentieth century we lost 75 per cent of agricultural seed diversity worldwide, not to mention a great deal of knowledge, so it's up to the next generation of seed-savers to maintain, save, and breed heirlooms to be handed down to future growers. Sowing seeds that were home-saved by yourself or a friend brings extra excitement and specialness to the already spectacular, magical feeling of watching your seeds germinate.

What are heirloom seeds?

Sometimes referred to as "heritage" or "open-pollinated", heirloom varieties are genetically diverse and have been handed down from generation to generation. They are developed over long periods by growers who hand-select plants that demonstrate particular traits, resulting in varieties that not only produce tastier food but also are resistant to local pests, diseases, and weather patterns. Many researchers and scientists consider protecting and preserving heirloom seeds to be a critical part of maintaining the genetic diversity of the world's food crops. Unlike F1 (hybrid) and GMO (genetically modified) plants, which produce unviable seed or are illegal to propagate, heirloom seeds can be saved and grown by anyone, anywhere, to

A flower head like the one on this lettuce plant will produce a good crop of seeds for sowing next year.

continue the tradition of collecting seed from their favourite plants and preserve genetic diversity for the next generation of growers.

The six easiest

There are six vegetables that are relatively easy to save seed from. This is because only one strong and healthy plant is required, and because they rarely cross-pollinate. These crops are the perfect entry point into the world of seed-saving, and any grower can give one a whirl and continue the cycle of life.

Common beans

These beans are self-pollinating, so plants grown from saved seed are unlikely to cross-pollinate. Select the best-performing plant and leave the pods on the growing plant to dry and turn brown, tan, or yellow. The beans should rattle inside when it's time to harvest. Pick or cut off all the pods and discard any that are damaged or mouldy, then leave the remaining pods in a well-ventilated place to continue drying. Once they are completely dry, shell the beans and discard any small, wrinkled, discoloured, or insect-damaged seed. Air the shelled beans for a few days before storing for the following season.

Garlic

This is not technically seed-saving, but garlic is one of the easiest crops to propagate from home stock, and always grows true to its parent. Simply keep back the best-performing bulbs to plant as separate cloves in autumn for next year's crop. There is no need to isolate the varieties; just label them clearly.

Lettuce

Choose the best-performing lettuce plant and allow it to flower and produce seed heads. Once the seed heads become dry, crispy, and brown, snip them off and pop

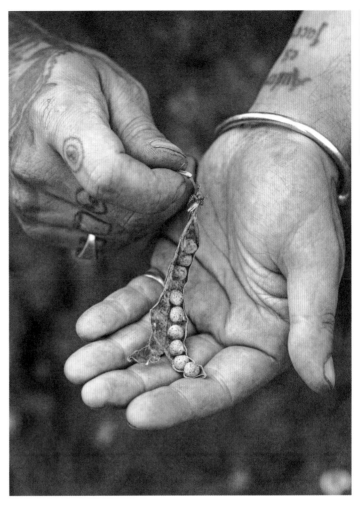

them into a paper bag or container. Shake, bash, or rub the seed heads to coax out the seeds, then leave to air-dry for a few days before transferring them to a sealed packet or airtight container and storing them in a cool, dry place.

Peas

Saving peas is done in the same way as growing peas to be dried for the kitchen (see page 313). Allow the pods to mature fully and dry out on the vine, until they become brown and brittle. Harvest them by gently snapping them from the plants, then open them and remove the seeds. Discard any seed that has been spoiled by pests, then dry the seeds fully in a cool, well-ventilated area before storing.

Wait until the pod is completely dried and shrivelled before removing peas for seed-saving.

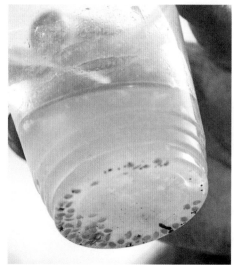

Home-produced tomato seeds require special treatment before they can be sown. After scooping out the seeds (above), soak them in water to break down the gel coating (top right), then spread out on baking paper and allow to dry (bottom right).

Potatoes

Again, not technically seed-saving, but it's super simple to save and plant your home-grown potatoes as you would seed potatoes in the spring. When harvesting spuds, put aside any that have turned green from exposure to the sun and use these as seed potatoes the following year.

Tomatoes

Start by identifying the strongest plant and removing a fully ripe, healthy fruit from it. Cut open the tomato and scoop out the seeds into a small lidded container. Add enough water to submerge the seeds, pop the lid on, and leave at room temperature for a few days. This will kick-start a process of fermentation that breaks down the tomato seed's characteristic jelly-like membrane. This coating contains substances that inhibit germination, preventing frost-tender wild seedlings from emerging in the autumn or winter. Stir the mixture daily for between five and seven days, and don't worry if a layer of mould forms on the surface. After about three days fermentation should be complete; rinse the seeds thoroughly in a small sieve or tea strainer under cold running water to remove the gel. Spread the seeds out to dry on baking paper or a paper plate and leave for a few days before transferring to a non-stick surface, such as a small china plate or metal tray, to continue drying in a cool, dry place, out of direct sunlight, for two or three weeks. The seeds can then be kept in an envelope in a cool, dry place.

Seed-saving tips

Only save seed from open- (naturally) pollinated varieties; Fl hybrids will not grow true to the parent, and many are protected by patenting restrictions.

Always save seed from the healthiest plant with the best fruit. When we save seed we become part of the process of natural selection, so choose wisely.

Give fruit that is being harvested for seed time to ripen completely on the plant, to ensure the seeds are fully mature.

Collect seed heads as soon as they mature, ideally on a dry day after the morning dew has evaporated.

Clean harvested seed thoroughly to remove and separate the chaff and other debris, which could cause the seeds to rot and become unviable.

Ensure the seeds have dried out thoroughly before you store them for later sowing; damp seeds will go mouldy over the winter.

Watch out for rodents, which will gladly steal your precious home-saved seed from the plant or when it's drying out undercover.

Label as you go; you don't want to grow something unexpected next season, so include the plant name and variety, along with the date of harvest.

Dried, cleaned seeds must be stored correctly. I keep mine in paper packets or envelopes, usually in an old tin in a cool frost- and moisture-free room in the house. Excess heat or moisture can quickly cause seeds to deteriorate or perish.

If you're unsure about the likely germination rates of your home-saved seed, perform a basic germination test by placing a few seeds inside a folded, damp paper towel to see if they spring into life.

Part 2.

plant guide

Bulbs & Stems

Offering distinctive, robust flavours, these crops are the backbone of the larder and the veg patch.

Celery

Apium graveolens

Also known as Apio, Kereviz, Sedano, Sellerie

Celery deserves the utmost respect, despite becoming an overlooked ingredient in home kitchens. Heirloom celery is considerably more flavourful than shop-bought, and the tall, straight stalks have a refreshing texture and succulent bite.

History

Celery as it is known today is descended from a plant of boggy marshland that is believed to be native to Asia and the Mediterranean. Archaeological evidence suggests that humans carried and traded celery seeds as early as 4,000 BCE. The leaves are incredibly bitter in their wild form, and the stalks thin and hollow. Despite this, the wild ancestor of celery was used for medicinal purposes in early civilizations. The ancient Greeks considered it a potent "love food" that enhanced libido and increased androsterone in men. The Romans, who are believed to have developed a taste for the plant after discovering it growing wild, chomped on raw celery stems to cure a hangover and clear a thick head after a heavy night on the tiles.

Celery's historical credentials as a frisky food can also be traced back to the eighteenth-century Italian adventurer Giacomo Casanova, who is often dubbed the world's greatest lover; he consumed celery in large amounts to improve his sexual stamina. More recently, in an attempt to add a dash of spice to the vegetable market, Hassy's Garden Fresh Celery (once a leading British celery supplier) made a lasting impression with an audacious promotional campaign that featured raunchy photographs of pin-up girls posing seductively with, and playfully nibbling, whole celery stalks.

Over the ages, celery has found itself on podiums with elite athletes when crowns were fashioned and woven from

61

its leaves in a similar way to the bay-leaf crowns at the Olympic Games. The celery headpieces were worn by the champions of the Nemean Games, an ancient athletic competition and musical celebration held in honour of the Greek god Zeus.

In the seventeenth century, Italian farmers domesticated celery as the vegetable that is familiar today. Over time, they improved both the taste – by reducing its bitterness – and the texture – by selecting plants with thick, juicy stems compared to the thin, hollow stalks of its wild precursor.

As celery became an essential base ingredient for many cherished dishes, it was also a hit in the drinks industry. A Brooklyn-based soda company started bottling celery-flavoured fizzy pop in the late 1860s. It has a flavour comparable to the sharp spiciness of ginger beer, yet with a prominent whack of celery that's seriously powerful and intense. The drink, known as Cel-Ray, became popular in Jewish delicatessens on the east coast of the United States and, 150 years later, is still popular in Jewish neighbourhoods.

It is said that the Bloody Mary, a cocktail initially concocted as a breakfast brew to cure a hangover, was invented in 1921 by the French bartender Fernand Petiot, who was working in New York at the time. However, Fernand's early versions lacked what is now considered the fundamental inclusion of a celery-stick

---

In the kitchen

These elegant stems are a fundamental part (with onion and carrot) of *mirepoix* and *sofrito*, the bases for countless sauces, soups, stews, and braises in cuisines worldwide. For me as a former chef, working with home-grown *mirepoix* or *sofrito* is one of the most satisfying cooking and gardening crossover moments.

---

garnish. In the 1960s, as an impatient guest at a swanky Chicago hotel waited for a bartender to fetch a swizzle stick for his cocktail, his frustration grew until he grabbed a celery stalk from a nearby garnish station – a seemingly small act that made history.

Culinary uses

Preparation

To enhance the flavour and improve the texture when cooking large chunks of celery, use the flat side of a knife to lightly crush and gently split the stalks.

Dishes

It's not surprising that celery has lost its popularity; the plastic-wrapped stuff that is sold in supermarkets is generally unappetizing and lacks flavour. However, this humble vegetable that is so often relegated to a supporting act in recipes can play the primary role, particularly when you discover the delicious taste of home-grown heirloom varieties.

Celery is a common ingredient in Chinese cuisine, although the varieties used in China differ from those found elsewhere in being smaller and crunchier, with a more robust flavour. They are usually not eaten raw, but braised or stir-fried with aromatic additions. In one of the country's most popular celery dishes the vegetable is stir-fried in a wok with flavouring ingredients, such as fresh chilli, soy sauce, rice-wine vinegar, and chicken stock, before shredded pork is added. This quick dish has the perfect balance of sweet, salty, and spicy, which works eloquently with the tender celery and crispy pork.

Celery sauce was a popular accompaniment to poultry dishes, particularly pheasant, in eighteenth-century Britain. The simple condiment is traditionally made by gently simmering chopped celery in water seasoned with

Celery can be so much more than the tall, pale green stems familiar from the supermarket. The three varieties shown here are (from left to right) 'Gigante Dorato', 'Chinese Pink', and 'Liyang White'.

66

The tall, straight stalks have a refreshing texture and succulent bite.

mace blades, thickened with butter and flour, and finished with a dash of cream.

In an article in the *San Francisco Chronicle* in 1919, the paper's cookery editor Belle De Graf shared a recipe for fried celery similar to onion rings. According to Mrs Graf, this recipe is a great way to make use of the tough outer stalks. To prepare, cut celery into 8 cm (3 in) lengths and parboil gently until soft and tender but not broken. After cooling, dip the stems into a fritter batter, deep-fry, and serve with tomato ketchup.

Growing

Propagation

Celery and its knobbly cousin celeriac (see page 266) are some of the trickiest veg to raise from seed. Their small, dainty seeds require warmth and light to grow, and even a small scattering of compost on top can hinder sprouting. To improve germination, sow sparingly in small trays on top of pre-watered compost. Gently press the seeds down to ensure good contact with the medium, but they must remain on the surface. To keep the seeds

63

Cardboard is a less intrusive way than trenching to blanch celery.

Growing at a glance

Sow Early–late spring,
15–20°C (60–68°F)

Plant out Late spring–early summer

Spacing 20–30cm (8–12in)

Harvest Summer–autumn

frost has passed completely. Dib a hole slightly deeper than the base of the plant so that they're buried, as this provides some protection from wind. Water the plants well and consider using horticultural fleece or mesh to protect them from pests for the first month or so, until established.

Aftercare

Traditionally, celery is grown in trenches and earthed up to blanch the stems, which helps to reduce bitterness and produces a more tender crop. Trenching is a very invasive process for the soil, however, and an easy alternative that stays aligned to no-dig practices is to encase the stems in a sleeve made from cardboard, secured with jute twine or a rubber band. This is a quick and effective way of blanching celery, and it should be done three or four weeks before harvest.

As the plants grow, remove any side shoots from the base to keep them growing uniformly. The trick to growing the tenderest, sweetest-tasting celery is to provide the plants with ample water throughout their life, and especially as they begin to bulk up. If rainfall is scarce, water celery thoroughly three times a week, and even if the plants look lush, abundant, and healthy, provide them with an extra burst of moisture to keep the stems crisp and succulent.

hydrated, cover them with a clear cloche to lock in humidity while allowing light to penetrate. Avoid using a traditional watering can, even one with a delicate rose attachment, which can easily wash the seeds away; use a fine spray bottle instead to mist the surface of the compost.

It usually takes two weeks for celery seeds to begin sprouting. Once the first set of leaves appears, remove the cloche. Allow the plants to grow for another two or three weeks, until they are large enough to handle and can be transplanted into individual seed cells. Celery plants are sensitive and often flower prematurely if exposed to cold conditions while young and tender, so it is crucial to keep new sowings in a bright, frost-free location. Leave them to grow for an additional four or five weeks after transplanting, and plant them out in the garden once the risk of

Well-watered celery
plants will produce
deliciously tender,
juicy stems.

66

This humble vegetable that is so often relegated to a supporting act in recipes can play the primary role.

Plant problems

Aphids, blight, celery leaf spot, leaf miner, rabbits, slugs and snails (see pages 49–51)

Harvesting

For an early harvest, grow a few celery plants that can be treated as a cut-and-come-again crop, harvesting the largest outer stems as needed. Depending on sowing dates, the cropping of whole heads begins in the summer and continues until the autumn. All plants must be picked before the first frost. It's essential not to allow celery to mature for too long in the ground, or the stalks will become stringy and fibrous. When harvesting whole heads, use a knife to cut just below the soil surface. Shoots often sprout and begin regrowing from the root plate if they are left in the ground, so be sure to remove them.

Storage

To maintain the crispness and succulence of celery, remove the leafy tops (these can be used in flavourful stocks, stews, and soups) and store the entire stem in a bowl of water. You can even propagate extra celery plants by placing a stalk in a glass of water, to encourage roots to form. It generally takes two or three weeks for the roots to emerge, after which the new plant can be transferred to a pot to grow on in compost.

Cut off the whole head below the surface of the soil (opposite), making sure the root plate is harvested too (above).

Recommended varieties

'Chinese Pink' A vivid candy-floss-coloured, thin-stemmed celery from northern China, this variety is much earlier to mature and considerably easier to grow than larger-stalked varieties. The stems add colourful flashes of neon-pink to the veg patch and brighten up soups and stocks, while providing a crunchy texture and a pronounced taste that is sweeter and more robust than that of regular green varieties. Pink celery was all the rage in Europe in the nineteenth century, but it fell out of favour as new culinary trends sprouted. This variety is best served cooked, for a delicate, mellow flavour. This type of celery is seen as a high-end ingredient in China and is found on the menus of top restaurants in Beijing.

'Giant Red' An old-fashioned red-stemmed celery that's capable of reaching heights over 60cm (24in). First made available in England during the eighteenth century, this ruby-coloured gem is very reliable and moderately cold-resistant, making it an excellent choice for late autumn harvests.

'Gigante Dorato' A thick-stemmed, succulent green celery from the Alpine province of Alessandria in northern Italy. It is perfectly suited to being eaten raw, especially if the stems have been blanched, when they turn a superb pale yellow; because of this, locals know the variety as 'Golden Legs'.

'Golden Pascal' A cold-tolerant celery that's perfect for late autumn harvests and for growers in cooler climates. Dating from 1885, this French-bred heirloom with tall white stems is crowned with vibrant golden foliage that adds a flare of brightness to the garden. The stalks are solid, with a beautiful texture and nutty flavour when cooked.

'Hopkins Fenlander' This large, succulent celery was bred in the mid-twentieth century by Stanley Hopkins of Stretham near Ely, Cambridgeshire, using an older Fenland type, and it is one of only three celery cultivars to hold a Fenland Protected Geographical Indication (PGI). Fenland celery is a unique white winter type that is available for only a short period, in late autumn and early winter. A fundamental, honourable British heritage ingredient, it was highly sought after for the dinner tables of wealthy Victorian Londoners. The plant owes its delicate, sweet flavour and crisp texture to traditional growing methods and the peaty Fenland soil in which it is cultivated.

'Kintsai' A mainstay of Chinese kitchens, 'Kintsai' is a dark green, thin-stemmed celery that has been grown since at least the time of the Ming dynasty (1368–1644). With an intense, bitter, and slightly spicy flavour, the stalks and leaves are best consumed cooked, when the flavour becomes sweet, mild, and well rounded.

'Liyang White' A slender, snow-white celery that has been grown for more than 800 years in the wetlands of Changzhou in eastern China. The Ministry of Agriculture of the People's Republic of China awarded it a PGI, signifying its importance in the region. 'Liyang White' is now transported to other parts of China, where it is marketed as a speciality ingredient and sold at premium prices. These pungent, brilliantly bright stems, perfect for soups and stocks, become even brighter if they are blanched for three weeks before harvest.

Fennel

Foeniculum vulgare var. azoricum

Also known as Finocchio, Florence fennel, Hinojo

Fennel's strong flavour, reminiscent of liquorice, is certainly not everyone's cup of tea, but the unique, fragrant flavour of this divisive vegetable enhances many dishes. Much like an onion, it produces a succulent bulbous heart composed of aromatic overlapping layers. Tall green stems emerge from the crown, with feathery leaves that sway gracefully in the breeze.

History

In its wild form, fennel is native to the shores of the Mediterranean, where it thrives naturally in the region's arid soil. The cultivated variety was bred in the seventeenth century in Italy.

The word "marathon" comes from the Greek word for fennel *máratho*. It's said that during the famous Battle of Marathon in 490 BCE, the war zone was a field of fennel. Despite being heavily outnumbered, the Athenian army managed to defeat the Persians. A Greek herald was sent running the 42km (26 miles) from Marathon to Athens to deliver news of the triumph, and this is supposedly how the race was born.

In medieval times the roots of fennel were used as a remedy for the bite of a mad dog. People traditionally hung whole fennel plants over doorways to ward off evil phantoms, and, for added magical protection, seeds were stuffed into keyholes to stop spirits from creeping through.

Culinary uses
Preparation
The key to serving fennel raw is to slice it as thinly as possible; for best results, use a mandoline to shave off fine slivers. Don't throw away the tops. These subtle-tasting, feathery leaves can be served as a herby garnish, tossed into salads, or whizzed into pesto and other sauces.

> **The unique, fragrant flavour of this divisive vegetable enhances many dishes.**

'Romanesco'

Dishes

Fennel bulbs are crisp and succulent with a pronounced anise taste, a bitter edge, and a tangy, citrusy zing. The refreshing, clean flavour makes fennel a great addition to many recipes, balancing and rounding off heavier-tasting ingredients. Eaten raw, it complements slaws and salads, such as the Sicilian classic *insalata di finocchi e arance* (fennel and orange salad). This dish is often eaten in Sicily as a celebration of the orange harvest. There are many versions, but my favourite includes thinly sliced fennel, fresh oranges, and black olives, and is topped with mint leaves, crushed walnuts, and a splash of olive oil.

Once cooked, fennel bulbs become tender and buttery, and the prominent aromatic smack softens considerably, to be replaced by a luxurious nutty, sugary flavour with only a suggestion of aniseed. For me, fennel is at its culinary best when roasted until golden brown and caramelized. This mutes its liquorice twang considerably and elevates the sugary notes, making it more palatable, and it is a wonderful way of introducing this vegetable to people who turn their noses up at anything aniseedy. Finishing off freshly baked fennel with a glug of balsamic vinegar adds a rich complexity to round off the sweetness of the roasted bulb.

69

The green devil

Absinthe is a distilled spirit made with Florence fennel, anise, and wormwood. It has a long history dating back to ancient Greece, where a wormwood-flavoured wine known as *absinthites oinos* was used for medicinal purposes. However, the first official account of absinthe, concocted with fennel, is from the eighteenth century. Initially created as a medicinal elixir in Switzerland, absinthe gained popularity as an alcoholic drink in Europe during the nineteenth century, when it was a favourite of the bohemian art circles in many capital cities. It was banned for a time in many countries owing to claims that it caused hallucinations and acted as a psychoactive drug, but has since come back into favour, after these claims were found to be spurious.

Growing

Despite being troubled by very few pests, fennel is often considered a challenging crop to cultivate, because it tends to bloom before it produces a bulb. However, you can increase your chance of success by carefully selecting sowing dates and choosing the correct heirloom varieties.

Propagation

Fennel's tendency to bolt before the bulbs develop fully is caused by the fact that its natural flowering time falls in midsummer.

Healthy fennel plants will produce dark green foliage and a crisp, bright white bulb.

The key is in the sowing date. Late winter or early spring is a good time to sow fennel; any later and the bulbs may not have time to bulk up before the plant bolts. However, early sowings require protection from frost when young, so you can also sow at midsummer, for autumn harvesting.

Early sowings will need warmth if they are to germinate, so keep them indoors on a sunny windowsill. Once sprouted, they can be moved out to a cold frame, greenhouse, or polytunnel for roughly four weeks, but do bring the tender seedlings into the house for protection if frost is forecast. Summer sowings grow much more quickly and are usually ready for transplanting in as little as three weeks.

Fennel seedlings have long, delicate stems that snap easily. To keep them safe from strong gusts of wind while they settle in, dib a slightly deeper hole than required and bury the base of the stem.

Aftercare

Cover spring-planted fennel seedlings with horticultural fleece to safeguard against frost and strong wind. The fleece can be removed in late spring, depending on when the last frost is likely. By then, the plants should be robust and healthy.

Water the newly transplanted seedlings generously, and monitor moisture levels. If the weather is dry, water them regularly until they become established. When spring-planted bulbs begin to swell, in early summer, provide them with ample water

Growing at a glance

Sow Late winter–early spring; midsummer, 10–20°C (50–68°F)

Plant out Mid-spring–late summer

Spacing 20cm (8in)

Harvest Early summer–mid-autumn

**Fennel bulbs need plenty
of water to swell.**

'Di Parma sel. Prado' This variety with squat, wide, flattened bulbs, named after the Italian city of Parma, is best sown late. It produces dense heads of succulent, delicious flesh and abundant foliage.

'Mantovano' These large, heavy fennel bulbs are quicker to mature than most, and slow to bolt, making them perfect for the first sowing of the year. This variety yields a deliciously sweet white bulb with a prominent flattened edge.

'Montebianco' A variety with tightly packed snowy-white bulbs, named after the highest Alpine peak, Mont Blanc. The plants resist premature bolting, but are still best sown late. This vigorous variety has intensely green leaves and a prominent globe-shaped bulb.

'Romanesco' Originating in Florence, this reliable heirloom variety yields plump, oval bulbs, dense, tightly coiled stems, and a large crown of feathery leaves. Perhaps the most popular variety, it's often considered the most beautiful, and its bulbs are prized for their sweetness, tenderness, and juiciness. A versatile type that performs well in both sowing periods.

to help them plump up. Autumn rains may mean that later-sown batches do not require watering during the swelling stage.

Plant problems

Rabbits, slugs and snails (see pages 49–51)

Harvesting

Timing is everything when harvesting fennel. There is a perfect moment when the sweet aniseed flavour and delicate texture are at their peak. Harvesting too early can result in less dense bulbs, while waiting too long can allow the bulbs to elongate, becoming fibrous and woody. The ideal bulb is plump, robust, and in good condition. Whatever happens, autumn-cropping fennel must be picked before the first frost. Harvest the whole plant by slicing it at soil level with a knife, leaving the roots in the ground.

Storage

Summer-harvested fennel is best eaten shortly after picking, and will keep for only about a week in the fridge. Autumn-harvested bulbs can be stored for longer, lasting two to three weeks in a wooden crate in a shed or other outbuilding. When storing, remove the tops but leave some of the roots attached to the root plate.

Flowering fennel

Don't worry if the plants start to bolt; as they begin to flower, they produce pollen, which can be harvested. Known for its strong aniseed flavour, fennel pollen is a sought-after ingredient in high-end establishments. Bolted fennel also produces a crop of sweet, fragrant seeds after flowering, and these can be harvested, dried, and added to the spice rack. Fennel seeds are fundamental in Indian cuisine and a crucial ingredient in *mukhwas pan masala*, an aromatic mixture of herbs and nuts that is commonly eaten as a palate-cleanser and also acts as a digestive aid after a meal.

Garlic

Allium sativum

Also known as Camphor of the poor,
Russian penicillin, Stinking rose

Love it or hate it, this pungent
plant is fundamental to almost
every cuisine worldwide.
Renowned for its strong aroma,
garlic is spicy and intense
when eaten raw and mellows
significantly to a robust, sweet,
nutty flavour when cooked.
Garlic bulbs comprise many
small, wedge-like segments
called cloves, encased in
a papery skin that can be white
(sometimes with purple stripes),
beige, tan, red, pink, or purple.

History

Garlic, one of the world's oldest crops, is native to Asia, possibly originating in the region between western China and Kazakhstan (although this is a matter of debate). Archaeological evidence has found preserved garlic in caves, suggesting that hunter-gatherers used garlic some 10,000 years ago. The ancient civilizations of Mesopotamia, Egypt, the Indus Valley, China, Greece, and Rome valued this plant as a food crop and medicinal plant. In addition, ancient Egyptians are thought to have worshipped garlic and are known to have buried pharaohs with it; when King Tutankhamun's tomb was excavated in 1922, there were several heads of perfectly preserved garlic nestled among his treasure. Garlic was also a form of currency in Egypt. In ancient Greece and Rome, athletes and gladiators ate the pungent cloves as a performance-enhancer before competitions and battles. More recently, garlic was used during both world wars as an antiseptic, rubbed on to open wounds to prevent infection.

Culinary uses
Preparation

Garlic must be used correctly to make the most of its pungent, punchy flavour. Too much of it overpowers dishes, and burning makes it bitter. Whether to crush or chop it depends on what you're using it for. Crushing with a press produces a very intense flavour, while slicing or finely chopping gives a mellower, subtler result.

Chopped garlic is best used as the base of sauces, soups, and stews, and is less likely to burn than crushed garlic. I use the flat part of the knife to crush the clove very lightly, making it easier to remove the skin, then slice through the garlic as thinly and evenly as possible.

When preparing uncooked sauces – such as chimichurri, salsa verde, and pesto – or garlic butter, I prefer to use crushed

'Violet de Cadours' (also called 'Rhapsody Wight') is a popular softneck garlic variety.

73

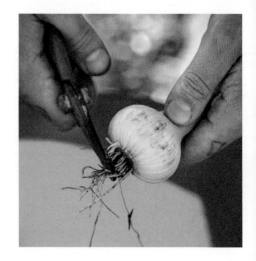

Trim the roots (right) before storing the garlic bulbs.

Seasonal garlic scapes (below) are rarely available to buy, so a home-grown source of these delicious greens is a treat.

garlic. I don't use a garlic crusher or press. Instead, I make a paste by chopping garlic into small pieces, sprinkling with salt, then using a large knife laid flat to work the garlic and salt together. This gives a much finer, softer, smoother result than you get from a crusher.

In both cases, it's crucial that you don't add garlic to the pan too early, or it may burn. I generally add it a minute or so before I add liquid, such as stock, wine, or passata, as this reduces the temperature and chance of the garlic burning.

Dishes

Of course, countless recipes call for garlic, but here I want to share some dishes where garlic is the stand-out star. First up is aioli, an intensely flavoured sauce made from raw garlic, lemon juice, olive oil, water, and salt. Another garlic-centric sauce is *bagna cauda*, a simple northern Italian dipping sauce made with fried garlic and anchovies, which is served warm alongside raw vegetables and bread.

There are various ways of preserving garlic. Laba (see panel opposite top) is a Chinese delicacy. In Korea, black garlic is a preserve made by exposing whole garlic bulbs to a low heat with controlled humidity for more than a month. The result is an ultra-sweet flavour with a garlicky, Marmite-like kick and a sticky,

Laba garlic

Have you ever seen bright green garlic? If not, let me introduce you to laba garlic: a pickled condiment, popular in northeastern China, that has a sweet-and-sour flavour and spicy edge. It's made by submerging raw peeled garlic in rice-wine vinegar and a touch of sugar and storing it in an airtight jar until the garlic turns green, like jade or an emerald – a process that takes about 20 days. In China, laba garlic is served with dumplings, but if you're looking for an unusual snacking dish that really has the wow factor, I'd recommend serving it as an appetizer, as you would olives or cornichons.

date-like texture. It's perfect slathered on crusty sourdough bread and topped with tomatoes and herbs.

An old French way of preserving garlic is a slow-roasted garlic confit, which involves cooking peeled garlic cloves, olive oil, and herbs in a low oven for 1½ hours or even longer. It's delicious mixed with balsamic vinegar for an indulgent dipping sauce for bread, and the garlic-infused oil can be substituted in any dish that calls for olive oil.

Fermented garlic honey is another simple and delicious way to preserve garlic. It may sound like an unusual combination, but it's a great addition to a salad dressing, drizzled over roasted carrots, or as a glaze for pork. Peeled garlic cloves are submerged in honey and stored in an airtight jar at room temperature for 3–12 months; the mixture must be stirred every few days to release the gases.

Growing

Garlic is a fun, easy crop to grow and it stores well. There are two main types: hardneck and softneck. Strong-flavoured hardneck varieties have a hard, woody stem that runs through the bulb, which is made of up a few large cloves, making it

Garlic is one of the world's oldest crops.

easier to use in the kitchen. Softneck types, which are a little milder, have a central stem made up of leaves rather than a tough stalk, and a bulb composed of many smaller cloves. Hardnecks require exposure to cold weather to form bulbs, while softnecks grow better in warm climates. Softnecks are usually quicker to mature and have a longer shelf life than hardnecks, which is why you're more likely to find softneck garlic in supermarkets. There are numerous subtypes of both, and I recommend growing a mixture so that you can have garlic to feast on throughout the year and a range of flavours that are suited to different dishes.

Propagation

The easiest way to grow garlic is to plant cloves directly in the ground in their final growing location. Always purchase seed garlic for growing from garden centres or online nurseries, rather than using cloves from the supermarket.

Scapes

In late spring and early summer, hardneck garlic varieties produce a scape – a thin, curly stem topped with an unopened flower bud. The scape must be removed as soon as the bud begins to form, so that the plant's energy is channelled into the bulb rather than into producing a flower. Simply snap off the scape as far down the stem as you can.

The tender green scape stalks are a delicious seasonal delicacy that are rarely found in shops. They can be treated in the same way as asparagus, and taste very similar but with a garlicky hit. I like to sauté them in olive oil and eat them for breakfast with scrambled eggs.

Growing at a glance

Sow/plant Mid-late autumn/
early winter; early spring.
0–10°C (32–50°F)

Spacing 10cm (4in), in rows
30cm (12in) apart

Harvest Late spring–
midsummer

Garlic is usually sown in mid- to late
autumn or early winter, before the ground
freezes. Some varieties are best sown in the
spring; these are usually labelled
"spring-sowing garlic" and should
be planted early in the season.

Sowing garlic in a no-dig system is
super easy. Choose a sunny position with
light, well-drained soil. Separate the cloves
carefully from the bulb and discard any
particularly small or thin cloves. Dib holes
5cm (2in) deep, pop the cloves into the
holes, pointed side up, and cover with
compost. Ideally, cover the bed with
a layer of compost 5–10cm (2–4in) thick.

Garlic can also be grown in pots placed
in a sunny location. Use high-quality
compost and ideally add perlite to improve
drainage. Sow three cloves in a 15cm (6in)
pot, six cloves in a 20cm (8in) pot, eight
cloves in a 25cm (10in) pot, and so on.
The pot should be at least 15–20cm
(6–8in) deep. Space the cloves equally
around the container and not too close
to the sides, to allow room for growth.
Because garlic is typically sown in early
winter, a pot of pre-planted garlic makes
the perfect Christmas present in the
northern hemisphere.

Aftercare

Water your garlic (particularly if you are
cultivating it in pots) during dry periods
for most of the growing season, but
stop watering during the last few weeks,
to avoid rotting. Weed regularly around
the plants.

Plant problems

Allium leaf miner, onion fly, onion
white rot, rust, stem and bulb nematodes
(see pages 49–51)

Harvesting

Most hardneck varieties are ready to lift in
early or midsummer. Softnecks are usually
ready three or four weeks earlier, as the
stems begin to flop.

Harvest garlic before the leaves turn
yellow. Feel in the soil to check if the bulb
has divided fully before lifting. Use a trowel
to prise the bulbs gently out of the soil,
and never pull the stem, or it may snap.
With the stem still on the bulb, peel back
the bulb's outer layer, exposing the clean
white skin below, then trim the roots using
a sharp knife.

Storage

Garlic is usually "cured", or dried, to
extend its shelf life. Choose a dry, well-
ventilated area, such as a shed, garage, or
shaded porch. Lay the bulbs on a bench,
table, or sheet of wire mesh, ensuring
they have adequate air circulation and are
raised off the floor. Curing takes between
20 and 30 days. If the weather is good, you
can dry the bulbs in the sun first to speed
things up.

Once cured, garlic can be plaited
and hung up in a well-ventilated place.
I hang mine in the kitchen for easy access
when cooking.

You may wish to keep some garlic to
be eaten fresh, rather than curing it all.
Known as "wet garlic", uncured garlic
has a delicate burst of flavour without
the pungent smack, and is delicious halved
and grilled on a barbecue. After harvesting
and cleaning the bulbs, trim the stems
roughly 10cm (4in) above the bulbs and
store in the fridge.

Hardneck garlic

Asiatic

Compared with other hardneck types, Asiatic garlic varieties are relatively quick to mature and many store for longer. They're hot and spicy when eaten raw, and sweet when cooked.

'Korean Red' A rich, intensely flavoured garlic that originates in the picturesque mountainous peninsulas of Korea, this has large, rounded bulbs covered with a magnificent display of purple stripes. The plants are tall and vigorous, reaching 45–50cm (18–20in) high.

Creole

Originally from Spain, Creole garlic was spread around the world by the Spanish conquistadors. Creole types generally have solid dark purple to pink or red cloves encased in a paper-white skin. They're rich and sweet, so ideal for eating raw.

'Morado de las Pedroñeras' This striking purple-skinned garlic is grown in the Spanish autonomous region of Castilla–La Mancha, where it's been an indispensable ingredient for at least 200 years. The cloves have a stronger, spicier flavour than most Spanish garlics.

'Rose de Lautrec' Often considered France's best garlic variety (see panel above), this has a unique, piquant flavour reminiscent of Dijon mustard.

'Rossa di Sulmona' Beneath the white skin of the bulb lurks a vibrant red-clove garlic named after the Italian city of Sulmona in the Peligna Valley, Abruzzo, where it's been cultivated since the eighteenth century. Its delicate, sweet taste makes it a go-to for recipes that call for raw garlic, particularly bruschetta.

Garlic is a foundational ingredient in cuisines around the world.

The legend of 'Rose de Lautrec'

Legend tells of a merchant who wandered the Tarn region in southern France and couldn't pay for his supper at a local tavern. His pockets empty of cash, he came to a compromise with the landlord and settled his bill with a bag of mystical-looking pink garlic. The garlic was planted and tended by the landlord, and has been a mainstay in the area ever since.

Porcelain

Considered the most intense and flavoursome of all garlic, porcelains usually produce fewer but bigger cloves, which make for easy peeling, and usually have a longer shelf life than many other hardnecks. The sheath colour varies from purple to brown, with a thick white or purple-striped, parchment-like bulb wrapping.

'German Giant' This extra-hardy garlic variety made its way from Italy, possibly via trading routes during the Roman empire, to northern Germany, where it was developed to tolerate colder growing conditions. It produces exceptionally large ivory-white bulbs. The cloves are loosely wrapped in a dark red skin that is easy to peel. Because of this variety's high sugar content and large size, it's one of the best types for roasting.

'Music' The name of this reliable, easy-to-grow variety derives from Al Music, a Canadian tobacco-grower who decided to delve into the world of garlic and imported the seed stock from Italy in the early 1980s. It has large white bulbs with a robust flavour, which is spicy when raw and aromatic and full-bodied when cooked.

Purple striped

Renowned for their vivid purple-striped or blotchy skin, these varieties are considered by many to be the oldest and most similar genetically to the garlic that was grown centuries ago. They have a sweet, rich taste when eaten raw, without the sharp, spicy flavour of many other garlics.

'Chesnok Red' An easy-to-grow garlic prized for its sweetness when roasted, this variety produces large plum-coloured bulbs. The variety is also known as 'Shvelisi', after the town of Skhvilisi in the southwestern Republic of Georgia, close to the

'Morado de las Pedroñeras' is a strongly flavoured hardneck garlic from Spain.

Turkish border, where it was originally grown. When the Russian Red Army invaded Georgia in 1921, the Soviets renamed it, *chesnok* being the Russian for garlic.

'Persian Star' ('Samarkand')
A sweet, complex and distinctive heritage garlic, this variety became popular after it was discovered at a bazaar in Samarkand, Uzbekistan – one of the oldest inhabited cities in Central Asia. The allium was acquired in 1989 by John Swenson, a respected US garlic aficionado who travelled the world in pursuit of new varieties and has donated more than 150 varieties of garlic to Seed Savers Exchange's seed bank, to be maintained and preserved.

Marbled purple striped
These produce a small number of large, richly flavoured cloves. The skins that surround the bulb are usually a mottled purple rather than striped, as the name might suggest.

'Bogatyr' When Soviet medical supplies ran short during World War II, this Russian variety was used as a substitute for antibiotics for injured soldiers, earning garlic the name "Russian penicillin". It wasn't until

the collapse of the Soviet Union in 1989–91 that these striking purple- and violet-striped bulbs were made available to growers outside the former USSR. Touted as one of the spiciest of all garlics, this profusely pungent variety produces huge maroon cloves.

Rocambole
These rounded bulbs are favoured by chefs for their deep, complex flavour. With their loose clove wrappers, they're much easier to peel than other varieties, too, but they're among the shortest storing garlics around (usually just three or four months).

'Italian Purple' This striking purple-striped garlic has a rich flavour that isn't overpowered by the hot, spicy notes sometimes associated with garlic. Popular with growers for its early harvest, it requires a cold winter if the bulbs are to develop properly.

Turban
Known for their hot, spicy flavour and squat, plump bulbs, turban varieties usually have a colourful outer skin ranging from vivid purple to purple stripes. They ripen considerably earlier than other types of garlic, but most have a relatively short shelf life (about five months).

'Basque' This beautiful variety is from the Navarre region in the Spanish Basque Country, where the squat bulbs are used to make the traditional smoky *sopa de ajo* (garlic soup). It's medium spicy but turns very sweet when cooked.

'Sonoran' Named after the Sonoran Desert in northwestern Mexico and the southwestern United States, this musky-flavoured variety is cultivated on the Mexican side of the border, where it's become a mainstay of local cuisine. It packs a seriously pungent, spicy punch when eaten raw but mellows considerably when cooked. The skin has a silvery, paper-like appearance with purple stripes.

Softneck garlic

Artichoke
Named for the overlapping clove formation, which is reminiscent of an artichoke, these types are vigorous and produce large bulbs that can be packed with up to 20 cloves. The skins are pearly white and papery, with the occasional shimmer of purple. They have a mild, pleasant flavour, rather tame when compared to that of the more pungent hardnecks, and a shelf life of 8–10 months.

'Lorz Italian' This large, robust bulb is named after the Lorz family, who introduced it to the United States when they emigrated from Italy in search of the American dream in the nineteenth century. They settled in Washington State, where they continued their tradition of growing garlic, and this variety is now popular with growers in the US. Prized for its pungent, bold flavour, it suits Italian cooking.

'Tochliavri' ('Red Toch') Originally grown in the small town of Tochliavri in the Republic of Georgia, this variety produces large, flat bulbs and cloves that have a sweet, mild yet complex flavour with minimal heat. The thick outer casing of the bulb is white with striking red streaks.

Variety	Type	Subtype	Number of cloves per bulb	Storage time
'Basque'	Hardneck	Turban	6–8	5 months
'Bogatyr'	Hardneck	Marbled purple striped	4–6	up to 9 months
'Chesnok Red'	Hardneck	Purple striped	8–12	up to 6 months
'German Giant'	Hardneck	Porcelain	4–6	up to 10 months
'Italian Purple'	Hardneck	Rocambole	up to 8	6–8 months
'Korean Red'	Hardneck	Asiatic	6–8	5–6 months
'Morado de las Pedroñeras'	Hardneck	Creole	8–10	8 months or more
'Music'	Hardneck	Porcelain	4–6	3–6 months
'Persian Star'	Hardneck	Purple striped	8–12	6–8 months
'Rose de Lautrec'	Hardneck	Creole	6–10	up to 8 months
'Rossa di Sulmona'	Hardneck	Creole	10–14	4–5 months
'Sonoron'	Hardneck	Turban	6–8	4–6 months
'Lorz Italian'	Softneck	Artichoke	12–15	up to 8 months
'Rose du Var'	Softneck	Silverskin	10–18	12 months or more
'Sicilian Silver'	Softneck	Silverskin	up to 15	about 12 months
'Tochliavri'	Softneck	Artichoke	up to 18	6–7 months
'Violet de Cadours'	Softneck	Artichoke	10–12	up to 8 months

'Violet de Cadours' ('Rhapsody Wight') A stunning violet garlic traditionally grown on the sunny slopes around the village of Cadours near Toulouse, France, this is one of the fastest-maturing softneck garlics and stores well into the early winter.

Silverskin

The silverskin group has the longest shelf life of any garlic (12 months or more). Cultivars vary in size and colour, but most have a spicy, musky, complex flavour. Unusually for softnecks, silverskins sometimes produce a scape (see page 75).

'Rose du Var' Highly sought-after by garlic breeders, this beautiful rose-pink bulb from France stores for a long time. The cloves have the perfect balance of sweetness and spice. Several registered cultivars derive from this heirloom, including the popular 'Cristo'.

'Sicilian Silver' This has been grown for generations on the Italian island of Sicily, where it's adored for its hot, spicy flavour. The intense, sharp-flavoured cloves are a smart choice if you're after a long-storing variety that will see you all the way through to your next garlic harvest the following year.

Garlic bulbs are laid out to finish drying before they are stored.

'Bulgarian
Giant'

Leeks

Allium porrum

Also known as Hawar, Negi, Poireaux

These tall, elegant stems with grand green foliage really do look phenomenal protruding from the soil, especially in the dreary depths of winter. Leeks are more than a mere background ingredient; they are a true culinary powerhouse, capable of enriching dishes by providing depth and complexity of flavour.

History

This ancient crop is thought to be native to the eastern Mediterranean and the Middle East, its wild precursors domesticated and cultivated by early civilizations, such as the Sumerians, Assyrians, and Egyptians. These peoples didn't just grow leeks for food, but also believed that they contained chemical compounds that could delay and even "cure" greying hair. The ancient Romans believed that consuming leeks regularly would improve the throat and singing voice, an idea that ultimately led Emperor Nero famously to feast on leeks in such excess that he gained the nickname Porophagus (leek-eater). In the Middle Ages leeks became a staple in Europe thanks to their ability to provide fresh food throughout the cold, dark winter months, when little else was available.

The name "leek" derives from the Old English *leac*, however, of the British nations, leeks are most famously worshipped by the Welsh. Legend has it that King Cadwaladr of Gwynedd ordered his warriors, on the eve of a great battle with invading Saxons, to display leeks on their helmets and armour to differentiate themselves from the enemy during the fight. The Welsh were triumphant in these savage battles against the Saxons, and subsequently the leek became a symbol of the country. There is some debate about when leeks landed on Welsh soil, however. Some historians believe they arrived on the great *gauloi* trading ships manned by Phoenician sailors searching for tin in about 1100 BCE, while others credit the Romans with introducing leeks after their brutal invasion of the British Isles in 43 CE.

Culinary uses

Preparation

As leeks grow soil tends to become trapped between their tight layers, so if you intend to use the leek whole, for braising, roasting, or grilling, discard any bulky foliage, remove the roots (leaving the root plate intact), and cut lengthwise through the green end of the leek, leaving the white end whole. Gently prise open the layers, fanning out the leaves, which can now be rinsed easily under running water to wash out any dirt or grit. Cut off the tough green leaves before cooking, but keep them to add to stock, rather than composting them; the dark green foliage is jam-packed with flavour, and sometimes difficult to come by since supermarkets tend to sell ready-trimmed leeks.

Dishes

Since they belong to the same family as onions and garlic, it's no surprise that leeks bear many of the same tasty and versatile characteristics as their kin, but they do possess unique characteristics that allow them to complement and elevate a diverse range of dishes. Much milder, sweeter, and lighter in flavour than onions, leeks are a common aromatic addition to such hearty meals as casseroles, stews, soups, pies, and risottos. When eaten raw, leeks have a crisp and crunchy texture with a subtle oniony aftertaste; best sliced thinly, they can be incorporated into salads, slaws, and krauts – just think of them as an alternative to spring onions. Cooked into stock, stews, and sauces, leeks act as a base ingredient, providing a sweet and savoury depth of flavour. Braised or roasted whole leeks can take centre stage or become the perfect succulent side dish.

Charred leeks are also certain to ignite the taste buds, and braising them gently in a stock spiced with an assortment of aromatics before banging them on the barbecue doesn't just cut down the cooking time, but also creates a better char on the skin while seasoning the vegetable throughout. The result is a more caramelized charred leek, remarkably tender and bursting with flavour.

Growing

Propagation

The different varieties of leek mature at varying times of year. I grow a diverse range, some of which are ready for harvest in late summer and autumn, and others that withstand the depths of winter. The latter varieties are the reason that leeks are a treasured asset in the patch, providing hearty harvests in the harsh and bitter months.

These slow-growing plants are best multi-sown into seed cells in batches of four in mid-spring; any earlier might induce premature bolting, because of unsettled weather early in the season.

Zeytinyağlı pırasa

Leeks bring a subtle oniony essence with rich and savoury notes that elevate any dish without being overpowering. A treasure of a recipe that sings the praises of this vegetable is the traditional tangy, sweet-and-sour, slow-braised leek dish called *zeytinyağlı pırasa* (leeks with olive oil) that is popular in Turkish cuisine. To make it, braise leeks low and slow with the addition of carrots and bulgur wheat or rice, and finish with fresh parsley and lemon juice for a zesty note. It is tasty eaten hot, but even better if allowed to cool, kept in the fridge for a day or so, and served at room temperature.

Growing at a glance

Sow Mid-spring, 10–32°C (50–90°F)

Plant out Early–midsummer

Spacing 30cm (12in)

Harvest Late summer–mid-spring

About four weeks after germination, pot on the multi-sown clumps into 7–9cm (3–4in) pots to grow on for a further four weeks. When planting out, leave 30cm (12in) between clusters. To grow jumbo leeks, sow, grow, pot on, and plant out single leeks 10cm (4in) apart, for extra legroom that will allow thicker, straighter stems. To grow leeks with more of the sweet white leaves, plant the seedlings deeply, burying the roots and stem 5–10cm (2–4in) beneath the soil surface.

Aftercare

Leeks are thirsty customers, and require a generous drink during dry conditions. It's also crucial to provide ample water from late summer until autumn, since that's when leeks begin to swell rapidly.

Plant problems

Allium leaf miner, mildew, rust (see pages 49–51)

Harvesting

Leeks can be harvested at any size. Baby leeks are a seasonal delight, and I often set aside a handful of seedling clusters to grow purely for this purpose. The key is not to let the summer and autumn varieties stay in the ground for too long, or they will rot and keel over in cold weather. All summer leeks must be harvested in late summer or early autumn, while the autumn types will be ripe and ready between mid-autumn and early winter, and the hardy winter varieties will be at their finest from late winter to mid-spring. A brilliant way to keep track of when to harvest your leeks is to plant early-maturing types at the front of the bed and work back, planting the winter varieties behind. Either harvest the whole cluster by lifting them gently out of the soil with a trowel, lifting the plants delicately to ensure a reasonable amount of root is still attached, or prise out the biggest of the bunch, leaving the remaining plants to continue fattening up.

Storage

Best harvested as and when they're needed, leeks can also be stored for up to six weeks, and the biggest ones store best. Without cleaning off the soil, removing any foliage, or cutting off the roots, store the leeks in a box in a cool but frost-free garage or other outbuilding, in dappled light.

To grow leeks with more of the sweet white leaves, plant the seedlings deeply.

Recommended varieties

'Bartek' This late-maturing Polish heirloom is the oldest of all the leek varieties bred in Poland, and dates back to the mid-nineteenth century. An excellent cold-hardy winter leek with delightful dark green foliage on a chunky white stem, 'Bartek' has good resistance to disease and can endure the harshest weather.

'Bleu de Solaise' A reliable winter leek with distinctive, dazzling bluish foliage that turns dark purple after a frost. This nineteenth-century French heirloom variety produces short, broad stems that are bursting with taste, while their sensational plum-shaded foliage provides a much-needed splash of colour in the patch during the cold months. A super-hardy variety that will power on through the worst winter.

'Bulgarian Giant' Cultivated in Eastern Europe for more than 100 years, this is one of the tallest leeks available. This fast-growing, thin- and long-stemmed variety produces pale green leaves with a suggestion of yellow. Ready for harvest from the summer onwards, it is a quick-maturing leek that has a delicious flavour and cooks down quickly. One of the most popular varieties to grow for competitions, since it can reach a staggering 1m (3ft) in height.

'Carentan' An old-school leek that's become something of a rarity. This French heirloom variety, which has been grown in Normandy since the nineteenth century, produces high-quality, short, stout stems that are capable of withstanding crazily cold winters. A crisp and mild-tasting leek, its flavour improves considerably after the first frost.

'Esther Cook' Saved from the brink of extinction by Suzanne Ashworth, who acquired the seeds from Esther Cook at a vegetable competition in Sacramento, California, in the 1980s, this is a real treasure that was nearly lost. The seeds had originally found their way to the United States when Cook's family moved there from Yugoslavia earlier in the twentieth century. This winter variety is considerably thinner and taller than other cool-season varieties, with a sweet, mild flavour.

'Jaune du Poitou' A rare and beautiful leek from the historic region of Poitou in western-central France. It dates back to the 1850s and produces unique pale yellowish-green foliage on a thick, meaty stem. With a tremendously tender texture and excellent flavour, 'Jaune du Poitou' is early to mature. It is not specifically a winter type, but is known to tolerate some cold.

'Long de Mézières' A long leek from the small town of Mézières, near Rennes in northwestern France. It is a significantly cold-tolerant variety that will sail through the harshest winter and into early spring. The lengthy stems are crowned with dark teal leaves, bringing height and contrast to the garden in the winter.

'Lyon Prizetaker' An old English classic that dates back to 1886. As its name suggests, it is ideal for the show bench. The mild-flavoured leeks are reliable and easy to grow, producing long, thick, uniformly white stems that can reach heights of 90cm (35in) and are ready for harvesting in early autumn. Grow these leeks singly to see them in all their glory.

'Monstrueux d'Elbeuf' Also going by the name 'Eel Head', this is a French heirloom variety that was originally grown in the alluvial plains of the River Seine in Normandy. It's a quick-maturing leek that's packed with flavour and ready to harvest from late summer until late autumn. Expect short, dense, chunky stems capped with brilliant bright green lolloping leaves.

'Musselburgh' A reliable Scottish heirloom dating back to the nineteenth century, developed by Dutch immigrants living in the small town of Musselburgh, near Edinburgh. Famous for its thick, tender stem and snow-white bulb with a beautifully mellow flavour, this is one of the easiest leeks to grow and can tolerate the harshest of winters.

'Poireau de Liège' A cold-resistant breed that also goes by the name "cork leek". This Belgian heirloom comes from the hilly Ardennes region in the southeast of the country, and is just as beautiful as the landscape in which it was developed. The tall stems are adorned by long, dark blueish-green leaves that can be cropped all the way through the winter and into the spring.

'Verdonnet' This very old, brilliantly bright green giant leek from Geneva, Switzerland, was named after the market gardener who developed it. Extremely quick to mature, it is usually one of the first leeks to be ready for harvest, although it can also tolerate cold winter conditions. A really handsome, elegantly tall leek with a notable flavour.

'Esther Cook' (left)
and 'Jaune du Poitou'

Onion

Allium cepa

Also known as Bulb onion

The humble onion is one of the most beautiful and fascinating vegetables to grow, and hugely versatile, a mainstay of dishes from numerous cuisines. Available in many shapes and sizes, it is the starting point for countless sauces, stocks, soups, stews, pickles, and preserves. Onions are generally cheap to buy from the supermarket, but growing your own allows you to try out more unusual varieties.

Made up of many fleshy layers with a thick, papery skin, the bulb of an onion in fact consists of modified leaves that grow underground and surround the bottom of the plant's stem. These scale-like layers grow from the inside, pushing the older layers outwards to create the bulb. Onion bulbs have evolved as a storage organ, allowing the plant to overwinter and flower in its second year.

History

The onion is one of the oldest cultivated vegetables in human history, having been farmed for more than 5,000 years. As with many important foods, its precise origin is debatable; some archaeologists believe onions were domesticated in central Asia, while others think it was in the Middle East, in what are today Iran and western Pakistan. One thing is for certain, however: the ancient Egyptians worshipped onions because they believed the network of rings symbolized eternal life, and they were known to bury their dead with onions as well as garlic (see page 72). Aside from being used as a form of ancient currency, often more valuable than money, the most unusual use of an onion is probably that of Roman gladiators, who would rub fresh onions over their body to stimulate and tone their muscles. Cultivated bulb onions made their way across the world when trade routes opened up from the mid-sixteenth century onwards. Until that point, Indigenous people in the Americas consumed only wild onions, which are now considered a weed in some areas.

Culinary uses
Preparation
Chopped or sliced onions are the first ingredient in endless recipes, and the best way to reduce tears is to minimize the time you spend working with onions. If you're not confident with a knife or have a lot of

The onion may be a very familiar vegetable,
but it comes in a startling array of shapes,
sizes, colours, and flavours.

flavour, these are distinctively shaped, like a tiny flying saucer. Given their mild flavour and the fact that they are pickled in balsamic vinegar, this type of pickled onion is much sweeter and richer than those you might be used to, making it the perfect accompaniment to any cheese board.

Another favourite of mine is *cebolla curtida*, a Mexican-style pickled red onion with lime juice instead of vinegar. This super-tasty and easy-to-make pickle turns the red onions a beautiful bright pink that brings contrast to the plate. Simply slice some thinly, sprinkle with a pinch of salt, cover with freshly squeezed lime juice, and leave to sit for 30 minutes. These vibrant pickles are traditionally served on tacos, but their zesty flavour also makes them an excellent garnish for chilli con carne and nachos.

Oven-roasted onions are the flavours dreams are made of. A quick tip when roasting onions is to peel the bulbs and simmer them gently for 10–15 minutes first. This will tenderize the layers and make them sweeter. Then you can simply slice the parboiled onions in half and place them cut side down in a roasting tray. You may want to roast them simply, with olive oil and salt, but a fantastic alternative is to pour double cream over them, season with fresh thyme leaves, salt, and cracked black pepper, finish with a generous handful of grated Parmesan, and bake for about 30 minutes until the onions are golden.

You could go one step further and make stuffed onions, otherwise known as Roscoff onions. Traditionally filled with cheese, cream, and breadcrumbs and served alongside roast beef, this dish is a French culinary classic. The best onion for it is 'Rose de Roscoff', a sweet, pearly-pink onion that's been grown in Brittany, northern France, since the seventeenth century. It's full of flavour and melts in the mouth.

onions to dice, try using the coarse side of a grater. It's surprising how quickly you can process an onion in this way.

Dishes

Onions are often used as a base ingredient, but there is no shortage of dishes that foreground this versatile vegetable, from classic French onion soup and puff-pastry onion tart to caramelized chutneys and sticky jams.

Preserved onions come in many forms, and pickles are my personal favourite; whether you like a strong, malty pickled onion chip-shop-style or the less pungent mini silverskins that are commonly served alongside a ploughman's lunch, I believe there's a pickled onion for everyone. A much-loved pickle of mine is traditional Italian balsamic onions. For this dish the small, flat 'Borettana' variety (also known as *cipollini* in Italy) is used. Prized throughout Italy for their mellow, sweet

Growing at a glance

Sow Mid–late winter,
10–32°C (50–90°F)

Plant out Early spring

Spacing 30–40cm (12–16in)

Harvest Midsummer–early autumn

If pickled and roasted onions aren't your thing, how about fried? Who doesn't like a deep-fried onion ring, whether in breadcrumbs, tempura, or beer batter? Perhaps the most delicious type of fried onion is the bhaji. Originating in the southern Indian state of Karnataka, onion bhajis are made by smothering finely sliced onions in a simple, fragrantly spiced batter and frying them to crispy perfection. The best onions for fried dishes are sweet, less pungent varieties, such as 'Walla Walla' and 'Mauis'. On the subject of fried onions, let me introduce you to the Persian kitchen staple *piaz dagh*, a crispy, crunchy fried onion that's sometimes spiced with saffron. Mainly used to garnish classic dishes, such as the noodle soup *aash reshteh* and *adas polow* (Persian rice with lentils), they're the crispiest fried onions I've ever tried, and are made by slicing yellow onions as thinly as possible and frying them to potato-crisp crunchiness.

Sumaklı soğan salatası (sumac onions) is a super-quick and simple way to prepare onions that are bursting with flavour. A mainstay of Turkish cuisine, it provides a sour, acidic punch that cuts through grilled meat and kebabs. It is also a wonderful side dish and works well served with barbecued food, roasted fish, grilled halloumi, and falafels. Slice red onions thinly, sprinkle with salt, and leave for 5 minutes. Then rinse off the salt with cold water and pat the onions dry with a clean tea towel. Put them in a bowl, add lemon juice, olive oil, freshly chopped parsley, and lots and lots

Onion types

Yellow/brown onion The everyday onion. If a recipe calls for onion without specifying the type, you can safely assume it's this one. These old faithfuls have thick, brown, parchment-like skin and ivory-white flesh with a pungent flavour. A true workhorse in the kitchen that won't dissolve into mush even after long cooking.

Red onion The prettiest of all, and sweet enough to be eaten raw, the flesh of red onions ranges from deep magenta to rosy pink. They are great for adding splashes of colour to salads. Try soaking them in iced water for 20 minutes before serving to crisp them up and remove some of the sharpness.

White onion Covered in a pale, thin, papery skin, white onions are softer and sweeter than yellows and reds, with less of the sulphurous aftertaste. Very popular in South and Central America and Mexico, they are perfect to eat raw in salsas and guacamole.

Sweet onion Larger and slightly flatter than yellow onions, with a paler, less opaque skin, sweet onions have a higher sugar content, making them perfect for caramelizing. Their size and flavour make them ideal for onion rings.

Pearl onion These very small onions can be white, yellow, or red, and are renowned for their sweet, delicate flavour. Usually served pickled as an accompaniment, they can also be stewed and roasted, although – being so teeny – they can be a chore to peel.

Cipollini Bred in the Italian countryside and with a name that means "little onion", these squat, flat-topped bulbs in fact look strikingly different from their *Allium cepa* cousins. This is the traditional onion that's used to make the famous balsamic pickled onions in the region of Emilia-Romagna. Easy to cook whole, they are well suited to roasting and fabulous when skewered up and flame-grilled over a barbecue.

of sumac, and leave to macerate. You may wish to add a dash of pomegranate molasses for a sweeter variation, or some chilli flakes for a spicy kick. I prepare my sumac onions an hour before I want to eat them, then keep them in the fridge to develop flavour and become cold and crisp. Yum.

Growing

Onions are one of the most fun crops to grow, and a great storing vegetable that you can feast on throughout the year.

Rows of onions curing in the midst of a burgeoning patch (opposite) are a satisfying sight.

Manicuring (see page 52) can be done as you harvest to prepare the veg for the kitchen (right).

Growing different types will unlock your ability to experiment with oniony flavours you have never tried before.

Propagation

I sow my bulb onions in late winter. (Overwintering onions can be sown in late summer and planted out in early autumn, but I tend to overwinter only spring onions.) I've found the best way to grow onions is by multi-sowing them six seeds to a cell. This results in several medium-sized bulbs, and it makes the most of the growing space. Keep the trays in the house until the seeds have germinated. Grow them on in the potting shed for a few weeks before planting them out into the ground, usually in early spring.

Aftercare

Onion seedlings are surprisingly hungry, considering their slender appearance, so it's best to get them into the ground while they're still small. Dib holes deep enough to half-submerge the seedlings, then cover the rows with a layer of horticultural

A tear in the eye

Why do onions – nature's tear gas – make you cry? These tears are not from emotion, of course; they are stimulated by the enzymes and sulfenic acid released when onion skin is broken. This is a defence mechanism for the plant, to deter creatures, such as voles and mice, from munching on the roots, tubers, and bulbs. These volatile chemicals vaporize into the atmosphere, and when they come into contact with our eyes they cause a burning sensation. As a way of protecting our eyes from these airborne irritants, the brain triggers a tear response to wash away the offending chemicals, leaving us puffy-eyed and damp-cheeked.

fleece. Onion seedlings are cold-hardy to a certain extent, but the fleece should stop birds from pulling out and pecking at the tender young plants.

In May, gently thin out the clumps, leaving three or four seedlings in each. The plants you remove can be used in the kitchen as spring onions, while those left in the ground will continue to grow and bulb up. If you choose not to thin your onions, you will get a harvest of more bulbs, but they will be smaller. It's useful to have a mixture of clumps of three, four, and six plants, to give a wide variety of onion sizes. Bulb formation begins around the time the days begin to shorten, so planting out your onions as soon as possible will give them time to develop a good root system and healthy amount of foliage in preparation.

Plant problems

Birds, mildew, onion root fly, rust (see pages 49–51)

Harvesting

Five or six months after sowing, it's time to harvest the booty. But how do you judge exactly when to harvest an onion? A good indication is that the stems of the onions topple over and lie on the ground. After

When harvesting, the roots should come out with the bulbs. The onions can then be left to dry outside or under shelter, depending on the weather. This variety is the ever-popular 'Bedfordshire Champion'.

Sets or seeds?

Onions can be grown from sets (immature bulbs), but almost all the varieties I recommend here will not be available to buy in this way. In fact, I steer clear of onion sets for a number of reasons. For a start, plants grown from sets tend to harbour more disease than those grown from seed. Onions are biennial plants, meaning they flower in their second year. Sets are in theory tiny onions grown the previous year and heat-treated for several months to prevent them from bolting the following year. I believe this process is unnecessary and too energy-intensive, and can be easily skipped by choosing to grow from seed. If you are growing from sets, avoid planting before the spring equinox to mitigate the risk of bolting.

about two-thirds of the plants have fallen, bend the remaining ones over at a right angle, to soften the neck and allow them to dry better and store for longer. Keep an eye on the swelling of the bulbs and their colour, too, since they often darken as they approach maturity.

Harvest the onions by pushing down gently on each bulb and twisting it out. There is no need to trim off the foliage; you will need it later to plait the onions into bunches.

Storage

Harvested onions must be dried and cured to help them store well. If the weather is good, line them up to dry on top of their beds; if wet weather is forecast, stack them in crates and store them in a shed, greenhouse, or other outbuilding, leaving plenty of room for air to circulate around the leaves. Drying and curing should take two or three weeks, after which the necks should be thoroughly dry and the outer bulb scales should make that familiar rustle you hear when peeling an onion. At this point the bulbs can be plaited together and hung in a warm, dry spot inside the house, ready for feasting on throughout the year.

Recommended varieties

Yellow/Brown

'Amish Bottle' A very hardy and long-storing onion grown by the Amish people of Pennsylvania from the late eighteenth century onwards. As the name suggests, these onions are elongated and look somewhat like an old-fashioned bottle. This fantastic yet rare variety, which is now difficult to find, is sweet enough to be eaten raw but robust enough to withstand long cooking. It is encased in a shiny golden-brown skin and tastes pleasingly nutty.

'Bedfordshire Champion' Bred in Bedfordshire, in the east of England, this variety produces large, golden-brown globe-shaped bulbs. Having won countless veg-growing competitions in its day, it is versatile in the kitchen and reliable in the garden, so it's no wonder that it has remained popular among growers for more than 200 years.

'Buan' A piece of Irish horticultural history. The name is from Irish dialect and translates as "long life", and this variety certainly lives up to that, storing well into the following spring and often until the summer. It's a good-quality onion, robust and resilient, that stands strong and performs well in adverse conditions. It is not technically an heirloom yet, however, since it was bred by Barnie Crombie in the 1980s, but it is open-pollinated and well on its way to becoming an heirloom. A great choice for growers in challenging climates.

'Dorato di Parma' This gorgeous golden-skinned, globe-shaped variety has been grown in the Italian region of Emilia-Romagna for hundreds of years. Renowned for its long storing abilities, it has a great flavour that intensifies the longer it's matured. You can expect bulbs of this rare heirloom to keep throughout the winter and, stored correctly, you should still have a stash by the time you sow more seeds the following spring.

'Jaune Paille des Vertus' This hard-to-come-by antique variety has been grown in the Champagne region of France since the late eighteenth century and is named after the village of Vertus. It has been a favourite for centuries thanks to its outstanding storage ability. The flattened, bronze-skinned bulbs look really beautiful when plaited and hung in the kitchen, while the flesh is a distinctive yellow colour and has a mild, sweet flavour.

'Ramata di Milano' Traditionally cultivated in the Lombardy region of northern Italy, 'Ramata di Milano' is one of the most unusual onions around. Shaped like a big, broad bronze egg, this general-purpose onion stores well and tastes fantastic. Beneath the coppery skin lies pinkish-white flesh that's sweet, well balanced, and rich, making this a perfect choice both cooked and raw.

Red

'Bronze d'Amposta' This variety is named after the small medieval city of Amposta in northeastern Spain, where *granjeros* (farmers) grow these pinky-bronze beauties that are delightful both to look at and to eat. The off-white flesh shimmers with pink tints that give the onion a glossy appearance. It is well suited for eating fresh, since it's not super spicy and stores well.

'Di Genova' An endangered variety from Zerli in northwestern Italy, traditionally eaten raw, with a sweet flavour that is second to none. A true culinary delight, and one of the best red onions around. One reason for its decline is that these squat, flat bulbs were once considered a nutrient-hungry crop, and many landowners prohibited the *contadini* (peasant farmers) from growing this particular variety of onion.

'Red Creole' A proper red onion, pungent and spicy. Commercially grown in Louisiana from the 1850s until World War II, this heirloom variety was subsequently replaced by sweeter types. The partially flattened bulbs are excellent for storing and will last up to seven months. For a spicy zing, and particularly if you want to cook Cajun food, this is your onion.

'Rose de Roscoff' Strictly speaking, this Breton variety is pink not red, but it is one of the finest onions around, being very versatile, with a sweet and fruity flavour when eaten raw and richly complex when cooked. These gorgeous onions were the type sold by "Onion Johnnies", the Breton farmers who cycled over to Britain laden with onions and garlic to sell for a higher price. Now almost impossible to buy in supermarkets, 'Rose de Roscoff' is prized by top chefs.

'Rossa di Toscana' A glossy magenta red-skinned onion with a powerful flavour, this Italian heirloom has been cultivated for hundreds of years in Tuscany. Not only is it prized for its long storage ability – it keeps for 8–10 months – but also it's said to be one of the most nutritious cultivars, brimming with immune-boosting antioxidants. The flattened bulbs are big and bold, and look beautiful when plaited.

'Rossa Lunga di Firenze' Also known by the English version of its name, 'Long Red of Florence', this onion is rooted in Tuscany, particularly the area around that most famous city. Consumed locally for centuries, it has gained recognition for its distinctive deep purple bulbs, which are long and narrow, with a bulge in the middle. It is an integral ingredient in local cuisine, such as the classic recipes *ribollita* (white bean soup) and *panzanella* (bread salad). As delicious as these torpedo-shaped onions are, they have a fairly short shelf life and are best used within three or four months.

'Rossa Lunga di Firenze'

'Rouge Pâle de Niort' A pale red vintage onion from Niort in western France, this variety has round, flattened bulbs that are coppery red on the outside and pale purple inside. They have a good shelf life and are versatile in the kitchen, with a delicious, mild flavour that is suited to eating raw or cooked. Still popular among locals in France, this fabulous onion is otherwise becoming hard to find.

'Violet de Galmi' Originating in the Ader Valley of southeastern Niger, this variety with its flat, thick, purplish pink bulbs is now popular for growing in several African countries. Very pungent and spicy, with a complex flavour when cooked, it is an excellent storing onion and well adapted to growing in hot climates. One of the best onions for curry pastes and other spicy sauces.

'Wethersfield Red' A true piece of American horticultural history, this once-popular variety dating back to the eighteenth century was a lucrative commodity crop sold by the Yankee traders of New England in the nineteenth century. The large, flattened purple bulbs are well suited to being eaten raw in salads. Not particularly good for long storage, so consume within a few months of harvest.

White

'Bianca di Maggio' A small, flat, creamy-white antique onion from Italy, this is a real speciality ingredient that fetches a pretty penny at market. It's best harvested a little early so that its full sweetness can be appreciated. Great eaten raw in salads, or pickled, roasted, or grilled whole.

'Gujarati White' This giant pure-white onion looks rather like a snowball. It has a mild, sweet flavour and is used widely to add a sweet-and-sour taste to dishes. White onions are very popular in India, and some of the best are grown in the state of Gujarat in the west of the country.

'Tonda Musona' A gorgeous big white onion with a brilliant shelf life of up to seven months. Originating in the ancient hamlet of Tonda, Tuscany, this is one of the sweetest and best-tasting white onions. It is a very hardy cultivar that can be sown in September and overwintered for an extra-early crop, or sown as normal early in the year.

'Unzen Flat' Originating in the Japanese city of Nagasaki and now a prized ingredient throughout Japan, this variety gets its name from the majestic volcano that overlooks the city. The thick, extra-juicy, flattened white bulbs are often enjoyed in salads for their crunchy texture and sweet flavour.

Sweet

'Kelsae' A massive Scottish heirloom bred in the 1950s, 'Kelsae' holds the Guinness World Record for the largest onion in the world, weighing in at mammoth 6.8kg (15lb)! It's pleasantly surprising to find a huge onion that still has a sweet flavour and fine texture. 'Kelsae' grows well in cold climates, and stores for a long time. It's a fun crop to grow, but give it plenty of room; avoid multi-sowing if you intend to grow mega bulbs and put your gardening game to the test at your local vegetable show.

'Mauis' So sweet it can be crunched into like an apple, this variety is often eaten raw and is considered a delicacy in Hawaii, where it is grown in the volcanic soil of Mount Haleakalā. This variety is considered the sweetest onion in the world, and it almost completely lacks the sulphur that causes the strong, sharp taste associated with onions. It started out as a hybrid of the variety 'Yellow Granex'. The cross was stabilized and has been grown by locals since the early twentieth century.

'Valenciana Tardiva' It's no secret that Spanish onions are regarded as some of the tastiest in the world, and the very best come from Valencia, on the east coast. One of the most sought-after is this one, a show-stopping all-purpose onion with a terrific shelf life and a properly robust, sweet flavour, suitable for eating raw or cooked. You can't go wrong with this big golden globe.

'Walla Walla' One of very few non-hybrid sweet onions. Named after the Walla Walla Valley in Washington state, this variety originated in Corsica and was brought over to the United States on boats by European settlers in the 1880s. The growers of Walla Walla Valley selected seed season after season to develop a larger, sweeter, rounder bulb. These mild, crunchy bulbs don't keep well and are best eaten straight out of the ground.

Other

'Borettana of Parma' A truly wonderful *cipollini*-type onion that can be traced back to the fifteenth century. Primarily grown in Boretto in the Emilia-Romagna region of northern Italy, these small, flat bulbs are traditionally pickled in balsamic vinegar.

Egyptian walking onion An onion that will quite literally walk out of the vegetable patch. Also known as tree onions, these plants produce little bulbs or topsets at the ends of their stems. Once the topsets become laden with bulbs, they topple over with the weight and the bulbs root into the ground, starting the process all over again. The whole plant is edible, and if you don't want them to walk out of the garden you can harvest the topsets before they topple over – although it is fun to watch them run away.

'Onion de Paris' These are the little white pickled onions, also known as "silverskins" or "cocktail onions", that you find in jars on the supermarket shelves. A French heirloom variety dating back to the 1850s, this is quick to mature and has a delicate, sweet flavour. The small, pure-white bulbs are not just great for pickling, but also work fantastically eaten raw in salads and cooked whole in soups and stews.

'He Shi Ko'

Welsh Onion

Allium fistulosum

Also known as Green onion, Japanese bunching onion, Scallion

Perhaps the most underrated member of the allium family, the Welsh onion is closely related to the common bulb onion, but its flavour is a gentle oniony whisper rather than a potent, powerful bark.

History

The common name "Welsh onion" is a misnomer, since this vegetable has absolutely no connection to the land of song. "Welsh" derives from the old German word *walsch*, meaning foreign or non-native, referring to the species' origin in Asia. Welsh onions have been cultivated in China for centuries, and are a flagship food crop there, one that's embedded in native cuisine. References to it in ancient Chinese literature can be traced back to the third century BCE. It is also cultivated in many other countries, including Japan and Korea.

Culinary uses

Preparation

The hollow, pencil-shaped leaves of the Welsh onion can be eaten raw or cooked. To make curly ribbons for a tasty green garnish, open out the foliage by splitting the tube-like stem lengthwise and flattening it out. Slice the leaves as thinly as possible into ribbons, then transfer them to a bowl of ice-cold water for 5 minutes. The thinner the ribbons, the better the curl induced by the chilly water.

Dishes

Welsh onions are an indispensable and ubiquitous ingredient in Asian cuisines and are used in an array of dishes. They're added to breads, dumplings, and ferments, and tossed into hotpots, stir-fries, and noodle soups to provide intensity of flavour, colour, and contrast, and to balance and round off dishes.

Welsh onions or spring onions?

Welsh onions are sometimes called spring onions, because their stalks are similar. However, spring onions as most people know them are usually immature bulb onions, which are biennial, while the Welsh onion doesn't develop a bulb and is perennial (and as such belongs to the group known as scallions). In terms of flavour, spring onions pack a much stronger, more intense punch than these mellow, sweet-tasting, soft-textured culinary superstars.

The savoury pancake *cong you bing* – a Chinese breakfast classic traditionally served alongside a glass of soy milk or rice porridge – really does sing this onion's praises. It's crammed full of the sweet, subtle leaves, which have been cooked until crisp, and is served with a dipping sauce of black vinegar and soy. The pancakes are made using a laminated dough (which consists of many thin layers separated by fat, like croissant dough), rather than a batter. The result is a flaky pancake that balances crunch with chewiness.

Pa-kimchi (green onion kimchi) is a Korean salty-sour ferment that fizzes with flavour. It calls for whole raw Welsh onions, which are fermented in fish sauce with *gochujang* chilli paste and other flavourings. It's the perfect accompaniment for broths and braises, and is also good chopped and stirred through rice, adding a zingy, spicy kick and a deep, sweet onion flavour.

The white parts of Welsh onions, at the base, can be chopped, fried until crisp, and used as a salad topper or garnish. They provide a delicate crunch and a sweet, oniony kick with just a tinge of bitterness.

The Welsh onion's habit of forming a clump means that your stock will increase year on year.

Growing

Welsh onions are low-maintenance and easy to grow, bursting back into life year after year. They grow as a clump, which gradually multiplies to form a bigger cluster that can be divided and replanted to form new colonies. Their compact nature means they don't take up a lot of room, and they're heroically hardy, capable of withstanding temperatures well below freezing. Being evergreen perennials, in most places they can be harvested all year. The decorative, ivory-white, globe-shaped flower heads that appear in the summer are fragrant and edible, and irresistible to bees and other pollinating insects.

Propagation

Multi-sow the seeds in clusters of 6–8 and plant them out once they are growing strongly, 4–6 weeks after germination.

'He Shi Ko'

Growing at a glance

Sow Early spring–summer, 10–32°C (50–90°F)

Plant out Late spring–early autumn

Spacing 35–45cm (14–18in)

Harvest Midsummer–autumn

Aftercare

The compact nature of Welsh onions allows them to be nestled among herbs, planted between rows of crops, and generally tucked into tight spaces throughout the garden. Water well, especially in dry spells, and deadhead as the flowers begin to fade.

Plant problems

Allium leaf miner, onion fly, onion white rot (see pages 49–51)

Harvesting

Welsh onions grow quickly and are usually ready for harvesting any time from about 55 to 70 days after transplanting. The simplest way to harvest them is to cut off the foliage at soil level. After a few weeks they will begin to resprout, producing more flavoursome leaves that can be harvested in the same fashion.

From China to an Italian classic

Legend has it that the *cong you bing* pancake was the inspiration for pizza. It is said that when the Italian merchant and explorer Marco Polo toured China in the thirteenth century, the pancake was one of his favourite foods. After returning to Italy, he developed the recipe with a Neapolitan chef, who decided to put the filling on top of the dough rather than hiding it inside, and voila! the first pizza was born – or so the tale goes.

> ## Welsh onions are low-maintenance and super easy to grow.

Alternatively, you can lift the whole plant, although this is generally done only when you intend to use the onions whole, or to eat the more pungent, pale root end.

If you have large clusters of mature plants that require dividing, this presents a terrific opportunity to reap the whole plant without compromising your supply. Gently lift the entire cluster using a spade or trowel, harvest what you need, and split and replant smaller clumps in the desired location. Although this can be done at any time of the year, it is generally best to divide mature plants in the spring.

Storage

Welsh onion leaves are best eaten shortly after picking. However, when harvested whole, the plants can be wrapped in a damp paper towel or cloth, placed inside a plastic bag or container, and stored in the fridge. The moisture will provide the humidity needed to keep them fresh for up to a week. Alternatively, if the roots are intact, the plant can be placed in a jar of water like a bouquet of flowers, where it will keep for up to two weeks if the water is refreshed every few days.

Dae-pa The thumpingly thick stems of this allium have a rich, deep flavour and a robust texture that's well suited to cooking. It's also known as the Korean leek, thanks to its size and the fact that it was developed in Korea, where it became a staple. Today, it's used extensively there, including in broths and soups, such as *seolleongtang* (a milky ox-bone soup) or *galbitang* (made with beef ribs). Its defiantly oniony flavour has a lingering garlicky sweetness that is much stronger than in most other varieties.

'He Shi Ko' This old Japanese heirloom, developed in the 1880s, is one of the most popular types grown today. It's resistant to pests and tremendously hardy. The long, slender, bottle-green foliage becomes silvery towards the root. The lower part of the plant is pleasantly pungent when eaten raw, making it a top choice for salads.

'Kyoto Kujo Negi' This long, lofty, ancient Japanese heirloom is believed to have been introduced to Japan from China's mainland via Korea during the Nara period (710–84 CE). It emerged in Osaka and was transported to and developed in Kyoto Prefecture, an area well known for culinary innovation. With its mild flavour, this variety has become a valued ingredient of daily meals, including the hotpot *sukiyaki* and noodle dishes.

'Red Welsh' The magnificent bulbous magenta root ends of this variety are very decorative, with a more potent flavour than the white-rooted varieties. 'Red Welsh' is extremely hardy and also capable of battling hot, dry conditions. The stem and leaves have a punchy flavour and are delicious wilted into soup.

'Shimonita Negi' Named after a quiet little town in Japan's mountainous Gunma Prefecture, this is called "King of the Negi", owing to its very large, fat root. It's a single-stalk variety, so it doesn't form clumps and can't be divided. Documents dating back to the Edo period (1603–1867) reveal that it was so prized in local cuisine that the *daimyo* (feudal lords) were willing to pay an unlimited fee to have its succulent stems delivered. For king-sized stems, sow seeds individually. Leave the plant to grow for at least 6 months before harvesting, or 12 months for it to reach its full potential.

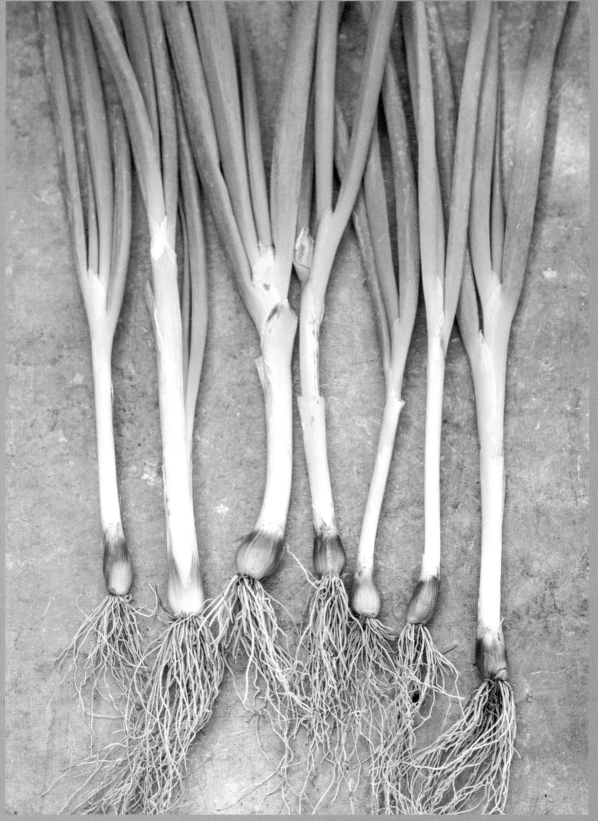

'Red Welsh'

Shallots

Allium cepa Aggregatum Group

Also known as Eschalot, Multiplier onion, Sambar

The shallot transforms dishes with a subtle flavour. It's seen by chefs as a secret weapon that adds a delicate yet complex taste, milder than onions, with a sweet garlicky back note. Like all alliums, shallots are remarkably versatile, sweet enough to use raw in salads and robust enough to handle cooking and caramelizing. These small onion-like bulbs range from pale purple and pink to golden brown, their off-white flesh tinged lavender, grey, pink, or green.

History

Shallots are perhaps most famous for their significant role in the development of French gastronomy. Countless classic French sauces and dishes call for the distinctive flavour and versatility of these alliums. The French began cultivating shallots in the twelfth century, mainly in Brittany and Anjou, the prized bulbs having arrived on European shores with crusaders returning from war in the Middle East. So, while shallots are closely associated with traditional French cooking, their roots are much further afield. The name itself derives from *escalogne*, the Old French term for shallot, from the Latin *Ascalonia caepa* (onion of Ascalon) after the ancient city (now Ashkelon, in Israel) where the ancient Greeks believed shallots to have originated.

But in fact, shallots are thought to have developed somewhere in Central or Southeast Asia, and their history dates back thousands of years, spanning a vast number of cultures and regions. They were considered a sacred plant by the ancient Egyptians, who portrayed them in artworks and included them in offerings to the gods. During the later Middle Ages shallots gained popularity throughout Europe, especially among the nobility, who grew them in their gardens and used them extensively in cooking. The cultivation of shallots spread to other parts of the globe as trade and exploration expanded from the fifteenth century onwards. Today, shallots have found their way into the cuisines of numerous cultures, and have become an integral ingredient for many.

The *eschalot grise*
or grey shallot
(left) and 'Longor'

Culinary uses

Preparation

The typical way of preparing shallots for cooking, especially when it comes to French cuisine, is *brunoise*, a knife technique that dices produce into 3mm (¹/₈in) cubes. This is a much finer cut than is typically used for an onion, and it takes some practice. Leave the root end on the bulb to keep the layers from separating while you slice and dice. Sauté shallots low and slow for best results; they will caramelize like onions but have a tendency to overcook rapidly and turn bitter, in a similar way to garlic.

Dishes

The divine flavour that's waiting to be unlocked within the shallot can be used in everything from pastries and tarts to pickles, pastes, sauces, and salads. Shallots are an integral ingredient of French sauces ranging from the ever-so-simple emulsified butter sauce *beurre blanc*, developed in nineteenth-century Nantes, to the luxurious Bordelaise sauce, a classic reduction of red wine and shallots, named after Bordeaux, the wine capital of the world. In Thailand shallots are used so frequently that they are often bought in bulk, and families commonly stock up for the whole year. They are the starting point for almost every Thai curry paste and sauce, and are used almost as frequently as garlic. While they can be used as a base ingredient or garnish, for me, one of the best ways to unlock the natural flavours of shallots is to slow-roast them whole with their skins on in a medium oven for 35–45 minutes until tender, adding plenty of fresh thyme and black pepper towards the end of the cooking time.

Growing

Although I typically plant home-saved shallots as a set that will multiply into a cluster of 8–10 bulbs the following year, shallots can be cultivated from seed. Whether you decide to grow from sets or seed will depend on whether the variety you wish to grow can be obtained only as seed; there are also some, such as 'Zebrune' (see page 107), that do not divide and so must be grown from seed.

Propagation

From sets

Sets often mature more quickly than seeds and can be acquired online or from a garden centre, or saved from last year's crop. They are best planted outside; simply dib a hole and pop in the bulb, root side down, with the tip barely poking through the surface of the growing medium. These shallow-rooting bulbs need space to divide and bulk up over the coming months, and you can expect anywhere from 6 to 12 shallots to form from each set planted. Birds may peck freshly planted sets out of the soil, so cover the sets with netting until they have sprouted.

As with onions, shallots can begin curing in the patch if the weather is fine.

Shallots are fairly shallow-rooted and should be harvested as the foliage starts to yellow, but before it dies back entirely.

Growing at a glance

Sow/plant Late autumn, late winter–early spring (sets, in situ); early–late winter (seeds), 10–32°C (50–90°F)

Plant out Early spring (seedlings)

Spacing 30cm (12in)

Harvest Midsummer–autumn

From seed

Seeds are cheaper to buy than sets, however, unlike sets, one seed will produce just one bulb. Multi-sow seeds in cells in clumps of five or six on a windowsill indoors or on a hotbed (see page 28). Although shallot seedlings look weak and flimsy, often growing very slowly to begin with, they are pretty hardy and will quickly transform into resilient plants. Plant them in their clumps directly into the garden, covering them with horticultural fleece for the first few weeks to protect them from pecking birds and harsh weather while they are young. Like onions and leeks, shallots are hungry seedlings, so be sure not to keep them growing in seed cells for too long.

Aftercare

These resilient plants require moist but free-draining soil and plenty of sunshine, and are relatively easy to care for once established. I water mine only during prolonged dry spells, and stop watering altogether once the bulbs have swollen in midsummer. All alliums are shallow-rooted plants, so it is crucial to remove weeds, which will compete with them for water and nutrients. Take care when weeding, especially if using a hoe, and ideally pull out weeds by hand. If any flower stems appear on your shallot plants, remove them and note which plants they came

Rub off the outer papery skin (left) to clean off the soil before curing and storing your shallots.

The *eschalote grise* (below) is ready for harvesting in early summer.

from; these bulbs will not store so well. One of the causes of bolting can be low temperatures in the spring.

Plant problems

Birds, rust, mildew, onion fly, onion neck rot, onion white rot, slugs and snails (see pages 49–51)

Harvesting

Shallots are ripe and ready for harvest as the foliage begins to turn yellow and flops over. Ensure that you harvest the bulbs before the foliage dies back completely. Gently twist or prise out the bulbs with a trowel and break up the clusters into individual bulbs. They must then be dried and cured in the same way as onions (see page 93), which will take anywhere from 10 to 20 days, depending on temperature and humidity.

Storage

When the shallots are ready for storage, the skin should be shiny and papery and the foliage crisp and dry. Store only pristine, undamaged bulbs, since these will keep the longest. Either plait the foliage and hang the shallots in bunches in a dry spot in the house, or cut off the foliage and keep the bulbs in mesh sacks in a light, cool, dry, well-ventilated place. Avoid storing any allium in the dark, since this tends to encourage sprouting.

Recommended varieties

Eschalote grise (*A. oschaninii*)
An ancient shallot originating in the
mountains of Kazakhstan, this species
has been affected little by human
selection and still closely resembles
its wild ancestors. Also known as the
grey shallot, it is the most sought-after
shallot at market by top chefs, for its
intense flavour. The thick-skinned
khaki bulbs are best planted from
mid-autumn to early winter and
harvested in early summer. The dense
skin and solid flesh make these bulbs
excellent winter storers.

'Hative de Niort' Also known
as the Niort shallot, this elongated,
pear-shaped variety is rooted in the
town of Niort in western France, where
it has been cultivated for generations.
The region is now renowned for its
shallot production. Its pretty pink flesh
is prized for its exceptional flavour,
which is sweet, mild, and crisp. The
variety is popular among exhibition
growers looking to showcase the
uniformity of these perfect bulbs.

Hom daeng (**Thai red shallot**)
This small, pungent bulb is prized
in Thailand for its unique flavour, and
has been cultivated in Sisaket and
Chiang Mai provinces for generations.
Smaller and rounder than its Western
cousins, with a sharper and stronger
taste, this culinary powerhouse will
keep for six months if stored correctly.
It is the perfect shallot to enhance the
authenticity of traditional Thai food.

'Longor' A very long banana-shaped
shallot that can be cultivated from a
parent bulb and split, when it grows
a crown of new bulbs. 'Longor' is a
French selection of 'Jersey Long',
famed for its robust, sweet flavour
and long storage capacity.

'Zebrune' (**'Cuisse de Poulet
du Poitou'**) Grown in the town
of Vienne, south of Lyon in eastern
France, this is a banana or eschalion
shallot, a cross between an onion and
a shallot that has inherited the best
qualities from both sides. Banana
shallots are larger than regular shallots
and therefore easier to handle, much
milder and nuttier in taste, and superior
to any onion. Classified botanically as
A. cepa (onion), these types do not divide
and must be grown from seed. The very
mild, sweet bulbs look as elegant as
they taste, although the name translates
from French to the rather inelegant
"chicken leg", from the shape of the
bulb. These meaty bulbs are heavy
yielders and, if stored correctly, will
keep for at least six months.

'Longor' (**left**) and
eschalote grise

Flowers

Giving both beauty and nutrition, flowering crops grace the plate with wholesome goodness and vibrant hues.

Broccoli

Brassica oleracea var. italica, B. o. botrytis cymose

Also known as Algentem, Brokalee, Tenderstem

Broccoli showcases Mother Nature's culinary prowess perfectly. Its quivering, firework-like florets, when perfectly cooked, are tender yet meaty, crisp, and lightly crunchy, providing an earthy sweetness with a welcome touch of bitterness and soaking up sauces like a sponge. Bursting with vitamins and minerals, broccoli is a powerhouse that offers numerous health benefits.

History

Born in Italy, a domesticated offspring of the landrace (ancient) wild cabbage (*Brassica oleracea*), broccoli is thought to have begun its horticultural odyssey with the help of the ancient Etruscan people, who were gardening geniuses. The people of this once-flourishing civilization, which occupied Tuscia (present-day Tuscany, Umbria, and northern Lazio), were famous for being skilled seafarers and renowned for embarking on trading expeditions to other Mediterranean civilizations. It is believed that, before their downfall at the hands of the Romans, the Etruscans were responsible for distributing early forms of broccoli throughout Greece and Phoenicia (roughly present-day Lebanon), along with the islands of Sicily, Sardinia, and Corsica.

The ancient Romans cultivated and consumed these cruciferous vegetables (named for their cross-shaped flowers), and the plant featured in Apicius' *De re culinaria*, one of the earliest-known recipe books. This Roman cooking compendium, thought to have been compiled in the fifth century CE, is a collection of techniques and recipes. The text recommends preparing broccoli by boiling, then seasoning "with a mixture of cumin and coriander seeds, chopped onion, plus a few drops of oil and sun-made wine". At the same time, it was said that patricians and the wealthy snacked on raw broccoli before banquets, since it was believed it would help the body to absorb alcohol.

The dispersal of broccoli outside Italy and into the rest of Europe began shortly after 1533, with the marriage of the Florentine noblewoman Catherine de' Medici to King Henry II of France. The new queen – only 14 years old at the time – arrived in France with a brigade of Italian chefs loaded with ingredients from her native Tuscany.

Breeding development ramped up swiftly, particularly in southern Italy and Sicily, and the very first variety of broccoli to be cultivated as it is known today is thought to be Calabrese broccoli. Italian horticulturists also produced other forms, such as *cime di rapa* (turnip tops), from a different lineage of domesticated *Brassica*.

Broccoli now comes in a variety of forms. The oldest is known as sprouting broccoli and belongs to the Italica group. These types produce many small, tender shoots, instead of a single large crown. "Standard" or "Calabrese" broccoli – the large, compact single heads that are often seen in markets – is a refinement of the old sprouting forms and belongs to the Botrytis group. Another variety of "broccoli" is raab (*cime di rapa*, also called *rapini* or *brassica ruvo*), a speciality in Italy, which is harvested and eaten like broccoli but is in fact more closely related to the turnip.

Culinary uses

Preparation

The delicate florets are traditionally steamed or boiled for only a few minutes, but roasting brings out a nutty, umami flavour. Be sure to use the whole vegetable. The stalks – which are far too often thrown away unnecessarily – can be chopped and added to soups, or fried with other goodies, such as garlic, chilli, and pancetta. This combination is perfect when tossed into a creamy sauce for pasta.

The maturing florets are full of promise, but keep the plant well watered as they grow and swell.

Dishes

This treetop-shaped vegetable, so frequently touted as a superfood, is just as highly regarded for being a universal ingredient that has been embraced by cultures all over the world. From Puglian pastas to Thai-style stir-fries and Japanese tempura tenderstems, broccoli is an indispensable green that rounds off dishes of all styles.

A go-to vegetarian filling for countless dishes, whether baked into quiches, mixed into frittatas, or scattered on pizza, broccoli provides sustenance, body, and bite. Embracing its softer side, the heads can be slow-roasted whole, garnished with cheese, nuts, seeds, and herbs, and served as a vegetarian centrepiece. A simple celebration of this vegetable is the traditional Neapolitan Christmas dish *broccoli di Natale*, in which the stems are boiled gently until al dente, splashed with extra-virgin olive oil, and seasoned with garlic, chilli, and lemon juice.

> **Bursting with vitamins and minerals, broccoli is a powerhouse that offers numerous health benefits.**

'Early Purple Sprouting' is a robust and delicious variety, capable of withstanding harsh weather.

Growing

Many cross-breeds have been developed to produce quicker-growing broccoli-like plants, usually with smaller florets and longer stems. These can be grown in broadly the same way as other broccoli, although the final spacing and sowing times may need to be adjusted accordingly.

Propagation

It's a good idea to stagger sowings of standard and raab-type broccoli throughout the season, sowing every couple of weeks to reap a continuous harvest.

Young brassicas are particularly susceptible to pests, so keep the seedlings undercover. Transplant them into their final home three or four weeks after germination, adhering to the spacings given in the panel overleaf and bearing in mind that closer spacing will produce smaller heads. Use a dibber to make a hole deep enough to bury the long stems, to brace the plant and provide extra support in windy weather.

Aftercare

No matter the type, protecting crops from pests, using row covers, is necessary

Growing at a glance

Sow Late winter–mid-spring or mid–late summer (standard/raab); early spring–early summer (sprouting). 6–30ºC (43–86ºF)

Plant out Early–late spring or late summer–early autumn (standard/raab); mid-spring–midsummer (sprouting)

Spacing 30–50cm (12–20in) (standard); 25–35cm (10–14in) (raab); 50–60cm (20–24in) (sprouting)

Harvest All year round (various types)

for a successful harvest. Water young transplants until they are established, after which they will require very little extra irrigation until they begin sprouting, at which point the watering regime can be ramped up, especially if the weather is dry. Keep the base of the plants free of weeds, and remove any dead or dying foliage as it begins to discolour, to reduce pressure from slugs and snails.

Plant problems

Aphids, cabbage root fly, caterpillars, flea beetle, leatherjackets, pigeons, slugs and snails (see pages 49–51)

Harvesting

Being made up of countless immature buds, the bubbly heads of broccoli must be harvested while they are still luscious and green, before the little yellow flowers begin to burst into the world. Keep a close eye on the developing florets, checking every few days, since it's always better to harvest broccoli too early than too late. The young stems are sweet and tender with a crisp snap, while older stems become fibrous and stringy.

To encourage a second flush of smaller, tender stems on standard broccoli types, harvest the central head, by slicing it off with a knife, while the broccoli beads are still tightly compact and slightly premature

(when they have grown to roughly two-thirds of their mature size). Before long, side shoots will start emerging from the main stem, and these can be snapped off easily by hand.

Check sprouting types twice a week once they begin to flower. Frequent pickings will encourage continuous blooms. When young and tender, the florets can be quickly snapped off by hand for an efficient harvest.

When harvesting raab types, if you carefully leave the lower stems and leaves intact, the plant may well resprout and bloom, providing a second and even third bounty.

Storage

With its tendency to discolour and turn yellow in a matter of days, broccoli is best eaten freshly picked. Large heads have the longest shelf life – roughly a week when kept in the fridge; for longer storage, blanch and freeze the florets.

Cima di rapa (***B. rapa sylvestris esculenta***) The name translates as "turnip top", since these broccoli-esque brassicas are in essence a turnip green that produces a cruciferous crown, although there are also *senza testa* (headless) varieties. This renowned ingredient is highly prized throughout Italy, particularly in the south. The long, tender florets produce slightly serrated leaves that spiral out of the stalk. Their flavour is stronger and noticeably more bitter than that of other broccoli, with a subtle spinachy essence, mixed with a sweet smack of greens. Within the *cima di rapa* family, there are a variety of types, each maturing at different rates, and it is often said that the longer the variety takes to grow, the better its quality. The most common are Quarantina, Sessantina, Novantina, and Centoventina, or 40, 60, 90, and 120, referring to the number of days it takes for each to reach maturity. There are also 130- and 150-day varieties, and a host of regional heirlooms, such as the Sel Fasano types, among them 'Natalina di Fasano Cima Grande' from Puglia. These are known locally as *cima grossa* (large head), since they produce big, robust florets.

'Di Ciccio' An old-fashioned Italian broccoli with an incredibly refined flavour, this is regarded as one of the most superior-tasting varieties. Grown since the nineteenth century, it's a compact but very productive plant that is quick to mature, producing a deep bluish-green asymmetric crown, followed by an enormous number of tender side shoots. Harvest the head when it reaches 8–10cm (3–4in) in diameter, to encourage side shoots to form.

'Early Purple Sprouting' Historically bred for overwintering to produce food during the "hunger gap" (see page 229), purple sprouting broccoli is extremely hardy, capable of tolerating temperatures well below freezing. Instead of developing one large central crown, it produces a mass of small, purple-headed side shoots, providing an abundant and continuous harvest from winter until spring. Sprouting broccolis have a tendency to tumble over in the high winds of autumn, but more often than not the plant will survive if the roots are still embedded in the soil. Instead of staking or supporting the stems, you can leave the toppled plants on the soil; they will quickly recover and grow upwards again.

'Piracicaba' While most broccoli varieties wither and wilt in the midsummer heat, 'Piracicaba' will thrive. Bred to withstand the sweltering temperatures of inland Brazil, the variety was developed at the Escola Superior de Agricultura Luiz de Queiroz, the country's oldest agricultural university, in Piracicaba, São Paulo state. A heavy-yielding plant that grows with phenomenal vigour, this type produces several side shoots rather than one big head. The sweet, succulent florets are much larger and looser than those of other types, and require a much shorter cooking time.

'Ramoso' This tremendously tasty Italian heritage broccoli from Calabria, in the south of the country, is a reliable cropper that's quick to mature. The plants are compact but produce a substantial harvest: first a single delicately flavoured, rich green head, then a profusion of large, individual spear-like side shoots that can be picked continuously for weeks.

'Spigariello a Getti di Napoli' Best grown in the spring and autumn, this is an ancient broccoli-esque variety from Naples. If allowed to mature, it will bloom with white petals, instead of the butter-yellow of other broccoli. Cultivated widely throughout Campania – an area celebrated for its climate, fertile land, and astonishingly beautiful landscape – these plants produce mild and sweet-flavoured crinkly, elongated, twisty blue-green leaves that are used in a similar way to kale (see page 225). Plants go on to provide a heavy crop of lateral tender-stemmed shoots, which grow back quickly after harvesting. The plant gets its name from the fountains (*getti*) of leaves that look like water cascading down the central stem. The flavour is sweet, and more similar to that of broccoli than is the full-bodied *cima di rapa*.

'Waltham 29' Developed in the 1950s by researchers at the University of Massachusetts, this variety is named after Waltham Field Station in Massachusetts, where it was bred specifically to withstand and thrive in the cold climate of the Pacific Northwest and the east coast of America. A highly sought-after broccoli with a dark blue-green complexion, it's a flavourful type that produces solid, dense medium-sized heads, followed by a fine crop of side shoots once the main head has been harvested.

'Palla di Neve'

Cauliflower

Brassica oleracea var. *botrytis*

Also known as Cyprus colewort

The aristocrats of the brassica family, cauliflowers are among the most refined masterpieces in the veg patch. Their elegant heads are composed of undeveloped flower buds, known as curds, in a multitude of colours and forms, including vivid purple, rounded clusters, and extraordinary green fractal florets. This versatile vegetable has a meaty texture and a rich, nutty flavour with a delicate, sweet aftertaste.

History

Like all domesticated brassicas, cauliflower descends from the hardy wild cabbage (*Brassica oleracea*), native to the coastal shorelines of southern and western Europe. The earliest records can be traced back to the writings of the Roman naturalist and philosopher Pliny the Elder, who died near Pompeii during the volcanic eruption of Mount Vesuvius in 79 CE. Pliny described a plant called *cyma* (believed to be an early form of cauliflower), which he called the most pleasant-tasting of all brassicas, while also noting the unfortunate fact that boiling the vegetable produces foul-smelling water.

In the twelfth century the Arab botanist Ibn al-ʿAwwam wrote that cauliflower was thought to have been developed in the town of Kythrea, on the Mediterranean island of Cyprus. This perhaps explains why in the Middle Ages cauliflower was referred to as Cyprus colewort in Britain and *choux de Chypre* (Cyprus cabbage) in France. Many historians credit the Levant region more broadly for cultivating the cauliflower, before it reached Europe.

As cauliflower's reputation spread, it became a delicacy in Europe, taking centre stage on the grand tables of the nobility, perhaps most famously that of the French king Louis XIV in the seventeenth century. It was also very fashionable in Victorian Britain. In the 1820s, the British introduced the cauliflower to India, where it has become an indispensable ingredient of the local food culture and one of the nation's most widely cultivated crops.

> **Cauliflowers require attention to detail if they are to be cultivated successfully.**

Check your cauliflowers carefully as harvest time approaches, to prevent them from over-maturing.

Culinary uses

Preparation

Cauliflower has a superior texture and flavour when grilled or roasted rather than boiled. Cook the florets from raw (there's no need to parboil), and don't be afraid to really crisp them up. The idea is to create caramelized, crunchy florets that are delightfully sweet and nutty. Don't throw away the leaves – they're a deliciously robust green packed with goodness. Those closest to the centre are the sweetest and most flavoursome. Cauliflower leaves can be used as an alternative to other leafy greens, such as cabbage and kale (see pages 196 and 225), and are especially tasty when roasted or stir-fried.

Dishes

In Britain, cauliflower has long been associated with cauliflower cheese – the classic, mouth-wateringly indulgent accompaniment to the Sunday roast. The vegetable fell out of favour for a while, but in recent years it has seen a renaissance in popularity at home and on restaurant menus. It's become a hearty constituent of vegetarian and vegan cooking, thanks to its flexibility, fresh flavour, and robust texture. Whether it's roasted, grilled, or stewed in casseroles, used as an ingredient in pickles, preserves, soups, and purées, or chopped finely and cooked as a low-carb alternative to rice and other grains, there are many ways to use cauliflower in cooking.

Cherished in India for its ability to absorb rich flavours, cauliflower can be found in an array of curries (such as *aloo gobi* and *gobi masala*), stir-fries, and preserves, including the sweet-and-sour winter pickle *gobhi gajar ka achar*, which is popular in Punjab, and the decadent, thick, coconut-based curry *gobi gashi*, which originates in the coastal region of Mangalore. Cauliflower is also commonly eaten for breakfast when grated, spiced, and stuffed into a paratha (a flaky, buttery flatbread).

When cauliflower is sliced into steaks and grilled over an open flame, its full-bodied, robust texture slowly tenderizes into a succulent treat, substantial enough to be served as the headline ingredient. Charred cauliflower steaks are cracking covered in salsa verde or other fresh herb sauces. Another creative vegetarian dish is spicy buffalo cauliflower wings – a twist on the classic meaty snack or appetizer.

Growing

Often considered a demanding and problematic crop to grow, cauliflowers certainly require attention to detail if they are to be cultivated successfully. There are three types – summer, autumn, and spring (see pages 118–19) – and if you choose a range of varieties, you could be harvesting cauliflowers most months of the year.

Propagation
Cauliflower should always be sown under cover. There are three main sowing windows, and the timing will depend on the cultivar (see Recommended varieties, overleaf).

Aftercare
The young plants can be transplanted to their final home approximately six weeks after germination, spaced according to the size of head you wish to achieve. Space plants at 40cm (16in) for small cauliflowers, 50cm (20in) for medium-sized heads, and 60cm (24in) for large heads. If you are short on bed space when planting out spring varieties in July, try interplanting cauliflower with crops that are close to being harvested.

Cover early plantings with horticultural fleece to protect them from frost, and ensure the young plants are well watered

Growing at a glance
Sow Late winter–early spring (summer types); late spring–early summer (autumn types); midsummer (winter types), 6–30°C (43–86°F)

Plant out Early–mid-spring (summer types); early–midsummer (autumn types); late summer (winter types)

Spacing 40–60cm (16–24in)

Harvest Spring–autumn

until they have had time to establish. Once the roots have taken hold and the plant is growing vigorously, water sparingly. However, when the curds begin to form and swell, ensure you give them plenty of water, especially during hot weather.

While some cauliflower varieties are self-blanching, others will need to be blanched by hand. Blanching refers to the technique that protects cauliflower heads from direct sunlight, which can cause the yellowing of curds and a more bitter taste. The process simply involves tying the cauliflower leaves together gently (I use thick rubber bands) to create a protective hood over the developing

'Purple Cape'

heads, safeguarding them from becoming over-exposed to sunlight. Blanching is usually done when the heads have just begun to form and are 5–8cm (2–3in) across. For best results, tie the heads on a dry day to prevent mould from developing inside the leaves.

Plant problems
Birds, butterflies, cabbage root fly, club root, flea beetle (see pages 49–51)

Harvesting
Cauliflowers are best picked while the curds are firm and compact, and before the florets start to grow away from the core. Don't allow them to mature on the plant for too long, or they will begin to flower, creating an inferior, airy, spongy texture. It's important to be vigilant, since in the summer, the heads can reach full maturity in as little as one or two weeks; during the cooler seasons, curds can take four weeks to reach their prime.

To harvest, slice the head off the main stalk along with several of the leafy layers below, to prolong the head's shelf life. The remaining growing stalk can now be removed from the bed, chopped, and thrown on to the compost heap.

Storage
Cauliflowers discolour quickly after harvesting and are best kept in the fridge or a cool, dark place, where they will last for about a week.

Summer types
Generally considered to be the easiest to cultivate successfully, the cauliflowers that are ready for harvest in the summer are fast-growing – usually ready for harvest in four or five months – and produce relatively small heads. Sow indoors or on a hotbed.

'Di Jesi' This stunning heirloom variety stems from Jesi, in the Marche province of eastern Italy, where it's known locally as "snail cauliflower". The spiralling florets are loved for their exceptionally beautiful geometric patterns and sweet, earthy flavour. It's a fast-growing, compact plant that produces crisp, creamy-white heads packed with fractal florets. It can also be grown for autumn harvesting.

'Palla di Neve' The name of this fast-maturing variety from the Italian Dolomite mountains translates as "snowball" – a reference to its perfectly round, solid, pure white heads. The plants are short-stemmed, compact, and versatile, performing well in both cool and warm temperatures.

Autumn types
Slightly slower-growing than summer varieties, and bred to withstand the high temperatures of summer, autumn varieties should be harvested before the arrival of the first frost.

'Di Sicilia Violetto' This is a truly stunning deep purple cauliflower from the sunny Italian island of Sicily. The psychedelic purple colour turns to green when the flesh is boiled, so try pickling or roasting it to retain some of the cosmic colour. It grows into a large plant and sometimes forms side shoots after the main head is harvested, providing a bumper bounty of tenderstem cauliflower. Give this crop plenty of space when planting out, to accommodate side-shooting.

'Gigante di Napoli' This huge cauliflower from Naples, which grows

'Di Jesi'

The cauliflower went on to win a First Class certificate from the Royal Horticultural Society in 1873. It produces enormous heads with huge florets, perfect for roasting and cauliflower cheese.

'Purple Cape' A show-stopping purple-headed cauliflower that has been grown in South Africa since 1808 and produces large, robust heads with an excellent flavour. This cultivar is exceptionally rich in beneficial anthocyanins.

'Tardif d'Angers' This fabulous, hardy French heirloom, developed in the region of Pays de la Loire, develops very large, pure white heads of the highest quality.

'Verona Tardivo' One of the most exceptionally flavoured of all cauliflowers, this ivory-white cultivar, with a pronounced, flattened head, has a sweet, floral taste with rich, earthy, nutty tones, and a creamy texture. Originating in the foothills of Italy's Lessini Mountains, these tall, vigorous plants are rarely grown commercially outside the area around Verona.

on tall, vigorous plants, produces dense snow-white rosettes that can turn yellow if they are left to mature for too long. It's the traditional cauliflower used in the time-honoured Neapolitan Christmas salad *insalata di rinforzo*, with peppers, pickles, anchovies, and olives.

'Romanesco' Utterly mesmerizing, 'Romanesco' is made up of enchanting lime-green florets set in a hypnotic spiral pattern. The remarkable heads display an example of the Fibonacci sequence – a mathematically perfect series of numbers, in which each number is the sum of the two previous numbers – at work in nature. Debate rages among horticulturists on whether 'Romanesco', which has been cultivated in the Lazio region of Italy since the fifteenth century, is a cauliflower or a broccoli. Whatever the case, it's not just a delight on the eye but also a treat for the table, with its nutty, sweet flavour and crunchy texture.

'Verde di Macerata' Originating in the province of Macerata on the Adriatic coast, this neon-green heritage

cauliflower is a highly prized ingredient throughout Italy. Its attractively coloured curds won't fade after cooking, so it's a chef's favourite for bringing visual contrast and a delicious nutty note to dishes.

Spring types

These hardy varieties, which are sown in the summer, overwinter, and are harvested from early spring, are a great choice of crop as they provide food during the "hunger gap" (see page 229). They're slow-growing plants that are wider and broader than other varieties, with larger heads. Often growing for six months or more, these types require a wide spacing to allow the plants room to bulk up.

'Leamington' This old English cultivar is also known as 'Mr Perkins', after a Mr F. Perkins of Regent Street, Leamington Spa. Perkins is believed to have first developed this cultivar in the late nineteenth century, and sold the seeds of his prized crop to locals.

The electric daisy's unusual, apparently petal-less heads will provide a talking point in the patch.

Edible Flowers

Flowers are fascinating, complex organisms that play a crucial role in sustaining life on Earth by providing nourishment for pollinators and other insects – while making the world a more joyful, colourful place. Many flowers also have exciting properties that can be harnessed to provide new flavour sensations or edible dyes, or simply brighten up a plate of food.

Cosmos
(*Cosmos sulphureus*)
Yellow cosmos

Renowned for its striking, fire-red flowers, cosmos blooms abundantly during the summer. The petals of this ornamental edible have a faintly sweet taste and crisp texture that make them perfect for garnishing salads and decorating cakes.

Growing

Sow singly in seed cells. Give these tall, bushy plants plenty of space (about 45cm/18in) and stake or provide other support if necessary.

Electric daisy
(*Acmella oleracea*)
Pará cress, Brazil cress

Mother Nature's natural popping candy. This native of the Amazonian rainforest, has been used for centuries by Indigenous people to relieve toothache by chewing on the flower heads, which release a burst of citrus followed by a buzzing jolt of electricity that numbs the tongue and makes the mouth water. This anaesthetic quality is caused by a compound called spilanthol, and usually lasts for 5–10 minutes. Its delicious flavour and numbing property make it just as useful today.

Growing

This is a tender perennial, tolerant of partial shade and low-growing, with a sprawling habit. Start the seeds off in cells, and transplant into the garden 35cm (14in) apart once all risk of frost has passed.

Variety	Good for	Conditions	Sow	Plant out	Harvest	Height
Cosmos	Garnish	Full sun; moist but well-drained soil	Early spring	Early summer	Summer/ autumn	10–50cm (4–20in)
Electric daisy	Cocktails	Sun or partial shade; light, sandy soil	Mid-spring	Late spring	Summer/ autumn	10–50cm (4–20in)
Safflower	Spicing; dye	Full sun; any well-drained soil	Early spring	Late spring	Summer	50–100cm (20–39in)
Arikara	Seeds; dye	Full sun; moist but well-drained soil	Mid-spring to early summer	Early summer	Summer	2.5–4m (8–13ft)
Hungarian breadseed	Poppy seeds	Full sun or partial shade; any well-drained soil	Early spring	Late spring	Summer	1–1.2m (3–4ft)
Butterfly pea	Tea	Full sun; moist but well-drained soil	Early spring	Late spring	Summer	1–1.2m (3–33ft)

Safflower
(*Carthamus tinctorius*)
False saffron

The vivid orange flowers of these fast-growing thistle-like plants can be used as a substitute for saffron, yet with a much softer and sweeter taste with hints reminiscent of chocolate. They're known in Japan as *benibana* and have traditionally been used dried, as a dye in textiles, pottery, art, and cosmetics.

Growing

This drought-tolerant annual (a plant that completes its life cycle in a single year) is best sown singly into seed cells and planted out once large enough to handle. Harvest the flowers regularly to encourage more blooms; they can be cut at any stage, and often turn a deeper orange as they ripen. Hang whole flower heads upside down to dry, to keep the petals long and straight.

Cosmos is an exquisite flower with deliciously sweet-tasting petals.

The slender petals of safflower look like saffron and can be used in a similar way, to colour and gently flavour rice and other dishes.

Arikara
(*Helianthus annuus*)
Common sunflower, Comb flower

Cultivated by the Indigenous Arikara people of what are now North and South Dakota for its nutritious, oil-rich seeds, this historic single- and multi-headed sunflower variety can reach remarkable heights. Large seeds can be eaten whole, while the small seeds were traditionally toasted and pounded into a fine meal that was made into energy balls carried by warriors as sustenance on their travels. The "Hopi black dye" or *tceqa' qu' si* is another significant historic variety of sunflower with a dual purpose. The heads produce tasty black seeds that are also used by the Hopi people of Arizona to make dye that is used for textiles and pottery, and body paint for ceremonial dances and rituals.

Growing

Space the seedlings generously (about 45–65cm/18–26in) when planting out. These tall plants are susceptible to wind damage, and the seeds risk being feasted on by birds and squirrels as they mature.

Hungarian breadseed
(*Papaver somniferum*)
Opium poppy, Balewort

The go-to poppy for cultivating a supply of delicious home-grown seeds for cooking and baking. These tall plants produce stunning purple and mauve flowers and bulky seed pods. Allow the pods to dry and turn silver on the plant before harvesting; once the seeds rattle inside, pick the pods and hang them indoors to continue drying.

Growing

These poppies are best direct-sown, and it can be helpful to mix the fine seeds into a handful of compost before scattering them over a weed-free bed. The seedlings are easy to identify and can be thinned if you have too many. This is a fantastic crop for sunny borders and partly shaded areas.

Butterfly pea
(*Clitoria ternatea*)
Blue vine, Pigeon wings

This tropical perennial is usually grown as a half-hardy annual in temperate climates. Its intricate vines produce an abundance of intensely blue-lobed flowers that boast a colour-changing property when brewed into tea. The caffeine-free tea's natural blue pigment undergoes a fascinating chemical transformation when the pH is decreased (made more acidic) with the addition of lemon juice, for example, changing from deep blue to vibrant violet or hot pink. This plant is famous all over Southeast Asia, particularly in Thailand, where the tea is known as *an chan* and is thought to possess anti-ageing properties.

Growing

Sow single seeds in cells and plant out the seedlings 30cm (12in) apart once all risk of frost has passed. These tall climbing vines need the support of a trellis.

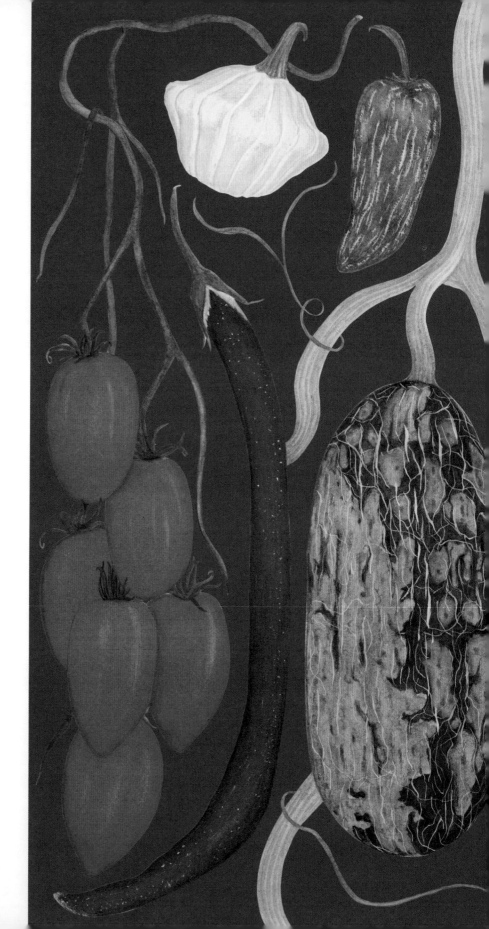

Fruit

With their sweet. fruitful harvests.
these crops reward our patience with
an abundance of delicious produce.

Aubergine

Solanum melongena

Also known as Brinjal, Eggplant, Garden egg, Melanzana, Melongen

Used in a wide variety of cuisines around the world, the aubergine is an incredibly versatile vegetable. It's great at soaking up flavours and works well in stews, soups, and curries, but is also perfect for grilling, roasting, frying, and barbecuing.

A sweet, tender vegetable that is actually technically a fruit, the aubergine is covered with a shiny skin that comes in many colours. The most common variety, 'Black Beauty', is dark glossy purple and black, but there are types that are mauve, red, yellow, white, or green, and even one with lilac and purple pinstripes. In terms of shape and size, aubergines are very varied: long and slender, short and squat, small and round, oval or pear-shaped. All types require a long, warm growing season and are at their prime in mid- to late summer and early autumn.

History

The evolution of this member of the nightshade family is a topic that poses more questions than it answers. Scientific research had indicated that aubergines were first domesticated in China and India thousands of years ago. However, recent studies have proved that the cultivated varieties are in fact related to a wild species that is native to the African savannahs, leaving experts scratching their heads about how aubergines made it from Africa to Asia millennia ago.

Without doubt aubergines are an important ingredient for many Asian cultures and cuisines today, but they have also been used historically throughout that continent, especially in China during the fifth century, when affluent and aristocratic ladies would stain their teeth black with dye made from the skin of aubergines. Aubergine seeds arrived in Europe after the Moorish invasion of Spain in the eighth century, and the vegetable has been used extensively throughout Mediterranean cooking since.

Known in Britain as aubergine, this crop is more commonly recognized around the word as eggplant. The latter name stems from their first introduction to Europe, when they were typically white or yellow with an elliptical shape – looking uncannily like a large bird's egg.

Culinary uses

Preparation
Aubergines require little preparation. They don't need peeling, but if you prefer to remove the skin, peel lengthwise down the fruit, leaving a strip of skin between peeled sections. This way, the aubergine is less prone to collapsing and turning to mush when cooked.

Traditionally, aubergines are sliced and salted before cooking to reduce bitterness from the flesh. Many varieties listed in this book have had the bitterness bred out of them, so salting isn't essential. However, if you're planning on slicing and pan-frying aubergines, or if they're large with lots of seeds, salting draws out the moisture, helping them to caramelize and crisp up, as well as improving the flavour.

Dishes
Classic aubergine dishes include ratatouille, a vegetable stew from the South of France; moussaka, a baked dish from the Levant (eastern Mediterranean) comprising layers of aubergine and a sauce of tomato and spiced lamb, topped with béchamel; and *parmigiana di melanzane*, a southern Italian baked dish made from layers of aubergine, mozzarella cheese, Parmesan, and tomato sauce. One of my favourites is baba ghanoush, a creamy, smoky dip that is a staple of Levantine cooking. It involves roasting or grilling the aubergines (ideally over an open flame) until the skins are charred, then chopping the flesh and combining it with olive oil, lemon juice, and tahini.

There are other, lesser-known dishes in which aubergines are given a starring role, including the Persian pickle *torshi bademjan*. For this, aubergines are stuffed with garlic, herbs, and spices (mint, dill, tarragon, chilli powder, coriander seeds, and nigella), then simmered in an aromatic liquor of flavoured vinegar. The mixture is transferred to preserving jars and left to ferment for at least 48 hours. Believed to aid digestion, *torshi* is traditionally served with meat kebabs or stews, but also works well with mezze, such as falafel, hummus, and tabbouleh.

Other favourite aubergine dishes are *baingan bharta* – a spicy, smoky, tangy curry from Punjab, India, made from charred aubergines – and *nasu dengaku* – a Japanese dish made with sliced aubergines coated in a sweet and savoury miso sauce, then baked.

Most recipes call for aubergines to be cooked. However, the Japanese cultivar 'Senshu Kinukawa Mizu' (see pages 130–31), which has soft, buttery flesh, is used raw in aubergine sashimi.

Growing

Aubergines can be tricky to grow in a temperate climate because they require warmth, but don't be put off. If you follow some simple rules, you'll be rewarded with a long-lasting, bountiful harvest.

Propagation
In temperate climates, it's recommended to start seeds off in a heated propagator, on a heat mat or warm windowsill, or in

Warning

The stems, leaves, and flowers of aubergines often have spikes that are as sharp as needles, so consider using gloves when handling plants.

66
All aubergines require a long, warm growing season.

'Ping Tung' (left) is almost outlandishly long and thin.

'Senshu Kinukawa Mizu' (below, top left), 'Nagasaki Long' (top centre and right), 'Ping Tung' (bottom left and right), and 'Listada de Gandia' (bottom centre)

an airing cupboard. Move them to a bright spot as soon as they germinate, and when the seedlings are large enough to handle (usually about two weeks after germination), prick them out into modules. Allow the seedlings to grow on for another three or four weeks, then pot them on into 7–10cm (3–4in) pots. Keep the pots indoors on a sunny windowsill or in a heated greenhouse. Once all risk of frost has passed, plant them out into their final growing positions.

Aftercare

Aubergines do better in a sunny position, ideally under cover. They can be grown in pots, grow bags, or directly in the ground. If you're growing them in containers, use a good-quality organic, peat-free compost and water well – at least once a day in the summer.

I grow aubergines as bushes with a support or stake in the middle, since the plants are prone to falling over when heavily laden with fruit. Ideally, stake at the time of planting or while they're still small, to avoid damaging the roots. Once the

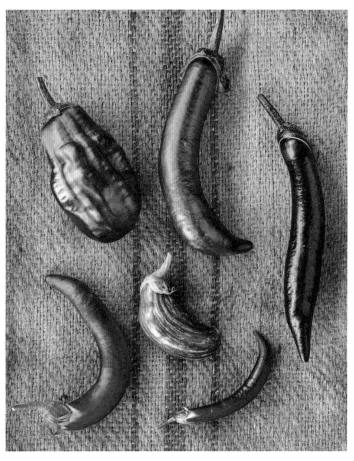

Growing at a glance

Sow Late winter–early spring, 20–30°C (68–86°F)

Plant out Mid-spring (heated greenhouse);
late spring (unheated greenhouse/polytunnel);
early summer (outside)

Spacing 40–60cm (16–24in)

Harvest Midsummer–mid-autumn

plants have reached 30–40cm (12–16in) high, pinch out the growing tips to encourage side shoots. When they start to set fruit, allow only five or six aubergines to develop per plant, removing any new flowers that form and pinching out any extra side shoots that develop, so the plant can focus its energy on maturing the fruit. Remove old petals and dead leaves regularly to reduce the risk of mould and disease.

Aubergines can also be grown as cordons, which grow continually on a single stem and must be trained on a support. Start by selecting one of the strongest stems to train, then prune the rest, removing the side shoots and lower leaves. Continue to train the main stem up the support as the plant grows. Growing aubergines in this way is great for saving space, and the restricted growth should make the plant concentrate its energy into producing fewer but better-quality fruit.

Plant problems

Aphids, blossom end rot, red spider mite, thrips, whitefly (see pages 49–51)

Harvesting

I recommend picking aubergines when they are ever so slightly immature, unless you're planning to stuff them. Smaller aubergines have a sweeter taste, thinner skin, and more flesh. When they are fully mature, the skin becomes dull and wrinkly, the flesh bitter, and the texture airier.

Harvest when the fruit reaches a decent size, has a glossy skin, and feels firm when squeezed gently. Cut the stems using a sharp knife or garden snips. Ideally, leave a short piece of stem attached to the fruit, to increase the aubergine's shelf life. Frequent harvesting will promote continued cropping and heavier yields.

Storage

Aubergines don't store well (the flavour starts to deteriorate after three or four days), so use them as soon as possible after harvesting. If you have a glut, try making *torshi bademjan* pickles (see page 126). Raw aubergines don't freeze well, so cook them into a meal before freezing.

'Ping Tung' (opposite) and 'Thai Round White'

'Aswad' This is an Iraqi variety that is believed to have been grown by the people in the ancient civilizations of Mesopotamia. It produces huge purple-black fruit, each weighing a whopping 1kg (just over 2lb) or more, on plants that can reach 1m (3ft) high. The fruit, which is short and stout, with very glossy skin and sweet, creamy flesh, is perfect sliced and grilled on a barbecue as a veggie steak or used in the classic Sudanese dish *salata aswad be zabadi*. *Aswad* is Arabic for black, and also happens to be the Sudanese word for aubergine.

'Blanche Dourga' Originating in France, this is an ivory-white variety that starts producing fruit early in the season and continues into late autumn. These compact plants grow to around 60cm (24in) high, making them good for containers. The fruit, which grow to 10–15cm (4–6in) long, are sweet and creamy with an almost mushroomy flavour.

'Lao Lavender' An old-school variety from the majestic mountains of Laos, Southeast Asia. These productive plants produce an abundance of tiny globe-shaped

'Aswad'

fruit just 2.5cm (1in) wide. The dainty aubergines are handsome with their luxurious marbled lavender skin, dappled creamy white. Best served whole as a bite-sized treat, they can be skewered and barbecued or tossed into stir-fries and stews.

'Listada de Gandia' A true treasure, this aubergine produces stunning purple fruit with white streaks. The name refers to its origin in the eastern Spanish town of that name, where it is used to make the classic Andalusian sweet-and-savoury tapas dish *berenjenas con miel* (aubergine with honey). The plants grow to 35cm (14in) high, do well in containers, and produce many thin-skinned, oblong fruit.

'Melanzana Rossa di Rotonda' Utterly scrumptious, the round, bright red fruit of this variety have a unique, piquant flavour that is like a cross between a tomato, a pepper, and an aubergine. Grown mainly in the province of Potenza in southern Italy, they are traditionally used to make the Sicilian sweet-and-sour relish caponata. The variety first appeared in Italy in the 1930s, when Italian colonists introduced the seeds from Ethiopia. When fully mature, the fruit resembles a tomato and has a bitter, tangy taste, so it is usually harvested while still orange (rather than red), with green streaks. Plants grow to around 80cm (32in) high.

'Nagasaki Long' A Japanese heirloom variety to rejoice over. It has long, tapering, jet-black fruit that are intensely flavoured with super-sweet notes and almost no bitterness, produced on plants that can reach about 1m (3ft) in height.

'Ping Tung' One of the most unusually long aubergines around. Named after the town of Ping Tung in southern Taiwan, China, this variety has slender fruit 25–40cm (10–16in) long with vivid violet skin and creamy-white flesh that is so sweet and tender it can be eaten raw. The plant provides an abundance

'Rosa Bianca' (left) and 'Violetta di Firenze'

of fruit and is good for containers, being relatively compact at 70cm (28in) high. It is an ideal candidate for stir-fries and tempura, as it cooks quickly.

'Ronde de Valence' Known for their unique slightly flattened, spherical shape and dazzling dark purple skin, these aubergines originate in the quaint southeastern French city of Valence, nestled on the Rhone River. A very productive and disease-resistant variety that produces tender, mild fruit the size of grapefruit (10–15cm/4–6in) on plants capable of reaching a height of 1m (3ft) or more.

'Rosa Bianca' This variety stems from the Italian island of Sicily, where the fruit is adored by locals for its mild, creamy flavour and tender, meaty texture. The name means pink and white, referring to the fruit's alluring skin, creamy-coloured with pinkish purple blushes. The extravagantly ostentatious round, ribbed fruit averages 12cm (5in) long, while the plants can reach heights of almost 1m (3ft).

'Senshu Kinukawa Mizu' Also known as "silk skin", the sashimi aubergine has a thin, delicate skin, extremely soft, succulent white flesh, and a sweet flavour, enabling it to be eaten raw. It originates in Osaka, Japan, where it has been traced back to the Muromachi period (1338–1573), but it is now grown in other parts of the country. The deep purple, almost black fruit, about 12cm (5in) long and carried on plants just under 1m (3ft) high, is best consumed straight after harvesting. It is traditionally scored, then split into strips lengthwise and served with miso, wasabi (see page 302), or soy sauce. It is also a popular choice for the salty, slightly sour *shibazuke* pickle. Take care not to bruise or score

the delicate fruit when pruning and training, and be sure to keep them well watered – they are traditionally grown in the corners of rice paddies.

'Thai Green' Frequently found growing throughout northern Thailand, where it is known as *makhuea*. This is a very productive, attractive variety that produces countless tiny green-and-white-striped fruit, about 2.5cm (1in) long, ideal for grilling on skewers or cooking whole in Thai curries. It's a bushy plant that grows to about 35cm (14in) high, making it perfect for compact spaces and growing in pots.

'Violetta di Firenze' A prized Italian heirloom from the city of Florence, this is a firm favourite with chefs for its mild, creamy taste that is always sweet and never bitter. The beautiful bicoloured fruit, about 15cm (6in) long, is a rich purple fading to white, with a stocky, crinkled, oval shape. The plants grow to about 75cm (30in) high and produce fewer spikes than other varieties. Reliable and great-tasting, this is well suited to roasting, stuffing, or slicing.

'Senshu Kinukawa Mizu'

Cucumber

Cucumis sativus

Also known as Cuke, Cetriolo, Kheera, Pepino

With an undeniable cool that sets them apart in the patch, cucumbers have a refreshingly crisp, crunchy flesh. They are much more than a mere addition to a salad; their unique flavour, slightly sweet and faintly salty, works gloriously in dips and soups, as well as in a gin and tonic and the quintessentially British alcoholic drink Pimm's.

History

It is a challenge to pinpoint the exact origin of the cucumber, but many researchers agree that it originated in the Himalayan foothills of northern India and Nepal thousands of years ago. The fruit spread slowly, entangling itself in the various cuisines of neighbouring civilizations, particularly the Sumerian cities hugging the Euphrates River, as well as China, where it's often claimed that pickled cucumbers were first developed for workers building the Great Wall. Inscriptions written almost 4,000 years ago on tablets XI and XII of the Mesopotamian Epic of Gilgamesh talk about a "thorny plant that grows beneath the waves, called How-the-Old-Man-Once-Again-Becomes-a-Young-Man". That plant is believed to be a form of old-school cucumber, and it certainly lived up to its name, as Gilgamesh, king of Uruk, was viewed as a demigod with superhuman strength, and is said to have lived for an astonishing 126 years.

Cucumbers later spread into ancient Egypt (where the vines were grown along the Nile using an irrigation system diverted from canals) before ending up in the hands of the Romans, who welcomed the plants warmly. The first-century emperor Tiberius demanded to be served fresh cucumbers every day of the year. To cater for his constant craving, winter cucumbers were cultivated in an early form of manoeuvrable greenhouse that could be positioned in the sunniest spots; these growing structures were given extra illumination via the careful positioning

> 66
> **It's often claimed that pickled cucumbers were first developed for workers building the Great Wall of China.**

of mirror stones around the garden. The cucumber spread to the Caribbean, South, and North America when Spanish boats sailed across the Atlantic and the explorer Christopher Columbus brought the seeds in 1494 to what is now Haiti.

Culinary uses
Preparation
Cucumber can be grated, sliced thinly, chopped into more rustic chunks, cut into batons, or left whole. It can be eaten raw, cooked, or pickled (see page 136), and its tantalizing, thirst-quenching, mild, crunchy

flesh collaborates with other ingredients and elevates dishes to new heights, whatever the cuisine.

Dishes
Raw cucumbers have a cool, revitalizing, crisp texture that works wonders in salads, sandwiches, and garnishes, perfect in the summer. They can be incorporated into dips, such as tzatziki, and cold soups, such as gazpacho. Pickled, no matter the time of year, cukes add a scrumptious snap of sweet acidity that cuts through the fattiness of a burger. At the other end of the spectrum, cooked cucumbers – which are

The variety of cucumber shapes and sizes is as wide as its culinary uses.

133

Train the growing tips gently around the support strings.

popular in Asia – take on a completely different character. They remain mild, subtle, and sweet, but the biggest difference is the texture, which becomes soft and tender. Sliced thinly on a mandoline, the cucumber refines and harmonizes dishes, as when it's used as a bed for an elegant smoked-mackerel rillette. Left chunky, cukes have texture, body, and bite, and their cool flavour neutralizes salty ingredients, such as the feta and olives found in Greek salad. The quintessential cucumber sandwich, with soft white bread, dates back to 1840, when the concept of afternoon tea was first introduced to England, and served only to the wealthy. Now, no tea party would be complete without these terribly posh sarnies, the Mad Hatter's included.

Perhaps the ultimate way to enjoy the refreshing flavour of home-grown cucumbers is to smash them. Traditionally paired with the spicy food of Sichuan province to balance and cut through the heat, smashed cucumber is an ancient Chinese preparation of raw cucumber chunks lightly crushed and tossed in a mixture of garlic, rice vinegar, and soy sauce, among other seasonings, and topped with sesame seeds. The smashing creates a tastier cucumber by cracking the skin and releasing the natural juices. Crushed cukes absorb flavours and sauces better, since aromatic ingredients can work their way into the nooks and crannies. Smashed cucumbers can also be prepared in a minimalist way; simply cut the flesh into chunks, crush and lightly salt them, and leave them in the fridge for 30 minutes. The pale centre will become a vibrant fresh green, while the flesh is bursting with flavour and perfectly seasoned throughout.

Growing

The beauty of growing only open-pollinated heirloom cucumbers (rather than F1 hybrids) is that you don't need to remove the male flowers, and they won't go bitter if you grow several types in the same area. These plants are very frost-tender and thrive in warm weather, so in a temperate climate they perform best when grown under cover. Having said that, there are varieties of outdoor cucumber that can be very productive when left to sprawl across the ground, even in cool climates.

Propagation

Cucumbers are best sown singly in seed cells from about three weeks before the last frost is likely; don't start them any earlier, or the plants will take up too much space before you can plant them out. Cucumber seeds need constant warmth to coax them into life, so for more successful germination, keep the trays inside the house or on a heat mat. The newly emerging seedlings grow swiftly and will require potting on into 9cm (4in) pots in as little as 10 days. Young cukes don't like having wet feet – their stems will quickly

damp off if they have too much moisture – so pay close attention when watering. Even inside an unheated polytunnel or greenhouse, transplant cucumbers only when the risk of frost has passed completely. For outdoor sprawling types allow 60 cm (24 in) between plants, and if training the vines up a string, allow a spacing of at least 75cm (30in). When planting climbing types out in a polytunnel or greenhouse, plant them deeply to support their succulent stem, burying the support twine under the roots before securing it to the top of the structure.

Fresh-tasting Barattiere or Armenian cucumbers are actually a type of melon.

Growing at a glance

Sow Mid–late spring, 16–35°C (60–95°F)

Plant out Early summer

Spacing 60–75cm (24–30in)

Harvest Midsummer–mid-autumn

'Aonaga Jibai'

These ferociously fast-growing plants need plenty of water. Even outside crops need a good soaking twice a week during dry weather, and cukes under cover appreciate a generous drink every three days.

Plant problems

Mildew, mosaic virus, slugs and snails, spider mite (see pages 49–51)

Harvesting

Once the vines start bearing fruit, you may get as many as one cucumber a day from each plant. Pick frequently so that they continue producing. To avoid a glut, pick cucumbers while still small, sweet, soft-skinned, and not too seedy.

Storage

Cucumbers are most scrumptious when eaten freshly picked, but they will keep happily for up to a week in the fridge, or several weeks for the thick-skinned storage types. For long storage, try pickling them. Ensure extra-crunchy pickles by slicing off 1.5cm ($^1\!/_2$in) from the blossom end of the cucumber (the end the flower grew from) before fermentation, since it contains enzymes that soften pickles. Another natural way to keep pickles crisp is by incorporating tannins in the brine. Fresh vine leaves are most commonly used for this purpose, but horseradish, blackberry, and raspberry leaves also work perfectly, as does green or black tea.

Aftercare

Train climbing cucumber plants to grow straight up by twisting the support strings around the main stem. Alternatively, train them up trellising.

To encourage a strong root system, cut off all small, undeveloped fruit and flowers until the plants are well established or at least 50cm (20in) tall. As the plants grow, remove every other side shoot – the fruit forms on these side shoots, so don't discard them all. The size of these side vines can be controlled by pinching out the fuzzy growing tips once they have grown to a length of 1m (3ft) or more. Once the main growing tip reaches the top of the support, curve it over and allow the plant to continue growing back towards the ground. With outdoor cucumbers, pinch out the growing tip once the plant has developed seven sets of leaves, to encourage side shoots; the side shoots' growing tips can also be pinched out to encourage even more vines.

> 66
> **These ferociously fast-growing plants need plenty of water.**

136

True cucumbers

These differ greatly in shape and size, from teeny-tiny prickly cornichons to long, smooth-skinned slicing varieties with very few seeds. Typically white or green at the eating stage, most turn a glowing golden-yellow or russeted brown as the fruit ripens fully and the seeds mature.

'Ancashino' It's thought the seeds of this classic Peruvian cucumber were brought to South America from Spain in the sixteenth century. Being adapted to the cool climate of the Andes, it is a great choice for growers in cool areas. Highly productive and a glorious deep green, it is famous for its resilience to pests and mildew, and its ability to continue cropping late in the season.

'Aonaga Jibai' Vigorous and hardy, capable of tolerating heat, drought, and mildew, this splendid heirloom variety has been handed down for generations by a local family in Beppu, on the southern Japanese island of Kyushu. The long, slender dark green fruit has an irresistibly sweet, tender, and unnoticeable seed mass, with no hint of bitterness.

'Boothby's Blonde' This eye-catching warty-skinned, creamy-white cucumber is shaped like a large egg. A family heirloom variety from Livermore, Maine, it yields many medium-sized

'Boothby's Blonde'

fruit, best picked when about 10cm (4in) long. There's no need for peeling, since the white skin is thin and tender, while the lime-green flesh has a mild taste and crisp, crunchy texture.

'Boston Pickling' These vigorous vines produce an abundance of small, slightly tapered, smooth fruit with black spines, perfect for making chunky dill pickles. This is my go-to fermenting cuke, since the thick flesh remains crisp while taking on the full flavour of the pickling spices. The seeds were introduced in 1877 by the US-based seed supplier D. M. Ferry & Co., which described it as "the only pickler you will ever need to grow".

'Çengelköy' A prolific thin-skinned traditional salad variety from Turkey, this performs well in temperate areas. It's named after a neighbourhood on the east bank of the Bosphorus in Istanbul, a region that was well known for its small cucumber farms, many of which have been forced out by urban sprawl. This once-popular variety is now somewhat of a rarity. For best crunchiness, harvest the fruit small, while the skin still has a green tinge. Naturally containing very few seeds, these sweet cucumbers are perfect for snacking on whole, or dipping into hummus or tzatziki.

'Chinese Yellow' A beautiful yellow cucumber that is considered rare, even in its native China. It is used there to make *lou wong kua tong* (old cucumber soup), a traditional sweet-and-sour soup that is said to have anti-ageing properties. It produces abundant fruit that start off green, transforming into a variegated orange and yellow skin that's free of bitterness. The crisp white flesh tastes mild, with a subtle sweet, zesty sourness when ripe.

'Crystal Lemon' The lucrative history of this round cucumber, which looks like a lemon, began when the nineteenth-century heirloom was brought to the USA late in that century. Fraudsters seized the opportunity to persuade unsuspecting people to pay well over the odds for the golden-yellow

'Little Potato'

fruit, claiming it was a genuine cross between a lemon and a cucumber. It is one of the most productive varieties I have ever grown, its fruit sweet and crisp, with dense white flesh and a zingy flavour. It grows well when left to sprawl, rather than trellised. It is very similar to 'Richmond Green Apple', an easy-to-grow small, round Australian heirloom that starts off green like an apple, but quickly turns lemon-yellow.

'Eden's Burpless Tasty Green' A wonderful "modern heirloom", this is a stabilized and improved selection of the twentieth-century F1 hybrid 'Burpless Tasty Green'. The open-pollinated version is the work of Eden Weiss at St Giles' Farm in the New Forest, Hampshire, just 1.5km (a mile) from my garden. On visiting Eden at his farm, where he was busy growing and saving seeds of countless crops, I learned that he had spent many years carefully selecting cucumbers to stabilize the variety, and ended up with a ridged cucumber that has an intense, complex flavour and is highly resilient and well adapted to growing outdoors or in a polytunnel or greenhouse. The seeds have now been made available via Real Seeds.

'Little Potato' (*khira balam*) As the name suggests, the fruit of this variety looks more like a potato than a cucumber. A robust, semi-bush type that is commonly cultivated in West

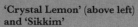

'Crystal Lemon' (above left)
and 'Sikkim'

Bengal and southern India, it pumps out a hefty quantity of round, brown, russeted fruit that are great for storing, keeping for up to 70 days after harvest. They remain crunchy and crisp, with a pronounced citrusy zing.

'Parisian Pickling' A reliable and productive late nineteenth-century French heirloom originally called 'Parisienne Cornichon de Bourbonne', this is said to be the number-one pickling cucumber. Bred to grow in the cool regions of northern France, it produces fruit with firm, thick flesh and a small, inconspicuous seed mass, perfect for fermenting. Pick young for cornichons, slightly bigger for gherkins, or let them grow on for slicing and eating raw, although at this stage the skin turns thick and may need peeling.

'Poona Kheera' A beautiful age-old cucumber from the Poona region of India. The fruit starts off pale green, turning burnt orange and finally a rich brown as it matures. Often sold as a refreshing roadside snack in the searing heat, 'Poona Kheera' has a unique flavour that is more savoury than a regular green cucumber. Well suited to being cooked, it is used to make the south Indian cucumber curry *dosakaya masala*. The fruit can become bitter with age, so harvest before or during the golden-orange stage.

'Sikkim' An ancient variety originating in the Himalayas, with a cracked exterior that looks as though it's made from alligator skin. The fruit can reach enormous sizes, often weighing up to 1kg (just over 2lb). This storing variety can be kept for up to a month after harvest. The unusual-looking fruit is delicious eaten raw, or chopped and fried with spices.

Armenian cucumbers

Sometimes also called Barattiere cucumbers, these are in fact botanically melons (*Cucumis melo* var. *flexuosus*). They have a melon texture but taste fresh, like a cucumber, if sweeter. This is because they lack cucurbitacin, a compound that makes classic cucumbers slightly bitter and difficult to digest. Armenian cucumbers are believed to have been cultivated first in the fifteenth century in western Asia, particularly Armenia, before spreading into Turkey and towards Egypt. Seed arrived in Italy in the sixteenth century, and the fruit gained popularity there, particularly in the south and on Sardinia and Sicily. It comes in myriad lengths, colours, and markings.

'Facussa' This variety was grown in Sardinia from 1541, after the seeds arrived with Tunisian settlers. It is still grown in the fishing town of Carloforte, on a small island off Sardinia's southwest coast. These heat-loving plants produce a continuous harvest of long, beautiful fruit decorated with jazzy zebra stripes.

'Metki Dark Green' Sometimes referred to as "snake cucumber", this old Armenian heirloom can produce fruit of serpent-like length. The slender, dark green fruit is best harvested when 30–45cm (12–18in) long, although if left on the vine it can grow much larger, up to 1m (3ft). Thin-skinned, mild, and sweet, it's absolutely delicious.

'Mezzo Lungo di Polignano' The "half-long of Polignano", originating in southern Italy, is one of the earliest cucurbits to ripen. The squat, cylindrical fruit, ridged prominently along its length, is a vibrant light green and covered in tiny hairs. This soft fuzz is easily brushed off before enjoying the sweet, crisp and tender, bitter-free flesh.

'Scopatizzo Barese' A vigorous classic Puglian variety that's super early and productive. Produces cylindrical green fruit with deep crosswise ridges, a firm, smooth skin, and crisp white flesh with very few seeds.

'Tondo Massafra' This round, tennis-ball-sized sweet treat has a deliciously complex, sugary flesh that could be the tastiest of the Armenian types. Stemming from the city of Massafra in Taranto province, it has an arty skin, embellished with subtle stripes and spots in shades of green.

Other

Many other cucurbits are grown in a similar manner to cucumbers. Several are now all but forgotten, yet they are an incredible source of food, a world of unexplored culinary flavours and rich history. All those listed below are best grown undercover with the aid of trellising or strings. They require warmth to germinate, and should be planted out only when the risk of frost has passed completely.

Achocha (*Cyclanthera pedata*)

Also known as the stuffing cucumber, achocha is native to the Andes and was an important food for the Inca. Its deep green, palmate foliage can easily be mistaken for that of an *Acer* (maple) tree or cannabis plant. The sprawling vines produce curved, tapered fruit that resembles a slipper, almost like a cucumber crossed with a pepper. Best harvested immature (when the fruit is 5–8cm/2–3in long) for consumption fresh, when the taste and texture are similar to those of a cucumber, with a soft, edible seed mass and crisp, fresh flesh. Left to mature fully, the fruit becomes hollow and flat and the seeds turn hard and black; at this point they

African horned cucumber (*Cucumis metuliferus*)

A prehistoric-looking plant, also known as the Kiwano jelly melon. This ancient fruit is native to the steppe-climate regions of the Kalahari Desert in southern Africa, where it is deeply rooted in the diets not just of the Indigenous Khoisan people, but also of several wild animal species, such as elephants and giraffes, which chow down on it as a natural digestive aid. The Khoisan eat the flesh – which is 80 per cent water – raw, and roast the rind and leaves. The fruit has brilliant storage capabilities, its thick, burnt-orange spiky skin providing the perfect protection for the flesh within for up to a staggering six months, although it must be kept out of the fridge. With its sweet, refreshing, tangy, lime-like flavour, this cucumber is one of very few sources of hydration in the desert during the dry season.

Luffa (*Luffa aegyptiaca*)

Used for food when small and green, or left to ripen fully on the vine until it turns a brilliant golden-yellow, fading to a rich brown, after which the fruit is dried and peeled to reveal a matrix of tough, fibrous, spongy tissue. Luffas

are removed and the fruit stuffed and baked, intensifying in flavour, almost identical to roasted green peppers.

were used in the early twentieth century as oil filters for diesel engines, and today are still employed in many places as a natural sponge, to stuff mattresses, for insulation, or to filter water. The luffa's origin is unknown, but most scientists agree that it originated in Asia and was grown early in India. Luffas need a long season, so sow them several weeks before cucumbers and keep them inside until all risk of frost has passed. To harvest as a sponge, leave the fruit on the vine as long as possible to ensure maximum development of the fibres, but do pick before the first frost.

Mexican sour gherkin (*Melothria scabra*)

Also known as cucamelon, *pepquiño* and *sandita*, this grape-sized, oval, smooth-skinned fruit looks exactly like a teaspoon-sized watermelon. Native to Mexico and Central America, it tastes mildly tart and sour, not sweet, with a distinct fresh aroma of cucumber. It can be thrown into salads, sautéed in olive oil, or pickled to accentuate the flavour. Very delicate when young, the plants should be spaced 15cm (6in) apart and grown up a trellis. They also produce underground tubers that can be lifted and stored over the winter. Growing cucamelons from tubers gives you a head start in the spring and results in an earlier and much larger harvest.

West Indian burr gherkin (*Cucumis anguria*)

Native to eastern and southern Africa, where a wild, bitter variety occurs naturally, the West Indian burr gherkin was introduced to the Caribbean as a result of the slave trade in the seventeenth century, and a non-bitter variety of the plant was developed in Jamaica and released in 1792. The bright green, oblong fruit has a spiny jacket, and the inner flesh is whitish green with a delicate flavour that's like a cross between cucumber and courgette. The long, trailing vines require trellising. As the fruit matures, it develops a strong and bitter taste, while the outer flesh becomes tough and develops long, rubbery spines that turn into spikes. Once regarded as the ultimate and true pickling gherkin, it is best picked young and fermented or made into relish.

'Scopatizzo Barese'

Achocha

Melon

Cucumis melo

Also known as Muskmelon

The magical realm of home-grown melons is one of spellbinding flavours. Their luscious, sugary flesh is subtly perfumed; some varieties carry delicate hits of honey, or a suggestion of pear, while others give off distinctly tangy, tropical aromas. As the fruit ripens the rind transforms from a simple green skin into an abstract piece of natural art.

History

Melons and their seeds were among the commodities sold by traders travelling by camel or on horseback along the caravan routes of the old Silk Road through southern Asia, Persia, and the Arabian Peninsula. There's debate about the fruit's native land, though. Some botanists consider it to be the Levant and ancient Egypt, others Iran, India, and Central Asia, and yet others maintain that it is of African ancestry. Wild melons still grow in several East African countries, among them Ethiopia, Somalia, and Tanzania.

"Muskmelon" derives from the Persian *musk* (perfume). Ancient Iran was an epicentre for the development and production of melons, along with the South Caucasus regions, Afghanistan, and India; the vines then twined their way into China and East Asia via the mountainous Western Himalayas. The oldest records of this fruit date back to ancient Egyptian funerary art of 2400 BCE, which appears to depict what experts have identified as a melon. The ancient Greeks and Romans are known to have cultivated melons, since both Pliny and the Greek physician Galen described the fruit.

The vines sprawled westwards, and by the late fifteenth century melons were commonly found in Spain and France. Christopher Columbus embarked on a second transatlantic voyage in 1493, and on that journey melon seeds were introduced to La Isabela, Spain's first stronghold in the Americas, on the northern side of the island of Hispaniola (now in the Dominican Republic). Soon afterwards, the plants were distributed through Central and North America.

Culinary uses

Preparation

To peel a melon safely, slice off a tiny sliver from either end. This will provide you with a flat surface so that you can easily remove

> **"**
> # Melon harvests are a summertime joy more than worthy of a celebration with friends.

the skin with a knife without it rolling or slipping. Scoop out and discard the seeds before slicing or chopping the flesh.

Dishes

Melon harvests are a summertime joy more than worthy of a celebration with friends. There is no better way to enjoy the vibrant tropical flavours of this fruit than eating it fresh off the vine, still warm from the sun. But melons are much more versatile than you might think. They're a magnificent ingredient that can be integrated into a medley of dishes – not just sweet treats, such as fruit salads,

sorbets, and smoothies, but also savouries. Wrapped in a slice of prosciutto ham for a tasty antipasto or tossed into a tangy Greek salad, their sweet, musky flesh lends itself perfectly to accompanying bold, salty foods, such as sheep's cheese and cured meat.

In savoury dishes, melons provide a refreshing element that cleanses the palate and elevates the food. The ultimate way to combat the heat of summer is with a gazpacho of cantaloupe melon and tomato, combining classic Spanish flavours with the cantaloupe's sweet, subtle, refreshing tanginess. A perfect accompaniment for this delicious cold soup is a thin slice of toasted

'Banana' may look like its namesake on the outside, but the luscious flesh within is juicy and spicy.

sourdough bread topped with the sweet, almost fruity, creamy, and spreadable Majorcan cured meat *sobrasada*.

Kavun dolma (stuffed melon) dates back at least to the fifteenth century. This noble dish beloved of the sultans was served on special occasions in the palaces of the Ottoman empire. Meat, traditionally lamb, is combined with rice, pistachios, herbs, and spices. The melon tops are removed – as when carving a pumpkin – allowing access to hollow and stuff the cavity with the meat mixture before the lids go back on, ready for roasting in the oven.

Growing

Every year, I anxiously anticipate the brief moment when a delightful, exotic fragrance can be detected wafting through the air of the polytunnel. Melons are undoubtedly one of the most rewarding crops to grow. However, this warmth-loving fruit is best cultivated under cover, especially in climates with damp, chilly, or unpredictable summers.

Propagation

Sow individually in cells. Melon seeds require constant warmth to germinate, so keep them indoors or on a heat mat. They must be exposed to sunlight, however, or the seedlings will quickly become tall and fragile. Melon seedlings are prone to

After potting on, keep the young plants in a frost-free place before planting them out in their final location.

damping off, so don't overwater, especially in overcast weather. Transfer the young plants to 7–9cm (3–4in) pots a few weeks after germination and keep in a frost-free, well-lit area. Only after all danger of frost has passed should they be transplanted into the polytunnel, greenhouse, or garden.

Aftercare

When transplanting melon seedlings, bury the stem deeply in the soil to reinforce the fragile central stalk. I prefer to train mine up strings or supports, in which case I make sure to bury the support string under the root ball when transplanting. However, they can also be left to sprawl along the ground.

Once in the ground, melons grow seriously fast. If using a string support, train the central stem around it every other day to ensure the vine is fully supported before it begins setting fruit. Melons set fruit on side shoots, so allow these to develop three sets of leaves before pinching out their growing tips. Plants sprawling on the ground can be left to run rampant, but you can encourage faster ripening by pinching out the tips of the side shoots once the plants begin to set fruit.

Melons require regular watering, especially in hot summer sun, but reduce the watering when the fruit begins to ripen, in late summer. This will enhance the flavour and reduce the risk of splitting.

Plant problems

Aphids, mildew, slugs and snails, spider mite (see pages 49–51)

Training melon plants up support strings is an efficient way of growing them in a limited space.

Harvesting

Melons may look ready for harvest, but do be sure before snipping off the fruit. An indulgent aroma will perfume the air when they are ripe, and the stalk connecting the fruit to the vine should look woody and cracked. Leave a short segment of the stalk attached to the fruit to help it store better.

Storage

Melons' perfumed flavour diminishes quickly and their flesh becomes soft, so eat them as soon as possible after harvesting or keep in the fridge for a few days.

Recommended varieties

'Banana' This variety was all the rage across the United States in the late 1880s, when the fruit attracted a great deal of attention at agricultural fairs – and for good reason, since it looks like a giant banana. Encased in the lemon-yellow skin is finely coloured salmon-hued flesh with a pungent aroma and sweet, almost spicy flavour. These melons can exceed 60cm (24in) in length and weigh up to an impressive 4kg (nearly 9lb), making them generally unsuitable for growing up strings. Best eaten fresh off the vine.
(Matures in 90 days)

'Bateekh Samara' This melon boasts an unusual flavour that is almost reminiscent of citrus. It is an ancient variety that dates back to the Golden Age of the Abbasid Caliphate, an empire that spanned the Middle East, western Asia, and northeastern Africa, with Baghdad as its capital. The name translates as "old melon of Samarra", the Iraqi city from where it originates and where it has been cultivated for more than 1,000 years. Sadly, owing to war, 'Bateekh Samara' is becoming rare in its native land. The fruit is a distinctive, unusual oblong shape with one rounded and one pointed end, its skin a mottled brownish-green and the flesh a stunning lime-green.
(Matures in 95 days)

'Queen Anne's Pocket'

'Blenheim Orange' An English heritage melon bred in 1881 in the greenhouses of Blenheim Palace in Oxfordshire, the birthplace and ancestral home of Sir Winston Churchill. Dating back to the mid-nineteenth century, this variety produces fruit with grey-green-netted skin and distinctive green stripes. Inside is a terrific tangerine-coloured flesh with a quintessential melon flavour. This was a highly sought-after and greatly admired variety in the Victorian era, particularly among affluent households who owned greenhouses.
(Matures in 90–100 days)

'Casaba Golden Beauty' A Turkish heirloom variety with a tough, wrinkled yellow rind and succulent, sweet white flesh. Stores very well.
(Matures in 120 days)

'Delice de Table' A classic French melon that has been around since the eighteenth century but is now very rare and difficult to find outside its home country. The fruit has a lovely ribbed appearance with smooth orange skin reminiscent of a pumpkin. It's called "delicious table melon" for a reason; the thick, orange flesh is sweet and tasty, with musky undertones that fill the kitchen with a beautiful aroma.
(Matures in 85 days)

'Eden's Gem' An open-pollinated cantaloupe variety with lively green flesh, developed in 1905 in Rocky Ford, Colorado. These little melons are relatively quick to ripen, making them an excellent choice for growers with short seasons. 'Eden's Gem' is an all-time favourite of Amy Goldman – a saver of heirloom seeds and author of *Melons for the Passionate Grower* (2002) – because of its complex flavour, which she says may cause you to drool.
(Matures in 65–75 days)

'Jenny Lind' An 1840s heirloom melon from the Philadelphia seedsman William Henry Maule, renamed as part of a plan to capitalize on the famous Swedish opera singer Jenny Lind's tour of the United States in the 1850s. The creamy green-fleshed fruit was almost forgotten, but is now making a return thanks to its deliciously sweet flavour and short maturing time.
(Matures in 75 days)

'Kajari' Stemming from the Punjab region of northern India, this is an age-old honeydew melon like no other. The botanical explorer and ecologist Joseph Simcox introduced it to the United States in 2014, after spending more than eight years tracking it down in India. It's a unique, striking melon that's great for its decorative value and flavour. The small, round fruit has green and ivory-white stripes that develop into a beautiful display of green, white, and bright orange as it matures. The flesh is just as colourful, dark green near the rind and fading to creamy white near the seeds. Despite its small size, this melon has dense yet succulent, sweet-smelling flesh. It's exciting to find such an unusual melon growing outside India, and it performs well even in temperate climates.
(Matures in 70–75 days)

'Kiku Chrysanthemum' This unique, attractive, and rare Japanese melon gets its name from its resemblance to the chrysanthemum flower, which is commonly used as a floral offering for the Buddha. This productive plant yields many small, creamy-white-skinned fruit with a sweet, spellbinding aroma and a delightful flavour similar to that of lychee or Asian pear. Considered a luxury food in its native Japan, these melons can be eaten straight out of the hand, just like an apple, owing to their soft, thin skin. Developed in Shiga Prefecture, Japan, using a silver *makuwa uri* (Oriental melon) from China, this mini melon is quick and easy to grow.
(Matures in 60 days)

'Kolkhoznitsa' Also called by the English version of its name, 'Collective Farm Woman', this Crimean heirloom variety is well known for its ability to thrive and produce bountiful harvests before the onset of autumn frosts in northeastern Europe. Bred in the 1930s to grow in these shorter seasons, it quickly gained immense popularity among Moscow's *dacha* gardeners, and remains the nation's top choice. It takes its name from a woman who was part of a collective farm and who gave the seed to the American Seed Savers Exchange in the 1990s. The fruit has a green and golden-yellow rind and

'Petit Gris de Rennes'

sweet white flesh, matures quickly, and can be stored for several weeks after harvesting, making it an excellent choice for cool climates and slow eaters. (Matures in 80 days)

'Noir de Carmes' This pumpkin-shaped cantaloupe variety is one of the oldest French types around. It was developed in monastery gardens by Carmelite monks, who recorded it in the nineteenth century, although experts believe it has been around for much longer. The fruit is round-ribbed, dark green, sometimes almost black, and takes on a distinctly golden tinge when nearing ripeness. The juicy orange flesh has an irresistible flavour that made it highly valued by French market gardeners in the nineteenth century. It's simple to cultivate and does well in cool regions. (Matures in 75 days)

'Petit Gris de Rennes' This variety was discovered in 1636 growing freely in the garden of the Bishop of Rennes, France. It is believed to be a descendant of 'Noir de Carmes' (see above). Its name, which means "little grey", refers to its small size and its grey-green exterior when immature. Its petite size, delectable flavour, and soft, sweet, orange flesh made it a sought-after fruit by the eighteenth century, and it was marketed as a luxury. It was cultivated extensively throughout the west of the country to meet demand, particularly along the Finisterre coastline. (Matures in 85 days)

'Prescott Fond Blanc' This variety is truly one of a kind, with its unconventional shape. It is often mistaken for something from a pumpkin patch, owing to its prominent ribs and warty appearance. The flesh is dense, with an excellent pattern that transitions from lime-green to a beautiful peachy-orange towards the centre. Its strong, musky aroma really sets it apart. This French heirloom has been cultivated for more than 200 years and is typically left to grow on the ground. However, I have successfully cultivated it using strings. (Matures in 75 days)

'Prescott Fond Blanc'

'Tiger'

'Queen Anne's Pocket' Also known as 'Plum Granny', this tiny fruit has a fascinating history. These highly fragrant mini melons are fun to grow, and so mighty that one can perfume an entire room. In the days before deodorant, upper-class Victorian women often carried them in their pockets, to scent themselves. They are named after Queen Anne, who is said to have always done so. The velvety orange rind is striped with maroon and gold, making the fruit just as pleasing to the eye as to the nose. While the fruit is edible, however, it is bland compared to its exquisite, unforgettable scent. (Matures in under 70 days)

'Tiger' Like the big cat, the tiger melon's smooth rind displays a distinctive pattern of rusty orange and yellow. This variety is believed to have originated in Armenia, where it was found growing in the fields of the mountain valleys along the Tigris River. It was probably cultivated and refined over time, and spread slowly to neighbouring regions through the efforts of travelling merchants. This ornamental fruit has creamy, off-white flesh that is both juicy and sweet. The flavour is reminiscent of a pear with a tantalizing, powerful aroma. (Matures in 80 days)

'Zatta' Known in Italy as "Brutto ma Buono" (Ugly but Good), this old heritage melon comes from Padua in the Veneto. First described by Giacomo Castelvetro in 1614 in his book *The Fruit, Herbs and Vegetables of Italy*, this scabby, warty melon has been cultivated for well over four centuries and probably a lot longer. Once you cut into the "ugly" exterior, you are met with the "good" in the form of an inviting, vivid orange flesh that's intensely fragrant and super-sweet. Each fruit can weigh up to 2kg (4½lb). (Matures in 85–90 days)

Peppers

Capsicum annuum

Also known as Biber, Gochu, Mirch, Peperoncino, Phrik, Pimienta

Sweet and spicy capsicums are a fundamental ingredient for many cuisines across the globe. Their flavour has transformed the culinary world, providing cooks with a lively, aromatic ingredient capable of igniting the taste buds with a fiery whack or a sugary smack. With great immune-boosting properties, peppers of all kinds are rich in vitamin C and other powerful antioxidants, minerals, and nutrients.

History

Capsicums originated in Central and Southern America, their wild seeds spreading via bird droppings. They have been consumed and cultivated for millennia and are considered one of the oldest farmed crops, with evidence suggesting that they were grown independently and simultaneously as far back as 6,000 years ago across the Amazon region and in Mexico. Sweet peppers, often shaped like bells, have been known as bell peppers since the late seventeenth century at least.

Christopher Columbus is credited with bringing peppers to Europe on returning from his famous voyage of exploration in 1493. The spicy chilli first landed on Asian shores with Portuguese traders, who introduced it to Goa, India, in the sixteenth century. It spread across the continent and quickly became a sought-after ingredient among Indian, Chinese, Thai, and other Asian cooks, who were already making use of such spicy, aromatic flavours as cumin, ginger, lemongrass (see page 218), galangal, and Sichuan and black pepper.

The word "chilli" has its roots in the Aztec Nahuatl language. Chillies were highly regarded in Aztec, Maya, and other Indigenous cultures across Central and South America, all of which believed that eating the fiery fruit was a way of honouring their gods. These peoples used chillies to treat various ailments, including asthma, coughs, and sore throats, believing that the heat generated by the fruit cleared the airways and improved breathing.

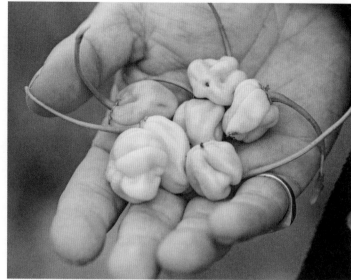

'Leutschauer Paprika' (left) and 'Malaysian Goronong'

Chilli peppers are known for their fiery taste and the burning sensation they cause in the mouth. It is a result of the chemical capsaicin, which is absent from sweet peppers. When capsaicin comes into contact with receptors in the mouth and tongue, it triggers a series of reactions, sending signals that trick the brain into reporting pain or burning. Capsaicin is hydrophobic (does not mix with water), so drinking water will not wash it away, but instead distributes it around the mouth and exacerbates the discomfort. Instead, balance the burn with acidic foods, such as lemons, oranges, or tomatoes.

Culinary uses

Preparation

Sweet peppers can be peeled by lightly oiling the flesh and flashing them whole over an open flame on the hob for several minutes until blackened (if you don't have gas, use a screamingly hot grill). Place the charred peppers in a bowl, cover with a clean tea towel, and leave to steam for a few minutes, after which the skin should slip off easily.

Both sweet peppers and chillies should be trimmed of their stalk and seeds before being chopped. Trim the tops off peppers that are to be used for stuffing. Rehydrate dried chillies by soaking them in water for 10–15 minutes. For a deeper flavour, toast them lightly for a minute or two in a hot frying pan, before soaking, to release the natural oils from the skin.

Dishes

Chillies reconstructed culinary traditions as they spread across the globe, and it's now hard to imagine preparing Indian curries, Hungarian goulash, Thai stir-fries, or Tunisian harissa without the addition of these fiery capsicums. *Mole* is a deliciously rich and flavourful sauce from Mexico, which is served over meat, vegetables, or rice. It is known for its fruity, fragrant aroma, which is achieved by adding chilli peppers, spices, fruit, nuts, and sometimes chocolate. There are seven distinct variations, each with its unique flavour profile and ingredients, and recipes depend on the region or cook preparing it. From the sweet, spicy, and smoky *mole poblano*, which is considered the national dish of Mexico, to the lively *mole verde*, concocted with coriander, jalapeños, and tomatillos, *mole* is deeply entrenched in the Mexican lifestyle, and one of the seven types, *mole chichilo*, is reserved for when someone has passed away. The deep black colour and complex taste of *mole* are achieved by charring the ingredients before cooking, which results in a burnt gravy-like flavour.

Sweet varieties of pepper are succulent in texture, with sugary notes, and can be pickled, roasted, or stuffed whole with savoury fillings for a stand-alone centrepiece. Chopped or sliced, they work perfectly tossed into stir-fries, curries, salads, and casseroles, such as the sunny southern Italian classic *peperonata*. This gorgeous Calabrian dish can be served hot or cold, as a side at a barbecue, or as a hearty summer snack on top of crusty bread. A colourful mixture of juicy sweet peppers is sautéed in olive oil with tomatoes and onions, and slow-cooked until tender. The dish is often flavoured with garlic and other aromatic ingredients, such as basil, mint, capers, and chilli flakes.

Growing
Propagation

These crops require a long growing season and are well worth giving a head start. All capsicums are best sown early in the year, but they are frost- and cold-tender, so they must be kept in the warmth of the house until the weather outside is palatable for them. For optimum results, I grow all chillies and peppers in the polytunnel, safe from the great British weather. However, once they are safely germinated and growing strongly, a sheltered south-facing wall, sunny balcony, or windowsill will provide them with the protection they need to thrive in a temperate climate.

Pepper seeds can be slow to sprout, so start them early in the season. Place the seed trays on a heat mat covered by a cloche, in a bright spot inside the house. Roughly four weeks after germination, transplant them into 7cm (3in) pots to continue growing, then transplant them into slightly larger pots (9cm/4in) pots four

weeks later. Young capsicums are prone to damping off, so make sure they do not become waterlogged and guard them from cold draughts from windows and doors. Only once the risk of frost has passed completely can these heat-loving crops be planted out in their final home. I grow most of my capsicums in large (11 litre/ 3 gallon) square pots, in a rich compost loosened with vermiculite or perlite to promote better drainage. The square containers align neatly along the paths of the polytunnel and allow me to crop extra plants without overwhelming the soil in the polytunnel with roots. Another advantage of pots is that they can be easily moved around or taken outside when room is needed to prune or train the other crops in the tunnel. Whether you grow capsicums

Peppers that are ready to harvest should be richly coloured and feel firm but not wrinkly.

Growing at a glance

Sow Late winter, 21–34°C (70–93°F)

Plant out Summer

Spacing 35–45cm (14–18in) in soil

Harvest Summer–autumn

in pots or directly in the soil, bury the stems deeply to provide support.

Aftercare

Although peppers and chillies love heat, they require much less watering than other summer crops, such as cucumbers and tomatoes. A deep drink weekly once the plants are established is often sufficient for those growing directly in the soil. For those in pots, lift the container to test the weight and water accordingly – this might be necessary once or even twice a day in hotter weather. As the flowers emerge, give them a generous glug of water to help the plants set fruit. Large sweet peppers also benefit from added moisture as their fruit begins to swell. Reduce watering for all capsicums as the summer cools to

encourage the plants to focus their energy on ripening fruit rather than producing new foliage and flowers. Capsicums grown in pots benefit from a liquid seaweed feed as the flowers begin to set fruit, followed by another feed in two weeks, although feeding is not essential.

As the plants become laden with fruit, their branches may snap or crack under the weight. Stake them with a bamboo cane and tie them in loosely with jute twine to avoid cutting into the stems as they grow; you may need to tie several points along the stem to provide enough support for extra-heavy yielders. This is best done once the plants are about 30cm (12in) tall; it is also a good time to pinch out the growing tips to encourage side shooting and, in turn, more flowers and fruit. Towards the end of summer, prune out new shoots and undeveloped flowers to maximize the plant's ripening efforts.

Plant problems

Aphids, blossom end rot, slugs and snails, spider mite (see pages 49–51)

Harvesting

Pick peppers and chillies as they ripen, since they can rot and spoil if left on the plant for too long. Although they can be quickly snapped off by hand, this can damage the main branch, so consider using snips for a clean cut.

Storage

Large sweet peppers can be kept in a cool larder or fridge for several weeks after harvest. Chillies can be dried in the sun, a dehydrator, or a low oven, and kept whole or flaked (using a blender or a pestle and mortar) in airtight glass jars for more than a year. Chillies also keep well whole in the freezer for later use "fresh"; they will defrost quickly as you chop them.

A *poblano* chilli (left) and 'Paradicsom Alaku Sarga Szentes' ('PASS')

Sweet

'Aconcagua' This Argentinian heirloom variety is named after the highest mountain peak in the whole of the Americas, Aconcagua, in Mendoza province. These large, conical peppers are very long and highly productive. They ripen from green to orange and then red but are often a variegated mixture of all three. Very sweet and great for frying.

'Albino Bullnose' Creamy yellow, almost bone-white peppers with a crinkled, wrinkled shape. The fruit starts out ivory-white and ripens to a peachy orange; it is delicious harvested no matter the colour, and a fantastic type for stuffing.

'Beaver Dam' A conical red pepper with just a suggestion of spice. Named after the Beaver Dam in Wisconsin, it was grown by Joe Hussli, a Hungarian immigrant who brought the seeds from his home country in the early twentieth century and shared them with locals. Today, the annual Beaver Dam Pepper Festival is held in honour of these delicious fruit, with vendors, growers, and locals joining the celebrations.

'Golden California Wonder' A delightful golden pepper with a sweet, subtle taste. Introduced in the twentieth century, it's perfect for areas with short, cool seasons.

'King of the North' An easy-to-cultivate variety that is well suited to cool regions with short seasons. Developed in the early twentieth century, it is a heavy yielder of great-tasting red, bell-shaped peppers.

'Lesya' A romantic palm-sized, heart-shaped fruit, deep red, sometimes blotched with black, and with a prominent pointed tip. Strongly flavoured, this Ukrainian open-pollinated beauty is extra sweet and has thick, dense flesh.

'Paradicsom Alaku Sarga Szentes' ('PASS') These stocky, low-growing plants produce beautiful

'Zulu' (left) and 'Albino Bullnose'

squat, ribbed, golden-yellow fruit that look like miniature pumpkins. A culinary delight used for stuffing, eating raw, or pickling, this rare heirloom was developed in southeastern Hungary, in Szentes, a town by the Tisza River.

'Quadrato d'Asti Giallo' This classic Italian heirloom from the Alpine region of Piedmont is one of the most enormous, producing bulky square peppers. The fruit, which ripens to a brilliant banana-yellow, is also one of the most delicious sweet peppers, with its thick, juicy flesh. A large red variety with the same delicious traits, 'Quadrato d'Asti Rosso', is also available.

'Rotunda Gogoshari' A fiery-red, heavily ribbed, flattened heirloom variety that resembles a tomato, this is a prolific producer of juicy, fleshy peppers that are well suited to cooking or eating fresh.

'Sweet Banana' These vibrant yellow, elongated fruit look strikingly similar to little bananas. They are officially considered hot peppers, but their spice level is often so low as to be undetectable. Traditionally

pickled, they make an excellent finger-food snack, salad garnish, or pizza topping.

'Sweet Chocolate' Developed in 1965 at the University of New Hampshire by the plant scientist Elwyn Meader, these richly coloured chocolate-brown peppers are an intense red inside. They thrive in cool regions and ripen early in the season.

'Sweet Nardello' Long, thin, and red, these look like spicy chillies but have a charming candy-sweet flavour. The plants are highly productive, and the fruit is best suited to grilling or frying and eating whole. This Italian heirloom was grown by the Nardello family in the southern region of Basilicata in the nineteenth century. The seeds were donated to the Seed Savers Exchange by Jimmy Nardello, whose parents had brought them to the United States.

'Zulu' A jet-black heirloom pepper of unknown origin, but believed to be of Polish descent. These peppers have a boxy appearance and are perfectly suited to eating raw, having a delicate, sweet flavour and crisp, crunchy flesh.

Scoville Heat Units (SHU) and the Scoville scale

In 1912 Wilbur Scoville, a pioneer in pharmacology, created a groundbreaking method for measuring the spiciness of peppers and chillies. His eponymous scale is based on the concentration of capsaicin, the compound that is responsible for the pepper's pungency. The scale, which is now widely accepted as the standard for measuring the heat intensity of chilli, is calculated in Scoville heat units, more commonly called scovilles:

Mild 100–1,500 scovilles

Warm 1,500–5,000

Medium 5,000–15,000

Hot 15,000–30,000

Extra hot 30,000–100,000

Blazing hot 100,000–300,000

Blisteringly hot 300,000+

Hot

Aleppo pepper (*pul biber*) Named after the Syrian city of Aleppo, an area devastated by modern conflict. These large red peppers are used widely across the Middle East, particularly in Turkish and Levantine cuisine, owing to their distinctive sweet, tangy flavour with just the right amount of spice. Traditionally, they are dried and crushed into flakes to season grilled meat and kebabs. (SHU: 8,000–10,000)

'Bhut Jolokia' A northeastern Indian fireball! These wrinkled, warty red chillies play a crucial role in Naga and Assamese cuisine thanks to their complex, fruity flavour. Sometimes known as the ghost chilli (*bhut* is Hindi for "ghost", alluding to the way the heat sneaks up on you), they are one of the most unforgivingly spicy peppers available. (SHU: 1 million+)

'Cascabel' Small, spherical chillies with a refined, nutty, earthy flavour and moderate heat. These peppers have a deep red skin that turns almost black when dried, and they are considered a speciality ingredient, hard to find outside Mexico. 'Cascabel' is named after the cascabel rattlesnake, because the maraca-like sound of the dried fruit resembles the sound made by the snake's rattle; the chillies are often used by children as musical toys. (SHU: 1,000–2,500)

Chile de árbol (tree chilli) A thin red chilli that originated in the town of Yahualica de González Gallo in the western Mexican state of Jalisco. Sometimes referred to as the "rat-tail chilli", it is traditionally sundried to intensify its already spicy flavour, which is deliciously smoky. (SHU: 30,000–50,000)

'Chile de Comida' A traditional Mexican drying type used for making *mole*, this medium-sized red chilli is richly flavoured with deep fruity undertones, and is now becoming hard to find. (SHU: 3,000–5,000)

Dedo-de-moça A South American heirloom beloved in Brazil, this chilli is used extensively throughout the country in such classic dishes as *moqueca de camarão*, a spicy seafood and coconut stew, and *feijoada*, a rich braise of pork and black beans. This tall plant produces orange-red citrus-flavoured fruit with a prominent spicy whack. (SHU: 10,000–15,000)

'Hong-Gochu' This bright red chilli is used extensively throughout Korea for *gochugaru*, a coarsely ground chilli flake that is an essential ingredient (alongside fermented soybeans, sticky rice, and salt) of the classic spice paste *gochujang*. (SHU: 4,000–8,000)

Jwala The name translates as "intense flame", and for good reason; these prolific producers yield an abundant bounty of long, thin, wrinkled red fruit that possess a blazing hot and wickedly fierce heat with a delightfully rich flavour. This is one of the most popular varieties of chilli in India. (SHU: 30,000–50,000)

Dried 'Leutschauer Paprika'

'Leutschauer Paprika' A premium paprika variety commonly grown in the Mátra mountains of Hungary after being introduced from Slovakia in the nineteenth century. The fruit is dried and milled to produce a sweet, mildly spicy paprika powder that is an essential ingredient of the Slovakian sauerkraut soup *kapustnica*. (SHU: 1,000–2,500)

'Malaysian Goronong' A glorious golden chilli with a wavy, wrinkled appearance. These may be small but they pack a viciously spicy punch, with flavours reminiscent of citrus and tropical fruit. This rare variety, similar to habanero, was developed in Malaysia and produces an abundance of gnarly, twisted peppers. (SHU: 250,000–400,000)

'Mirasol' A mainstay of Mexican cuisine, these peppers are dried and smoked to produce *guajillo* (using the same process as for chipotle, the dried and smoked version of jalapeño). They're essential in traditional intensely flavoured *moles* owing to their fruity, berry-like flavour and tangy, subtle heat. (SHU: 2,500–5,000)

Poblano This chilli is thought to have originated in Cholula, Mexico's oldest inhabited city, in the mountainous state of Puebla. The large, wide peppers are a glossy dark green, mildly spicy, and bursting with fruity flavour; they have a thick skin and are the number-one

'Zapotec Jalapeño'

pepper for *chiles rellenos*, a traditional Mexican dish that involves stuffing the peppers with cheese and meat, roasting them, then dipping them in a light batter and frying until golden. (SHU: 1,000–1,500)

'Prik Kee Noo' This ferociously fiery chilli with a humorous name – "mouse poo pepper" – may sound unappetising but is a beloved ingredient in Thailand. Also known as "bird's eye", this little red chilli brings immense heat, and its unique flavour adds complexity to a range of traditional Thai dishes. (SHU: 50,000–100,000)

Ramnad mundu A famous globe-shaped chilli from the state of Tamil Nadu in southern India. The name translates from Tamil to "fat and round", hinting at its distinctive shape. The drought-resistant plant produces aromatic, intensely flavoured, seriously spicy fruit. (SHU: 30,000–50,000)

Rezha (vezeni piperki) This Macedonian heirloom variety has a tough russet skin that is roughened through an effect known as corking,

and indeed the word *rezha* means "embroidered", referring to this bark-like skin. With an unpredictable heat similar to that of padron peppers, this long, red, generally mild fruit is best suited to grilling or roasting, since the rough exterior protects the flesh from charring. (SHU: 1,200–5,000)

'Serrano' An exquisite variety from the magnificent highland regions of Mexico's Puebla and Hidalgo states. The name, which means "mountain dweller", is derived from its natural habitat. These little firecrackers are usually harvested early, while still green. (SHU: 10,000–25,000)

'Zapotec Jalapeño' An ancient heirloom variety cultivated by the Indigenous Zapotec people, who occupied land in the valley of Oaxaca, Mexico, from 700 BCE to 1521 CE. This heritage chilli has a superior, full-bodied flavour, with a noticeably spicier hit than any other jalapeño on the market. It produces abundant fruit that ripens to a glossy dark red, with deep striations on the skin. Perfect for pickling. (SHU: 5,000–10,000)

Paprika

Unlike other varieties, paprika chillies offer a mild, sweet flavour that elevates many dishes. Once dried they can be roasted or smoked for a more intense flavour, or simply deseeded and ground into the spice-rack essential paprika powder, for use in sauces, stews, and chilli con carne, to season oven-roasted squash, beetroot, and carrots, sprinkled on top of hummus, or tossed through sautéed potatoes.

Summer Squash

Cucurbita pepo

Also known as Calabacín, Courgette, Kabak, Marrow, Zucchini

Summer squash is the crop you can never keep up with – in the blink of an eye they seem to double in size. Often, the only variety available in stores is long and green, but these soft-skinned, creamy-textured, sweet, nutty-tasting fruit boast much more enthralling attire, flavours, and textures, from heavily wrinkled and warty, custard-yellow, crooked courgettes to pale pear-coloured, flat pattypan squashes.

History

Summer squash are rooted in the American continents, specifically the historical region of Meso-America, and were domesticated by Indigenous people some 10,000 years ago. The long zucchini we know today, with its smooth, green skin and sausage shape, was bred sometime during the nineteenth century in northern Italy, about 300 years after the introduction of summer squash from the Americas. The first recorded reference to this type of zucchini appeared in a Milan publication in 1901. Farmers throughout the country bred varieties that were named after the cities in which they were grown, such as 'Zucchino di Faenza' and 'Zucchino di Napoli'. Today, an annual celebration is held throughout Italy in honour of this squash, Fiera Nazionale della Zucca, defining the vegetable's importance to the country's cuisine and culture.

These squash are known as marrows when left to grow to full size, yet everyone ponders what to do with these obtrusively large fruit. A genius idea has sprung up at countless farmers' markets in North America, where hundreds of zucchini races take place. Competitors hit the tarmac with homemade, model-sized marrow trucks, cars, and karts decorated to the highest of fashions. There are different rules at different venues, but traditionally the racers are separated into categories by age and weight of fruit.

Summer squash are available in a wonderful variety of shapes, colours, and sizes.

Culinary uses

Preparation

Summer squash are delicious eaten raw when young and tender, but marinate them briefly before serving so that they soften but remain crisp with a slight bite. Cut lengthwise into ribbons using a vegetable peeler, toss them lightly in dressing, and leave to stand for no longer than 20 minutes.

The trick to making extra-crisp squash fritters and pakoras is to grate the vegetable into a colander, sprinkle with sea salt, and leave to stand for about 10 minutes, allowing them to release their juices.

Dishes

Even if you have only a few plants, the quantity of fruit ripening at the same time can feel overwhelming. Luckily, there's a long list of creative ways to cook with courgettes. Barbecue or grill them in chunks for a meaty, wholesome main course, shave them into thin strips and marinate them before adding them to a salad, simmer them in summertime stews like the French classic ratatouille, or incorporate them into baking in a similar way to carrots. For *calabacitas*, a traditional Mexican side dish that's comfort food at its best, sauté courgettes with fresh corn, herbs, and spices and pair with wickedly spicy grilled meats and a stack of tortillas.

Summer squash can be hollowed out, stuffed, and roasted with a delightful selection of savoury fillings. *Kousa ablama* is a traditional Lebanese recipe that is famous in the Middle East. A fragrant and flavourful mixture of meat, pine nuts, tomatoes, and aromatic spices is stuffed into a courgette, baked in the oven, and served with rice and yoghurt. Long courgettes are used for this dish, but they are not split in half lengthwise but rather hollowed out, creating a concealed chamber within which the flavours can marry.

A popular way of cooking summer squash is to whip them into fritters and bhajis for a crunchy snack. A zesty version that hums with the fresh flavours of the Mediterranean sun is the Greek dish *kolokithokeftedes*, in which grated courgette

'Gelber Englischer Custard'

Growing at a glance

Sow Mid-spring–early summer, 16–32°C (60–90°F)

Plant out Late spring–midsummer

Spacing 75–90cm (30–35in)

Harvest Summer–autumn

'Benning's Green Tint'

Blooming delicious

Both the male and female flowers of courgettes are edible. They are seen as a seasonal delicacy and used extensively throughout the culinary world. Although most commonly stuffed, they can also be chopped and incorporated into salads and pasta. It is easy to distinguish the two types: female flowers have a tiny courgette at the base, which is absent in male flowers. Whatever the type, they are best harvested just before they open.

is blended with zingy feta cheese, garlic, onions, and punchy fresh herbs, such as dill and mint. The mixture is bound with egg and flour, rolled into balls, fried until crisp, finished with a squeeze of lemon, and served with cooling tzatziki.

Growing

Propagation

There's no need to sow these bushy, sun-loving, frost-tender crops too hastily. Starting early often results in patchy germination and a house full of plants with nowhere to rehome them until the weather warms up, and because they're ferociously fast-growing, later sowings catch up in no time. If you really want to get a head start, the earliest chance to sow is two weeks before the last frost (often in mid-spring), yet they can be sown until early summer.

Sow one seed directly into each cell. Squash seeds are particularly prone to rotting in wet soil, so consider adding perlite or vermiculite to the potting mix to improve drainage, and steer clear of sprouting seeds in pots, which hold more water and pose a greater risk of rotting.

To encourage germination, cover them loosely with a clear cloche to lock in warmth, but keep them ventilated and in a warm, bright place. Early sowings will benefit from a heat mat to coax the seeds into life.

Allow the seedlings to grow for two weeks after germination, then transplant into 9cm (4in) pots. This allows them to develop into strong and robust plants and provides wiggle room for earlier sowings if there's still a chill in the air. The risk of rotting doesn't pass with germination, so keep a close eye on moisture levels throughout the early stages of growth, to prevent damping off.

Although in many places the risk of frost has not entirely passed, late spring is often considered a safe time to begin planting out summer squash if the weather forecast looks kind. They can be covered with a protective layer of horticultural fleece if there's a risk of late frost, high winds, or low night-time temperatures. Using a trowel, create a neat planting hole large enough to bury the roots and a section of the stem, for support.

Aftercare

If the weather is dry, water the plants generously and provide a deep drink every few days until they have settled in and are growing strongly. Summer squash bulk up rapidly with the long, hot days. They are thirsty customers and require ample moisture if they are to produce fruit during dry spells.

Warning

The stems and fruit of courgette plants are adorned with sharp little needles – some varieties more spiky than others – that can irritate the skin, so consider covering up when handling them.

Plant problems

Aphids, mildew, mosaic virus, slugs and snails, spider mite, whitefly (see pages 49–51)

Harvesting

If fruit forms on young plants, harvest it immediately to allow the plant to focus its energy on growing and provide a greater bounty later on. Using a knife, slice the fruit off at the main stem, leaving a section of the stalk attached to the fruit to prolong its shelf life. Pick baby zucchini while the blossom is still attached. Courgette plants often provide their bounty until the first frosts, by which time all fruit should be harvested.

Storage

These soft-skinned squash will keep for up to two weeks if stored whole in a paper bag in the crisper drawer of the fridge. Unlike their more robust winter relatives (see page 174), they can't be kept long term, but they can be pickled if you need to use up a glut.

'Benning's Green Tint' A delightful lime-green, flat squash. Introduced in the early twentieth century, it was bred in Benning, Washington, DC, by Charles N. Farr, who was taken aback by its creamy green colour. Super sweet and earthy-flavoured, it is best harvested young. (Ideal length at harvest: 7–10cm/3–4in)

'Cocozelle' A traditional green-skinned zucchini from Naples, bred in the nineteenth century. The long, lightly ribbed dark green fruit are gracefully painted with pastel green markings. This is one of the tastiest courgettes, with a deep nutty flavour, and a terrific choice to be harvested as baby zucchini. (Ideal length at harvest: 15–25cm/6–10in)

'Crookneck' One of the oldest heirloom courgettes available, grown by Indigenous American peoples before records began. Outstandingly ornamental and profoundly appetising, the long, crooked lemon-yellow courgettes have a bulbous bottom and thin, warty skin. (Ideal length at harvest: 15–20cm/6–8in)

'Desi' This open-pollinated pale greenish-yellow Indian summer squash is a profuse producer of neat spheres that pack a sweet, nutty punch. To keep up with the production of fruit, harvest

'Cocozelle'

when small. (Ideal length at harvest: 7–12cm/3–5in)

'Gelber Englischer Custard'
There isn't a word to describe these custard-yellow, round, flappy-fingered flattened squashes, they are so oddly shaped. A German heirloom variety from the village of Gatersleben in central Germany, the plants are robust, resilient, and productive. (Ideal length at harvest: 7–12cm/3–5in)

'Kamo Kamo' A rare, heavily ribbed, stocky, round heirloom variety speckled green and white and grown by the Maori people of New Zealand after squash was introduced to the islands by European settlers in the nineteenth century. A long, trailing type that will claw its way out of the vegetable patch, it can also be left for harvesting as winter squash, when the skin turns a rich burnt orange with green pixelated stripes. (Ideal length at harvest: 10–15cm/4–6in)

'Nano Verde di Milano' A luscious, solid dark green, almost black zucchini from the Lombardy region of northern Italy – a classic. The courgettes are long, slim, and delicious. (Ideal length at harvest: 15–20cm/6–8in)

'Odessa' A delicious variety that produces short, thick fruit with a

'Kamo Kamo'

slightly bulbous base. These thin-skinned off-white or pale green courgettes are a Ukrainian heirloom cultivated on the shores of the Gulf of Odessa, in the Black Sea. Productive, sweet, and robust. (Ideal length at harvest: 20–30cm/8–12in)

'Patisson Panache Vert et Blanc'
These round, ribbed, scallop-shaped squash are prolific producers of fruit that flaunt creamy-white jackets with vivid green stripes and splashes. In 1856 the cultivar was included in *Les Plantes Potagères* by the French seed company Vilmorin Andrieux. (Ideal length at harvest: 7–12cm/3–5in)

'Pineapple' A peculiar and perplexing mint-green starfish-shaped squash with ten "fingers". This stunner, introduced in 1884 by the American seed company Burpees, has a pleasant flavour and smooth, refined texture. It is terrific for stuffing and roasting whole to make a showy vegetarian centrepiece. (Ideal length at harvest: 7–12cm/3–5in)

'Ronde de Nice' A fast-growing southern French heirloom variety that is an abundant producer of small, thin-skinned, pale green spheres, at

their best when harvested at the size of a tennis ball. An outstanding option for baking and stuffing. (Ideal length at harvest: 5–10cm/2–4in)

'Rugosa Friulana' Gnarly and warty, these are some of the most gruesome yet gorgeous squash. Originating among the Dolomite Mountains in northern Italy, they have an incredible nutty flavour and silky-smooth texture. The long, wrinkled, heavily pimpled fruit start out pale yellow and deepen in colour as they mature, although they are best harvested when on the small side. (Ideal length at harvest: 15–20cm/6–8in)

'Rugosa Friulana'

Tomato

Solanum lycopersicum

Also known as Love apple, Pomodoro, Rajče, Tamatim, Wolf peach

Tomatoes ripen leisurely on the vine, kissed by the summer sun. These sweet, tangy treasures go far beyond the familiar red spheres. Some are brown-toned, others brilliantly bicoloured, and there are orange oxhearts, snow-white beefsteaks, and golden cherries that twinkle like gems. Ranging in shape from elongated plums to long, slender, tapered forms, some ribbed like the bellows of an accordion, they serve as both fresh superstars and essential ingredients for saucy masterpieces.

History

This iconic fruit is native to a region stretching from the western Andes north through Central America and Mexico. They were originally much smaller, tarter berries, and the plants that bore them rambled and scrambled over the ground. They were known as *xitomatl* in Nahuatl, and it is the ancient Aztec who are credited with domesticating and cultivating them into the form that is familiar today. These Indigenous peoples regarded tomatoes as a potent fertility aid, and they became a popular gift for newlyweds.

In the sixteenth century European explorers returning from the Americas introduced the seeds of the tomato, to a mystified reception. Despite its delightful taste, it was initially grown only for ornamental value, being thought of as poisonous or for use in witchcraft. It was even claimed that witches transformed people into werewolves using tomato-based elixirs, leading to the common name "wolf peach". Not for many decades did the tomato gain widespread acceptance in Europe as a delicious culinary ingredient.

Tomatoes have long been a popular projectile for public shaming. The practice of pelting unworthy actors with rotten fruit was most often associated with Shakespeare's Globe theatre, but such scenes were not limited to London. La Tomatina, a juicy onslaught held every year in the small town of Buñol in eastern Spain, is one of the world's most bizarre events. Thousands of festivalgoers gather to engage in an epic tomato fight, throwing the squishy fruit at one another until buildings, walls, streets, and people are covered in juice and pulp. The tradition arose after a street parade in 1945, when a heated argument between individuals quickly turned into a full-blown street brawl, knocking over a vegetable stand and kicking off a food fight. Over subsequent years, the group who had

" Tomatoes serve as both fresh superstars and essential ingredients.

participated in the original shenanigans returned to the scene during the annual parade, and tomato-tossing war was declared again.

Culinary uses

Preparation

To remove the skin without damaging the flesh, cut a small X into the blossom end (the end opposite the stem) of the fruit and dunk it in a pan of boiling water for 30–60 seconds before refreshing it in ice-cold water. After this, the skin will peel off easily.

Dishes

Tomatoes are fundamental to culinary creations in every corner of the world. They can be snacked on straight from the vine (especially if they're the little cherry types), chopped into salsas, sliced into sandwiches, and tossed into Italian salads, such as Caprese (see page 215) and panzanella (bread salad). It's hard to imagine the Italian and indeed the Mediterranean diet more widely without them. Nothing beats bruschetta with vine-ripened tomatoes and potent home-grown garlic, bound with olive oil and ample fresh basil for an aromatic hit.

Rich and delicious, tomatoes have been bred to provide a shape, size, and colour suitable for almost any dish.

Growing at a glance

Sow Late winter–mid-spring; 16–32°C (60–90°F)

Plant out Early–midsummer

Spacing 45cm (18in)

Harvest Midsummer–autumn

Another dish that is certain to tempt the most discerning dinner guest is *pomodoro al forno con basilico* (roast tomatoes with basil), which uses the same four simple ingredients. The tomatoes are cut in half, the pulp is removed, and they are stuffed with chopped basil, finely chopped garlic, olive oil, and salt, then roasted in the oven for about an hour. The result is similar to a sundried tomato, yet much tastier and more elegant, ideal for finger snacking or as a side dish.

Another terrific baked tomato plate is a savoury tarte Tatin, perfect with a puff-pastry base and lashings of balsamic vinegar and Madeira to replace the fudgy caramel layer of the more traditional apple version. To avoid the dreaded soggy bottom, it's best to skin and deseed the tomatoes for this, and choose less watery plum types. Alternatively, fresh tomato tarts make a beautiful display and a refined alternative to a salad. Blind-bake pastry in a dish, allow to cool, and spread with a thin layer of ricotta or other soft cheese, followed by a colourful contrasting layer of sliced tommies. Top the tart with sea salt, olive oil, a generous crack of black pepper, and splashes of fresh pesto for a lively finish.

In their saucy form, tomatoes can be used in pasta dishes, thirst-quenching gazpachos, and sweet ketchup, or juiced for a wickedly tangy, hangover-curing bloody Mary. Their sweet nature naturally counterbalances the spiciness of chilli peppers (see page 147), and this pairing works wonders in fiery *arrabbiata*, slow-cooked barbecue beans, and the authentic, irresistible Mexican *tinga de pollo*. This

Puebla phenomenon, served in corn tortillas, consists of shredded chicken simmered in a zingy, sweet, smoky, spicy sauce of tomatoes and chipotle peppers. Even though the flavour profile is complex, this is an easy dish to cook at home and certain to please. Another sizzlingly spicy and sugary sweet tomato and chilli combo is the Trinidadian breakfast dish tomato *choka*, a simple meal bursting with flavour. Onions, peppers, chillies, and spices are sautéed before pre-poached tomatoes are thrown into the pan to take on the flavours. The tomatoes are then shredded with a fork and the soupy mixture served with the flatbread *sada roti*.

Growing

Tomatoes are sensitive to frost and adore the warm, dry weather of summer. In a temperate climate, they perform best when grown in a polytunnel or greenhouse, although they can be grown outside in pots in the very warmest areas. They can be separated into two categories. Determinate types are bushy, low-growing plants that can be left unpruned and loosely tied and supported with a bamboo cane, and perform well in pots and containers. Indeterminate varieties

'Cuore Antico de Acqui Terme' is an enormous heart-shaped sauce tomato with few seeds. Being so heavy, its stems must be trained around the supports with extra care.

produce long vines that must be trained up strings and have their side shoots or suckers removed regularly. The latter types often yield a much greater bounty.

Propagation

If space permits and you want to get a head start, you can sow tomatoes in very late winter. However, plants sown in early spring often catch up because of the lengthening daylight hours. All seeds should be sown by mid-spring. A heat mat and clear cloche can be beneficial for early sowings, but remove the cloche as the seedlings begin to emerge. Keep the trays in a sunny location or the plants will quickly become leggy and fragile. Tomato seedlings are prone to damping off, so keep a close eye on moisture levels and avoid overwatering.

Two or three weeks after germination, transplant the seedlings into 7cm (3in) pots, burying the stem deeply. Allow to continue growing for another three weeks before transplanting into 9–11cm (4–5in) pots, again burying the stem deeply. Transplanting them in this way helps to produce short and stocky plants with a good root system, capable of finding their feet quickly once they go out into the polytunnel.

Only once all risk of frost has passed can tomatoes be planted in their final home. Using a trowel, make a planting hole deep enough to bury a portion of the plant stem. This will provide extra support and encourage a bigger root system, since new roots will sprout from the buried section. For indeterminate types, bury twine under the roots of the plant before securing it to the top of the support structure. Determinates can be supported in the same way or simply staked with a bamboo cane and tied in as the flowers emerge.

Aftercare

To train indeterminate varieties, gently encourage the growing tip to twine around the support string by twisting the stem around as it grows. To keep the plants neat and growing on a single stem, snap off side shoots regularly by hand. As the plants scramble up the string, remove the lowest leaves to allow easier access to the base of the plants for watering and weeding, while also improving airflow and reducing the risk of blight.

Remove any flowers that emerge before the plants have reached at least 30–35cm (12–14in), so they can focus their energy on producing roots. Cut off the growing tips in late summer to encourage the plants to focus on ripening fruit rather than

Once the plants are growing strongly up their supports, remove the lower leaves to improve ventilation as the fruit develops.

163

producing new growth that will not have time to mature.

Tomatoes are temperamental when it comes to watering, and often have more problems when overwatered than when dry. A good rule of thumb for those growing directly in the soil in the polytunnel or greenhouse is to water twice a week, or three times if the weather is very hot. Irregular watering or overwatering will cause the fruit's skin to split, so try to maintain a routine. Water the plants around the base, and avoid splashing the leaves, to reduce the risk of blight. Tomatoes in pots may need watering twice daily in the hottest weather. As the summer comes to a close, reduce watering to once a week to encourage the plants to finish ripening fruit rather than making new growth. A liquid seaweed feed mid-season is a brilliant natural boost, but isn't necessary for producing luscious fruit.

Plant problems

Aphids, blight, blossom end rot, slugs and snails, spider mite (see pages 49–51)

Harvesting

Tomatoes taste best when they are left to ripen on the vine, but they must be picked

Pinch out the side shoots to maintain growth on a single stem.

before they overripen and take on an acidic, fermented edge. Alternatively, they can be harvested once they reach full size but before their colour has fully ripened, and left to mature slowly at room temperature inside the house. Handle the fruit with care to avoid bruising and, using snips for a clean cut, remove single fruit, leaving the green leaves attached to the fruit, to prolong storage. Snapping tomatoes off by hand can damage the rest of the truss (bunch), particularly on big beefsteak types, which tend to have fibrous stems. As the hours of sunlight shorten in mid-autumn, harvest the remaining fruit, remove all plants from the polytunnel or greenhouse, and compost them.

Storage

Never keep tomatoes in the fridge; they contain an enzyme that reacts to cold, causing the cell membranes to break down and resulting in mushy fruit. Store them at room temperature, out of direct sunlight, but do not keep them in a wicker basket or they will bruise. Avoid storing them next to bananas, which emit a gas that causes them to spoil rapidly.

'Thorburn's Terracotta'

Recommended varieties

Slicing
These varieties are perfect for salads, sandwiches, garnishes, and eating fresh.

'Aunt Ruby's German Green'
A German heirloom brought to the United States in the early twentieth century, this large beefsteak tomato is without a doubt the best-tasting of the types that are green when ripe, with its citrusy sweet-and-savoury edge. It often matures with yellow blossom ends.

'Canestrino della Garfagnana'
A classic Italian gem, grown for more than 100 years in the province of Lucca, Tuscany. The plants produce an abundance of squat, fiery red, aubergine-shaped fruit that may have grassy green shoulders. The firm flesh is very meaty, the perfect choice for sun-drying or roasting.

'Chadwick Cherry' Bred in the twentieth century by the legendary master gardener Alan Chadwick, this superabundant large red cherry tomato has brilliant disease-resistance and a robust, proper tomato flavour.

'Cherokee Purple' A beefsteak tomato in purple, red, and black hues, this is one of the best-tasting heirlooms historically grown and stewarded by the Indigenous Cherokee nation of North America.

'De Colgar' A long-storing tomato that can be left to hang in the kitchen. The name of this old Spanish heirloom variety even means "to hang", and clusters are harvested while unripe and left to mature in a cool, dry place inside the house. The red fruit is typically cut in half and mashed over toast with garlic for a tasty snack, but the skin is discarded, being much tougher and thicker than that of most other slicing types.

'Earl of Edgecombe' A noble fruit that arrived on British soil in the 1960s. When the 6th Earl of Edgecombe in Cornwall passed away, the title was inherited by a long-lost relative, a sheep farmer from New Zealand. When the new earl came to England to claim his title, he brought with him his favourite tomato, cultivated on his farm for generations. An orange variety with a smooth, meaty texture, it is rich, sweet, and tart.

'Gold Medal' This large fruit has stunning yellow flesh that takes on a strawberry hue towards the blossom end. In 1921 the horticulturist John Lewis Childs of Floral Park, New York, introduced it as 'Ruby Gold'. It was renamed by the tomato enthusiast Ben Quisenberry in 1976.

'Hillbilly' This mega-sized beefsteak tomato is an ornate bicoloured beauty, its orange-yellow flesh blushed and splashed with magenta. It originated in the mountains of West Virginia in the late nineteenth century. The dense flesh is tropically sweet, with suggestions of apricot and tangerine.

'Igleheart Yellow Cherry'
This little golden cherry has been grown by the Igleheart family in Connecticut since the 1960s, when they received a handful of seeds from their Italian-born gardener, who spoke highly of its flavour. The plants are vigorous and the fruit has a complex flavour, the perfect balance of sweetness, fruitiness, and acidity.

'Jaune du Lac de Bret' Although technically a sauce tomato (see page 167), this teardrop-shaped, fiery orange fruit is terrific as a sweet slicing type. A very rare heirloom from Lac de Bret in Switzerland, it is superabundant and decorative.

'Manx Marvel' A prolific yielder of small, round red fruit that is early to mature, this variety was bred on the Isle of Man. It was thought to have become extinct, but the seeds were rediscovered in the early twenty-first century in an American seed bank by Dr Russell Sharp of Lancaster University. The flavour is nothing to write home about, but this is a rare British variety and worth growing for that reason alone.

'Montserrat' Grown for generations in Catalonia, this grand variety is named after the region's holy mountains, the Serra de Montsant. The big, bulky, ribbed fruit is the top choice for stuffing, since the seeds can be removed easily and replaced with flavourful fillings.

'Nebraska Wedding' This big orange beauty was first distributed through Nebraska in the late nineteenth century, when settlers moved westwards across the rugged terrain in horse-drawn wagons, carrying seeds with them. It became popular among brides, who received the seeds to symbolize hope for a prosperous marriage. The apricot-coloured fruit is bulky and sweet, with a subtly tart edge.

'Negro Azteca' A complex-tasting dark brown cherry tomato with unmistakable notes of smoke and red wine. This plump little fruit, which matures early, is believed to be of ancient Aztec origin.

'Red Calabash' Native to Chiapas, Mexico, this flattened, ribbed treasure has gleaming purple-red skin and a wonderfully sweet flavour.

'Reisetomate' One of the most unusual-looking tomatoes, this looks like a fused-together bunch of grapes. Known as the traveller tomato, it was bred for trekking across the Andes, its bobbly structure allowing segments to be torn off and the rest popped back into a bag without leaking juice. It is strongly flavoured, with a pleasantly acidic taste. The French breeder Philippe Rommens has recently introduced yellow and green versions, known as 'Phil's One' and 'Phil's Two'. It is well worth growing for its incredible appearance, although the fruit can spoil quickly on the vine.

'Sutton's White' This rare English heirloom was bred in the 1920s by

Variety	Use	Vine type	Size	Colour	Ripening time
'Aunt Ruby's German Green'	slicing	indeterminate	beefsteak	green	85 days
'Canestrino della Garfagnana'	slicing	indeterminate	beefsteak	red	80 days
'Chadwick Cherry'	slicing	indeterminate	cherry	red	75–80 days
'Cherokee Purple'	slicing	indeterminate	beefsteak	purple/black	80–90 days
'De Colgar'	slicing	indeterminate	small	red	80 days
'Earl of Edgecombe'	slicing	indeterminate	medium	orange	75 days
'Gold Medal'	slicing	indeterminate	beefsteak	yellow	75–90 days
'Hillbilly'	slicing	indeterminate	beefsteak	orange	85–95 days
'Igleheart Yellow Cherry'	slicing	indeterminate	cherry	yellow	70–80 days
'Jaune du Lac de Bret'	slicing/sauce	indeterminate	oxheart	orange	70–80 days
'Manx Marvel'	slicing	indeterminate	medium	red	70 days
'Montserrat'	slicing	indeterminate	beefsteak	red	70–80 days
'Nebraska Wedding'	slicing	determinate	medium	orange	85–90 days
'Negro Azteca'	slicing	indeterminate	cherry	brown/red	75–80 days
'Red Calabash'	slicing	indeterminate	small	purple/red	68 days
'Reisetomate'	slicing	determinate	small	red	60–80 days
'Sutton's White'	slicing	indeterminate	beefsteak	white	80 days
'Thorburn's Lemon Blush'	slicing	indeterminate	medium	yellow	75 days
'Thorburn's Terracotta'	slicing	indeterminate	medium	red/brown	75 days
'Tonodose des Conores'	slicing	indeterminate	cherry	dark red	75–85 days
'Zapotec Ribbed'	slicing	indeterminate	beefsteak	red	80–90 days
'Amish Paste'	sauce	indeterminate	medium	red	80 days
'Banana Legs'	sauce	determinate	medium	yellow	75 days
'Cornue des Andes'	sauce	indeterminate	long plum	red	75–80 days
'Dad's Barber Paste'	sauce	indeterminate	medium	red	80+ days
'Jersey Devil'	sauce	indeterminate	medium	red	90 days
'King Umberto'	sauce	indeterminate	medium	red	55–65 days
'Moyamensing'	sauce	indeterminate	medium	red	85 days
'Old Brooks'	sauce	indeterminate	large round	red	75–85 days
'Plate de Haiti'	sauce	indeterminate	small	red	80 days
'Salvaterra's Select'	sauce	indeterminate	medium	red	70–80 days

the British seed company Suttons. The large, squat beefsteaks are snow-white with a suggestion of creamy yellow and an unmistakably lemony flavour.

'Thorburn's Lemon Blush' With luxurious, bulky lemon-yellow fruit blushed peachy pink and a wickedly citrusy, sweet flavour, this variety was developed by the breeder Elbert S. Carman in 1893. It was thought to have been lost until the heirloom seedsman extraordinaire William Woys Weaver received the seeds in the 1990s from a rare collection, grew stock, and made it available through Baker Creek Heirloom Seeds of Mansfield, Missouri.

'Thorburn's Terracotta' Almost lost from circulation in the early twentieth century, this terracotta-coloured tomato with orange and green flesh was released in the 1890s by the breeder James Thorburn of New York. His seed house was forced into bankruptcy during the Great Depression of 1920–21, taking its inventory with it. In 1993 the seeds were given to William Woys Weaver's Roughwood Seed Collection by a farmer who had stewarded countless heirlooms and wanted to ensure that they found a safer home. This medium-sized, productive variety has a deep, acidic, smoky flavour.

'Tonodose des Conores' This extremely rare and endangered heirloom cherry tomato is prolific, producing dark red fruit with an orangey interior. With an explosion of flavour that lingers in the mouth, this is one of the best-tasting cherries.

'Zapotec Ribbed' An Oaxacan heirloom cultivated by the ancient Zapotec civilization in what is now Mexico. Ripening late, this bulky red, deeply ribbed beefsteak is great for slicing, or for stuffing and roasting.

Sauce
Sometimes called paste tomatoes, these varieties are robust and hearty, best for cooking into sauces, pastes, and soups.

'Amish Paste' Although delicious when sliced and eaten raw, this teardrop-shaped, sweet, brick-red variety truly shines in sauces. It has been grown since the nineteenth century and is said to have originated in the Amish communities of Wisconsin, but was later discovered among the Amish of Lancaster County, Pennsylvania.

'Banana Legs' With canary-yellow, elongated cylindrical fruit that have a citrusy, acidic, tropical edge, this offers a striking contrast to regular red tomato sauce, is superabundant, and ripens early in the season. It is relatively new, named and introduced in the 1980s by the seed-saver John Swenson of Illinois.

'Cornue des Andes' A rare large tomato that looks like a giant red pepper. Thought to be one of the original Andean tomatoes, it was imported to France by early European seed collectors searching for cultivars in South America. Highly productive, it has outrageously tasty fruit with a thick, fleshy texture and very few seeds.

'Dad's Barber Paste' This elongated ruby-red tomato with a pronounced nipple on the blossom end is productive and very sweet. Fantastic for soup.

'Jersey Devil' This variety was developed, named, and introduced by the Tomato Seed Co. of Metuchen, New Jersey, in the 1980s. Distinctively shaped, it resembles a little red banana and has a juicy, meaty texture that is perfect for flavourful sauces. It yields an abundance of fruit with surprisingly few seeds, adding to its saucy appeal.

'King Umberto' A luscious and succulent little tom fit for a king, bursting with robust, tangy flavour. In 1878, during the visit of Umberto I di Savoia, King of Italy, to Naples, the local people named the tastiest tomato variety in honour of the occasion. A true Italian gem, it produces small plum-shaped fruit with a delicious flavour and ruby-red sheen.

This royal fruit is acknowledged to be the ancestor of the world-famous 'San Marzano' variety that is commonly used for canning.

'Moyamensing' ('Spring Garden Jail') The story of this variety is shrouded in mystery, with its origins in a criminal past. It is believed that it was first grown in either Moyamensing Prison or Eastern State Penitentiary, both in Philadelphia. The seeds were eventually donated to the Roughwood Seed Collection in 1982 by one Mrs M. J. Grooms of Philadelphia, the great-granddaughter of a prison cook. The story goes that the tomato had been grown for the prison kitchen by convicts since the nineteenth century. A fiery red, medium-sized tomato, it is a top choice for soups, sauces, and canning.

'Old Brooks' An old heirloom variety that boasts truly impressive resilience to blight, blossom end rot, and drought. It is highly productive, with a bountiful harvest of large, spherical, full-flavoured rosy-red fruit that is acidic, making it the perfect choice for sauces.

'Plate de Haiti' A fascinating variety with a rich and complex history, 'Plate de Haiti' produces tons of fruit that is delightful when cooked or used in sauce. With a peachy red hue and a perfectly round shape, it is similar in size to a golf ball. Records show that it has been cultivated in the Caribbean since at least the sixteenth century. The Haitian Revolution began in 1791, when Haitians enslaved by the French fought successfully for independence. Some French colonialists who managed to escape brought with them seeds and plants to Louisiana and Cuba, and it is believed that it was this tomato that first entered traditional Creole cooking.

'Salvaterra's Select' Cultivated in Hazleton, Pennsylvania, for more than half a century, this variety was from the 1980s under the stewardship of Charles Salvaterra, who donated it to the Seed Savers Exchange. It is a superior sauce type with incredible flavour, its rich red fruit oval and of good size.

An array of melons (clockwise from top left) 'Silver Yamato', 'Moon and Stars', 'Jánošík', 'Wilson's Sweet', and 'Kaho'

Watermelon

Citrullus lanatus

Also known as Batikh, Pastèque, Sandía, Suika, Tarbooj

There's nothing like biting into a succulent watermelon. This juicy diva springs on to the summer scene in an explosion of fresh, sugary sweetness. Far beyond the most familiar strawberry-red flesh, these varied fruit come in an array of hues from silvery white to gold and orange. But it's the skins that steal the show, intricately textured in shades running the gamut from deepest seaweed-green to pale mint or earthy-toned stripes.

History

Watermelons quenched the thirst of ancient Indigenous civilizations in the sun-drenched African landscapes of the Kalahari Desert, known as the "land of great thirst". However, archaeologists have uncovered 5,000-year-old watermelon seeds at the Neolithic site of Uan Muhuggiag in the Libyan Sahara, suggesting that the plants were more widely distributed than first thought. Early watermelons had a bitter taste and tough, hard rinds that were difficult to open. After twining their way into the hands of the ancient Egyptians, they began to be improved by selection for sweeter fruit, as is shown by the seeds and paintings that have been unearthed from tombs. The ancient Greeks used the fruit's cooling rind as a cooling compress on the forehead to treat heatstroke.

In the early sixteenth century European colonists introduced watermelon seeds to America, where it was grown by Indigenous peoples after early encounters with the Europeans. After the American Civil War (1861–65) watermelons took on a complex role, becoming more than just a refreshing fruit. Former enslaved African Americans, now free individuals, embraced the cultivation, consumption, and sale of watermelons as a symbol of their resilience and new-found freedom. The fruit came to signify the sweetness of liberation. However, this narrative took a bitter turn as some Southern white people, threatened by the visible assertion of Black freedom, transformed the watermelon into a symbol

Growing at a glance

Sow Early–mid-spring,
22–32°C (72–90°F)

Plant out Late spring–early
summer

Spacing At least 120cm (47in)

Harvest Midsummer–early
autumn

laden with derogatory stereotypes. The
fruit became a target, embodying racist
notions reflecting the struggles and
prejudices of a society grappling with
the aftermath of slavery and the quest
for racial equality.

A more light-hearted association for
the fruit is skiing. This winter sport is not
limited to the alpine slopes, and there is

a realm of passionate watermelon skiers
in the arid Australian outback. The main
event is the biannual Chinchilla Melon
Festival in Queensland, where discerning
festivalgoers arm themselves with
protective headgear before inserting each
foot into a carved-out watermelon boot.
Gripping a rope, they struggle valiantly to
maintain their balance as they are pulled
across the slithery rubber slope – made
more slippery with splatters of the previous
contestant's melons.

Culinary uses
Preparation

Eaten as a stand-alone star, watermelons
are the juiciest fruit you can sink your teeth
into, simply cut into wedges. A Southern
speciality in the United States is to sprinkle
sea salt over fresh watermelon before
chowing down. This draws out some of
the moisture and enhances the sweetness.

Dishes

Watermelons are an ideal candidate for
summery fruit salads, yet their sweet and
refreshing edge also lends itself to salty
additions, such as olives and feta, and
a fresh zip of mint. Cubed and tossed
sparingly into Greek-style salads, they pass
the sweet-and-salty combination test with
flying colours. The same principle applies
when the flesh is frozen and blitzed into
spicy salt-rimmed iced margaritas for
a tasty alcoholic tipple. Set in moulds,
the frozen pulp can also be turned into
ice lollies for a healthy, refreshing treat –
perfect when pottering around the patch.

**Watermelons need a great
deal of water as they grow,
to produce their famously
succulent flesh. This one is
'Blacktail Mountain'.**

Growing

Propagation

While they are one of the trickier crops to grow in a temperate climate, watermelons are tremendously rewarding to cultivate at home. To optimize my chances I grow them only undercover, in the polytunnel, since they love heat and high humidity. Sow individually into seed cells. They require constant warmth to germinate, so keep sowings indoors or on a heat mat. Do ensure they are exposed to sunlight, however, or the emerging plants will quickly become spindly. Melon seedlings are prone to damping off, so be sure not to overwater. Transfer the young plants to 7–9cm (3–4in) pots a few weeks after germination. Then they can be grown on in a frost-free, well-lit area to produce bushy seedlings, and only after all risk of frost has passed should they be transplanted into the polytunnel, greenhouse, or garden.

Aftercare

Unlike other melons, these are best left to sprawl along the ground, like summer and winter squash (see pages 154 and 174). To make the most of the space in the polytunnel, I allow watermelons to scramble along the edges and underneath my string-trained melons. Using a trowel, bury the young plants deeply at an ultra-wide spacing. Water the plants generously and once they find their feet they will grow rapidly. They can be left to run rampant, but once a few fruits have set, it is possible to encourage faster ripening by pinching out the tips to contain the growth and focus the plant's energy on swelling.

Watermelons require ample water, especially during hot summers. However, decrease watering a little when the fruit begins to ripen and the foliage begins to fade; this will reduce the risk of the fruit splitting and enhance its natural sweetness.

'Cream of Saskatchewan'

66
The fruit came to signify the sweetness of liberation.

Plant problems

Mildew, rodents, spider mite
(see pages 49–51)

Harvesting

Scampering rodents will gnaw their way into ripe fruit, so be vigilant and beat them to the booty. The many varieties ripen at different times, however, and although they may look ready, do consider other indicators before harvesting. The first is the thump test. Give the fruit a knock with your knuckles, and if it is ripe it should produce a deep, hollow sound. Next, examine the field spot, the point where the fruit rests on the ground. On a ripe watermelon, the field spot usually develops from green-white to a creamy, yellowish orange. Finally, watch the curly tendril closest to the stem of the fruit; when it turns brown and starts to wither, the watermelon is probably ready to harvest.

Storage

Watermelons can be stored for three weeks and sometimes even longer when left whole and kept in a cool, dry place.

'Moon and Stars'

'Art Combe's Ancient' This is a magical tale. In the early 1920s Art Combe, a plant expert from the American Southwest known locally as "The Wizard", made a remarkable discovery. Inside an abandoned sandstone cave in the breathtaking scenery of the awe-inspiring Mogollon Rim region of Arizona, he stumbled on a pot containing a treasure trove of bright red watermelon seeds. He managed to sprout them, and the melons they produced were oddly shaped, crooknecked, unlike any that had been seen before, and brilliantly sweet. Over time Combe selected the largest, roundest specimens, and the result is a magnificent extra-large watermelon with vibrant red, super-sweet flesh, brilliantly resistant to drought.

'Blacktail Mountain' An open-pollinated type developed in the 1970s by Glenn Drowns of Sand Hill Preservation Center in Calamus, Iowa. The fruit is greenish-black with muted red flesh, among the earliest to mature, and, with its brilliant resistance to cool temperatures, a great choice for cold climates.

'Clay County Yellow Meat' A real beauty rolling out of Clay County, Alabama. The globe-shaped fruit, pale green with dark stripes, contains sweet, pastel-orange, meaty flesh that is considered by many to be the tastiest of the golden types. An annual festival is held in honour of these wicked watermelons in Ashland, Alabama.

'Cream of Saskatchewan' The seeds of this variety arrived in the prairies of the Western Canadian province after which it is named with Russian settlers in the early twentieth century. This is a fantastic watermelon with a thin rind and pearly white flesh that's creamy-textured and brimming with sweet citrusy tangs. Early to mature and great for cool, short-season climates.

'Georgia Rattlesnake' Producing bulky oblong fruit with a snake-like patterned skin, this variety boasts

Variety	Size	Flesh colour
'Blacktail Mountain'	Small	Pink
'Cream of Saskatchewan'	Small	White
'Kaho'	Small	Golden
'Silver Yamato'	Small	White
'Small Shining Light'	Small	Red
'Art Combe's Ancient'	Medium	Red
'Jánošík'	Medium	Yellow
'Nancy'	Medium	Pink
'Royal Golden'	Medium	Pink
'Sweet Siberian'	Medium	Orange
'Wilson's Sweet'	Medium	Red
'Clay County Yellow Meat'	Large	Orange
'Georgia Rattlesnake'	Large	Red
'Moon and Stars'	Large	Pink
'Scaly Bark'	Large	Pink

rich rosy-red flesh and was bred in Georgia, USA, in the 1830s. It is a highly productive old Southern fruity-star.

'Jánošík' A prized golden-yellow, crisp-fleshed Polish heirloom, bursting with flavour. It is named after a seventeenth-century Slovak highwayman, Juraj Jánošík (known as "the real Robin Hood"), who was executed at the age of 25 and became a legendary hero of Slovak, Polish, and Hungarian folklore. He symbolized resistance to oppression in Central Europe, and his name was used by an anti-Nazi resistance group during the Slovak National Uprising in 1944.

'Kaho' Oblong fruit with peachy orange flesh and pale green, lightly snakeskin-patterned rind. Developed in Asia at some time before the twentieth century, it is quick to mature and has a fruity, sugary taste.

'Moon and Stars' Dark green fruit with cosmic patterns of starry golden-yellow splashes. Once nearly lost from cultivation, these wacky oblong watermelons are believed to have originated along the Volga River in Russia during the nineteenth century.

'Nancy' A cracking watermelon that is believed to have been discovered growing freely in a Georgian cotton field in the 1880s by one Nancy Tate. It boasts excellent resistance to drought, and its fruit is oval with pretty pink flesh and a stripy green rind.

'Royal Golden' This majestic variety looks like a squash with its burnt-orange skin, yet inside is charming coral-pink flesh. It was developed from the now extinct watermelon variety 'Pumpkin Rind'.

'Scaly Bark' A rare old US heirloom variety whose name is a nod to its rough, tumbled bark-like skin. With delightful salmon-pink flesh and a thick skin, it keeps for a long time after harvest.

'Silver Yamato' A spectacularly sugary silver-fleshed sensation with a delicate citrusy twang. This Japanese heirloom from the hilly northeastern edge of the Nara Basin produces ornate, pale green fruit with a thin rind patterned in thick dark stripes.

'Small Shining Light' A lovely little watermelon, this Russian heirloom is super quick to mature, often one of the first to be ready for harvest. The fruit is a deep dark green, almost black, with stunningly juicy, sweet rosy-red flesh.

'Sweet Siberian' Originating in the chilly Russian region of Siberia, where it was cultivated widely before the seeds made their way to the USA in the late nineteenth century, this oblong variety boasts a luscious golden flesh complemented by an appealing apple-green rind. It is an excellent choice for regions with short, cool growing seasons.

'Wilson's Sweet' This variety was nearly lost before being reintroduced by Glenn Drowns of Sand Hill Preservation Center, who received a sample of the seeds in the post from a grower who had maintained it. The early-maturing fruit boasts a unique marbled, mottled skin and deep red flesh, but the rind is thin and fragile.

Winter Squash

Cucurbita spp. *maxima, mixta,* and *moschata*

Also known as Calabaza, Gourd, Joumou, Kabocha, Pumpkin

Squashes exhibit extraordinary shapes, sizes, and shades, from neat green globes or creased white cubes to gigantic golden spheres blistered with rusty warts. Some look like big beige bananas while others have long, curled, trombone-like bodies. Yet they are not just a sight to behold; they are also a phenomenally tasty, versatile ingredient. Beyond this, they store very well, providing sweet, nutrient-rich fruit for months after harvest.

History

Squash's long tendrils took root in Meso-America before unfurling throughout the American continents about 10,000 years ago. Ancient agriculturists honoured its ability to provide food and adapt to diverse landscapes and climates, from the Andean valleys to the arid American Southwest, and over time this important crop wove its way into cultural practices.

The Indigenous peoples of northeastern North America had a sacred way of cultivating their land, which included growing squash as part of the "Three Sisters" system. Gourd plants were allowed to sprawl on the ground, providing natural cover for the soil, and were interwoven with corn, which supported climbing beans. This trio was not only practical but also held special meaning, representing a spiritual connection with the cycles of life. The three were seen as inseparable sisters who could grow and thrive only together.

Indigenous people also used the hard shells for practical purposes, including containers, bowls, bottles, and utensils, and for the musical instruments, such as rattles and drums, that had a place in ceremonial dances and spiritual practices. They carved, painted, burned, or embellished intricate, symbolic designs into the skins.

Today, pumpkins are not just carved into Halloween jack-o'-lanterns but also made into vessels for the Windsor Pumpkin Regatta, held every October on Lake Pisiquid, Nova Scotia. Some sailors dress up as pirates or don cumbersome pumpkin suits before taking to the lake for a 0.8km ($1/_2$ mile) row-off. The gourd craft are restricted to a weight of 250–350kg (550–770lb), and there are strict rules against pushing, barging, and shoving.

Culinary uses
Preparation
No matter the preparation method, don't throw away the seeds, which are edible

"There are endless possibilities for preparing the vibrant orange flesh.

with or without the hull. Once thoroughly washed and dried, they can be lightly coated in olive oil and baked for a crunchy snack or a topper for soup or salad. After roasting, they can easily be popped out of the hulls for pepitas-style seeds.

Dishes

It's an exciting moment slicing open a home-grown squash. There are endless possibilities for preparing the vibrant orange flesh, from soups and stews to savoury purées and sweet pies. Today's pumpkin pies are made with sweetcrust pastry, but the earliest were rather different: whole pumpkins with the tops cut off and the seeds scooped out, the cavity filled with a sweet egg-custardy mixture, seasoned with spices. The top was popped back on and the fruit baked, left to cool, and cut into slices, like a regular pie.

Another squashy sweet treat is *calabaza en tacha*, a Mexican dish traditionally served during the Day of the Dead celebrations. The fruit is chopped and gently simmered in a syrup spiced with cinnamon, cloves, and *piloncillo* (raw, pure cane sugar).

Among many ancient cooking techniques for squash is slow-roasting whole over an open fire or among the embers. The rugged exterior provides the perfect barrier from heat, and the smoky flavour penetrates the flesh and provides a pleasant barbecue taste that is impossible

to replicate in an oven. Just be sure to turn the fruit so that it cooks evenly.

Growing

Propagation

It's worth giving this crop a head start, since it requires a long season with plenty of sunshine. If space permits, sow seeds up to a month before the last frost is likely, for bulky plants that are ready to find their feet outside the moment the weather warms. Sow one seed per cell or directly into small (7cm/3in) pots by pushing the seed into the compost until it is submerged; some

Winter squash provide a robust, nutritious bounty that will keep fresh for a long time after harvest.

people recommend sowing squash seeds on their side, although I've found they sprout with no problems whether sown flat or side on. The seeds require warmth to germinate, so consider using a heat mat or putting the trays in a cosy place, such as an airing cupboard. Do not allow them to become waterlogged, since they are susceptible to rotting in cold, damp compost. You may find it helpful to add vermiculite or perlite to the potting mix for extra drainage. Protect from rodents with a cloche or keep in a pest-free zone.

Provide the seedlings with as much sun as possible, and, if necessary, move them to 7cm (3in) pots once the first set of true leaves emerges. At this point, if you have a greenhouse or polytunnel, it's worth moving the plants into it during the day to catch the rays, before taking them back inside as the temperature drops in the evening. It may be necessary to pot them on a second time if they outgrow their home as you wait for frost to pass. Don't let them become waterlogged or they will wilt and damp off.

Only once all risk of frost has passed can the plants be set out in the patch, spaced widely so as not to restrict their growth. Use a trowel to make a planting hole, and bury a section of the fragile stem to provide extra support.

Aftercare

Keep an eye on moisture and give the young plants a generous drink as necessary until they are established; this may be

The thick, hard skins of winter squash make these fruit excellent storers.

required every other day in hot, dry weather. In temperate climates, squashes tend not to need extra water once established, but in extremely arid, hot areas it may be necessary to water them as the fruit begins to set and swell. If bad storms are forecast shortly after transplanting, protect them with a layer of horticultural fleece or mesh, but remove it the moment the weather warms up, to avoid scorching the plants.

The long vines may need to be picked up, repositioned, or cut back if space is short; however, squash grows best when left to ramble and run rampant, making it one of the lowest-maintenance crops you can grow. I never prune my plants, instead allowing them to sprawl far and wide.

Don't be alarmed if you discover undeveloped fruit decaying underneath the plants; squash often produce more fruit than the plant can handle, and they self-prune to keep things under control. As late summer approaches, you may spot signs of mildew on the older leaves; this is part of the natural cycle and no cause for concern if the plant is growing strongly.

Growing at a glance

Sow Mid–late spring, 20–35°C (68–95°F)

Plant out Summer

Spacing 80–100cm (31–39in)

Harvest Autumn

Plant problems

Mildew, rodents, slugs and snails (see pages 49–51)

Curing squash

Curing allows water to evaporate slowly from the squash, concentrating the sugars and increasing the richness and complexity of the taste. It also hardens the rind, slowing the onset of disease and mould and allowing long storage. To cure squash, store it in a bright, sunny place, such as a windowsill or conservatory, ideally at 25–30°C (77–86°F) for at least two weeks. Note that although the polytunnel or greenhouse may seem a good place to cure squash, cold night-time temperatures and high humidity can cause the stems to rot, and the fruit is prone to being feasted on by rodents.

Harvesting

Harvest all fruit before the first frost or it may spoil or store poorly; it should be picked even if it isn't fully mature, and will still be edible, albeit less sweet. Before this, there are some signs that will tell you when to harvest. The leaves will die off naturally, the fruit's stem will become woody, almost like tree bark, and the rind will be thick, hard, and the correct colour for the mature fruit. Using secateurs, snips, or a sharp knife, cut the stem where it meets the vine, keeping as much as possible of the barky stem connected to the fruit. Take care not to damage the fruit's thick outer skin, or the shelf life will be shortened.

Storage

It's essential to cure squash (see panel above) to improve its storage ability and sweetness. It can then be kept in any warm, well-ventilated area that doesn't fall below 10°C (50°F). Many winter squash will store long into the following year. The timings given in the table overleaf are a rough guide, but as long as the fruit shows no signs of rot, it will be perfectly edible. In fact, the flavour improves after prolonged storing because the sugars continue to develop. Once open, a squash will keep for up to two weeks in the fridge.

Recommended varieties

Maxima

This species is believed to have originated in what are now Bolivia and Argentina. Rampant, long, bristly vines are adorned with large, prickly leaves, and the plants are tolerant of low temperatures, making them ideal for northern climates. The fruit is renowned for its impressive size – up to 20kg (44lb) in some varieties. The flesh is typically vivid yellow or orange, and the outer skin ranges from green to grey to orange.

'Boston Marrow' The precise origin of this variety has been the subject of debate. Some claim that its seeds originated in Chile, but there are indications that the seed was obtained in the United States by the nineteenth-century horticulturist John Mansfield Ives of Salem, Massachusetts. Ives collected the cultivar from someone who claimed it originated with an Indigenous people near Buffalo, New York. It was initially named 'Autumn Marrow' and became very popular in Boston for baking pumpkin pies, leading to the name change. It is characterized by a large, round dumbbell shape with a slightly flattened top, its rich orange skin lightly warted and wrinkled. With a sweet, nutty flavour, it is delicious in desserts.

'Flat White Boer' This South African heirloom variety is thought to have been introduced and developed by early Dutch settlers who arrived in the Cape of Good Hope in the seventeenth century. The bright orange flesh of these flat, ribbed, pure white pumpkins is irresistibly sweet.

'Galeux d'Eysines' This salmon-pink pumpkin – an old French heirloom – has brown cork-like warts caused by a build-up of sugar. The skin can be scored lightly while the fruit is growing to produce a decorative embroidery of brown scabs; some growers etch their name into the skin, which gradually turns into a thick, warty display as it matures. The sugary flavour is reminiscent of sweet potato.

'Gete Okosomin' This giant, ancient variety has a rich and fascinating yet miscommunicated history. It was famously known as the 800-year-old squash thanks to a legend that the seeds were discovered buried in ancient clay fragments unearthed in Wisconsin. Yet research has shown that this orange, banana-shaped Native American squash has been cultivated, carefully saved, and passed down for generations by the Indigenous Miami Nation of Indiana.

'Green Hubbard' Seeds of this thick-skinned variety first arrived on North American soil in Marblehead, Massachusetts, in the 1790s, when one Captain Knot Martin returned to port; it is thought that he had obtained them in South America or the Caribbean. The seeds found their way into the hands of Elizabeth Hubbard, a neighbour of the renowned nineteenth-century seedsman James J. H. Gregory, the "Seed King of Marblehead". In the 1840s Gregory listed the variety as 'Green Hubbard', in honour of his neighbour. For her part, Hubbard said this was "the best squash she'd ever tasted".

'Guatemalan Blue' An ancient South American squash believed to have been cultivated for millennia in the Guatemalan highlands. The silvery blue skin is streaked with pale grey and the flavour is among the finest and fruitiest of all squash.

'Hopi Pale Grey' A culinary gem with a wonderfully sweet, rich flavour, this variety was on the verge of extinction in 2003 after fire ripped through the seed bank of the Abundant Life Seed Foundation in California (the only organization that listed the variety at the time), destroying vast expanses of the inventory. Thankfully, a few home gardeners stewarded it, and the seed stock was rebuilt and offered to the public. Shaped like a giant silver rugby ball, this fruit was first cultivated by the Hopi people of what is now northwestern Arizona. It stores incredibly well, reportedly up to 24 months at room temperature.

'Iran' A large silvery blue squash with peach blotches, this mildly flavoured variety stores extremely well. The seeds were first collected in the 1940s in the northeastern Iranian city of Torbat-e Heydarieh.

'Marina di Chioggia' Originating in the seaside town of Chioggia, south of Venice, this warty dark blue-green variety is considered the king of all squash in Italy. The striking orange flesh has a nutty flavour.

Variety	Species	Size	Weight	Colour	Shape	Storage time
'Boston Marrow'	*maxima*	20–50cm (8–20in)	4–10kg (9–22lb)	Fiery orange	Squat	6 months
'Flat White Boer'	*maxima*	25–50cm (10–20in)	5–15kg (11–33lb)	Ivory white	Flat globe	6 months
'Galeux d'Eysines'	*maxima*	25–40cm (10–16in)	4–8kg (9–18lb)	Peach	Globe	3–5 months
'Gete Okosomin'	*maxima*	50–90cm (20–35in)	5–12kg (11–26$\frac{1}{2}$lb)	Fiery orange	Long banana	6 months+
'Green Hubbard'	*maxima*	30–50cm (12–20in)	4–9kg (9–20lb)	Green	Teardrop	5–6 months
'Guatemalan Blue'	*maxima*	30–45cm (12–18in)	2–5kg (4$\frac{1}{2}$–11lb)	Blue	Long banana	6 months
'Hopi Pale Grey'	*maxima*	30–45cm (12–18in)	4–7kg (9–15lb)	Silver/grey	Egg	9 months+
'Iran'	*maxima*	25–50cm (10–20in)	8–15kg (18–33lb)	Silver/pink	Globe	4–6 months
'Marina di Chioggia'	*maxima*	25–45cm (10–18in)	6–10kg (13–22lb)	Dark green ribbed warty	Flat sphere	6 months
'Moranga'	*maxima*	15–30cm (6–12in)	1–3kg (2–7lb)	Salmon-pink	Flat ribbed	3 months
'North Georgia Candy Roaster'	*maxima*	35–50cm (14–20in)	3–5kg (7–11lb)	Pinky peach	Long banana	6 months

Variety	Species	Size	Weight	Colour	Shape	Storage time
'Pikes Peak'	*maxima*	30–45cm (12–18in)	2–5kg ($4^1/_2$–11lb)	Grey-blue	Long banana	6 months+
'Queensland Blue'	*maxima*	20–40cm (8–16in)	2–5kg ($4^1/_2$–11lb)	Grey-blue	Ribbed square	4–5 months
'Red Warty Thing'	*maxima*	30–45cm (12–18in)	4–8kg (9–18lb)	Fiery red	Elongated sphere	5 months
'Turk's Turban'	*maxima*	20–40cm (8–16in)	2–3kg ($4^1/_2$–7lb)	Multicoloured	Squat sphere	4–6 months
'Ute'	*maxima*	20–30cm (8–12in)	2–4kg ($4^1/_2$–9lb)	Pale green	Squat sphere	6 months+
'Zapallito del Tronco'	*maxima*	5–10cm (2–4in)	0.4–1kg ($^3/_4$–2lb)	Dark green	Flat ribbed round	3 months
'Green Striped Cushaw'	*mixta*	25–45cm (10–18in)	4–6kg (9–13lb)	Green striped	Long bottle	6 months
'White Cushaw'	*mixta*	30–45cm (12–18in)	2–4kg ($4^1/_2$–9lb)	Ivory white	Long bottle	4–7 months
'Canada Crookneck'	*moschata*	15–25cm (6–10in)	1–2kg (2–$4^1/_2$lb)	Peach	Long bottle	5 months
'Futsu Black'	*moschata*	15–25cm (6–10in)	1–3kg (2–7lb)	Black/rusty brown	Warty squat square	6 months
'Long Island Cheese'	*moschata*	15–25cm (6–10in)	2–5kg ($4^1/_2$–11lb)	Tan/orange	Ribbed round	3–6 months
'Musquee de Provence'	*moschata*	30–50cm (12–20in)	5–10kg (11–22lb)	Golden-brown	Ribbed round flat	8 months
'Seminole'	*moschata*	15–25cm (6–10in)	2–4kg ($4^1/_2$–9lb)	Deep orange	Squat sphere	8 months+
'Shishigatani'	*moschata*	20–25cm (8–10in)	2–3kg ($4^1/_2$–7lb)	Green	Warty hourglass	2–5 months
'Sucrine du Berry'	*moschata*	12–15cm (5–6in)	1–2kg (2–$4^1/_2$lb)	Orange/green	Oval/pear	3–6 months
'Tahitian Melon'	*moschata*	35–55cm (14–22in)	5–9kg (11–20lb)	Peach	Long, curly, bulbous	9 months
'Tromboncino'	*moschata*	50–65cm (20–26in)	1–3kg (2–7lb)	Peach	Trombone, curly	2–3 months
'Violina di Rugosa'	*moschata*	20–30cm (8–12in)	2–3kg ($4^1/_2$–7lb)	Tan/orange	Warty violin	4–6 months
'Waltham Butternut'	*moschata*	20–25cm (8–10in)	2–3kg ($4^1/_2$–7lb)	Peach	Elongated pear	4–8 months

'Marina di Chioggia'

'Moranga' A rare Brazilian heirloom variety, heavily ribbed and flattened with a delightful salmon-pink skin, this is traditionally used to prepare *camarão na moranga*, a dish from the coastline of São Paulo state. This creamy prawn and seafood stew is served in the hollowed-out pumpkin for a striking centrepiece.

'North Georgia Candy Roaster' Developed and stewarded by the Cherokee Nation in the Appalachian Mountains, this pinkish-orange squash with blue tips looks like a giant banana. The long shape makes it easy to slice the fruit in half, scoop out the seeds, and roast the flesh. Simply delicious.

'Pikes Peak' Second to none for flavour, this elongated teardrop squash has a pale greenish-blue rind with dark green flecks. Believed to be native to the North American continent, it was made available commercially in 1887 by the seed company Hiram Sibley & Co. of New York, which had acquired the seeds from an elderly lady who had grown the squash for more than 50 years.

'Queensland Blue' An Aussie heirloom cultivated down under for more than 100 years, this plant is a prolific producer of dark greenish-blue fruit with a boxy, tapered shape and deep ribs. It has an outstanding texture

and mild, sweet taste. It is similar to the New Zealand squash 'Whangaparaoa Crown', which is rounder, less ribbed, and has a lighter, greyish-white rind.

'Red Warty Thing' Introduced in 1897 by James J. H. Gregory of Massachusetts as 'Victor', this peculiarly gruesome and beastly squash was later renamed for its striking fiery orange skin, which is ribbed and warty. It has a pleasant, sweet flavour and delicate texture.

'Turk's Turban' One of the most oddly shaped squash, this variety displays a rainbow of markings ranging from green to orange, pink, white, yellow, and even blue. The fruit is round and flattened, with a turban-like protrusion at the top end, hence the name. The colours and protrusions are irregular, so no two fruit look alike. An old heirloom variety dating from before the nineteenth century, this is not just a masterpiece to look at but also tastes great.

'Ute' An ancient Native American squash initially grown by the Indigenous Ute people of the territory now known as Colorado. With an attractive pale grey-green rind, it is distinctive to look at, with a protruding bottom that resembles a second squash growing out of the base. It is a culinary delight, bursting with sweet, complex, nutty flavours.

'Zapallito del Tronco' An old-school Argentinian heirloom with a semi-bush habit, this prolific variety produces small green-rinded fruit with delicate ribs. The fruit can also be harvested as summer squash (see page 154) when it is the size of an avocado. The variety was first listed by James J. H. Gregory in 1885, and is now rare and highly sought after.

Mixta

This species comprises an array of cultivars collectively called cushaws, which have been cultivated for centuries over a vast region stretching from Guatemala to the southwestern United States.

Mixtas **are of particular interest to growers thanks to their exceptional ability to tolerate drought. The flesh of *mixta* squash is noted for its pale colour, robust texture, and deep flavour.**

'Green Striped Cushaw' A work of art with an ornate appearance that is sure to impress, the fruit has a mammoth, bulbous bottom and a long, crooked neck with striking green and white stripes. Domesticated several thousand years ago, this variety was valued highly by the Indigenous Hopi people of Arizona, who considered it one of the most delicious and versatile squashes.

'White Cushaw' A rare, exquisite cushaw with stunning white skin that sets it apart from other varieties. The fruit has a long neck and a bulbous bottom, and the sweet, pale orange flesh has a delectable flavour and smooth texture.

Moschata

Native to the tropical lowlands of Central and South America, this species prefers areas with mild nights and high humidity. The plants have large leaves and sprawling, smooth stems, and the fruit is valued for its sweet taste, creamy texture, and dense flesh. The most commonly cultivated *moschata* variety is the famous butternut squash.

'Canada Crookneck' A long-necked butternut-shaped squash with a bulbous base. Now exceedingly rare, this rich, sugary variety is thought to have been grown and stewarded by the Indigenous Iroquois peoples of northeastern North America. Productive, pest-resistant, and delicious, it was first made commercially available in 1834 by the Boston-based seedsman Charles Hovey.

'Futsu Black' Easy to grow, early to mature, and superabundant, this squat, gnarly squash is prized throughout Japan but rarely sold outside the country. Beneath the scaly, almost black dinosaur-like skin, the flesh has a deliciously complex, intensely nutty flavour.

'Long Island Cheese' This old-school New York heirloom variety has sweet, finely textured flesh. Named for its resemblance to a wheel of cheese, it was nearly lost during the 1970s but rescued thanks to the heroic efforts of the Long Island plant-breeder Ken Ettlinger, who tracked down the few remaining growers who had preserved seed.

'Musquee de Provence' A French classic dating back to the nineteenth century and beloved by chefs for its sweet, nutty, spicy-edged flavour, this big, flat, rounded squash has deep ribs and an impressive golden-brown rind. Its fruit is the most picture-perfect pumpkin shape.

'Seminole' This variety is named after the Indigenous American people of Florida who cultivated it along tropical riverbanks and swamps and planted it underneath trees, which acted as natural trellising. The incredibly thick skin requires some care when cutting. The squat, round, pear-shaped squash is easy to grow and much sweeter than other *moschata* cultivars.

'Shishigatani' Knobbly and warty, with two bulbous ends and a narrow waist, this variety has been grown in the Higashiyama district of Kyoto, Japan, since the nineteenth century. Anraku-ji Temple has a long-standing tradition of celebrating the harvest and hosts an annual festival to celebrate this exceptionally tasty squash.

'Sucrine du Berry' A classic heirloom from the old region of Berry in central France, its name means "the sweet one from Berry" – and for good reason. Well adapted to harsh weather and cool summers, this plant produces pear-shaped squash that are delightfully tasty.

'Tahitian Melon' Seeds of this variety were initially passed to the UK-based Seedhouse in 1976 by the gardener George Patton, having been collected on the volcanic island of Bora Bora in the South Pacific, and 'Tahitian Melon' was introduced by the seed company Thompson & Morgan in 1977. These extra-large squash resemble giant butternuts with a sweet, nutty flavour.

'Tromboncino' This unique squash boasts a striking resemblance to an old-fashioned trumpet, with a long, curly shape that is a wonder to behold. It is the result of selective breeding in the mild climate and rolling hills of Liguria in northwestern Italy. It can be harvested while young, as a tender and delicious zucchini (see page 154), or left to mature, eventually attaining an impressive butternut-like shape.

'Violina di Rugosa' This southern Italian treasure is knobbly and warty with deep ridges and, as the name suggests, shaped like a violin. The fruit is incredibly sweet with a smooth texture.

'Waltham Butternut' Charles Leggett of Massachusetts is credited with developing one of the most sought-after strains of butternut squash. Seeking guidance, he brought his newly created squash to the Waltham Field Station, where the staff were astounded and charmed by it, describing it as smooth as butter and sweet as a nut. They advised Leggett to name it, and he chose the moniker "butternut squash".

'Tromboncino'

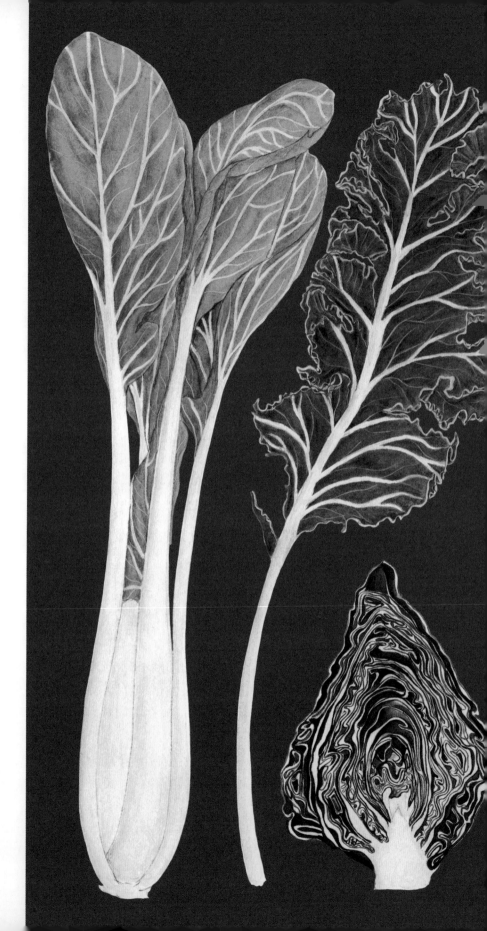

Leaves

From salad leaves to stir-fried greens, these crops bring a burst of freshness and nutrients to dishes.

Chinese Cabbage & Pak Choi

Brassica rapa subsp. *pekinensis* & *chinensis*

Also known as Bok choy, Napa

Sweet, crunchy, and tender, these crops contain more water than the thicker-leafed brassicas, bringing a wealth of culinary opportunities. The succulent heads of Chinese cabbage and juicy stems of pak choi can be fiddly to grow, but they are worth it, elevating Asian-inspired dishes with an authentic flavour unparalleled by most supermarket offerings.

History

These intriguing members of the brassica family trace their origins to China, specifically the Yangtze River Delta in the heart of Jiangnan region, one of the world's oldest agricultural landscapes. Chinese culture has a strong association with the white cabbage known in Mandarin as *bái cài* (one hundred wealth). Seen as a symbol of prosperity in the coming year, it is synonymous with Lunar New Year celebrations and is eaten extensively throughout the festivities.

The taste of home

A romantic folk legend tells of how the Chinese cabbage was introduced to Korea. A Chinese princess married a Korean king and, as part of her dowry, brought with her the seeds of her favourite leafy green, wanting to enjoy the flavours of home and contribute to the garden of her new household. This cabbage later become a crucial ingredient in kimchi, a staple of Korean cuisine. It is believed that subsequently the seeds spread to America through Chinese settlers arriving during the gold rush of the nineteenth century.

Culinary uses

Preparation

The trick to preparing any stir-fried dish with Chinese cabbages or pak choi is to tear the leaves rather than slicing with a knife; this creates haphazard, ragged-edged chunks that absorb more flavour.

Dishes

A staple ingredient throughout Asia, these crunchy greens radiate a delicate mineral flavour. They are often simply thrown into dishes as a last-minute addition, yet their culinary use is much wider. They are common shredded in steamed dim sum dumplings, often paired with sweet, juicy pork in these iconic Chinese snacks. *Suan la bái cài* is a fragrant, tangy hot-and-sour stir-fried cabbage dish that is very popular in China. Rapidly cooked in a sizzling wok, it has a bold and zingy aromatic punch provided by spicy chilli flakes, minced garlic, Szechuan pepper, soy sauce, and lashings of Chinkiang black vinegar.

Kimchi – Korea's national dish – has been a part of the country's cuisine for thousands of years, having developed as an ancient technique of storing vegetables during the winter. The meticulous process has been passed down through generations, with recipes varying from cook to cook and region to region. It is commonly made with Chinese cabbage, which is seasoned with a blend of aromatics and spices, typically garlic, ginger, and chilli. This combination and the process of fermentation give kimchi its unique taste, which can be described as tangy, spicy, and slightly sour. If fermenting Chinese cabbage into kimchi, try quartering the heads rather than shredding them. A vegan substitute for the fish sauce traditionally used in kimchi is a mixture of white miso paste and soy sauce, which adds umami and saltiness.

Pak choi is a sublime substitute for such familiar side dishes as kale and spinach, whether baked or roasted in halves or quarters (when it develops a crispy, crunchy exterior with nutty notes and caramelized edges and tender, succulent hearts) or slow-braised in stock with aromatic additions. It pairs with any cuisine, and is just as welcome in sweet and rich Chinese five-spiced pork as it is in delicate, zesty fish dishes and the boldest game pies and stews.

Fine-mesh netting helps to protect these heads of 'Granaat' Chinese cabbage from pests, such as birds, butterflies, and aphids.

Growing at a glance

Sow Mid–late summer, 6–30°C (43–86°F)

Plant out Late summer–early autumn

Spacing 30–40cm (12–16in)

Harvest Mid-autumn

Chinese cabbage
(*Brassica rapa* subsp. *pekinensis*)

Propagation

A lover of cool weather, these tender-headed cabbages can be tricky owing to their short sowing window and pest-prone nature. Keep sowings well protected from butterflies and flea beetle by raising them in a potting shed or greenhouse. Pot on the rapidly growing seedlings into 7cm (3in)

Chinese cabbage
'Golden Beauty'

66
These crunchy greens are a staple ingredient throughout Asia.

pots two weeks after germination, and plant them out in the patch 7–10 days after that. Bury the stems deeply to give extra support, and cover the plants immediately with fine mesh to deter pests.

Aftercare
These are exceptionally thirsty crops. If the weather is dry, ensure they receive a deep drink every two or three days throughout their life cycle; added water is usually not needed once the autumn rains arrive. Good housekeeping is critical to producing a bounty of these tender, lush cabbages. Remove dead, decaying, or yellowing leaves promptly, to deter slugs, and rummage around the base of the plant to find any of these slitherers hiding among the tender foliage.

Plant problems
Aphids, birds, caterpillars, flea beetle, slugs and snails (see pages 49–51)

Harvesting
There is a fleeting optimum harvest window in mid-autumn, when the hearts have bulked up and swollen. It's a balancing act, however, since they must be left to swell until large enough but picked before the first frost. Using a sharp knife, slice the whole head off at the soil surface.

Storage
The biggest, tightest heads can be stored whole for several weeks in a cool, frost-free shed or outbuilding, or fermented into delicious kimchi for prolonged storage.

Recommended varieties

'Golden Beauty' One of the most popular varieties, this has been cultivated in China for millennia. The squat, chunky heads with their rich chartreuse hue are tender and often regarded as the best-tasting Chinese cabbage.

'Granaat' A tall, tight, thin variety developed in Europe to be higher-yielding with a sweeter flavour. The plants are much more erect and elongated than other types, with serrated light green leaves.

'Nagasaki Late' (*tojinna*) An old Japanese heirloom from the island of Kyushu, this variety produces gloriously chunky white stems and large-lobed dark green leaves. It has been grown in the mountainous surroundings of Nagasaki for hundreds of years.

'Granaat'

'Tai Sai'

Pak choi
(*Brassica rapa* subsp. *chinensis*)

Propagation

To optimize success, pak choi is best grown later in the year, when there is less risk of the plants bolting and reduced pressure from pests. Sow seeds by broadcasting, and prick out once they are big enough to handle. These rapidly growing plants often need to grow for only two or three weeks before being transplanted into the patch. Bury the plants deeply, since their fragile stems are easily broken by breezy gusts.

Aftercare

As with all brassicas, cover them with fine mesh to keep off flea beetles, egg-laying butterflies, and pigeons. The luscious, crunchy-stemmed leaves require ample moisture as they rapidly swell and grow. If the weather is dry, give them a generous drink every few days. To deter slugs, maintain good housekeeping by removing dead, decaying, or yellowing leaves and keeping the base of the plant free of weeds.

Plant problems

Aphids, birds, caterpillars, flea beetle, slugs and snails (see pages 49–51)

Harvesting

Harvest whole heads by slicing off the stem at soil level with a sharp knife. Pak choi stands well in the ground during the cooler

Growing at a glance

Sow Late summer–early autumn, 6–30°C (43–86°F)

Plant out Mid-autumn

Spacing 25–30cm (10–12in)

Harvest Late autumn

autumn months, but should be harvested before any heavy or prolonged frost is forecast. It can also be treated as a cut-and-come-again crop; once the leaves are big enough to be picked, remove the outer ones regularly, leaving the central heart to continue producing. Harvesting in this way will generate three or four good crops of leaves.

Storage

The leaves are best eaten on the day of harvest for the most pleasurable crunchy texture, but they will keep for several days in the fridge if wrapped in a damp cloth or washed and popped in a plastic bag. Pak choi is also a perfect alternative to Chinese cabbage for storing as kimchi and other fermented preserves.

Making sure the young plants are clear of weeds and decaying leaves will keep slugs away from your precious seedlings.

Recommended varieties

'Hedou' A pocket-sized pak choi that is harvested when the heads can fit into the palm of the hand. It is believed to have originated in a small village near the city of Hong Kong, and local legend has it that the grower shared the seeds with his neighbours, but only on the condition that they not be passed on to people outside the village. Unfortunately, one night, the village seed stash was stolen, and the tiny pak choi were spread throughout the region, where they quickly became famous for their diminutive size.

'Maruba Santoh' Gloriously chartreuse-coloured, these golden-yellow to pale green brassicas are very quick to mature and produce large, leafy, tender heads that are sweet and crisp.

'Tai Sai' Big, bold, and beautiful, this rapid-growing variety has luxuriously long snow-white stems topped with broad, pear-green leaves. These vigorous plants can reach phenomenal heights, almost resembling Swiss chard.

Brussels Sprouts

Brassica oleracea var. *gemmifera*

Also known as Cavoletti, Rosenkohl, Sprouts

Never has there been a more divisive vegetable than the bittersweet Brussels sprout. It's a love-it-or-hate-it food, possibly because of a particular human gene that regulates the perception of bitterness and varies from person to person. But don't overlook it; it's rich in vitamins and, cooked correctly, brings an earthy, wholesome touch to the table. Brussels sprouts are among the veg patch's hardiest plants, providing bountiful harvests through the winter.

History

A descendant of the same wild species of *Brassica* as the cabbage, sprouts were bred for their edible buds. They are thought to have been developed near Brussels in the thirteenth century, while the area – part of a territory comprising present-day Belgium and the Netherlands – was controlled by the Duchy of Brabant. The seeds spread later to other cool regions of Europe, yet cultivation records can be traced back only to the late sixteenth century.

Brussels sprouts and Britain go hand in hand, and the UK consumes the most sprouts of any European country. More often than not, they're served with an "X" sliced into the stem end, but this is a technique born out of superstition, not a culinary trend. In the late Middle Ages, it was commonly believed that demons resided between the layers of leaves. To ward off these wicked spirits and their sorcery, a holy cross was cut into the base of the sprout, and the tradition has stuck.

Sadly, there is no compelling tale to explain why the sprout became one of the most loved (and hated) Christmas trimmings. Its spot on the festive table is perhaps a result of circumstance as much as anything else, since Brussels sprouts are naturally ready for harvest around 25 December. The vegetable's popularity in gardens spiked during the Victorian era, when the joyful and festive Christmas as we know it today began taking off across

Even haters should consider giving these crops a try – an entire stem of Brussels sprouts makes a charming festive present.

66

Brussels sprouts are among the vegetable patch's hardiest plants.

the British Isles, with many traditions – crackers, cards, and boiled sprouts – springing from this time.

Culinary uses

Preparation
If pan-frying or roasting, blanch Brussels sprouts for a minute or two in boiling water before refreshing in ice-cold water. This reduces any bitter notes and enhances their natural sweetness.

Dishes
Even if you find sprouts distasteful, give home-grown heirloom varieties a chance, since some are much sweeter and less intense than the standard supermarket type. These multi-headed cabbages perfectly accompany richly flavoured, gamey meats, such as venison, partridge, and pheasant. Their distinctively tangy flavour is reminiscent of the frost-bitten months, making hearty meals feel that little more wholesome. *Spruitjesstamppot* is a beloved Dutch dish typically enjoyed in the winter, in which Brussels sprouts and potatoes are boiled and mashed with butter and milk until smooth and creamy. Many versions call for a topping of crispy pork lardons, smoked sausage, and a few fried sprouts; apples and a touch of nutmeg can also be included for a fruitier hit and to pair perfectly with the pork. But the flavour of Brussels sprouts is far more versatile than you might think; their bitter edge works wonders when they are roasted

with spices and seasonings or dressed with hot sauces, as in the Chinese-inspired *kung pao* sprouts.

Growing

Propagation
Brussels sprouts are big, broad plants that can take up valuable growing space if they are sown too early in the season. Sow the seeds in the spring, to be planted out once beds become available in early summer. Roughly three weeks after sprouting, the seedlings can be transplanted into 7–9cm (3–4in) pots to continue growing for a few weeks. This helps the plants to bulk up and allows other crops to finish growing and vacate the vegetable beds. Spacing the plants generously, use a trowel to make a planting hole and bury the stem deeply to provide support while they establish.

Not every human likes Brussels sprouts, but pests certainly do; for an unblemished harvest, protect the plants with mesh or netting.

Aftercare

Water the young plants in thoroughly and keep a close eye on moisture levels as they grow, giving them a good drink regularly until they are established, since summer weather is often dry. Additional watering may be needed in the autumn if there is little rain.

Like all brassicas, Brussels sprouts must be covered with a layer of mesh or netting to protect them from pests. Towards the end of summer, support tall varieties or any on windy and exposed sites using a solid stake or a few thick bamboo canes. Maintain good housekeeping, removing any dead or yellowing leaves to discourage a slug feeding frenzy.

Plant problems

Aphids, birds, cabbage root fly, caterpillars, flea beetle, slugs and snails (see pages 49–51)

Harvesting

For early varieties, harvesting usually begins in mid-autumn, while later types start producing several weeks or even months later and are hardy enough to continue cropping into the spring; these later harvests are much sweeter, once the sprouts have been seasoned with a frost. Because sprouts mature from the bottom up, they should be cropped in this fashion, by removing the lower, fully ripe ones first. However, the lowest sprouts that emerge are often much smaller and rarely develop fully. Once plump and dense, sprouts can be cropped weekly either by pushing them down to snap them off, or by using a knife to slice them off cleanly. If any sprouts are blown and produce leafy, open heads rather than tight, dense buttons, harvest these promptly and eat them first. Once the plants have finished producing, a second bounty can be cropped in the form of the luxuriant, leafy crown, also known as the sprout top. Many growers and chefs agree that this is one of the tastiest leaves around, providing a flavour reminiscent of cabbagy spring greens and a suggestion of Brussels sprouts.

Storage

Sprouts store well for a few weeks when kept in brown paper bags in a frost-free shed, other outbuilding, or fridge.

Keep the plants well watered as the tiny buds start to swell.

Growing at a glance

Sow Late spring, 6–30°C (43–86°F)

Plant out Early–midsummer

Spacing 60–75cm (24–30in)

Harvest Mid-autumn–late winter

'Bedford Fillbasket' A famous English variety that is true to its name, often producing the densest, most enormous sprouts in the patch. A favourite among gardeners for years thanks to its robust nature and heavy yield, it can be harvested from the early autumn and continue into the new year.

'Catskill' Harris Seeds unveiled this variety in 1941, cultivated meticulously by the New Yorker Arthur White using a hand-picked selection from his personal collection of the variety 'Long Island Improved' (see below). It is compact in stature and yields abundant dainty but delicious sprouts.

'Evesham Special' An old British sprout from the market town of Evesham, in the rolling countryside of Worcestershire in the English Midlands. This is a desirable variety that yields a bounty of medium-sized, noticeably sweet, crisp sprouts that ripen early in the season and continue until Christmas. The plant is short and compact, well suited to exposed sites and challenging climates.

'Long Island Improved' Introduced to the United States by French settlers in the 1890s, this rapidly became the favoured cultivar in commercial agriculture before the advent of modern F1 hybrids. Thanks to its delicious taste, tender texture, and exceptional quality, it has become a household name for gardeners across the United States. A semi-dwarf type that is highly resistant to pests, diseases, and poor weather, it produces a bounty of dense sprouts.

'Red Rubine' This remarkable, vivid purple sprout captivates the eye in the garden and the taste buds on the plate. Its flavour is sweet and delightful, reminiscent of red cabbage. Historical accounts suggest that red sprouts have been cultivated since the 1930s, while this specific variety is thought to have been introduced in the 1940s or 50s.

'Roodnerf' An esteemed variety that has earned a reputation for being one of the best heritage sprout varieties still available. Bred in the Netherlands, it has a tall stature that allows it to produce an abundance of tight, medium-sized, sweet sprouts. 'Roodnerf' is known for its remarkable resistance to pests and diseases, making it a favoured choice among gardeners who want to ensure their crops remain healthy and abundant, with little input.

'Seven Hills' A rare English heirloom that was until recently on the verge of extinction, this is a short, compact variety that produces small, dense sprouts bursting with flavour. However, owing to limited or poorly maintained seed stock over the years, this cultivar can be unreliable.

'Wroxton' Developed by the green-fingered Mr Findlay, Lord North's head gardener at Wroxton Abbey, Oxfordshire, in the 1880s. Although introduced as a dwarf species, these plants have been known to grow to an impressive height of 1m (3ft). Robust and resilient, 'Wroxton' produces big, broad sprouts.

"

The Brussels sprout brings an earthy, wholesome touch to the table.

Four Acre Farm in Ringwood, Hampshire, is being slowly converted by Kate Forrester and Mollie Taylor with an emphasis on habitat. Having this natural meadow on the doorstep brings huge wildlife benefits to my no-dig garden on the site.

Cabbage

Brassica oleracea var. *capitata*

Also known as Chou, Karanb, Zele

These sweet-tasting big-leafed brassicas are majestic as they grow slowly and gracefully in the patch. They require love, care, patience, and attention to detail, but are fulfilling and gratifying to cultivate. Cabbages are also a cunning and creative crop in the kitchen, with a cracking flavour and brilliant bite whether cooked, raw, or fermented.

History

Cabbages were probably domesticated thousands of years ago along Europe's Mediterranean coastlines, although there is some evidence that they had been grown in China and Asia much earlier. The nomadic peoples of Mongolia and China are thought to have discovered the process of fermenting cabbage to preserve it. That also enhanced its nutritional value, making it an essential source of sustenance. This early form of sauerkraut was adopted throughout ancient China and was an important part of the diet of labourers constructing the Great Wall in the first millennium BCE. Conquering Hun and Mongol cavalcades may also have brought pickled cabbage to Europe.

The ancient Greeks called cabbage *krambe*, while the Romans knew it as *brassica*. Cato the Elder, a celebrated Roman statesman, writer, and public speaker of the second century BCE, was a true cabbage connoisseur. He promoted not only the habit of eating plenty of it, but also that of sipping on a cup of urine from those whose diet was high in the leaves. In the first century CE Pliny the Elder documented seven distinct varieties of cabbage that were farmed throughout the empire.

Despite cabbage's roots in the Mediterranean and Asia, the Celtic people of northwestern Europe acquired such a deep knowledge of it that the Roman name for it actually came from the Celtic *bresic*. It is possible that the Celts played a more significant role than the Romans in its spread. Older types of cabbage formed partial heads, rather than the dense, round heads we are familiar with today; it is thought that these developed in colder parts of Europe. The round-headed cabbage was first documented in England in the fourteenth century, while the crinkly savoy varieties were developed in the sixteenth century in the Alpine region once ruled by the Italian house of Savoy.

" The wide variety of cabbages brings exciting opportunities for chefs.

An old wives' tale in medieval times was that boiled red cabbage could tell the gender of a foetus. The mother's urine was mixed with the liquor of boiled cabbage; a purple colour indicated that the baby was a girl, while pinky-red was believed to show a boy. The age-old French saying "*Mon petit chou*" ("my little cabbage") conveys love and admiration, and throughout the country, postcards and memorabilia are decorated with cabbage-patch babies. Meanwhile, an old Irish proverb, "No use boiling your cabbage twice," is a reminder that it is unproductive to regret and dwell on one's mistakes.

Culinary uses

Preparation

I'm not a fan of soggy cabbage and believe it's best cooked like pasta: al dente, soft, and succulent, with a little bite. Don't throw away the outer leaves, particularly those of the savoy – they can be used as the casing for *holishkes* (see overleaf).

Dishes

For some, cabbage revives memories of rancid school dinners or Grandma's overboiled Sunday roast. However, there are countless ways to enjoy this versatile vegetable. The tender, sweet leaves

'Sapporo Taikyu' is one of the largest varieties, a truly impressive cabbage with a multitude of uses in the kitchen.

'Kalibos' (top left, bottom right) and
'Rouge Tête Noire'

enhance many dishes, from sour ferments and creamy coleslaws to savoury spiced braises and stir-fries.

Cabbage is front and centre of Irish national cuisine. An iconic St Patrick's Day celebration dish features slow-boiled bacon and cabbage cooked in the ham liquor, giving it a rich, meaty flavour. Another Irish cabbage feast is colcannon, which is similar to the Brits' prized bubble and squeak. Colcannon is creamed mashed potato loaded with cabbage and butter, perhaps with the addition of spring onions or leeks. Bubble and squeak, on the other hand, is a mixture of leftover vegetables, including cabbage, traditionally saved from a Sunday roast then mashed and fried to create a crispy, caramelized crust.

The wide variety of cabbages brings exciting opportunities for chefs. Robust red-heads require longer cooking and are suited to braising with earthy spices and citrus for a sweet-and-sour kick. The small pointed hispi or sweetheart types can be grilled, fried, or roasted in halves, and maintain their shape, flavour, and texture even after long cooking. The wrinkled savoy absorbs sauces, and its texture is perfect for the traditional Jewish dish *holishkes* (stuffed cabbage leaves). The

Growing at a glance

Spring (overwintering) cabbages
Sow Late summer, 6–30°C (43–86°F)
Plant out Early autumn **Spacing** 20cm (8in) (spring greens)/30–35cm (12–14in) (hearts)
Harvest Late winter–late spring

Summer cabbages
Sow Early–mid-spring, 6–30°C (43–86°F)
Plant out Mid–late spring **Spacing** 35cm (14in)
Harvest Late summer–early autumn

Autumn cabbages
Sow Mid–late spring, 6–30°C (43–86°F)
Plant out Late spring–early summer **Spacing** 40–50cm (16–20in) **Harvest** Mid–late autumn

Winter cabbages
Sow Late spring–early summer, 6–30°C (43–86°F) **Plant out** Midsummer **Spacing** 50–60cm (20–24in) **Harvest** Late autumn–late winter

whole leaves are boiled briefly so that they can be folded and stuffed with meats and spices, then carefully wrapped before being braised in a rich, tangy tomato sauce.

Growing
Propagation

The various cabbages are ready at different times, so with careful planning you can grow cabbage all year. Spring cabbages form small heads and can be sown in late summer for overwintering. Summer cabbages are bred to withstand heat and are ready for harvest at the height of the season. Autumn cabbages can be stored for use in the winter, and winter cabbages provide a valuable, long-storing crop that can withstand harsh weather.

Brassicas grow tall and leggy quickly, so keep the seedlings in a bright location. Pot them on into 7cm (3in) pots two weeks after germination, burying the stem deeply if the plants have grown spindly. Allow them to continue growing for two or three weeks to give the plant more room to bulk up before being planted out, which is helpful if slugs are a problem in your garden. It's always a good idea to keep a few spare seedlings, since the soft, succulent leaves of young cabbage plants are particularly prone to slug onslaught.

Four or five weeks after germination, the cabbage seedlings are ready for planting out. Bury the stems as deeply as possible to provide extra support.

Aftercare

Brassicas rarely require extra watering, but summer and autumn varieties may need a deep drink if the weather is dry as their hearts form. They are vulnerable to pests, so keep a close eye and cover them with mesh or fine netting from seedling to harvest. Ensure that none of the foliage touches the net, or the cabbage white butterfly will still lay eggs. Summer cabbages planted out early in the year require additional protection and should be covered with horticultural fleece until May, to safeguard them from wind, cold weather, and flea beetles. Remain cautious with later unprotected sowings growing in a shed, polytunnel, or greenhouse, since butterflies will quickly sniff them out.

Plant problems

Aphids, cabbage root fly, cabbage white caterpillars, mildew, pigeons, rabbits, slugs and snails (see pages 49–51)

Harvesting

Picking cabbage at its most perfect requires trial and error. Spring types can be picked as spring greens in late winter or early spring or left to form a heart, but must be harvested while still creamy green, before they bolt. Summer cabbages should be harvested when their heads are firm; if left too long they are susceptible to insect damage, and their sweet flavour and tender texture deteriorate in hot weather.

Autumn types should be picked when their heads are substantial and dense; they will happily sit in the ground for weeks in their prime. Winter cabbages, the hardiest of all, will stay in optimum condition in the soil for several months. To harvest, use a sharp knife or small hand saw to cut the thick stem at soil level. Cut as low as possible, since brassicas can sometimes resprout and grow from the stump. Harvest autumn and winter types as late as possible if you plan to store them.

Storage

Keep autumn and winter cabbages in a cool, frost-free shed or other outbuilding for several months. Remove any big leaves and check thoroughly for slugs. Don't be disheartened if the outer leaves go mouldy; once a few layers are peeled back, there should be a pristine head hiding inside. Spring and summer types should be eaten within a few days of harvest.

A bounty of cabbages of various types will provide a long-lasting harvest.

Green

'Bacalan de Rennes' (spring/summer) This exceptional French heirloom variety with elegant oxheart-shaped pointed heads of wavy foliage was first cultivated in the early nineteenth century in Brittany, northern France, where it thrives in the mild coastal climate. Its green heads are renowned for their early maturity, delectable flavour, and delightful texture.

'Belarusian 455' (winter) A flat-headed variety from the Belarus–Poland border, this cabbage was documented in the Russian State Register of Plant Breeding in 1943, but is believed to be much older, bred from another Belarusian heirloom. It stores brilliantly and is impeccably cold-hardy, capable of being grown in any part of Russia. Very pale, tightly packed leaves that are tender and sweet.

'Brunswick' (autumn) An old German heirloom variety producing big, flat, heavy heads worthy of the show bench. Hardy, reliable, and uniform, it grows and thrives in a range of climates and soils, and is a choice cabbage for sauerkraut.

'Christmas Drumhead' (late autumn) This excellent compact heirloom variety from 1903, ideal for small gardens, produces solid, flat heads. The name is deceptive, since this is a late autumn-harvesting type, but it can sit in the ground until December. The leaves are tightly packed and soft, like those of butterhead lettuce, making it the perfect Christmas treat. Sadly, it is becoming increasingly difficult to find.

'Danish Ballhead' (autumn) This variety has brilliant storage potential, and keeps for extended periods after harvest. Dutch colonists developed it in the fifteenth century on the Danish island of Amager, east of Copenhagen. It has very tight, crisp heads with a delightfully mild, sweet taste and soft texture.

'Early Copenhagen Market' (spring/summer) A quick-maturing compact cabbage with a large, round head of blue-green foliage, developed by the Danish seed outlet Hjalmar Hartman & Co. of Copenhagen in the early twentieth century. The cabbage soon became popular among small farmers and greengrocers owing to its exquisitely sweet taste and the fact that it looks so handsome on display at market.

'Early Durham' (spring/summer) An old English heirloom variety that produces firm, pointed, well-flavoured hearts on compact plants. They are great for planting densely to overwinter, since they produce the most delicious spring greens early in the year. In the 1930s this variety was known as York cabbage, but it underwent a name change for a mysterious reason that remains unknown.

'Early Jersey Wakefield' (spring/summer) This rapidly growing cone-shaped cabbage is ready for harvest in early summer but hardy enough to be overwintered for spring picking. It is perfect for people with limited space, being more compact than many cabbages. The variety has some heritage in the UK but gained popularity in the US during the 1850s after being grown by Francis Brill and his neighbours in Jersey City. The cabbage was considered a natural cross between the 'Wakefield' cabbage from England and another cultivar that was commercially farmed nearby.

'Filderkraut' (autumn) An ancient, mammoth pointed cabbage with incredibly tender, deliciously sweet leaves, this is perfect for sauerkraut. According to records, monks in the small town of Denkendorf near Stuttgart, Germany, have cultivated it for 500 years, prizing it for its robustness, hardiness, and versatility in the kitchen. It is held in such high esteem in Germany that every October the nearby town of Leinfelden-Echterdingen holds a Filderkraut Fest in honour of its luscious leaves.

'Glory of Enkhuizen' (autumn) An excellent crisp, tender cabbage with tightly layered, medium-sized round heads. It was developed in the late nineteenth century by crossing two old German types ('Glückstadter' and 'Ditmarscher') and released in 1902 by the not snappily named Dutch seed company NV Sluis en Groot's Koninklijke Zaadteelt en Zaadhandel te Enkhuizen.

'Late Flat Dutch' (winter) This variety, which originated in the Netherlands in the 1840s, took American growers by storm after seeds arrived in the United States with European settlers. Touted by cabbage connoisseurs as one of the tenderest and tastiest winter types, it has large, blue-green, flattened heads tightly packed with dense layers of golden and white leaves.

'Sapporo Taikyu' (winter) Perhaps the world's most enormous cabbage, capable of growing to 20kg (45lb) under the right conditions, this Japanese heirloom variety has been documented since the nineteenth century and is grown exclusively on Hokkaido, Japan's northernmost island. It is an essential ingredient in the region's preserved foods, such as *nishin-zuke* (pickled herring and vegetables) and *izushi* (a dish made by pickling fish with rice and vegetables). This tender cabbage is also used in other popular Hokkaido dishes, such as soups, stews, and hotpots.

'Wheelers Imperial' (spring/summer) A long, pointed cabbage bred by George Wheeler of Warminster, Wiltshire, in the early to mid-nineteenth century. It thrives in cold and can be harvested in late winter for tender spring greens, or left to form a dense head. Also resilient to warm weather.

Red

'Kalibos' (autumn) A perfectly pointed cabbage developed in the former Russian Empire, in what is now Belarus, during the nineteenth century. Hardy, robust, and very pretty.

'Mammoth Red Rock' (winter) An enormous, hearty, rich red heirloom producing tight, flat, round heads that taste wonderful and are brilliant for storing through the winter. Perfect for pickling.

'Rouge Tête Noire' (late summer/early autumn) A reliable old French variety with a small, dense, deep purple, globe-shaped head that matures early.

Savoy

'D'Aubervilliers' (autumn/ winter) An old, gigantic drumhead savoy that originated on the outskirts of Paris and became popular in the early twentieth century. Its crinkly, compact heads are mild and tender.

'Des Vertus' (winter) An old French flattened-head savoy variety that has been grown since the nineteenth century, this is a deeply wrinkled, dark blueish-green cabbage that is extremely frost-hardy.

'Di Piacenza' (winter) Hailing from the picture-perfect region of Piacenza in northern Italy, this remarkable variety is exceptionally hardy. The leaves are a vibrant green and deeply wrinkled, forming dense, round heads. Some people regard this as the most delicious of all savoys.

'Ormskirk' (winter) A reliable, resilient, hardy old English heritage variety developed in 1899 and grown in the market town of Ormskirk, Lancashire. It has a pale green heart and there is an almost blue tinge to the larger leaves.

'Testa di Ferro' (autumn) A prized, quick-to-mature Italian strain that is also known by the English version of its Italian name, 'Ironhead Savoy'. The soft, tender, pale green, dainty round heads are highly sought-after throughout Italy.

'Violaceo di Verona' (winter) An exquisitely beautiful bicoloured savoy with rich green leaves dappled and splashed with purple, darkening after a frost. It originated in the region around Verona in northern Italy centuries ago from a cross between a savoy and another type of cabbage, and is tolerant of both heat and cold.

An array of cabbages (clockwise from top left) 'Ormskirk', 'Early Jersey Wakefield', 'Glory of Enkhuizen', and 'Testa di Ferro'

'Variegata di
Castelfranco'

Chicory

Cichorium intybus var. *foliosum*

Also known as Endive, Italian chicory, Radicchio

Bitter, tangy chicory is a staple throughout Italy, yet less common elsewhere. Many varieties tolerate frost and provide an abundance of nutrient-rich leaves when other crops are scarce. It is a fashionista in looks, from mottled, variegated globes in yellow, pale green, and burgundy, to ruby red rosettes and long, tall, pointed emerald-green heads.

History

Chicory developed from a wild species, a flowering plant in the daisy family that humans have used as food for centuries. Pliny the Elder recorded its ability to purify the blood and promote sleep. It contains various beneficial compounds, such as inulin (which acts as a prebiotic and helps digestion), antioxidants, vitamins, and minerals, making it a valuable addition to the diet.

The cultivated variety of chicory was developed and grown in the mountainous Veneto region in northern Italy. It quickly became an esteemed ingredient there, and can be seen in sixteenth-century artworks, including those by the painter Leandro Bassano. Legend tells of the plant first arriving in northern Italy via birds that flew overhead and dropped the seeds into a churchyard, luckily falling into the hands of monks, who have cultivated and protected them ever since.

In the 1860s, the Belgian botanist Francesco Van den Borre introduced to the Veneto the method of blanching chicory, which he had developed for the pale-leafed Belgian endive. This technique deprives the plant of light, causing its leaves to turn white and become less bitter. Many of today's named varieties were developed in the early twentieth century by farmers across northern Italy.

Culinary uses

Preparation

Bring wilted leaves back to life by refreshing them in a bowl of ice-cold water for an hour or so.

Dishes

Chicory is often considered a salad crop, and its crisp, crunchy, tangy leaves do work exceptionally well when dressed with sweet balsamic vinegar. Yet its true culinary beauty unfolds when it is cooked. It can be sautéed, grilled, roasted, or even braised in stock or ale with aromatic additions, such as fennel, lemon, and thyme. Served on crusty sourdough bread and topped with melted cheese – a strong variety, such as Gorgonzola or Comté – it works tremendously as a tasty lunch or a simple but effective dinner-party starter. The spicy, bitter notes of the leaves have found their way into pasta dishes throughout northern Italy. A creamy sauce is often seasoned with authentic *salsiccia* sausage or dry-cured speck to make an eloquent combination of sweet, bitter, and fatty flavours. Quartered or halved, chicory hearts are robust enough to withstand the intensity of flames from a hot grill, and will take on a delectable smoky flavour. When they are grilled or roasted, their succulent texture and rich bitterness harmonize brilliantly with the sweet-and-sour tang of *agrodolce*, a thick, glossy, sugary, yet tart Sicilian sauce made with dried fruit and nuts, red-wine vinegar, honey, and aromatics.

When to harvest

Different varieties of chicory have different shapes, leaf densities, and growing periods, so keep a close eye on the plants and ensure that none ends up spoiling by rotting in the ground. If you live in an area of harsh winters, consider harvesting and storing the heads, rather than leaving them to grow in the vegetable patch.

Growing at a glance

Sow Summer, 15–25°C (60–77°F)

Plant out Late summer–early autumn

Spacing 30cm (12in)

Harvest Autumn–winter

Growing

Propagation

This hardy, robust, pest-resistant cool-season crop performs best when grown in the autumn and winter, which means sowing over the summer. If sown in the spring, it may bolt before it has the chance to bulk up and produce a dense, leafy head. Broadcast-sow the seed and prick out into cells when the seedlings are big enough to handle. Allow the plants to continue growing for a further four weeks before planting them out in the garden.

Aftercare

The weather is often dry at this time of year, so monitor moisture and water generously until the plants are established. Chicory is a slow, steady grower, and the leafy crowns begin to bulk up with the arrival of autumn rains and lower temperatures. The heads can withstand cold, but some varieties will spoil if hit with a heavy or prolonged freeze. While chicory can be cultivated in the garden to full maturity without blanching, the process can be a fun job for winter. Such varieties as 'Rossa di Treviso (Tardiva)' and the popular 'Witloof' are often forced to produce sweeter, less bitter leaves in complete darkness. The easiest way to blanch chicory is by covering the plants with a bucket for a minimum of two weeks before harvesting. It is also possible to dig up the plants with a section of the root attached; the leafy head is removed, and the roots replanted in pots or crates of compost and left indoors in complete darkness to produce "chicons", the blanched hearts.

Plant problems

Aphids, mildew, slugs and snails (see pages 49–51)

Harvesting

Cropping begins in mid-autumn for early varieties, while late types are ready for picking in late autumn. The plants can tolerate temperatures down to about -5°C (23°F), so will survive well in the ground throughout the winter in milder regions, and can be harvested until late winter, when the plants begin to bolt. To harvest, use a sharp knife to slice off whole heads just above the soil surface. The outer leaves may look discoloured and shrivelled, but they can be pulled away to reveal the tender, luxurious heart beneath.

Storage

Whole heads of chicory store remarkably well, often staying fresh for five weeks or more when kept in a cool, frost-free shed or other outbuilding. They will keep for several weeks in the crisper drawer of the fridge.

The outer leaves can be pulled away to reveal the tender, luxurious heart beneath.

'Rossa di Chioggia' (overleaf, left)
and 'Pan di Zucchero' (overleaf, right)

Recommended varieties

'Orchidea Rossa' A stunning semi-open-headed type that looks like a beautiful flower, its magnificent leaves maroon with a glossy sheen. It matures quickly, and can be harvested as cut-and-come-again or as whole heads.

'Pan di Zucchero' These large, leafy green heads are much sweeter and less bitter than those of other varieties, hence the name, Italian for "sugarloaf". It is a rapid grower, yielding long, prominent hearts that should be harvested before heavy frosts.

'Puntarelle' Resembling a cluster of dandelion or rocket leaves, this unusual-looking, early-maturing variety is grown widely across the central Italian region of Lazio for its long, hollow stems, an essential ingredient in the kitchens of Rome today. One of the most popular uses for this crop is for *puntarelle alla romana*, a potent yet pleasantly full-flavoured salad dressed with garlic, anchovies, vinegar, and olive oil.

'Rossa di Chioggia' A fast-maturing variety that produces tight, round purple heads with snow-white veins. Crisp, crunchy, and subtly flavoured, it is an excellent choice for market gardeners because it is reliable, quick, and easy to grow.

'Rossa di Treviso (Tardiva)' A treasure in the world of chicory, this is a forcing type with elongated, pointed maroon heads that mature late and become even darker purple and glossier after being seasoned with frost.

'Variegata di Castelfranco' A true ornamental beauty that adds a little *je ne sais quoi* to the winter salad patch. The sweet custard-yellow leaves are speckled with wine-red flecks, and the plants form a wide-open rosette with tight, dense heads in the middle. This is one of the best flavoured of all varieties, and matures late.

'Variegata di Chioggia' With crisp, golden-yellow globes sprinkled with pink splashes, this ornate variety is among the hardiest and the latest to mature, ready for picking in the cold of late winter and standing well into early spring. Produces compact, dense heads.

Collard Greens

Brassica oleracea var. *viridis*

Also known as Colewart, Tree cabbage

Intensely flavoured with a subtle, bitter note, and a powerhouse of nutrients, collards are steeped in history. They have a lot to offer, from glossy, thick leaves similar to those of Swiss chard, to deep blue foliage with alluring, prominent purple stems, or the palest of green leaves that sometimes look yellow.

History

Collard greens are one of the oldest brassicas, springing from the sandy soils of the Mediterranean before wending their way into North Africa. Many brassicas were carried along the North African salt trade route from Morocco to Timbuktu during the Middle Ages, initially intended to sustain traders, but quickly becoming lucrative market crops in the Sahel. African societies had a strong connection with the consumption of farmed or foraged greens, and the leaves of bombax, okra, and African eggplant were a staple, often cooked with onions, tomatoes, and spices to create nutritious and delicious dishes. As European slave forts (trading posts) emerged in Africa, it became necessary to grow food to sustain those occupying them. Growing cabbages and turnips resulted in only limited success, but collard greens proved more fruitful and are mentioned frequently in letters and records discussing the forts and their kitchen gardens. From then on, the seeds of collard greens spread through various African countries.

On being taken forcefully to America, enslaved Africans cultivated collard greens to supplement their measly rations. Plantation owners would allocate "provision grounds" for the cultivation of such crops as sweet potatoes, greens, and yam, although these were often in areas of poor soil and far from the Africans' living quarters. The enslaved people slow-cooked collard greens with leftover scraps of meat from the plantation kitchen. The cooking

A freshly harvested selection of collard greens is a joy of the vegetable patch.

broth, known as "potlikker", was a crucial source of nutrients and provided a rich, savoury flavour.

Collards became an integral and important food for African Americans, and they have bloomed into a noteworthy representation of the rich cultural heritage of Southern and African-American communities. Beyond being a staple food in these regions, collard greens have also been recognized as a symbol of resilience, resourcefulness, and creativity in the face of adversity. Thelonious Monk – one of the most influential jazz pianists and composers of the twentieth century – displayed a fresh collard leaf in his lapel during his lively performances at jazz clubs in New York City, as a nod to his Southern roots. The leaf was a symbol of his heritage and a way to connect with the predominantly African-American audience who had migrated from the rural South to the urban North. Over the years, collard-green festivals have become an integral celebration of African-American culture, organized in various states to celebrate the community's rich and diverse heritage.

The leaves can be picked when young, for a tender feast, or left to mature, when they become robust and juicy.

Culinary uses

Preparation
Remove the rigid, tough central stem by slicing along either side of the stalk, or strip it off by hand. The leaves can then be stacked in a pile, rolled, and easily sliced crosswise into ribbons.

Dishes
With a subtle bitterness, less pronounced in taste than cabbage but sweeter than kale, collards are thick and sturdy. That makes them ideal for slow-cooking in braises, soups, and stews, and they release a rich and earthy flavour that's sure to satisfy, as in the delightful Turkish soup *karalahana çorbası*. One of the most significant dishes in the cuisine of the Southern United States is eaten for the New Year's Day celebrations, and is said to bring good fortune; traditionally made up of "mixed greens", black-eyed peas, and smoked meat, and served with cornbread to soak up the potlikker, it is a soul-food classic.

Throughout East Africa, *sukuma wiki* (Swahili for "stretch the week") is a popular dish that can be relied on to provide a nutritious and filling meal, even when supplies are scarce. Made from a combination of leafy greens, tomatoes, onions, and spices, it is easy to prepare and offers a delicious taste of East African cuisine. It is often served with *sima* or *ugali*, which is similar to polenta and a staple food throughout the region. *Feijoada*, meanwhile – the national dish of Brazil – blends African, European, and Indigenous American influences in a hearty, wholesome, slow-cooked stew that is typically made with black beans, a variety of meat, such as beef, pork, and sausage, and a zingy blend of spices. One of the critical components of *feijoada* is a side dish of collards, which provides a refreshing contrast to the rich, meaty stew.

> **Collard greens have been recognized as a symbol of resilience and resourcefulness.**

Growing
Propagation

A lover of cool weather, collards are robust and resilient but – like all brassicas – require love and attention. First sowings can be made in early or mid-spring to supply delicious greens until the summer, while later sowings should be made in the summer for autumn and overwintering, to continue cropping into the following year. Brassicas quickly grow tall and leggy if they get insufficient light, so keep the seed trays in a bright, frost-free location. Roughly three weeks after germination, the seedlings can be transplanted into the garden, but more often than not, I pot mine on into 7–9cm (3–4in) pots to continue growing for two or three weeks before transplanting; this produces more robust seedlings that are better prepared to withstand a slug attack.

Space the seedlings according to the way you plan to harvest the crop: 10cm (4in) apart for baby greens to be picked regularly; 25–35cm (10–14in) for cutting when half-grown, much like spring greens (see page 196); and up to 1m (3ft) to grow colossal collards. Bury the seedlings' roots deeply to provide these tall-growing brassicas with support as they mature.

Aftercare

Keep a close eye on moisture levels and water accordingly until the plants have established; after their roots have become entrenched in the soil, collards rarely need additional watering in a temperate climate, except during prolonged dry spells. Cover the young seedlings with mesh or horticultural fleece to safeguard them from insects and birds and, for early plantings, bad weather; once they are growing strongly, switch the covering to netting, which will deter ravenous pigeons

Inspect the rows as you pick, to look out for yellowing or decaying leaves that might encourage slugs and snails.

For a beautifully fresh cut-and-come-again crop, pull the lowest leaves individually as you need them.

from munching on the crop and cabbage-white butterflies from laying eggs. Remove yellowing lower leaves as the plant grows.

Plant problems
Aphids, caterpillars, flea beetle, mildew, pigeons, rabbits, slugs and snails (see pages 49–51)

Harvesting
Collards can be harvested in a cut-and-come-again manner by snapping off the lower leaves where they meet the central stalk, pushing them down to make a clean break. When picked in this way, collards will grow tall and produce a thick trunk with the primary growth confined to the top, much like kale; regular picking encourages new growth and keeps the plants cropping for longer. Alternatively, harvest entire plants when they are half grown (similar to spring greens) or fully grown.

Growing at a glance
Sow Early spring–midsummer, 6–30°C (43–86°F)

Plant out Late spring–early autumn

Spacing 10–100cm (4–39in)

Harvest Early summer–late winter

'Ellen Felton Dark' The Felton family from Eure, North Carolina, has preserved this variety of collards since 1935. Harrell Felton acquired the seeds from his mother, Ellen, who first cultivated the crop in Beaufort County. In 2003 the Feltons gave seeds to Dr Edward Davis, who was collecting heritage strains for preservation. It has large green leaves with brilliant white veins and stems bursting with sweet, fruity flavours. Hardy and resistant to frost.

'Georgia Southern' Introduced in 1885, this variety is robust and slow to bolt, making it ideal for warm climates. It is versatile, however, being also resistant to light frost. Its large, loose heads are packed with crinkled blue-green leaves.

'Green Glaze' One of the oldest known cultivars available, this produces glorious waxy leaves with a mirror-like sheen similar to spinach or chard. The thick, glossy leaves are delicious, boast some of the best resistance to pests, and cope well with warm weather.

'Miss Annie Pearl Counselman' Named in honour of a 94-year-old gardener from Clarke County, Alabama, who received seeds of this collard in the 1950s and has grown and stewarded it ever since. In 2012 she gave seeds to Tom Lambard of Mobile, Alabama, and three years later he donated some to Seed Savers Exchange. As a tribute, Lambard requested that the variety be named after her. Sweet and richly flavoured, they have a brilliant texture that is even better after a seasoning from frost.

'Moses Smith Yellow Cabbage Collard' Named after Moses Smith, an African American farmer and seed steward from Scotland Neck, North Carolina. Smith earned a reputation for growing the finest collards in the region and has been saving his seeds carefully since the 1990s, resulting in a highly sought-after strain. The enormous, broad, wavy leaves are a delightful yellowy green with a suggestion of blue on the outer foliage.

'Ole Timey Blue' A dark collard with big, deep blue leaves and rich violet-tinted stems, this bold and beautiful variety was cultivated and cared for by the late Ralph Blackwell of Jasper, Alabama, who was given the seeds by his mother, Ira. She had grown the collard for as long as Ralph could remember, and used the leaves for fermenting. The Blackwell family named it and believed it tasted far superior to other green-leafed collard types, especially after being seasoned by frost.

'Ole Timey Blue'

'Ellen Felton Dark'

Herbs

An essential part of both the vegetable patch and the kitchen, herbs add fragrance, colour, and flavour. The three described here have been chosen for their popularity, variety, and versatility in the kitchen.

Basil
(*Ocimum basilicum*)
Basilico, Herb royale, Reyhan, Vasilikós

The bustling world of basil is far broader than you might think, with hundreds of named cultivars. These soft-leaved aromatic beauties burst with sweet, spicy, floral tones that intrigue the taste buds. Some have a flavour reminiscent of lemon or rich aniseed, while others pack a cinnamon whack or even leave you with a tingling sensation that numbs the throat.

History

Basil and its relatives (see panel, page 217) are native to an area that stretches from tropical Africa through the Middle East to India and Southeast Asia. Basil played a significant role in ancient Egyptian funeral practices, its antibacterial properties and distinctive aroma making it an essential ingredient during embalming for slowing decay and masking the rotting smell. It was also believed to ensure safe passage for the soul to the afterlife. In ancient Greece it was considered a symbol of hatred, yet it also played an essential role in funerary practices. The Greeks believed that basil could offer peace and comfort to the deceased, and would place the herb in the hands of the dead as a final offering. They also crowned basil the king of herbs, as indicated by its name, which derives from vasiliás, "king". According to legend, the third-century Roman empress St Helena discovered basil in the Holy Land, at the foot of the newly rediscovered Cross of Jesus, after she stepped on the plant and released its potent aroma. In the Greek Orthodox Church, basil is blessed and hung in homes to bring health and prosperity.

In Europe in the sixteenth century basil was associated with scorpions, and it was recommended that it be handled with great care. Superstition held that a single basil leaf left under a pot would eventually hatch into a deadly scorpion. Later, in Italy, basil bloomed into a symbol of love. Unmarried women would adorn their hair with fresh sprigs of the fragrant herb to indicate their romantic availability.

Culinary uses

Preparation

Avoid chopping basil with a knife, since it will quickly discolour and lose its appeal. Either tear the leaves gently, moments before serving, or use them whole.

Dishes

Basil has a bossy flavour that is capable of enriching robust savoury dishes. It is adored throughout Italy for its ability to round off tomato sauces with a lively green kick, is used fresh in salads, such as the classic Caprese (with mozzarella and tomatoes), and takes the leading role when blended into *pesto alla Genovese*. Other varieties are a mainstay of cooking throughout Southeast Asia, and these types have a very different flavour from those associated with Mediterranean cuisine. The flavours of Thai cooking, bursting with fresh, aromatic, spicy, and sour notes, work wonderfully with these prominently liquorice-flavoured basils. Persian varieties can be concocted into a delightful and refreshing drink, *reyhan şerbeti* (basil sherbet). This traditional Turkish bevvy is typically made by boiling the leaves in water with honey to create a sweet, tangy syrup, which is mixed with cold water and served over ice.

Growing

Propagation

All basils are sun-lovers and perform best during the warmer months. They are perennial in their native lands, but in temperate climates they are usually grown as annuals. I recommend growing them under cover, especially in places with high

rainfall or cool summers; I grow all mine in the polytunnel as a companion plant with tomatoes (see page 40). The seedlings are very susceptible to damping off. To reduce the risk, use a half-and-half mix of potting compost and sand to create a free-draining medium for germinating seeds, and water very sparingly. Early sowings will need to be kept in the warmth of the house or on a heat mat to germinate. Sow two seeds per cell and thin out the weakest seedling roughly two weeks after germination, or leave the two to plant out as a pair. Plant out once all risk of frost has passed.

It is also easy to propagate new plants by placing freshly harvested stems in clean water until they grow roots, then transplanting them into pots and growing on as required.

Beautiful Persian basil has a complex flavour, combining notes of pepper and spice with citrus.

215

Growing at a glance

Sow Mid-spring–early summer, 18–24°C (64–75°F)

Plant out Early–midsummer

Spacing 20cm (8in)

Harvest Summer–autumn

Aftercare

Keep the new plants well watered; a good soaking twice a week over the summer is better than more frequent, less generous waterings.

Plant problems

Aphids, mould, root rot, slugs and snails (see pages 49–51)

Harvesting

To promote a bushier plant and prevent it from flowering prematurely, harvest frequently from the growing tips of each plant, removing roughly 5–8cm (2–3in). This encourages new side shoots to form. Continuing to gather from the new tops prolongs the plant's life and ensures a steady supply of succulent leaves.

Storage

You can't beat freshly picked basil, but longer stems can be kept fresh in a glass of water for a few days.

Standard basil

African basil (*Basilicum gratissimum*) This one-of-a-kind species from Ghana, known as *nunum*, boasts a unique flavour and aroma that blend basil's familiar taste and scent with a strong essence of oregano. The mildly spicy, supersized, serrated leaves with a slightly fuzzy texture provide a subtle punch of pepper and aniseed, and a sweet earthiness.

'Akoko Mesa' This intense, minty-tasting Ghanaian basil, the name of which means "chicken dance", is essential in poultry dishes, and creates a song and dance of flavours.

'Cinnamon' A dark, glossy green, sweet and spicy basil with a woody undertone unmistakably reminiscent of cinnamon, this is a popular ingredient in Mexican cuisine and is often known as Mexican spice basil.

'Dark Opal' Deeply hued in a luxurious shade of purple, this variety can also be elegantly mottled with mauve. The plantsmen John Scarchuk and Joseph Lent bred it in the 1950s at the University of Connecticut, with aesthetics and flavour in mind.

'Evivi Ntor' The Ewe people of Ghana cultivated this variety as a sacred plant. Its name means "very tasty", and indeed its dainty green leaves are bursting with flavours of hot pepper and floral notes of citrus. A symbol of cultural heritage and tradition, it reached the brink of extinction in the mid-twentieth century, but was made available more widely thanks to the efforts of a passionate Ghanaian seed-saver, Solomon Amuzu, who received the seeds from an 86-year-old Ewe elder who recognized the importance of preserving it.

'Foglie di Lattuga' These mammoth leaves are as large as dinner plates, and the name of the variety, "lettuce leaves" in Italian, is a nod to the sheer size of the sweet, aromatic foliage. The leaves are ideal used as a wrap or base for other ingredients.

Holy basil (*Ocimum sanctum*)

Holy basil is an aromatic perennial shrub in tropical climates and (like other basils) can be grown as an annual in temperate climates. Also known as *tulsi* (Sanskrit for "the incomparable one"). it is believed to have originated in northern India before spreading throughout Asia. It is considered sacred in India and is dedicated to the Hindu god Vishnu and his wife Tulasi, who was believed to be reincarnated as a basil plant when she came to Earth. It is part of the Hindu tradition to bathe the head of a deceased person in tulsi water, and a tulsi leaf is also placed over the heart. It has a light, aromatic scent and distinctive flavour, and the oval leaves with slightly sharpened tips are commonly dried and made into a sacred tea that is believed to encourage positive energy. This holy herb is also used in traditional Ayurvedic medicine to treat various ailments.

Tulsi has immense cultural and spiritual significance in Thailand. It symbolizes purity and protection and so is often grown around Buddhist temples. The leaves, which are rich in essential oils, are a popular ingredient in many of the country's dishes, including curries, stir-fries, and soups. *Pad kee mao* (drunken noodles), for example – a dish so spicy that it should be eaten with an ice-cold beer within reach – consists of extra-wide rice noodles stir-fried with meat, spices, and heaps of holy basil for a much-needed refreshing hit.

'Horapha Nanum' This delicious Thai basil is perfect for curries, braised dishes, and noodles, where its bold and spicy flavour can shine through. It has purple stems and luscious purple-tinted dark green leaves with a spicy hit of liquorice.

'Mrihani' A unique zigzag-edged basil from the tropical island of Pemba in the Zanzibar Archipelago, off the coast of Tanzania. This variety was discovered in 1990 by Richo Cech of Strictly Medicinal Seeds in southern Oregon during a visit to the northern part of the island, when he met a local farmer who was growing the crop. The alluring fragrance of this basil is reminiscent of a floral perfume.

'Mrs Burns' Lemon' A truly exceptional sweet basil with an unusual citrusy flavour. This heirloom has been meticulously cultivated since the 1920s and was initially grown by one Mrs Clifton of Carlsbad, New Mexico. She gave seed to the organic gardener Janet Burns, who introduced this incredibly aromatic herb more widely in 1939.

'Napoletano' Full of flavour, easy to grow, and prized in Italian cuisine, this large, crinkly-leafed basil is a staple in the kitchens of Naples, where – as the name suggests – it originated.

Persian basil (*reyhan*) A fantastic Middle Eastern basil with a peppery hit like star anise, balanced with a citrusy zing. This variety is a staple ingredient of the traditional Iranian dish *sabzi khordan*, a platter of fresh herbs, radishes, and sheep's cheese. This is certainly one of the prettiest basils, with glorious green leaves blushed violet.

'Sweet Genovese' This is the most popular variety of sweet basil in the world. Developed in Italy, it reliably produces extremely aromatic green leaves that are perfect for pesto and pasta sauces.

'Verde a Piccole Foglie' A small, dainty basil that packs a serious whack of flavour. It forms a compact, dense, bushy shrub covered in tiny leaves.

Holy basil

'Kapoor' This variety is used widely in Southeast Asian cuisine, where it is known as *kaphrao*, *bai gkaprow*, or Thai holy basil – not to be confused with Thai basil varieties, such as 'Horapha Nanum' (see left). 'Kapoor' has a unique peppery, clove-like flavour and a mouth-numbing effect similar to that of Sichuan pepper.

'Krishna' Sometimes known as "Shyama tulsi", these vibrant, purple-hued leaves and dark stems have a crisp, peppery taste that sets them apart from other varieties of tulsi. Although it is grown in various parts of India, it is scarcer than the green varieties.

'Rama' Also known as "Lakshmi tulsi", this emerald-green leaf is famous for its soothing, mellow flavour. Brilliant brewed into tea.

'Mrs Burns' Lemon'

Lemongrass
(*Cymbopogon* spp.)
Citronella grass, Malabar grass, Silky heads

A fragrant plant with an irresistible flavour, lemongrass is a staple in Asia, an essential part of many soups, stews, curries, salads, and tea. Versatile and delicious, it can be used in both savoury and sweet dishes.

History

Lemongrass has been cultivated in its native Asia for thousands of years for use in cooking and medicine. Through the slave trade in the late eighteenth century it reached Jamaica, where it is used to counteract the effects of fever and improve dental health. In some cultures, lemongrass was believed to have potent magical properties. In North America, enslaved African people who practised the folk magic known as Conjure or Hoodoo used the leaves to make potions that they believed would protect against evil and bring good luck in love.

Culinary uses

Preparation

Trim the base of the stalk and remove the hard outer layers. For soups and sauces, use the whole stalk, first crushing it with a rolling pin or other heavy object to release the oils. For a finer, smoother, more flavoursome curry paste, cut the stalk into very thin slices and pound with a pestle and mortar to shorten the fibres.

Dishes

The tender young leaves can be eaten raw – chopped and added to salads – or used as a garnish. They're also delicious thrown at the last minute into stir-fries or curries, adding a fresh, fragrant kick, and can be used dried in teas and soups. The chunky stalks are great for flavouring sauces. Lemongrass adds a citrus zing to many Southeast Asian dishes, including Thai curries and *rendang*, an explosively flavourful, slow-cooked dry beef curry from Sumatra in Indonesia.

Lemongrass is also great in desserts. One of my go-to summer puds is a creamy coconut-milk panna cotta infused with lemongrass. This Italian–Asian mash-up is made extra aromatic by adding makrut lime leaves during the steeping process. Another unusual take on a classic is lemongrass tart, made in the same way as regular lemon tart except that the double cream used for the filling is infused with lemongrass. This method can also be used for an Asian take on the classic Portuguese custard tart, *pastel de nata*. In all cases, crush the stalks with a rolling pin before infusing them.

In India, lemongrass is a main ingredient of *masala chai*, a sweet spiced tea made by simmering black tea leaves in milk flavoured with herbs and spices. For a more indulgent version, add cacao to give a chocolatey twist. I also like to make refreshing drinks from lemongrass, including iced tea and cordial (see panel below).

Growing

Although lemongrass is frost-tender, you can grow it in temperate climates, either as an annual in the summer only, or as a perennial in pots that are brought indoors in the winter. It thrives in full sun and likes rich, free-draining soil. If you have heavy

---

Lemongrass cordial

To make this simple, refreshing drink, dissolve 500g (1lb 2oz) sugar in 250ml (9fl oz) water in a small pan, throw in a few crushed lemongrass stalks and the grated zest of one lime, and bring to the boil. Reduce the heat and simmer for a few minutes, then leave the mixture to cool completely. For extra sourness, squeeze fresh limes into the cooled syrup.

You can use lemongrass cordial in all manner of funky drinks. One of my favourites is "lemongrassade". Dilute 1 part cordial in 4 parts sparkling water to create a fragrant, thirst-quenching fizzy drink. The cordial is also a great mixer in mojitos, margaritas, and other boozy potions.

**Handle your
lemongrass plants
with care – the
leaves can be sharp.**

Growing at a glance

Sow Late spring, 20–25°C
(68–77°F)

Plant out Summer

Spacing 85–100cm (33–39in)

Harvest Late summer–
autumn

clay soil that's prone to waterlogging, it's
better grown in pots. If planted in the
ground, it can reach a staggering 1.8m (6ft)
tall and 1.2m (4ft) wide in a single growing
season. The tall, slender blades work well
at the back of borders, providing beautiful
bursts of green.

Propagation

Lemongrass can be propagated by leaving
store-bought stalks to root in a jar of
water in a sunny place, but I prefer the
achievement of growing it from seed.
Don't cover the seeds with compost, since
they need light to germinate, but do cover
with a glass or plastic cloche to retain
moisture, and leave in a warm place.
Seedlings should emerge after 5–21 days.

The seedlings can be pricked out when
they are big enough to handle. If you
intend to plant them in the garden, prick
them out into modules to allow them to
grow stronger and establish before planting
out. If you intend to grow in pots, they can
be transplanted into their final home at
this stage. Use a pot at least 35cm (14in) in
diameter and plant only one seedling per
container. Whether growing in pots or the
ground, don't plant or place the seedlings
outside until all risk of frost has passed.

Plant the seedlings at the same depth
as they're already growing in their
modules. In pots, add horticultural grit

or small pebbles to the potting mix at a ratio of 1 part grit to 3 parts potting mix, to improve drainage.

Aftercare

Keep the soil moist throughout the growing season, but avoid waterlogging. Lemongrass is one of the easiest crops, preyed on by few pests because of the insect-repellent qualities of the citronella it contains.

A single lemongrass plant in the ground will provide an abundance of stalks – more than enough for one household. It tends to spread, but this isn't usually a problem in temperate climates because the winter frost will kill it off. In any case, it responds well to being cut back, so don't be afraid to give it a restraining haircut. Remove dead leaves from pot-grown plants to encourage more stalks, and keep an eye on the base of the pot; if roots start to show, move the plant to a bigger container.

Lemongrass plants will be going dormant by late autumn. Before the first frost, bring potted plants indoors and trim the foliage to roughly 10cm (4in) tall. It's crucial not to overwater in the winter. In the spring, new shoots will emerge and you can boost the soil fertility with a homemade plant food (see pages 38–39).

Plant problems

Rust (see pages 49–51)

Harvesting

Lemongrass grown outdoors must be harvested before the first frost. You can harvest at any time in the growing season, but in temperate climates it's best done in mid-autumn, to allow the stalks to fatten.

To harvest individual stems, snap them off or cut with a sharp knife. Bear in mind that the thick, edible part is at the base of the stalk, so be sure to include this. To harvest more stems, divide the plants. If growing in a pot, remove the whole plant, cut through the root ball, taking as many stems as you want, then replant the rest to carry on growing. If the lemongrass is planted outdoors and the first frosts are imminent, dig the whole plant out of the ground and harvest all the stalks. After harvesting, remove and discard the woody end, as well as the tough foliage.

If you want to harvest your lemongrass earlier, remove the older, thicker stalks first. The ideal thickness of stalks for harvest is 5–10mm ($^1/_4$–$^1/_2$in). It is especially important to leave stalks to reach this size if you want a thick, tender core (the soft, fleshy part under the tough outer leaves), which is the most fragrant and flavoursome part. Stalks that are harvested small may still have fibrous cores. This will be a problem if you're blending the stalks into sauces or pastes, but doesn't really matter if you're using them whole.

If you want to use the young, tender lemongrass leaves, harvest them before the plants reach 30cm (12in) tall, cutting the stems roughly 5cm (2in) up from the base.

Storage

Although most people use lemongrass fresh, the stalks freeze well and keep for up to a year in this way. Hang the leaves in a warm, well-ventilated area to dry.

Beyond the kitchen

Lemongrass is cultivated for the production of citronella, an essential oil that is extracted from its leaves and stems. Citronella has natural antiseptic properties and is used in perfumes, soaps, and disinfectants, and as an insect repellent. But perhaps the most fascinating use is in beekeeping. To lure a swarm of honeybees to a hive, beekeepers use a concoction of beeswax and lemongrass oil imitating the Nasonov pheromone that's emitted by worker bees to guide their colleagues home.

Citronella grass (*C. nardus*)
Cultivated to produce citronella oil, this species has reddish leaves that give off an incredible lemony scent when crushed. A rapid and prolific grower, it can reach a height of 2m (6½ft), making it the perfect choice if you want to grow lemongrass for ornamental purposes. Extracting citronella oil at home is a challenge, so this species is best grown ornamentally only.

East Indian lemongrass (*C. flexuosus*) The stems of this species, which are flushed purple towards the base, are thinner but more crunchy, pungent, and aromatic than those of the West Indian species. The plant is also denser and shows good resistance to rust. A vigorous grower, it can reach 1.5m (5ft) tall.

West Indian lemongrass (*Cymbopogon citratus*) Also known as "common lemongrass", this is the species most often used in Asian cuisine. The plant produces a thick lower stem and has a pungent flavour that's perfect for making pastes, sauces, and soups. A bushy plant and prolific grower, it can reach 1m (3ft) tall and wide in a single season. (Note: the name refers to the west of India, rather than the West Indies.)

East Indian lemongrass

Parsley
(*Petroselinum crispum*)
Maïntanós, Persil, Petersilie, Prezzemolo

A hardy backbone of the herb patch and a powerhouse in the kitchen, parsley has a clean green, grassy taste that pairs perfectly with vegetables, fish, and meat. There are various types, from short and plump curly-leaved varieties to gigantic plants with thick stems and long, luscious foliage.

History

From the same family as the carrot (see page 256) and native to the Mediterranean, these glossy green leaves have been grown for centuries. Parsley was regarded by the ancient Greeks as too holy to eat. Legend had it that sprigs of parsley sprouted from blood shed by the boy Archemorus as he was slain by a serpent, and the herb was used in wreaths to decorate tombs. The Greeks even used the phrase *De'eis thai selinon* (To need only parsley), similar to "knocking on heaven's door".

In ancient Roman culture, parsley was a symbol of the goddess Persephone, queen of the underworld. The Romans believed the herb could protect the dead on their journey to the afterlife, and used it in funeral ceremonies. In the Middle Ages, parsley was attended by many superstitions. One legend suggested that its seeds had to make a treacherous journey to the depths of hell and return unscathed before the plant could grow successfully, which might have been an attempt to explain why they are so slow to germinate.

Parsley is deeply symbolic in Hebrew Passover celebrations. The fresh herb is dipped in salty water during the Karpas ritual of the Passover Seder, to symbolize the tears shed during the Israelites' enslavement, and the parting of the Red Sea by Moses. Parsley is eaten at the start of the Passover feast, celebrating freedom and new beginnings.

221

Parsley root

Parsley root was mentioned in European cookbooks as early as the fifteenth century. Today, it's grown and eaten in Russia, Poland, and Germany. It looks like a parsnip (see page 272), with its beige skin and tapered shape. When eaten raw, it has a crisp, tender texture, and when cooked, it's smooth and creamy and tastes very similar to celeriac (see page 267).

Culinary uses

Preparation

A quick and efficient way of cleaning parsley is to swish the leaves in a bowl of water while they are still attached to the stems. The water can then be easily flicked off by holding the branches and swooshing the bunch, without the need for a salad spinner. Don't throw away the stems – they are an excellent addition to stock.

Dishes

The world's most popular herb has been a mainstay of Mediterranean and Middle Eastern cuisine for centuries. Its magical flavour marries ingredients by bringing a clean, fresh aroma to dishes, awakening the palate, cutting through bold flavours, and rounding them off with a herby hit.

Tabbouleh, an ancient dish from the mountains of Lebanon and Syria, applauds the herb's prominent taste. Typically made with chopped parsley, bulgur wheat, onions, tomatoes, mint, and lemon juice, it is usually served with grilled meat. In Italy, a popular condiment for vegetables, fish, and meat is the traditional bright-hued *salsa verde* (green sauce) of parsley, capers, garlic, and olive oil.

The quintessential cockney classic, pie and mash has been a staple of the cuisine of London's East End since the early nineteenth century. It is served with lashings of a zesty liquor, an authentic taste of the local culture. This thick sauce is made by boiling fresh parsley in eel liquor, the flavourful liquid left over from stewing eels caught in the River Thames for another London classic, jellied eels.

'Gigante di Napoli' (left) and 'Riccio Verde'

Growing

Propagation

These shy-to-germinate seeds can take several weeks to sprout, so don't give up on them too soon. Broadcast-sow a light scattering of seeds and prick out into seed cells once the seedlings are big enough to handle. A plastic cloche can assist with germination, maintaining humidity without rotting the seed. Allow seedlings to grow for four or five weeks more before transplanting them into the patch. Early sowings benefit from protection from the elements; horticultural fleece will keep

Growing at a glance

Sow Early spring–early summer, 5–32°C (41–90°F)

Plant out Early summer–early autumn

Spacing 30cm (12in)

Harvest All year round

them cosy while they establish. Although biennial parsley sometimes flowers at the height of summer, it's worth staggering sowings to ensure a constant supply of leaves in case the odd plant bolts; later plantings also overwinter better, often producing a continuous bounty until the spring. I usually grow a few plants in the polytunnel, since they produce more leaves undercover in the winter.

Aftercare

Once established, parsley requires little or no maintenance. Water sparingly unless the weather is dry, when you should provide a generous drink once a week.

Plant problems

Aphids, rabbits, slugs and snails (see pages 49–51)

Harvesting

Pick the outer leaves first, while doing the housekeeping of removing old or yellowing foliage. Harvest the whole branch, rather than just the leaves, by snipping or snapping close to the main stem. This will ensure a continued supply and keep the plant neat.

Storage

Curly-leafed parsley stores better than flat-leafed varieties, which have a tendency to go limp; both can be kept for a few days in the fridge, either wrapped in a damp cloth or with their stalks in water.

Recommended varieties

'Berliner' (*Petroselinum crispum* var. *tuberosum*) This is two crops in one. Above ground, the plant produces luscious green foliage, while below it a gigantic root (see panel opposite) forms, ready for harvest in roughly 100–130 days.

'Bezirci' A downright delicious flat-leafed heirloom variety from Turkey, oozing with fresh and zingy aromatics. Used extensively in traditional Turkish cuisine, this parsley is superabundant, resilient, and among the top of the list for flavour.

'French' A delicate variety, favoured throughout France, with flat, dark green, serrated leaves and a silky, refined flavour. It can withstand light frosts, but is less resilient than other varieties.

'Gigante di Napoli' A mammoth parsley from the area around Naples in Italy. Easy to cultivate and a staple ingredient throughout the region, it produces thick, long stalks and abundant chunky, delicious leaves. It is excellent for cooking.

'Hungarian' A rare European landrace parsley with an impeccable flavour – a true culinary delight. Robust and resilient, the plants have a distinctive, wild appearance and haphazard leaf structure. A vigorous type that's easy to cultivate and has none of the metallic taste that is sometimes associated with parsley.

Mitsuba (*Cryptotaenia japonica*) This perennial cousin of parsley is also known as East Asian wild parsley or Japanese parsley. It is popular in Japan, where it is cultivated extensively for its unique parsley-like flavour, with hints of coriander and celery. The plant also produces fleshy tapered roots, a popular root veggie nationwide. A deep, rich red, almost purple variety, 'Bronze', is also available. Mitsuba is usually grown as an annual.

'Riccio Verde' A compact, dark green, aromatic parsley with heavily curled and ruffled leaves that are drought-tolerant and cold-resistant. This robust type stays fresh for a long time after harvest.

Kale

Brassica oleracea var. *sabellica*

Also known as Borecole, Cail, Cavolo, Leaf cabbage

This sweet-leaved, nutrient-dense brassica is one of the most robust vegetables. Its cut-and-come-again nature and long growing season allow an abundant harvest, come rain or shine. Heritage kales range from ornate, frilly-leaved fancies and short, stocky bushes to towering varieties that were traditionally used to make walking sticks. Is there a box that these quietly confident crops don't tick?

History

Kales's roots run from the eastern Mediterranean through the Anatolia region of Turkey, where it has been cultivated as a food crop for centuries. In ancient Greece, both curly-leaved and flat-leaved varieties of kale were already being grown extensively as early as the fourth century BCE and were often chopped, boiled, and eaten as a hangover cure, as the philosopher Theophrastus noted in his book of plants in 600 BCE. The Romans referred to these old-school varieties as "Sabellian kale", and these types are widely believed to be the precursors of all present-day kales. This leafy green was once a staple across Europe, sustaining people and livestock, but it fell out of favour after the Middle Ages, when the cultivation and consumption of cabbages began to rise.

Scotland has a rich history of growing "kail", and the vegetable once played a significant part in every Scots household. The term "kail" was commonly used to refer to supper, and no Scots kitchen was complete without a "kail-pot", a metal cauldron used for various purposes, including boiling water for tea, simmering stews, and, of course, cooking kale. The term "kailyard" – slang for vegetable gardens or small cabbage patches – was used appropriately for the Kailyard school, a Scottish literary movement (1880–1914) that idealized rural life, focusing on the beauty of nature and everyday simplicity.

In the early 1940s, as World War II raged on, kale became a vital part of the

British government's "Dig for Victory" campaign. Its ease of cultivation and nutritional benefits made it an obvious choice for supplementing the meagre diets of civilians during rationing. After the war, kale again fell down the pecking order and was more commonly found in the cattle feeder than on the dinner plate. But as the twenty-first century dawned, kale began a renaissance and regained popularity, dubbed a "superfood" owing to its numerous health benefits. People worldwide were fascinated by this leafy vegetable, and its popularity soared. Today, food enthusiasts and health-conscious individuals celebrate International Kale Day in October.

Culinary uses

Preparation

Fully grown kale leaves can be tenderized and used raw in salads by being chopped and massaged for a few seconds with a drizzle of olive oil and a pinch of sea salt. Crispy roasted kale is delicious; throw a handful of oiled and seasoned chopped kale on to a baking tray and cook in a hot oven until crisp and crunchy.

Dishes

The tender texture and sweet, earthy, nutty flavour of home-grown kale make it just as versatile an ingredient in the kitchen as it is a robust and hardy veg-patch constituent. Tasting slightly more peppery when raw, the tender young leaves are delicious in salads but also offer an earthy twang when blended into pesto or chopped into a salsa, while large raw leaves can be fermented into krauts and kimchis. When cooking, the leaves can be roasted, steamed, stir-fried, sautéed, or even braised in meat stock low and slow for 30 minutes until tender and sweet, for the perfect accompaniment to a roast, pie, or fish dish.

In Italy, an old Neapolitan soup called *minestra maritata* (married soup), dating back

Snap off the lower leaves of kale as you need them.

> 66
> **This leafy green was once a staple across Europe.**

Growing at a glance

Sow Early spring–midsummer,
6–30°C (43–86°F)

Plant out Late spring–early autumn

Spacing 40cm (16in)

Harvest All year round

to Roman times, has curly kale as one of its main ingredients. This brothy soup traditionally involves the addition of *sofrito*, leftover meat or meatballs, and tiny pasta, braised in richly flavoured chicken stock. The term "married" refers to the harmony of the flavours of leafy greens and other ingredients that combine perfectly in this delicious dish.

Grünkohl und Pinkel is a traditional German dish that has been enjoyed for centuries in the north of the country and is a winter staple. It consists of kale (*Grünkohl*) cooked with onions, bacon, and stock until soft and tender. The Pinkel sausage is made with a blend of pork, oats, and secret spices, to a recipe that varies from village to village owing to the closely guarded trade secrets of the butchers who make it. It is added to the kale and the two are cooked together until the flavours have melded. The dish is usually served with boiled potatoes, mustard, and a large glass of cold beer.

Growing

Propagation

Kale is robust, heat-tolerant, and cold-hardy. By planning the sowing timeline carefully and selecting particular heirloom varieties, it can be grown and harvested nearly all year round. First sowings can be made in the spring to supply luscious leafy greens from summer all the way through to early winter; later sowings are made in the summer for overwintering, and will continue cropping into the following spring.

Brassicas quickly grow tall and leggy with insufficient light, so keep the seedlings in a bright, frost-free location. Roughly three weeks after germination, they can be transplanted into the garden; however, more often than not, I pot my brassicas into 7–9cm (3–4in) pots to continue growing for two or three weeks before transplanting; this produces robust seedlings that are more capable of withstanding slug attack. When planting, bury a section of the stem to provide these tall-growing brassicas with extra support as they mature.

Aftercare

Keep a close eye on moisture levels and water accordingly until the plants are established. Once its roots are entrenched in the soil, kale rarely needs additional watering except during prolonged dry spells. Cover young seedlings with mesh or horticultural fleece to safeguard them from insects and birds, and as soon as the kale is growing strongly, switch the covering to netting, which will deter ravenous pigeons and rabbits from eating the crop and cabbage-white butterflies from laying eggs. Taller varieties, such as 'Jersey Walking Stick' (see opposite), benefit from being staked to prevent them from being blown over in high winds. They may also need a bespoke brassica cage or high wooden structure for pest protection. Remove any yellowing lower leaves as the plants grow.

Cold-weather wonder

As with many brassicas and some other vegetables, kale does not simply withstand cold temperatures. It becomes noticeably sweeter after frost – which causes it to turn the starches in its leaves to sugars as protection against the cold – making it a valuable crop for those who garden in harsh climates.

Kale for salad

Baby kale leaves add a delicious and healthy touch to salads. To harvest kale for this purpose, sow two or three seeds per cell in mid- to late summer. The seedlings can be planted out as clusters for autumn and winter harvest. To ensure the plant keeps producing leaves and that the leaves stay small, pick the outer leaves continuously while they are petite and dainty.

Plant problems

Aphids, cabbage root fly, flea beetle, slugs and snails (see pages 49–51)

Harvesting

Kale is ready for its first harvest roughly a month after transplanting. It is harvested in a cut-and-come-again manner by snapping the leaves off where they meet the central stalk. Harvest the lower leaves, leaving the central heart to continue growing. Throughout the season, kale grows tall and produces a thick, tree-like trunk with main growth confined to the top; regular picking encourages new growth and keeps the plants cropping for longer. Any flowers that appear can be removed by twisting out or slicing the stem, or left to bud up, at which point these sprouting broccoli-esque tops can be harvested and enjoyed in the same way as tenderstem (see page 109).

Storage

Best eaten freshly picked, kale is at its most delicious straight off the stalk; however, curly types store well in a damp, clear plastic bag in the fridge for up to a week.

'Blue Curled Scotch' An old Scottish curly-leafed heirloom that dates back to the eighteenth century. These short, compact plants produce abundant wavy blue-green leaves with a hint of purple. A cold-hardy variety that grows well even in the harsh winters of Scotland, it produces crinkled leaves that are so pretty they could be grown for their ornamental value alone. However, this high-yielding plant also has a delicious, sweet flavour.

'Daubenton' This perennial kale from Montbard in the Burgundy region of eastern France is named after the eighteenth-century French naturalist Louis-Jean-Marie Daubenton, who wrote about it in his book *Advice to Shepherds and Owners of Flocks*. Shepherds typically planted fields of Daubenton's kale to feed themselves and their flocks throughout the winter. This cold-hardy plant rarely flowers, and it's believed that it has lost its ability to run to seed through being propagated by cuttings for so long. The plants grow short and wide, becoming shrubby, and the leaves are mild and nutty-flavoured and will continue to crop for several years. When production slows, simply snip off a branch and replant it. The flat, light green leaves have a serrated edge; 'Daubenton Panache' is a variegated version.

'East Friesian Palm' An ancient and rare landrace, kale was grown for thousands of years in Ostfriesland, northern Germany. A very hardy curly kale with a long cropping window, this variety can grow well over 1.5m (5ft) tall, producing a large quantity of green, crinkled leaves. It can be harvested from the late summer through winter and well into the following spring. It is perfect for making *Grünkohl und Pinkel* (see page 227).

'Greenpeace' A purple-stemmed Siberian-type kale that tastes delicious. This relatively new breed was developed at the Greenpeace Experimental Farm on Denman Island in British Columbia, Canada. The organic, self-sufficient farming community was formed in 1974 by

Greenpeace co-founders Jim and Marie Bohlen to develop farming techniques that produce food in a way that empowers local communities rather than transnational corporations, while simultaneously restoring and preserving the natural world. The frilly blue-green leaves with vivid purple stems and veins of this variety are stunning and look fantastic in the veg patch.

'Jersey Walking Stick' Also known as 'Long Jacks', these giant kales can reach 3.75m (12ft) in height and originate from the island of Jersey in the English Channel. In the nineteenth century, the Channel Islands would have been covered in groves of kale, but now they're few and far between. The crops were predominantly grown as fodder for the famous Jersey dairy cows; however, owing to the kale's long, sturdy stem, locals made it into walking sticks by drying the stalks before adding a lick of varnish and a knob as a handle.

'Madeley' With mammoth leaves that are sweet and tender, this rare English heirloom variety provides copious amounts of food throughout the winter and into spring. This productive plant, a relative of the ancient 'Thousand-Headed Kale', is frost-hardy and more resistant to pests than other varieties.

'Nero di Toscana' Also known as *cavolo nero*, this world-famous leafy green originated in the Apennine Mountains of Tuscany. Used to make *ribollita toscana*, a vegetable soup that's the traditional dish of Florence, it has reportedly been grown in Italy since 600 BCE. The distinctive dark, long, bobbled leaves are icy and hardy, and their flavour is considered to improve after a few frosts. Less appealing to slugs than other kales, 'Nero di Toscana' will crop from October until April and reach a height of just under 1m (3ft).

'Red Russian' Also known as 'Rugged Jack', this beautiful heirloom is originally from Siberia and dates back to 1855. The frilly oak-leaf-shaped foliage with attractive purple veins and stems reached Canada and the United States in the 1880s, when the plant became known by some American growers as Communists' kale, owing to its Russian heritage. This vigorous plant is a big hit in many gardens for its tender leaves and delicate flavour.

'Russian Hunger Gap' This kale is appropriately named after the period each year when winter crops are diminishing and spring crops aren't quite ready for harvest. A red Russian type, it has large, jagged green leaves with purple stems and veins. It's a super-hardy kale that can tolerate high and low temperatures and has become something of a rarity. It was introduced to England during World War II as part of the "Dig for Victory" campaign, because it's easy to grow, produces lots of leaves that are full of healthy vitamins and minerals, and provides an abundance of raab, a type of unopened flower bud similar to broccoli (see page 109), when it bolts during the hunger gap in early spring.

'Scarlet' A beautiful open-pollinated purple kale that produces an abundance of curly leaves rich in antioxidants and flavour. This plant could be grown for ornamental value alone, and the deep purple leaves add striking contrast, brightening up the garden during the winter. It is a curly type that reaches a height of just under 1m (3ft) with a spread of 60cm (24in).

'Shetland' A landrace perennial kale that is the oldest known vegetable to be grown in Scotland. It's been cultivated on the Shetland Islands since at least the seventeenth century. Traditionally eaten boiled as an accompaniment to mutton stew, the leaves have a sweet, peppery taste and are packed with vitamins. The older, more rigid leaves would usually have been fed to cattle and sheep during the winter, while the young, tender new growth would be destined for the soup pot. This is one of the hardiest kales around, but even these tough plants needed a helping hand to survive the harsh conditions of the northernmost region of the United Kingdom. They were often cultivated in "plantie crubs", small stone-walled enclosures designed to protect the plants from strong wind, harsh weather, and marauding sheep. These enclosures can still be seen dotted over the islands today.

'Taunton Deane' A perennial kale from the West Country of England, once a popular vegetable, but now a rarity. First described in 1753 by the celebrated Swedish botanist Carl Linnaeus, this short-lived perennial was preserved from extinction in the gardens of Knightshayes Court in Devon. The broad, flat, tender blue-green leaves with purple stems can be harvested all year round. A very prolific grower capable of reaching more than 2m (6½ft) in height and producing a thick, woody, trunk-like stem, this is in my opinion the tastiest of all the "perennial" kales.

'Torzella' This Italian kale, also known as *torza riccia* or *cavolo greco*, is one of the oldest kales to be grown in Italy, and is considered the ancestor of curly kale. 'Torzella' has been developed in that country for at least 4,000 years, but is now predominantly found growing in the Acerra and Nola areas of Naples. Plants reach an average of 1m (3ft) in height and produce a tremendous quantity of delicious, nutrient-dense, curly green leaves. The leaves are one of the main ingredients of *minestra maritata* (see pages 226–27).

Lettuce

Lactuca sativa

Also known as Rabbit food, Salad greens

One of the most widely consumed vegetables globally, lettuce is an easy-to-grow crop that can be cultivated all year round. Bursting with subtle, sweet flavours and with a delicately bitter aftertaste, it is abundant in vitamins and minerals. Lettuces are also among the prettiest vegetables in the patch, and very varied, from loose bundles of frilly, oak-leaf-shaped bronze foliage to compact, heavy bright green heads.

History

Lettuces were first cultivated about 6,000 years ago in the Caucasus region of eastern Europe. They were originally grown for their seeds, which were processed into oil, rather than for their leaves. In ancient Egypt, around 2000 BCE, lettuce was a sacred sex symbol associated with Min, the god of fertility, probably because its tall, erect growth habit – which resembled present-day romaine lettuces (see page 234) – was reminiscent of a phallus, and because a rather suggestive milky white fluid (lactucarium) seeped out of the base of the stems when they were cut. Inscriptions on the walls of the Temple of Edfu state that lettuce can help Min to "relentlessly perform".

Lactucarium had a narcotic effect rather like that of opium. For this reason, the Greeks and Romans ate lettuce leaves for their calming, sleep-inducing effect, and wild lettuce (*Lactuca virosa*) is still sometimes used in natural remedies as a sedative and to relieve pain. Since lactucarium has a bitter taste, it has been selectively bred out of salad lettuces over time, but all lettuces today contain a little of this tranquillizing, soporific compound.

Culinary uses

Preparation

Lettuce should be torn rather than cut with a knife, to avoid browning the cut edges. Wilted lettuce can be revived by bathing the heads or leaves in ice-cold water, or simply braised and used in soup.

Dishes

Lettuce is usually thrown straight into the salad bowl, but it can also be grilled, braised, and baked. In France, the classic dish *petits pois à la française* (French-style peas) – which consists of lettuce, fresh peas, and pork lardons braised gently in chicken stock – celebrates the arrival of spring. Grilled

lettuce halves (mainly romaine types) are also a real treat, especially when cooked on a barbecue. The outer edges become caramelized and charred, while the tender inner leaves remain crisp and fresh, with a distinctly sweet, smoky flavour. They can be doused in a dressing, such as sour cream and garlic, then topped with tasty extras such as Parmesan, anchovies, and pine nuts.

Grow a mixture of lettuce varieties and you will have leaves in contrasting tastes, colours, and textures to use in the kitchen.

Lettuce also has a long history of being made into soup, including the simple, delicate Cantonese lettuce and fish soup and the rich, robust French cream of lettuce soup.

Yedikule gardens

The Yedikule *bostans* (market gardens), which run along the southern edge of the fifth-century walls that surround Byzantine Constantinople (now Istanbul), have supplied vegetables for the city's residents since its earliest days. Although an important part of Istanbul's historical and cultural heritage, these ancient gardens are threatened by urban encroachment from a city restoration project. The Slow Food movement has spearheaded a campaign to retain the gardens and draw the world's attention to the famous 'Yedikule' lettuce (see page 234).

Growing

One of the most productive crops you can grow, lettuce will provide an abundance of tasty, colourful leaves. In a temperate climate, the plants are mainly harvested in the spring and summer, but by carefully selecting cool-season varieties and pinpointing the sowing dates correctly, you can harvest lettuce all year round.

Propagation

Lettuce seeds are best broadcast-sown into trays. They require dappled light to germinate, so avoid burying the seeds too deeply, and cover them lightly with a dusting of potting mix, perlite, or vermiculite. Bring winter sowings indoors to germinate, and keep summer sowings out of direct sunlight or very hot, unventilated areas. Prick out the seedlings when they are large enough to handle. Lettuce plants grow rapidly and are often ready to plant out in as little as three weeks. Winter sowings should be protected with horticultural fleece or grown in a greenhouse or polytunnel to protect them from frost.

Aftercare

Plant lettuces in staggered rows and water immediately after transplanting. In hot, dry weather, keep them well watered – a good drink every three days should be

Lettuces produce amazingly varied leaves. The red-speckled 'Forellenschluss', rounded 'Gustav's Salad', sharply pointed 'Strela Green', and purple-blushed 'Bronze Syrian' are a distinctive presence in the patch and on the table.

> ## 66
> # Wild lettuce is sometimes used in natural remedies as a sedative and to relieve pain.

sufficient. Avoid watering in the evening, or the wet soil and leaves will entice slugs and snails to chow down on your succulent salad overnight. Similarly, if watered in the morning, the leaves will dry off more quickly, reducing the risk of mildew.

Celtuce 'Purple Sword' and 'Green Mountain' (left)

When harvesting a lettuce whole (above), cut it off as close to the soil as possible.

Plant problems
Aphids, cutworms, grey mould, mildew, slugs and snails (see pages 49–51)

Harvesting
Lettuce is best picked early in the morning, and there are two main ways of harvesting. You can cut off whole hearts or heads at soil level, using a knife and removing as much of the stem as possible. Alternatively, you can use the cut-and-come-again method, which involves pulling or cutting off the outermost leaves and continuing to pick them as they grow.

The latter technique is the most economical and productive way to grow lettuce, but the tightly packed leaves at the heart of the lettuce are considerably sweeter and more succulent than the outer foliage. For this reason, I grow a mixture of lettuces: loose-leaf varieties for cut-and-come again harvesting and other varieties for their hearts. Remove and compost plants as they bolt, since the leaves will turn bitter at this stage.

Storage
Lettuces have a short shelf life and are therefore best kept in the fridge. Wash loose-leaf and cut-and-come-again lettuce immediately after picking, then dry gently, leaving a little residual water to prevent wilting. They can be stored in an unlidded plastic container with a damp cloth covering the leaves. Wrapping whole heads in a damp cloth will keep them crisp.

Growing at a glance

Sow Late winter, late spring, midsummer, early autumn (for cut-and-come-again); successively late winter–early autumn (for heads), 4–24°C (39–75°F)

Plant out 3 weeks after sowing

Spacing 30cm (12in)

Harvest All year round

Butterhead lettuces

Wrinkled, ruffled butterhead lettuces are often grown for harvest as full-sized heads. The heads are small, loose, and partially flattened, with a sweet, perfectly blanched heart.

'Grandma Hadley's' A fast-maturing, sweet, tender, crisp lettuce grown by one Grandma Hadley, who passed the seeds of this dashing dark purple-tinged butterhead on to her granddaughter Flossie Cramer in 1915. At 85 years old, Cramer gave the seeds to her great-niece Pam Andrews, who donated the variety to the Seed Savers Exchange in 1988. It's said to be a Hadley family favourite used in wilted lettuce salad with hot bacon dressing.

'Grandpa Admire's' This beautifully bronzed, loosely packed, wrinkled lettuce has a mellow flavour. It's named after the US Civil War veteran George Admire, who migrated west from Indiana to Putnam County, Missouri, in the 1850s. The seeds were maintained by his grandchildren in their own gardens as a tribute. In the late 1970s Admire's granddaughter donated the seeds to the Seed Savers Exchange. It's very heat-tolerant and slow to bolt, even in strong summer sun.

'Gustav's Salad' This refined, compact butterhead produces some of the softest, most succulent salad leaves. Grown and developed in the early twentieth century by a plantsman from the southern Netherlands known to posterity only as Gustav, the lettuce was called "Sla van Pa" (Pappy's salad) by local villagers. For more than 40 years, Gustav would cycle around on a bicycle laden with brimming baskets of melt-in-the-mouth butterheads destined for the dinner tables of the local community. Shortly before his death, he shared the seed of his signature salad with locals, and the variety is now sold commercially.

'Merveille de Quatre Saisons' With a name that means "four-season marvel", this historic French variety, which dates from at least the mid-nineteenth century, is easy to grow, performs well in a wide variety of climates, and can be harvested nearly all year round. The leaves, which are green with pinkish-purple tips, darken during the winter.

'Sanguine Ameliore' Also known as strawberry cabbage lettuce, this is a rare nineteenth-century French heirloom variety. *Sanguine* means ruddy, referring to the crimson splashes on the light green leaves. Although it will perform well in hot weather, it's best to grow it in the cooler months for a darker, more captivating colour.

Romaine/cos lettuces

The oldest known lettuces, dating back at least 5,000 years, romaine or cos varieties are recognized by their tall, oblong heads. The narrow leaves are crunchy, sweet, and succulent, and the inner ones are the crispest. These are the go-to lettuces for a Caesar salad.

'Bronze Syrian' This gorgeous green lettuce has foliage that is elegantly blushed with bronze and a silvery sheen, and violet stems. It originated in Homs, Syria, once a fertile, thriving city but which has since 2011 been experiencing extreme violence because of the civil war, resulting in massive loss of farmland and heirloom seeds. 'Bronze Syrian' is full of flavour and a very heat-tolerant variety that's slow to bolt.

'Forellenschluss' An old Austrian beauty that produces tender, buttery foliage with spectacular dark red freckles. The name means "rear end of a trout", paying homage to the lettuce's resemblance to this flamboyant fish. It performs well from spring to autumn and can even be overwintered under cover.

'Rouge d'Hiver' This beautiful, deep bronze-red lettuce, which has been a favourite since the eighteenth century, is quick-growing, slow to bolt, and impressively resistant to heat and cold. Fittingly, its name means "winter red", since it's perfectly suited to autumn and winter growing. The burgundy-tinged leaves darken in cooler weather.

'Yedikule' This ancient romaine lettuce has been cultivated for more than 1,500 years in Istanbul, in the historic vegetable gardens of Yedikule (see panel on page 232). Its long, tender apple-green foliage has a crisp, crunchy centre and sublime flavour. It's reported that locals consider the leaves so juicy and full of natural oils that they can be eaten without the addition of dressing.

Crisphead/iceberg lettuces

These compact varieties develop an abundance of overlapping, curved leaves, which create a tight, round head that resembles a cabbage. As the name implies, they possess a crisp, fresh texture. They are usually harvested whole.

'Reine des Glaces' A rough and ragged yet elegantly stylish variety more than 200 years old, this has

'Forellenschluss'

beautiful, strikingly green, incredibly frilly, crinkled leaves that almost look like green flames. Crisp and crunchy, bursting with robust flavour, it's superb when eaten in quarters, dressed generously with hot garlic butter. The name means "ice queen", and the variety does indeed perform well in the winter.

Loose-leaf lettuces

A loosely packed head of frilly leaves emanates from the stem of these lettuces. Their easy-to-cultivate nature makes them a gardener's favourite, as the leaves can be easily harvested using the cut-and-come-again method.

'Rossa di Trento' This large, soft-textured, loosely wrapped lettuce with a sweet flavour originated in the Alpine city of Trento, northern Italy. It's an early-maturing variety that produces attractive, large green leaves with rich ruby-red tips that are textured like a savoy cabbage (see page 196). It has a tendency to bolt, especially in hot weather, so it's best grown in the spring and autumn.

'Strela Green' A sensational, star-shaped rosette of slender, spear-like leaves makes this lettuce stand out wherever it's planted. The bright green, pointed foliage tastes as spectacular as it looks, with a crunchy texture, sweet tones, and almost no bitterness. Dating back to the sixteenth century, 'Strela Green' is relatively quick to mature and performs well in hot weather. It was reintroduced into the modern seed trade by Dr Alan Kapuler of Peace Seeds, Oregon.

Batavia/summer crisp lettuce

Milder in flavour and with a softer, more tender texture than some of its cousins, the Batavia lettuce is somewhere between an iceberg and a romaine. The seeds of Batavias are able to germinate in hotter conditions, and the plants are very slow to bolt, so they perform much better than other types in the summer heat.

'Grazer Krauthäuptel' Hardy enough to be cultivated all year round, this old Austrian heirloom from the city of Graz is an ornamental joy and deliciously tasty. The big, bright green heads have serrated scarlet tips.

Celtuce (*Lactuca sativa* var. *angustana*)

Believed to have originated in the Mediterranean, celtuce (also known as stem lettuce) was introduced to China during the Tang dynasty (618–907 CE), when it became a popular ingredient throughout the country and elsewhere in Asia. The plants contain up to 50 per cent more vitamins, minerals, and antioxidants than regular leaf lettuce, and although the leaves are edible, it's the long, thick, succulent stems that are the star of the show.

Celtuce can be eaten raw in salads or lightly stir-fried. The crisp yet tender texture resembles that of water chestnuts or apples, while the flavour is mild, nutty, smoky, and bitter. Peel away the bitter skin before slicing the stem thinly. Although the young celtuce leaves can be eaten when young, they turn bitter when mature.

Harvest celtuce when the stems reach at least 3cm (1¼in) in diameter, but before they start to split. In cool, damp conditions, the stems can be allowed to become 5–8cm (2–3in) thick, but during hot summers, it's better to harvest them when they are thinner.

'Green Mountain' Originating in mountainous regions of southwestern China, this vivid green celtuce produces swollen stems that can reach colossal proportions. They are crunchy, tender, and juicy, and have a fresh flavour reminiscent of cucumber. This easy-to-grow variety is best planted out in the late summer.

'Purple Sword' Specifically suited to cool-season growing, this plant has long, sword-shaped murky green leaves that fade to deep purple, while the skin of the stalk is an elegant lilac. The young leaves are often used in a similar way to pak choi (see page 188), while the lime-green inner flesh of the stem can be eaten raw or cooked.

Spinach

Spinacia oleracea

Also known as Épinard, Ismaloq, Ispanak, Paalak

These full-flavoured, robust deep green leaves have a tangy mineral taste that is beautifully suited for consuming both raw and cooked. They combine versatility and nutrition with an easy-going nature that makes them a winner in the patch.

History

Botanists believe spinach originated in ancient Persia more than 2,000 years ago, domesticated through the selective breeding of wild species. It spread to India before reaching ancient China by 647 CE. In the late Middle Ages the Saracens (a derogatory term used by Crusaders to refer to Muslims, regardless of background) brought it to Sicily. Once in Italy, it became a widely grown crop in the Mediterranean and spread rapidly across mainland Europe.

The greens became a favourite of nobility and royalty. Legend has it that the culinary term *à la Florentine* originated with the Italian noblewoman Catherine de' Medici, who married the future French king Henry II in 1533. Catherine, a food lover, brought a team of Italian chefs from Florence when she ascended the French throne, and introduced the court to her spinachy specialities. Some historians view this as more legend than fact, but still, the term "Florentine" is commonly used in French cuisine to describe dishes that involve cooked spinach.

The famous 1930s cartoon character Popeye sings, "I'm strong to the finish, 'cause I eats me spinach, I'm Popeye the Sailor Man!" Famously, after he cracks open and chows down on a tin of the greens, he gains superhuman strength. The show's popularity brought about a significant increase in spinach consumption throughout the United States. However, it is now fairly well known that spinach's legendary iron content is a misconception, stemming from a mathematical error. In 1870 the German chemist Erich von Wolf was studying iron in various vegetables. While recording his observations in a notebook, he accidentally misplaced the decimal point in the figure for spinach, writing 35mg instead of 3.5mg, with the result that the iron content of spinach appeared ten times higher than its actual value. German scientists identified the error in the 1930s, but by then the belief that spinach was a great source of iron had become deeply rooted.

Culinary uses

Preparation

An easy and fast method of wilting spinach without overcooking it is to place the leaves in a colander in the sink and pour boiling water over them.

Dishes

The beauty of growing your own spinach is the ability to harvest the larger leaves, which are packed with flavour and have a more robust structure than the "baby" leaves most commonly found in supermarkets. Home-grown leaves are much more versatile than mass-produced packaged spinach, which quickly turns to mush when cooked.

If perfectly wilted, the leaves shrink, losing their shape without becoming soggy. It's at this stage that spinach is at its best. *Fatayer bi sabanekh*, a tasty, crisp triangular Lebanese pastry filled with a tangy mixture of wilted spinach seasoned with sumac, pomegranate seeds, and pine nuts, is irresistible and the perfect veggie snack.

Spinach is commonly found in tapas throughout Spain, and the Andalusian *espinacas con garbanzos* (spinach with chickpeas) is one of Seville's most prized dishes. This hearty, wholesome stew, traditionally feasted on during Holy Week, combines chickpeas and spinach with such warming spices as paprika and cumin. Although it's known as a Spanish dish, it has Arabic roots and comes from ancient Persia, where the two ingredients originated.

Another veggie tapas delight is the classic Catalonian dish *espinacas a la Catalana*. This recipe has been around since the Middle Ages and can be found in many old Catalan cookbooks. Consisting of spinach, raisins, olive oil, pine nuts, and garlic, with a squeeze of lemon juice, it's often served with crusty bread.

Propagation

Spinach thrives in cool weather and there are two windows of opportunity for germination, of which the later one is more reliable and productive. If sown in the spring, they can yield a large quantity of greens, but the plants will bolt and flower as soon as summer arrives. If sown later, the leafy greens can be harvested continuously throughout the autumn. The leafy growth naturally slows during the winter, but leaves can still be picked until spring.

To grow large spinach leaves for cooking, sow two seeds per cell and discard

The robust leaves of spinach respond well to cooking but, when small, are tender enough to eat raw.

the weaker seedling after germination; for baby leaves similar to those found in supermarkets, plant three or four seeds per cell and grow them as a cluster. Keep early sowings in the warmth of the house to encourage germination, but transfer to a frost-free greenhouse, polytunnel, or cold frame shortly after sprouting. Early sowings are usually ready for transplanting in four weeks, while later sowings grow much faster, and are often ready for planting in as little as two weeks.

Spinach can withstand frost and harsh weather, but new plantings benefit from a protective covering of horticultural fleece in early spring to improve growth and protect from pests. While it is not mandatory, covering the later sowings with fleece at the start of winter can also promote faster growth and protect the leaves from extreme weather.

Aftercare

Water the new plants generously and keep the soil moist, especially if the weather is dry, until they are established. It's worth keeping spare plants to fill any gaps if crops are lost to pests. In the spring, when the plants are putting on growth, water at least twice a week in sunny weather. Autumn spinach typically does not require extra watering, unless the weather is dry.

Plant problems

Aphids, cutworms, flea beetle, leaf miner, slugs and snails (see pages 49–51)

The sting in the tale

One leafy green that is far richer in iron than spinach is stinging nettles. They have been used in cooking for millennia, and indeed nettle pudding is said to be Britain's oldest recipe, dating back 8,000 years. It was a staple among the people of Stone Age civilizations, who made it by mixing nettles with other foraged leaves, such as dandelion and sorrel, and binding the mixture with barley flour.

Harvesting

To harvest the leaves, pinch them off cleanly at the base of the plant, removing the entire stem. This will prevent damaged or tattered stems from decaying on the plant, which can attract pests – particularly slugs – and encourage disease.

As spinach plants mature, their leaves change in shape from round to a pointed arrowhead, signalling the end of their cycle and the start of bolting. Pinching out the flower stalk will not stop the plant from flowering. Once the flower stalk begins to emerge, continue to harvest the leaves for about a week, then remove the bolted plants by cutting them off at the base with a pair of secateurs or snips.

Storage

As with all leaves, spinach is best eaten freshly picked. However, the leaves can be kept for a few days in the fridge if you put them in a plastic box with a damp paper towel as a lid.

Growing at a glance

Sow Late winter–early spring; late summer, 7–24°C (45–75°F)

Plant out Early spring; early autumn

Spacing 25cm (10in)

Harvest Autumn–mid-spring

Flat-leaf

'Galilee' A tall Middle Eastern heirloom from the region of Galilee, which extends from northern Israel to southern Lebanon. Boasting impressive, vibrant green, arrowhead-shaped leaves that grow rapidly, it is exceptionally heat-tolerant, slow to bolt, and suitable for the Mediterranean climate. The leaves are noticeably paler green than those of other varieties.

'Gigante d'Inverno' The name of this Italian heirloom means "winter giant", and it produces bountiful harvests throughout the cold months. Its large, glossy, ruffled leaves have a fine texture and wonderful taste.

'Monstrueux de Viroflay' Prized for its ability to withstand cold, this variety produces an abundance of sizable, thick, juicy leaves. Introduced in 1885 by Vilmorin Andrieux, it holds significant heritage value. It was the top spinach variety sold at the old Les Halles market in Paris, and its desirable genes have played an extensive role in breeding programmes to create modern hybrids.

Savoy and semi-savoy

'Bloomsdale Long Standing' This variety was first brought to market by the D. Landreth Seed Company, Philadelphia, in 1826. It underwent selection for improvement in 1925 and has since maintained its reputation as one of the most highly regarded non-hybrid spinach varieties. It is a high-yielding, spectacular plant that produces large, deeply crinkled dark green leaves.

'Giant Nobel' Sometimes referred to as 'Long-Standing Gaudry', this variety was developed in 1926 by Zwaan and Van der Molen of Voorburg, the Netherlands' oldest city. Its large, thick, deep green leaves have rounded tips and a mild, buttery taste, noticeably sweeter than those of other varieties. Productive, slow to bolt, and great for spring sowing.

'King of Denmark' A Danish variety introduced in 1919, perfect for spring sowings. It is a hardy and robust type, with large, smooth, dark green leaves that are rounded and slightly bumpy. It is slow to bolt, and can be harvested for weeks after other spinach has flowered. The taste and texture

Spinach types

Spinach is divided into three categories: flat-leaf, savoy, and semi-savoy. Flat-leaf is the type most commonly found in supermarkets, and is great for picking as baby leaves. Savoy types are ideal for growers and market traders owing to their superior appearance, flavour, and long shelf life. Semi-savoy types, as the name suggests, are partially crinkled and so easier to wash.

are exceptional and the leaves store well, making it an excellent choice for market gardeners.

'Norfolk' This Canadian heirloom from cold Quebec produces dark green, heart-shaped, bubbly leaves resembling the texture of savoy cabbage. Bred in the mid- to late nineteenth century, it displays excellent resistance to cold and is well suited to both early and late sowings.

'Gigante d'Inverno'

'Bloomsdale Long Standing'

Roots & Tubers

These hidden treasures thrive under the soil, enabling countless culinary creations with their rich, earthy goodness.

Ancient Andean Tubers

Originating where the lush Amazon rainforest meets the Andes mountains, these tubers are not your common veg-patch personalities. Once the culinary staples of Indigenous cultures, they are now becoming popular among home gardeners for their unique flavours, textures, and aesthetics, and for their heritage. Tracking them down can be a quest, but they are becoming more widespread and easier to acquire through the internet.

Oca
(*Oxalis tuberosa*)
Apiña, Huasisai, Irish potato, Miquichi, New Zealand yam, Papa extranjera, Truffette acide

This plant really is a testament to nature's creativity. The tubers resemble pebbles painted with the enchanting colours of an artist's palette, from brilliant fuchsia-reds and muted pinks to sunny yellows and pearly whites. Some are oblong, others almost perfect spheres, the skin smooth and slightly waxy, with delicate, indented rifts and chinks. They also reveal their artistic flair through their foliage, which is formed from delicate heart-shaped leaflets cascading from the gracefully sprawling stems of these bushy plants.

History

The name "oca" derives from *uqa*, a word in Quechua, the primary language of the pre-Columbian Inca empire. Yet these gemstones of the vegetable world were cultivated by Indigenous Andean peoples hundreds of years before the Incas, and played a vital role as a staple food, becoming one of the most important food sources in the high elevations, second only to the potato. More recently, these Andean tubers were dubbed the "Irish potato", owing to their shamrock-shaped leaves,

241

The oca's shamrock-like leaves gave rise to the nickname "Irish potato".

It was also commonly stewed in soups with quinoa for a hearty, warming meal.

Growing

Oca tubers can be chitted in a similar way to potatoes (see page 280) from late winter, and rehoused in small pots once the eyes begin to form. This will produce small plants that can be planted out in the patch once all risk of frost has passed. Alternatively, the tubers can be chitted and planted directly in their final location once the weather has warmed and no more frost is forecast. Space the plants 30–40cm (12–16in) apart, burying the tuber 5–10cm (2–4in) below the surface.

Plant problems

Rodents (see pages 49–51)

Aftercare

Oca are relatively low-maintenance, except for weeding and the removal of decaying foliage; however, regular watering is crucial, especially during dry periods. The plants are known for their partially trailing nature, so allow them to sprawl. Tubers begin to form after the autumn equinox with the shortening daylight hours. Keep an eye on the base of the plants and earth up any exposed tubers to protect them from pests and increase the yield (although, unlike spuds, they will not spoil and become poisonous if exposed to sunlight).

Harvesting

Harvest as the foliage begins to die back after the first light frosts, usually in late autumn and early winter. Oca must be picked before the onset of heavy ground freezes, but if early frosts are forecast and the tubers still need time to bulk up, cover them with a double layer of horticultural fleece during the cold snaps. When harvesting, pull the plants up using the stem. The tubers are often connected to the web-like root system, but do fish

and they also became known as the "New Zealand yam" after being introduced to the Pacific Aotearoa Islands in the late nineteenth century as a competitor to the humble spud.

Culinary uses

In the kitchen, oca is an exciting alternative to the potato. Its delightful flavour – a unique fusion of sweet nuttiness and earthy notes, with a subtle but sharp tang – offers a broad spectrum of culinary possibilities. When raw, the flesh has a pronounced lemony, floral flavour with the crunch of a carrot. Yet oca is at its best roasted, when it takes on a clear-cut taste that I find pleasantly reminiscent of a chip-shop chip splashed with malt vinegar. The authentic ancient Andean way of cooking oca is to roast the tubers in their skins over open flames or hot coals, for a smoky flavour and delightfully crisp exterior.

around in the soil for any stragglers; the colourful "pebbles" are easy to spot against the dark compost.

Storage

Brush the tubers clean, spread them out on newspaper or in shallow crates, and leave them to cure on a sunny windowsill or in a conservatory for a week before eating or storing them. It has been found that exposure to sunlight reduces the levels of organic acids in oca, and improves and refines their natural sweetness. The tubers store well if kept in paper bags in a cool, frost-free place, and can be saved in this way for growing the following year.

Recommended varieties

'Bolivian Red'
'Dylan Keating'
'Golden'
'Hopin'
'Manzana'
'Mexican Red'
'Paloquemao'
'Puka Ñawi'
'Scarlet Red'

Oca produce many small potato-like tubers in a variety of jewel colours (above). Seen right are 'Scarlet Red' and the white 'Dylan Keating'.

Mashua

(*Tropaeolum tuberosum*)
Añu, Cubio, Isaño, Mazuko, Nabu

This charismatic ornamental edible is a tuber-forming member of the nasturtium family, with long vines that produce masses of heart-shaped leaves and fabulous fiery-red and burnt-orange trumpet-shaped flowers. They provide a lush backdrop when given trellis or other support to scramble over. They produce elongated ovoid tubers like hidden treasure in a vivid mosaic of charming colours, from the creamy and peachy hues of dawn to dusky regal purples. The tubers are smooth-skinned with deep crevices, mirroring the contours of the Andean landscape from which they originate.

History

It's believed that mashua was cultivated by Indigenous communities in the lofty heights of the Titicaca basin on the border between Peru and Bolivia, long before the rise of the Inca empire. It was traditionally acknowledged as a natural anaphrodisiac, reducing sexual desire and arousal. For this reason, the Incas fed their troops with vast quantities of the tuber in the hope of maintaining the soldiers' focus and energy on the battlefield and preventing them from being distracted by amorous thoughts about their partners left at home.

Culinary uses

Eaten raw, mashua leaves a peculiar spread of flavours on the palate, a cross between the pungent spiciness of radish and intense, sweet floral tones unmistakably similar to marzipan. The fiery flavour mellows when it is cooked, yet the blossom-like taste remains. Mashua can be baked, fried, stewed, or mashed, and it's claimed that freezing the tubers before cooking improves the flavour.

Similarly to nasturtiums, the leaves and flowers are also edible and bring a peppery punch to salads.

*Mashua's kinship with the nasturtium (*Tropaeolum majus*) is obvious from the appearance of its leaves and flowers.*

Growing

Although the taste is certain to split opinion, mashua's ornamental glory is sure to please and certainly makes growing this crop worthwhile. The production of tubers is triggered by shortening daylight hours, as with oca, so there's no rush to plant them out in the patch.

Propagation
Start the tubers off in early spring in small pots, pointed side down. Each

tuber will produce several sprouts, and the new plants are ready to be planted out after all risk of frost has passed. Alternatively, the tubers can be planted directly in their final location either in the ground or in large containers, such as wooden barrels, once the weather has warmed and no more frost is forecast. The leaves can lose water rapidly through transpiration in windy conditions, so plant in as sheltered a spot as you can if your garden is exposed.

Aftercare

The long vines require trellising or other support, and look particularly pretty when allowed to wend their way over fences and walls. Water the plants regularly during dry spells. You will find that cabbage white caterpillars enjoy munching on the leaves, but the sheer abundance of foliage means they are unlikely to do too much harm.

Plant problems

Caterpillars (see pages 49–51)

Harvesting

These plants will resist light frosts, and begin to form their tubers only after the autumn equinox, so it's best to let them grow for as long as possible. Harvest them after they have been seasoned by a light frost or two, which improves the flavour. Be vigilant, however, as harder frosts will damage and spoil them. Lift the tubers using a hand trowel or fork, ideally in the late autumn.

Storage

Once out of the ground, the tubers are prone to dehydration if they are stored in a warm place, but they will keep for months in paper sacks in a cool, dark, frost-free shed or other outbuilding. They can be saved and replanted the following year. If they begin to shrivel, wilt, and soften before the time comes to plant them, pot them up in moist compost; they will begin to resprout and can be kept in the warmth of the house until the time is right for them to be planted out.

Recommended varieties

'Blanca'
'Bloody Tears'
'Ken Aslet'
'Puca-Añu'
'Q'illu Isañu'

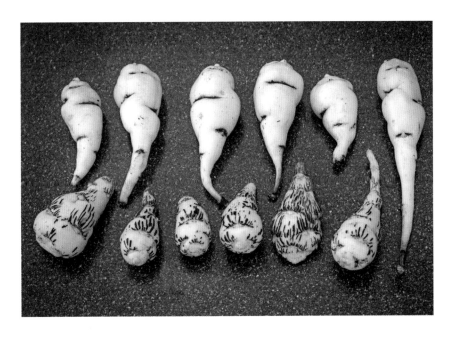

Mashua 'Blanca' (top) and 'Bloody Tears'

Yacón looks more like a prairie flower (left) than a vegetable, but after harvesting its culinary value becomes abundantly clear (opposite, top).

Yacón
(*Smallanthus sonchifolius*)
Bolivian sunroot, Llacon, Pear of the earth, Peruvian ground apple, Poire de terre

An ancient Andean gem, this burly tuber is deceptive. Although it resembles the sweet potato visually, it is the polar opposite of it in taste, texture, and culinary possibilities. Crisp, juicy, and succulent, it is comparable to a fresh apple or pear. Its unique sweetness, which is derived from inulin rather than starch, sets it apart from other tubers.

History

Known in the Aztec language as the "water root", yacón is a member of the daisy family and originated in the incredibly diverse Yungas region on the eastern slopes of the Andes, where the mountainous terrain gives way to the Amazon rainforest. The Moche, a pre-Inca civilization in northern Peru, revered yacón, which is depicted in their ceramics and stirrup vessels. The tuber's high water content makes it a natural source of hydration, and civilizations across the Andes planted it along messenger trails as a refreshing snack and source of sustenance for the parched runners, and in field margins as a revitalizing meal for farmers.

Culinary uses

Yacón is at its glorious best when eaten raw, a juicy sensation with the texture of water chestnut, bursting with natural sweetness. In this form it is perfect in refreshing fruit medleys or savoury salads, grated into slaws, diced into salsa, juiced in a smoothie, or simply eaten on its own as a crunchy snack. Its crisp texture means it absorbs flavours well, and it can be marinated in vinaigrettes and dressings for a few minutes before serving. Cut into batons and sautéed lightly until delicately caramelized, yacón can be incorporated into stir-fries, blended into sugar syrup, diced and baked into cakes, or cooked down with sugar and spices (such as cinnamon) into a sweet compote, ideal for crumbles and pies.

Growing

Plant the tubers direct, burying them 5–10cm (2–4in) below the surface. Alternatively, acquire clones (plants propagated from cuttings) from a plant nursery and plant them out in a sunny spot after all risk of frost has passed. Allow a wide spacing of 45–55cm (18–22in) between plants, which will grow bushy and produce an abundance of soft, fuzzy green leaves and small orange blooms. Yacón isn't fussy, but it does require regular watering, especially during dry spells.

Plant problems
Rodents (see pages 49–51)

Harvesting

Tuber formation is finished by late autumn or early winter, and the plants should be harvested before the onset of heavy ground frosts. Yacón often yields more than 4kg (nearly 9lb) of tubers per plant, but the tubers are large, clumped together, and difficult to pull up. First cut back the foliage, leaving a length of stem at the base to use as a handle to lever the tubers from the soil. Then, using a fork, lift the tubers, avoiding snapping or damaging them, since that will inhibit their storage ability.

Storage

Undamaged tubers store well in paper sacks in a cool, dry, frost-free shed or other outbuilding. They may sweeten over time, forming a thicker skin, which darkens and will need peeling as it becomes bitter. Eat the smallest first, since they have the shortest shelf life. Before eating, bring the tubers into the house to warm up and sweeten for a week or so.

Recommended varieties

'Cajamarca'
'Morado'
'Rojo'

'Morado' (bottom)

Beetroot

Beta vulgaris

Also known as Beet, Blood turnip

Vibrant and versatile, these bulbous roots have a distinctive flavour of candied sweetness and elegant earthiness. Although usually thought of as deep burgundy, they're available in various shades, as well as shapes, including damson-coloured discs, snow-white globes, and long, tapered roots. Packed with essential vitamins, minerals, phytonutrients, and antioxidants, beetroot are some of the most nutrient-rich food crops around.

History

Beetroot originated along the majestic coastlines of the Mediterranean. Derived from the wild sea beet (*Beta vulgaris* subsp. *maritima*), it was initially domesticated and cultivated for its flavoursome foliage by the ancient Greeks. Later, in the Roman era, it was also cultivated for the root, which was considered a powerful aphrodisiac. In the ancient Roman city of Pompeii, beetroot featured in the erotic frescoes that decorated the walls of the Lupanar brothel. At this time, horticulturists began selectively breeding the plants to develop larger roots. Ranging in colour from creamy white to scarlet and purple, these early beetroot had a much longer, more slender appearance than today's beetroot, similar to the tapered, parsnip-like roots of 'Rouge Crapaudine' (see page 253).

Breeding accelerated across Europe in the mid-sixteenth century to create beetroot that were larger, sweeter, more palatable, and with a softer texture. Several new varieties emerged, including the mangelwurzel (see page 254) – a huge beet used to feed livestock – and the extravagantly striking, concentric pink-and-white-ringed, delectably sweet 'Chioggia' (see page 254).

Extracting sucrose sugar from beets was discovered in 1747 by the German chemist Andreas Sigismund Marggraf. His discovery opened the door for the cultivation of sugar beet as an alternative to sugar cane, which could be grown only in tropical or subtropical regions. By the late nineteenth century, the production of sugar beet had become widespread in Europe and North America, and a major agricultural industry was born.

Culinary uses

Preparation

If eating beetroot raw, it's best to peel before grating or slicing, then squeeze over some lemon juice. This helps to reduce the chance of any possible adverse reactions to oxalic acid: a naturally occurring organic compound found in moderate quantities in beetroot and which can cause a reaction in some people, such as a burning sensation in the mouth or a scratchy, sore throat.

If roasting, boiling, or steaming, or salt-baking beetroot, I recommend keeping the beets whole with the skin on. This ensures even cooking, and the tough skin acts as a protective shield, helping to retain the beetroot's nutrients, texture, and vivid colour. Once cooled, the roots can be skinned effortlessly without the need for a knife or peeler.

Dishes

With its dense flesh, powerful flavour, and enticing colours, beetroot has found its way into variations of dishes worldwide, including the Scandinavian-inspired beetroot-cured salmon gravadlax and the lightly spiced, stir-fried beetroot *poriyal* from southern India. It can also be concocted into hummus, gnocchi, pasta, and other dishes, which take on the beetroot's earthy flavour and – in the case of scarlet and magenta types – deep purple pigment, resulting in a visually appealing plate of food that really stands out on the dinner table.

The roots are delicious paired with various types of fish and meat, or pickled or roasted and thrown into salads. They're also wonderfully refreshing when incorporated into juices and shakes, and are a great ingredient in cakes. One of the oldest recipes that celebrates beetroot is the hearty soup known as borscht, which originated in Ukraine but is also extremely popular in other Baltic and Slavic countries.

Beetroot responds well to multi-sowing.

Growing

Propagation

I recommend sowing beetroot under cover (in a polytunnel or greenhouse), since birds love nipping at the tender young leaves and will polish them off in the twinkling of an eye. The gnarly, knobbly seeds, which look like a ball of bark, are best sown into seed modules in groups of four seeds per cell (see opposite). Beetroot seeds can sometimes sprout several plants per seed, so may require thinning out to four or five plants per cell to give the plants space to thrive.

If you are making early sowings in late winter or early spring, when it is still cold outside, bring the seed trays indoors to germinate. If sowing in the winter, bear in mind that most varieties are likely to bolt before the root is big enough to harvest. Delaying sowing until the spring will reduce this risk.

Plant out the clumps of seedlings about four weeks after germination.

Aftercare

Early plantings are best covered with a layer of fleece to protect them from frost,

Growing at a glance

Sow Late winter–mid-spring, 10–30°C (50–86°F)

Plant out Mid-spring–early summer

Spacing 30cm (12in)

Harvest Early summer

while later plantings may require mesh to keep them safe from birds and rabbits. Newly planted beetroot should be watered every few days until the roots have established, then they can be watered sparingly (every three weeks or so during dry weather, and hardly at all if there is some rain).

Plant problems

Birds, rabbits (see pages 49–51)

Harvesting

With beetroot you have a double harvest, since the leaves are edible and can be used in the same way as chard or spinach. Harvest the leaves in a cut-and-come-again manner, although I tend not to take leaves from plants that I intend to harvest roots from, since this can make the roots turn woody. Use small leaves for salads and larger leaves for cooking. All beetroot must be harvested before early winter, or the

Multi-sown beetroot (left) may need thinning once the seedlings are growing strongly.

An array of stunning root colours and patterns (overleaf, left), and the oldest beetroot variety, 'Rouge Crapaudine' (overleaf, right).

Mangelwurzel

Mangel or mangold beets, also known as mangelwurzels, have a long history in England. Since the eighteenth century they have been used as animal fodder, and they have also been used in potent alcoholic brews. In addition, mangelwurzels have traditionally been used for sport (in mangelwurzel-hurling competitions) and as decorations for Punkie Night, the annual traditional West Country celebration, when the roots are hollowed out and carved to create mangelwurzel lanterns. Mangelwurzels are delicious – provided you harvest their smooth-textured roots when they're still young and sweet – and an excellent source of nutrients.

frost will turn the roots to mush. Select the biggest roots from each clump to harvest first, leaving the remainder to bulk up further. Simply push down and twist out the roots to cause the least disturbance to the soil.

Storage

Remove the foliage and gently brush off any excess soil. Avoid cleaning them too thoroughly, or washing, since this will remove the fine, waxy outer layer of the root, along with the soil that helps to keep the beetroot fresher for longer.

Muddy roots can be dried before being brushed off, and once manicured beetroot is best kept in a box or sack, in a cool, dark, frost-free shed or other outbuilding. Large roots will store the longest, so feast on the smaller ones first.

'Albina Vereduna' This ivory-white, globe-shaped Dutch heirloom beetroot, bred in the eighteenth century or earlier, is considerably sweeter and less earthy-flavoured than its purple cousins. In fact, it's so sweet that it can be used to make sugar. It's excellent for cooking, especially when paired with light-coloured foods, such as fish and poultry, because it doesn't bleed and stain the food.

'Bull's Blood' Derived from the ancient variety 'Rouge Crapaudine' (see opposite) and bred in the Netherlands in the 1840s, this striking, burgundy-leaved beet is often grown to be harvested as a salad leaf. The vivid blood-red roots are best picked as baby beets, when their flavour is richer and sweeter. This is a pretty plant that could be grown for its ornamental appeal alone.

'Cheltenham Green Top' This is one of the tastiest beetroot I've ever eaten. Bred during the 1880s in Gloucestershire, UK, the elongated, tapering, dark red roots, which can grow to 25cm (10in) long, contrast beautifully with their light green foliage. It's a great storing variety, with an outstanding flavour that doesn't diminish over time.

'Chioggia' (**'Candy'**) Bred in the nineteenth century or earlier in the tiny Italian fishing village of Chioggia, nestled on the shores of the Venetian lagoon, this is possibly the most striking variety of all. It has mesmerising concentric rings of milky white and pinkish-red stripes and a sugary-sweet, mildly earthy flavour.

'Covent Garden Red' Named after the famous London market, where it was once sold in large numbers, this rare British-bred beet has been grown since the 1880s at least. It has long, purplish-red roots with firm, juicy flesh.

'Crosby's Egyptian Flat' One of the earliest to mature, this is an improved version of its parent, 'Egyptian Flat', which is still available from seed companies today. 'Crosby's

Egyptian Flat', developed in Boston during the 1860s, was selected for its big, flat beets with a smooth skin. Flat beetroot was once widely available to buy. However, because of its squat disc shape it is less frequently cultivated today, since the flattened roots make it a challenge to harvest mechanically.

'Cylindra' ('Formanova') This nineteenth-century Danish heirloom is sometimes called the "Butter Slicer" owing to its soft texture. It's easy to prepare, being long and cylindrical, because it can be cut into uniform discs. The roots are best harvested when on the small side, while they're at their most tender. In Denmark, 'Cylindra' is traditionally pickled and served as a topping with pâté on *smørrebrød* (a type of open sandwich).

'Detroit Dark Red' Developed in Michigan and first sold in 1892, this is one of the most popular varieties cultivated by home growers and market gardeners today. It is fast-growing and one of the best types to harvest as baby beets, which are delicious eaten raw. It's also one of the darkest beets, and has uniform, smooth, ball-shaped roots that lack the distinct appearance of rings.

'Yellow Intermediate Mangel'

'Dobbies Purple' A hard-to-come-by nineteenth-century Scottish heirloom with a long, chunky root that can weigh up to 1.5kg (3lb) if allowed to grow. Even at this staggering size, the roots remain tender and don't become woody.

'Early Blood Turnip' One of the oldest surviving varieties of beetroot, this is becoming endangered. The gnarly roots are violet, topped with striking red stems with dark green leaves. Introduced to the US from Eastern Europe in the early nineteenth century, the seeds are believed to have found their way into the hands of President Thomas Jefferson, who grew this variety in the vegetable garden at Monticello, his plantation in Virginia. It's a complex-flavoured beetroot that starts with a hint of spice, followed by tartness and a rich, earthy finish. A hardy, reliable crop, it can be stored for up to eight months after harvest.

'Golden Detroit' A richly coloured golden beetroot that's ever so sweet and tremendously tender, this variety dates to at least the 1820s, when it was bred and selected as an improved variety of an ancient beetroot known as 'Golden Beet'. However, it wasn't until the 1940s, when the US-based seed company Burpee released 'Burpees Golden', that growing golden beetroot became popular among gardeners.

'Lutz' This heirloom originated in Germany and was popular among the Amish and Mennonite communities, finding its way to the United States with them in the late eighteenth and early nineteenth centuries. The sweet, pinkish roots can reach a considerable size without compromising their flavour or texture. The large, vigorous leaves, which grow on attractive red stems, can be used as greens and have a similar flavour to spinach or chard. Also known as 'Winter Keeper', this variety is often regarded as the longest storing of all beetroot.

'Mr McGregor's Favourite' Possibly named after the grouchy vegetable gardener Mr McGregor in

'Bull's Blood'

Beatrix Potter's *The Tale of Peter Rabbit* (1901), this exceptionally rare Scottish heirloom was once thought to be extinct. It's shaped like a long purple carrot, topped with a dazzling display of glossy, spear-shaped, dark maroon leaves. It has a good, old-fashioned, earthy beetroot flavour.

'Rouge Crapaudine' The oldest-known variety of beetroot available today, this French beet is thought to have been cultivated for 1,000 years or more. Its roots are long and pointed, and its flavour among the deepest and earthiest of all. Its name is derived from the French word for a female toad (*crapaudine*), although it is also known as the tree-bark beet. Both names refer to the thick, woody skin of the beet. In France, the roots are traditionally roasted whole on an open fire. After roasting, the skin peels away to reveal the striking purple flesh that has taken on the smoky flavour from the fire.

'Yellow Intermediate Mangel' This nineteenth-century French heirloom was traditionally grown as fodder. The attractive roots, with alternating white and yellow rings, are sweet and juicy, with a soft texture that's perfect for the dinner table – not just the cattle trough.

Carrot

Daucus carota subsp. *sativus*

Also known as Cairéad, Gizêr, Zanahoria

Carrots are a cheerful veg-patch classic, charming even when crooked, and the captivating colours and complex flavours of home-grown heirloom varieties make them even more compelling. There's always a feeling of excitement when unearthing a carrot bounty. More than confident in the kitchen, they are cherished by chefs as the heart of many culinary creations.

History

Wild carrots are native to Asia, the Middle East, and the Mediterranean, but it is believed that they were domesticated in ancient Persia, specifically in what is now Afghanistan, Iran, and Uzbekistan. However, there is evidence that a "domesticated wild carrot" type existed earlier, during ancient Greek and Roman times. The ancient Greeks gave the carrot an enchanting name, *philtron* (love charm). They believed that carrots possessed potent aphrodisiac properties, capable of making men more passionate lovers and women more submissive and promiscuous. The first-century Roman emperor Caligula was convinced, and forced the entire Senate to eat carrots, hoping to trigger an orgy or, as he described it, to see them "in a rut like wild beasts".

The domesticated carrots that are familiar today were brought to the Mediterranean, East Africa, and western Asia by Arabian traders along the Silk Road. These roots came in various colours, including creamy white, dark purple, and yellow. The orange variety, rich in the nutrient beta-carotene, is believed to have originated in Holland during the seventeenth century. It is said that Dutch horticulturists selectively bred the carrot to be orange as a gesture of respect for William of Orange (who ascended the throne of England, Scotland, and Ireland in 1689) and to represent Dutch resistance against Spanish rule. The orange carrot became associated with the House of Orange, and its cultivation was widespread in the Netherlands by the late seventeenth century.

There's no doubt that carrots contain compounds that are good for the eyes, but the popular belief that they improve night vision was born out of a propaganda

'Manpukuji' is
an impressively
long variety
that requires
deep soil.

Growing at a glance

Sow Mid-spring (early types); early summer (standard types); midsummer (late types). 8–30°C (46–86°F)

Spacing 5–8cm (2–3in) (after thinning), in rows 20–30cm (8–12in) apart

Harvest Early summer–late autumn

The feathery leaves of carrots are easily distinguished as the seedlings appear.

campaign during World War II. Wishing to keep the invention and use of radar secret from the Germans, the British Air Ministry released press statements popularizing the myth that British pilots were consuming a lot of carrots, which gave them superior night vision and was resulting in improved hits on German targets. Rabbits are also often associated with carrots, thanks to the iconic image of Bugs Bunny munching on one; however, this is another myth. Rabbits may nibble the tops of carrot leaves, but this vegetable is not a natural part of their diet. In the wild, rabbits primarily eat grasses, herbs, and leafy greens.

Culinary uses

Preparation

Carrots are great for practising knife skills and cutting techniques. The two methods I recommend are the oblique and the lozenge cut; both add a touch of class to dishes and will impress guests. The first, which is used widely in Asian kitchens, results in elongated pieces on a diagonal, and is achieved by cutting the whole carrot at a 45° angle and rolling the carrot a quarter turn before the next cut. The lozenge cut is an elegant diamond shape made by cutting rectangles that are then cut at an angle; however, this method creates a lot of waste, so use the offcuts in soups and stocks.

Dishes

The crunch of a raw carrot, sweet and earthy with a hint of aniseed, lends itself to use in an assortment of ways, adding a burst of freshness with plenty of bite. Unlike most other root veg, carrots are super sweet and palatable straight from the ground, so they can be snacked on whole, grated into salads and slaws, or sliced into crudités ready to dunk into creamy hummus or sour tzatziki. Yet they provide a different level of flavour and versatility when cooked. Their charismatic flavour and cheerful colours make them a striking addition and a treat for the taste buds in a myriad of dishes, including spiced soups, rich and velvety purées, and glazed medleys of roasted roots.

Kinpira gobo is a traditional Japanese side dish made by rapidly stir-frying thinly sliced carrots and burdock root in a mixture of soy sauce, mirin, sugar, and chilli pepper until tender yet still crunchy,

A varied crop

Carrots are often thought of as long roots, but in reality they come in a multitude of forms, from golf-ball-sized spheres to mammoth heart shapes, while some are as small and thin as a dainty little finger. Their entrancing colours are equally dazzling and diverse, from the familiar tangerine-orange to scarlet, ivory-white, purple, and canary-yellow.

> # 66
> # Unlike most other root veg, carrots are super sweet and palatable straight from the ground.

then garnishing with sesame seeds and spring onions for colour contrast, flavour, and texture. The name derives from the Japanese folklore hero Kinpira-sama, who was famous for his fiery temperament – a nod to the dish's spicy punch.

Tzimmes is an aromatic Ashkenazi Jewish stew typically made from tender carrots and dried fruit, such as prunes and raisins, which make it sweet and tangy. Other root vegetables are often added to this hearty dish to add greater depth of flavour and texture; some cooks also add chunks of meat to make it even more satisfying. *Tzimmes* is a traditional part of the meal for Rosh Hashanah, symbolizing hope for a sweet and prosperous new year.

The sweetness of these roots makes them a go-to ingredient for cakes, loaves, and cookies. In northern India a traditional carrot-based dessert is *gajar ka halwa*, which is made by slowly cooking grated carrots in a rich mixture of ghee (clarified butter), milk, sugar, and a blend of fragrant spices, including cardamom and cinnamon. The result is a mouth-watering dessert with a creamy texture. It is decorated with crunchy almonds, pistachios, and raisins and traditionally served hot during Hindu festivals, such as Diwali, Holi, and Raksha Bandhan.

Growing
Propagation
There are three main windows of opportunity to sow carrots, and with carefully planned sowings, these crunchy root veggies can be harvested throughout the summer and autumn and stored over the winter. Carrots are one of very few crops that I choose to sow directly, since sowing them in cells or trays inhibits or damages root growth and leads to a poor harvest.

Carrots benefit from a companion planting (see page 40) of marigolds.

259

'Pusa Asita' and
'Dragon' (opposite),
and 'Little Finger'
(above)

Create trenches 2cm (about 1in) deep using a dibber; the closer the rows, the smaller the carrots. If the soil or compost is dry, gently sprinkle the trench with water before sowing. Scatter the seeds thinly, two or three per cm (six or seven per inch), being careful not to over-sow. Backfill the trench gently and tamp it down to ensure good contact between soil and seeds. Carrots are notoriously slow to germinate, and once they do, they're very prone to attack by pests, so I always cover the sowing site with a layer of mesh or horticultural fleece. This is particularly important with early sowings, which also benefit from the added protection from the elements.

If the weather is dry, keep watering the sowing area until the seeds have germinated and are growing strongly. As the seedlings emerge, keep the site carefully weeded to prevent damage to the vulnerable young roots.

Aftercare

Once plants reach a height of 6–8cm (about 3in), or roughly three weeks after germination, you can begin thinning them. Start by watering the area thoroughly so the unwanted plants will come out easily, then remove the scrawniest, weakest seedlings. Finally, thin out the rest, leaving 2–3cm (about 1in) between plants. Repeat the process after another three or four weeks, leaving a final spacing of 5–8cm (2–3in) between plants. (The second

thinning may provide a harvest of baby carrots that are delicious pickled.) Carrots rarely need watering, but they may require an additional drink in early to midsummer, as they are establishing, or if the weather is particularly dry. As the roots start to swell, stop watering completely, since drier conditions will result in a far sweeter, more concentrated flavour.

Plant problems

Birds, carrot root fly, rabbits, slugs and snails (see pages 49–51)

Harvesting

Harvest all early sowings before the end of June, and be sure to pick later types before the onset of heavy and prolonged frosts. A clear and obvious sign that carrots are ready for harvesting is when they begin to protrude from the ground, revealing their crown and shoulders. If they are not displaying their crown, have a quick rummage around at the top of the roots, and you should get a clear indication of whether the carrots are big enough to be plucked from the soil. They are easier to harvest in moist soil, so if the bed is dry, give them a splash of water before picking. Pull the biggest first, to leave space for the smaller neighbouring roots to bulk up. They can usually be prised out by grasping the lower part of the foliage, giving them a quick wiggle and pulling. Larger roots may need encouragement from a hand trowel.

Storage

Early varieties are suited to eating fresh, whereas large "maincrop" carrots harvested later in the year are typically the best for extended storage. Under the right conditions, carrots will keep for four months or more. Remove the leafy tops and store the carrots unwashed in thick paper potato sacks or a box of sand, in a frost-free shed or other outbuilding.

66
There's always a feeling of excitement when unearthing a carrot bounty.

Early

'Chantenay Red Cored' Chantenay-type carrots have thick conical roots and were developed in northwestern France during the 1830s. 'Chantenay Red Cored' is the result of selection by the American breeder C. C. Morse & Co. to produce a carrot with a rich, dark red core, rather than the more common pale yellow core. It was introduced in 1930, and the company's catalogue from that time states, "The first time you pull this new carrot, you will want to eat it there and then." This is by far one of the best Chantenay types, and grows well in various soils.

'Danvers 126 Half Long' A timeless American heirloom variety that has been in cultivation since the 1870s and refined and improved over the years. In the 1940s the Eastern States Farmers' Exchange introduced strain 126, which boasted a richer orange colour, a smoother skin, better uniformity, and a more significant yield than its predecessors. It is renowned for its adaptability and reliability, and for its thick roots bursting with a rich, sweet flavour that will satisfy any carrot-lover's palate.

'Early Scarlet Horn' The oldest commercially cultivated carrot variety available, this was bred in the town of Hoorn, the Netherlands, and commonly found in the markets of Amsterdam in the early seventeenth century. The short, stumpy, rich orange roots mature quickly, making this the perfect variety for early sowing.

'Little Finger' A quick-maturing proper baby carrot developed in France specifically for pickling whole. These heritage mini roots, which have been grown for centuries, may be small but they pack a full whack of flavour and make the perfect snack straight out of the soil. Great for early sowing.

'Parisian Market' A small nineteenth-century heritage variety from France with a round, ping-pong-ball shape, only 5cm (2in) in diameter. It is perfect for challenging conditions, such as shallow, clay-rich or rocky soil, and for container gardening. It is smooth-skinned, sweet, tender, and juicy, making it popular for using whole in salads, stews, and roasted dishes. Its unique shape adds a fun element, making it a favourite among children. Legend has it that Parisian carrots were bred specifically to be petite and fast-growing, perfect for cultivation in the limited space of window boxes. In a city as densely populated as the French capital, where many people live in small apartments without access to outdoor areas, window boxes are a convenient way to cultivate flowers, herbs – and carrots.

'Touchon' A quick-maturing French heirloom variety dating back to the late eighteenth century. It produces long, sweet, crisp, deep orange, coreless roots with a fabulous flavour that makes them perfect raw or cooked. A great choice for early sowing.

Standard

'Blanche à Collet Vert' This beautiful Belgian heirloom variety produces ivory-white roots with grand green shoulders. First bred in the nineteenth century for animal feed, it is now considered the tastiest white variety. The long, pointed roots pack a delicious carroty punch, especially once cooked.

'Jaune Obtuse du Doubs' A bright and beautiful golden-yellow carrot, thick and tapering, with bottle-green shoulders. It originated in the nineteenth century in the quaint mountainous valley near the French riverside town of Doubs, near the

Intense and sweet, freshly pulled carrots are a revelation when compared to the watery specimens so often found in the supermarket.

263

border with Switzerland, where it was at first grown as cattle fodder. However, this striking carrot entered the culinary world because the slightly savoury roots are a real treat when stewed. Stores very well.

'Kuroda' A small, sweet, extra-juicy version of the Chantenay carrot that was refined and developed in Japan in the 1950s. Robust and widely adaptable to challenging conditions, these delicious deep orange, stubby, thick roots are great for juicing.

'Küttiger' A rare variety of white carrot introduced via trade from Afghanistan and cultivated in Europe since the fifteenth century, this was the mainstay of carrot production until orange types were introduced. However, it was kept alive for more than 300 years by farmers in rural Switzerland. Stocky and stout, with broad shoulders, it has excellent long-storage potential.

'Kyoto Red' A highly sought-after carrot that is hard to find outside Japan. The delectable, striking red roots have an incredibly fragrant and fruity flavour and an exquisite texture, making them easily one of the best carrots on the market. These ruby roots are highly valued, and are consumed during New Year festivities in Japan, when they are carefully carved into the shape of fruit blossom, *umebachi*, which symbolizes fertility and good luck. The brilliant colour becomes even more intense when this carrot is grown in lower temperatures, so it is best sown later in the year. The thick, exceptionally long roots can reach whopping sizes.

'Muscade' A delicious and relatively rare North African variety known for its thick, chunky, cylindrical roots that have a beautiful orange colour. Naturally heat-tolerant and boasting a wonderful texture that's crunchy and crisp, as well as an exceptional flavour, it's a wonderful all-rounder.

'Rouge Sang' An exquisite and rare French heirloom boasting a magnificent and ostentatious colour gradient from

deep, rich purple-maroon at the crown to warm, inviting sunset-orange at the tip. This hardy and robust half-long type has a sweet flavour and stunning appearance that make it a stand-out addition to any dish.

'St Valery' An exquisite bright orange carrot that has gained immense popularity among growers. As far back as 1885, the renowned French seed company Vilmorin referred to this variety as being grown in France, noting that it had already been in cultivation then for an extensive period. St Valery is a prolific, reliable, large-rooted heirloom variety that is ideal for winter storage. It is also highly sought-after for juicing owing to its sweet flavour and crisp, juicy, tender texture.

Late

'Dragon' A vibrant carrot, purple on the outside and deep orange within, and full of flavour, with an almost spicy sweetness. This variety was developed by the geneticist and plant-breeder Dr John Navazio.

'Gniff' A truly unique carrot with a psychedelic appearance. The deep purple of the short, tapering root's exterior seeps into the flesh but quickly becomes creamy white at the core.

'Gniff'

'Pusa Asita'

This is an ancient variety from the mountainous region of Ticino in southern Switzerland, where it is traditionally preserved in oil and vinegar and seasoned with garlic and aromatic herbs. This rare carrot was unearthed in the 1950s after a farmer sold the roots at market in the village of Brè, near Lugano. A particularly slow-growing root with a prominent savoury flavour and meaty, fibrous texture, it is best cooked, and offers a different eating experience altogether.

'Guérande' Also known as 'Oxheart', this magnificent French heirloom carrot is celebrated for its colossal, girthy heart shape, producing roots that are often as wide as they are long. Dating back to the nineteenth century, it's adored for its exceptional flavour and remarkable storing abilities. This versatile variety thrives in most soil types and is resilient and hardy.

'Manpukuji' Not your average carrot, this mind-boggling variety can grow enormously long under the right conditions. It is a descendant of the long carrot types that were famous during the Edo period (1603–1868) in Japan. The name is derived from a temple in Kyoto that is said to bring good fortune, and the carrot is believed to have the same effect on those who grow and consume it. It is a crucial ingredient in the traditional New

Variety	Type	Time to maturity	Colour	Average length of root
'Chantenay Red Cored'	Early	65 days	Orange	12cm (5in)
'Danvers 126 Half Long'	Early	75 days	Orange	15cm (6in)
'Early Scarlet Horn'	Early	65 days	Orange	10cm (4in)
'Little Finger'	Early	60 days	Orange	8cm (3in)
'Parisian Market'	Early	50 days	Orange	5cm (2in)
'Touchon'	Early	65 days	Orange	15–20cm (6–8in)
'Blanche à Collet Vert'	Standard	75 days	White	25–35cm (10–14in)
'Jaune Obtuse du Doubs'	Standard	75 days	Yellow	20–30cm (8–12in)
'Kuroda'	Standard	75 days	Orange	12cm (5in)
'Küttiger'	Standard	75 days	White	20cm (8in)
'Kyoto Red'	Standard	85 days	Red	30–40cm (12–16in)
'Muscade'	Standard	75 days	Orange	15–20cm (6–8in)
'Rouge Sang'	Standard	75 days	Multi	15cm (6in)
'St Valery'	Standard	75 days	Orange	25–30cm (10–12in)
'Dragon'	Late	85 days	Multi	12cm (5in)
'Gniff'	Late	95 days	Multi	15cm (6in)
'Guérande'	Late	85 days	Orange	12cm (5in)
'Manpukuji'	Late	85 days	Orange	80–150cm (30–60in)
'Pusa Asita'	Late	95 days	Purple	15–20cm (6–8in)
'Uzbek Golden'	Late	85 days	Yellow	15cm (6in)

Year celebration dish *namasu*, a salad of grated carrot and daikon radish marinated in vinegar, symbolizing good health and fortune for the coming year. 'Manpukuji' is an excellent choice for those who love growing giant vegetables. To cultivate it, I use a mixture of sand and compost in an old water butt with the bottom removed. This ensures that the roots have plenty of space to grow, leading to the development of giant carrots that are easily harvested.

'Pusa Asita' This Indian-bred variety is unique and striking in its aubergine-black colouring. The high concentration of the pigment anthocyanin makes these carrots so dark and inky that they bleed like a beetroot when sliced. The long, thin, tapered roots thrive in hot climates and have a rich, earthy flavour that sets them apart from orange carrots.

'Uzbek Golden' A cracking canary-yellow carrot with a distinctively short, thick root. Packed full of natural sweetness, it is delicious raw or cooked. This ancient Uzbekistani heirloom variety is used widely in local cuisine for *plov*, a hearty dish of rice, carrots, meat, and spices. This versatile and robust carrot yields delectably sweet roots even in challenging soils.

265

'Del Veneto'

Celeriac

Apium graveolens var. *rapaceum*

Also known as Céleri-rave, Knob celery, Sedano rapa

These knobbly, gnarly, soil-encrusted roots are constantly swept aside in the vegetable beauty pageant, but they are delicious when they roll into the kitchen, blending caramelly, nutty flavours with delicately aniseedy notes. Celeriac is considered one of the trickiest crops to grow: often challenging to raise from seed, and requiring fertile soil and a long growing season.

History

The lineage of celeriac is closely linked to that of celery, since they derive from the same Mediterranean marshland plant, wild celery. It's believed that the ancient Egyptians, Greeks, and Romans consumed early forms of celery for medicinal purposes. However, celeriac achieved significant culinary status during the Middle Ages and was first recorded as a gourmet ingredient in France in the seventeenth century. Technically speaking, these "root" veggies aren't roots at all. Instead, they develop an enlarged hypocotyl, the part of the plant's stem that is below the leaves and directly above the root system. Celeriac is now grown across the globe, including in Central America, Europe, and Asia, but it remains an underrated and unsung hero of the vegetable kingdom.

Culinary uses

Preparation

Despite its prehistoric appearance, celeriac is simple to prepare. The easiest way to approach peeling is to use a sharp knife and not fear losing some of the flesh. Peeled celeriac discolours quickly, so as you slice it, drop the pieces into a bowl of cold water acidulated with a squeeze of lemon juice or a small splash of white-wine vinegar.

Dishes

Celeriac is incredibly versatile. It has a rich, warming taste, a splendid sweetness, and a meaty texture when cooked.

However, it is suitable for more than just hearty stews and roasts. When raw, it remains crisp and crunchy, with an earthy flavour that makes it perfect for winter salads, such as the simple French classic celeriac remoulade. The key to a good remoulade is to julienne the celeriac into thin, uniform matchsticks. The traditional dressing calls for mayonnaise, mustard, lemon juice, and seasoning, and I like to add grated apple and toasted walnuts for extra sweetness and crunch. Celeriac purée is a deliciously nutty alternative to traditional mashed potatoes. For the sweetest, creamiest, most luxurious results, soften small cubes of celeriac in a generous amount of butter for five minutes before simmering them gently in seasoned milk until soft and tender. Separate the cubes from the cooking liquor and blend, gradually adding the milk until the mixture reaches the desired consistency. A squeeze of lemon juice at the end brings a zesty zing to cut through the richness.

Growing

Propagation

The seeds are as small as a grain of sand and notoriously tricky to germinate. For best results, scatter the seeds directly on to moist compost and leave them uncovered, because they need light to sprout. Pop a clear propagation cloche over the trays and keep them indoors on a windowsill or a heat mat with sufficient light. Exposing the seedlings to cold early on can lead to crop failure through premature flowering. To ensure the seeds stay moist, use a spray bottle to mist them gently as required. Remove the cover when the seedlings appear, about ten days after sowing. Once these slow-growing young plants have developed their first true leaf, usually after another three weeks, they can be pricked out into large seed cells or small pots. Grow the young plants in a polytunnel or greenhouse until the weather warms up in

late spring, at which point they can be safely planted out in the garden.

Celeriac thrives in rich, heavy soil that retains moisture. If your soil is light and free-draining, like mine, consider adding a thick layer of mulch to the beds before planting celeriac out in the garden. Bury them deeply and water them in thoroughly.

Aftercare

Celeriac requires ample moisture to swell, and young plants must be kept well watered, especially during hot spells. If your soil is chalky or sandy, you will need to water more than on heavy soils, especially as the "roots" begin to bulk up in the late summer and autumn. Watch out for aphids, and wash or brush off any that you see. Remove the older leaves from the crown to encourage the developing root to swell. This also helps to deter slugs.

Plant problems

Aphids, celery fly, celery leaf spot, mice, slugs and snails, woodlice (see pages 49–51)

Harvesting

After six long months or more, in mid-October, the plants are finally ready for the pot. Crops can be harvested as required; however, all celeriac should be lifted from the ground by late autumn, since they are susceptible to disease and to attack by slugs and woodlice.

To avoid damaging the soil, refrain from pulling up the crops. Instead, use a trowel to gain purchase underneath the bulbous and swollen hypocotyl, and, using a sharp knife, slice through the thick, entangled spiderweb-like root system as close to the soil as possible. Although the leafy tops are often tossed into the compost, they can be used in the kitchen in the same way as regular celery (see page 61), albeit with a stronger and more pronounced flavour.

Celeriac can also be harvested small, a little larger than a cricket ball, when it has a delicate, soft texture and a more intense flavour. Young celeriac has become popular in Peruvian cuisine, where it is traditionally served ceviche-style. Young celeriac roots provide a refreshing crunch and subtle sweetness that balance the acidity of the lime juice and the heat of the chilli, for a great vegan alternative to this traditional fish dish.

Storage

Celeriac stores exceptionally well over the winter. It tends not to shrivel, retaining its texture for months after harvest. To prepare it for storage, remove the leaves cleanly by snapping them downwards, but do not wash the celeriac; a little compost will help to lock in moisture. Keep the vegetables in a wooden crate in a cool shed or other outbuilding. Celeriac can withstand a light frost, but if heavy frost is expected, move it to a frost-free area.

Recommended varieties

'Del Veneto' Del Veneto celeriac has been growing in the romantic Venetian countryside for centuries. Northern Italians prize it highly as an ingredient, but it is far less common in the south of the country. This variety has snowy-white flesh that is delicate in flavour and smooth in texture, providing a delightful culinary experience.

'Giant Prague' Introduced in 1871, this variety quickly became a favourite among home growers and has maintained its position as one of the top-performing celeriacs. This Czechia heirloom produces massive knobbly roots that resemble a large globe with a flat base. They're highly regarded for their consistent growth, strong resilience, extended shelf life, and delightful taste.

'Monstorpolgi' This heritage celeriac has been grown in France since 1623 and is considered a rare find. It may be on the small side, but its firm, round "roots" are valued highly for their delicious, full-bodied, nutty flavour with a hint of sweetness and a subtle liquorice aftertaste. It is super hardy and stores extremely well.

> 66
> **Technically speaking, these "root" veggies aren't roots at all.**

Gradually remove the outer leaves (overleaf, left) as they flop, to expose the crown and allow it to swell.

'Giant Prague' and 'Del Veneto' (overleaf, right)

Parsnip

Pastinaca sativa

Also known as Chukandar, Pastinaca, Yaban havucu

The parsnip's spiced taste evokes nostalgic memories of winter. Its distinctive hearty, wholesome flavour is sweet, earthy, and nutty, and pairs perfectly with spices to create deep, robust layers of warming flavour against the bitter cold. Requiring a lengthy growing season, the gnarly, tapered, creamy-coloured roots provide substantial harvests at a time of slim pickings.

History

Parsnips originated in the eastern Mediterranean and northeast to the Caucasus. Their wild relatives – some of which are deadly poisonous – can be found growing in hedgerows across Europe, showcasing stunning displays of firework-like blooms that serve as a crucial source of food and shelter for numerous animals, birds, and insects.

The cultivation of parsnips is believed to have begun during Roman times, but there is limited archaeological evidence, and the confusion between parsnips and carrots – both of which were referred to as *pastinaca* at that time – is little help. Legend has it that Emperor Tiberius loved parsnips passionately, to the extent that he accepted them as part-payment of the tribute owed by the peoples of Germania. The imported roots grew abundantly along the Rhine, where the cold climate with its heavy frosts caused a more profound, sweeter flavour to develop in the parsnips, a taste that tickled Tiberius' fancy.

In the Middle Ages, before potatoes were introduced from the New World in the sixteenth century, parsnips were the preferred root vegetable in Europe. They were a significant part of the diet of humans and animals, and a valuable source of sweetener before the arrival of cane sugar. Additionally, home brewers commonly used parsnips to create old-fashioned, full-bodied, high-alcohol wine.

The white roots of parsnips have a complex flavour very different from that of other root vegetables.

273

> ❝
> **Parsnips are most delicious when roasted until golden and crisp.**

The first parsnips can be harvested in mid-autumn, but the crop will continue throughout the winter.

Culinary uses

Preparation

Young, home-grown parsnips are so tender that they often don't even require peeling. However, do peel and remove the central core from large roots, which can be tough and fibrous.

Dishes

Parsnips can be baked into cakes and mashed as an alternative to potatoes, and work exceptionally well in comforting soups, stews, and casseroles, imparting rich layers of flavour. With their delicately peppery taste and liquorice undertones, they are most delicious when roasted until golden and crisp, bringing out their signature rich caramel flavour. A wonderful way to elevate the humble roast parsnip is by preparing it in the same way as Hasselback potatoes. Small, tender roots work best for this. Start by cutting the parsnips in half lengthwise, then score deep lateral cuts every 0.5cm (¹/₄in) along the length of the vegetable, without cutting through the whole root. Sprinkle with olive oil, herbs, and other seasonings before roasting until crisp.

Interestingly, a simple parsnip recipe found in Apicius' *De re culinaria*, a Roman cookbook, can be seen as a predecessor to French fries with ketchup. In it, the knobbly roots are cut into chips, fried in olive oil, and served with a tangy dipping sauce known as *oenogarum*, consisting of reduced red wine, *garum* (fish sauce), and a generous amount of pepper, among other ingredients.

Growing

Propagation

Parsnips are often accused of being difficult to raise from seed, but really they are just slow to germinate. It can take 30 days from sowing for the young shoots to emerge, but the plants are relatively easy to care for once established. They are among the few seeds I like to sow directly into the soil, since transplanting or pricking

Growing at a glance

Sow Mid-spring–early summer, 10–20°C (50–68°F)

Spacing 2.5–10cm (1–4in)

Harvest Mid-autumn– early spring

out can harm the long taproot, causing it to fork or grow poorly. They prefer growing in loose, free-draining soil, and won't perform well in heavy clay.

In a temperate climate, parsnips are best sown once the soil has warmed up. Rake the beds gently and use a dibber to make a trench 3–5cm (1–2in) deep. Choose a calm day, since the light seeds will easily blow away in a breeze. Sow thinly, leaving a gap of about 1cm (¹/₂in) between seeds, but don't be afraid to over-sow, because germination can be unreliable. Backfill the trench carefully and firm down the compost gently to ensure good contact with the seed. The lengthy germination time means it is essential to keep the beds free of weeds and moist around the sowing site, especially during dry spells.

Aftercare

Once germinated, allow the plants to form a set of true leaves before thinning them out. Parsnips can be thinned out on a sliding scale, depending on the desired size of the root. Thin them to 2.5cm (1in) apart for small, dainty parsnips; to 5cm (2in) for

Warning

It's essential to protect your skin when weeding, maintaining, or harvesting parsnips. The sap in their leaves and stems contains a chemical called furanocoumarin, which sensitizes the skin to sunlight. A severe inflammatory reaction can follow, including irritation and blistering.

'Viceroy' (left) and
'Bedford Monarch'

a medium-sized crop; and to 10cm (4in) if you want hefty roots. Once established, they require little or no maintenance and no additional watering, since their roots can absorb moisture from deep within the soil; however, parsnips often perform better in wetter conditions and predominantly begin to swell and plump up during the rains of autumn. Make sure their shoulders are covered with soil at all times, to reduce the risk of canker; this is particularly important if you garden on heavy soil.

Plant problems

Aphids, canker, carrot root fly, rodents (see pages 49–51)

Harvesting

Harvesting begins in the autumn and continues until early spring. Parsnips become even sweeter and more flavourful after they've experienced frost, when the starches stored in the roots break down and are converted into natural sugars. Although the roots can be pulled up by hand in loose, sandy soils, I prefer to use a trowel to prise them out, to avoid damaging them and jeopardizing their storage ability.

Storage

Parsnips will keep in the ground over the winter and can be gathered as needed. However, if the soil becomes waterlogged or the roots have been infected by carrot root fly, they can be susceptible to canker or rotting. In that case it's best to pull them in early winter, brush off excess dirt (but don't wash them), trim the leaves, and store the roots in wooden crates or paper potato sacks, in the dark, in a frost-free shed or other outbuilding. If stored correctly, they will last for several months.

'**Avon Resistor**' A delicious, easy-to-grow parsnip that's highly resistant to canker and an excellent choice for clay and other heavy soils, owing to its short root. This is an old ex-commercial variety from the South Island of New Zealand, developed from an older heritage parsnip. The late seed-saver Henry Harrington kept the type alive and passed his collection on to Kōanga, the home of New Zealand's largest and most significant heritage food and plant collection. Seed of this variety is now sadly scarce and hard to come by, however.

'**Bedford Monarch**' A rare old English heritage parsnip from the east of the country. The exceptionally sweet roots are long with broad shoulders, and can reach mammoth sizes. This smooth, white-skinned variety is highly resistant to canker and extremely cold-hardy, performing well in the UK's frosty winters. Harvesting after a few frosts will increase the sweetness even further.

'**Guernsey**' ('**Half Long**') Despite its name, this is in fact a French-bred heirloom. This old treasure was introduced to England in the early nineteenth century, but it is thought to have been developed much earlier than that. 'Half Long' refers to its broad, chunky shoulders and short, chubby root, similar to a Chantenay carrot (see page 263). This makes it ideal for shallow or stony soils, producing sweet, high-yielding white roots that can be stored for a long time.

'**Hollow Crown**' One of the oldest commercially cultivated heirloom parsnips, dating from the nineteenth century and still farmed today. Its name comes from the sunken, crown-shaped hollow top, from which the leaves sprout. The roots can be up to 30cm (12in) long and have firm, creamy-white flesh that is exceptionally sweet, with a nutty edge. This has remained among the best-tasting varieties for centuries, and is particularly delicious roasted or mashed. It is a resilient variety and resistant to canker, making it reliable even during challenging seasons.

'**Kral Russian**' An unusual bulbous-shaped parsnip that looks rather like a beetroot or turnip. This sweet, crisp-flavoured Russian heirloom variety is extremely cold-hardy, capable of surviving the harshest winter weather. Its globed shape makes it a superb choice for growers with heavy and/or stony soil. These spherical parsnips are also easier to harvest; they can be twisted out easily with minimal disturbance to the soil, since no digging is needed to lift them.

'**Student**' An early nineteenth-century English heirloom developed by James Buckman, a botanist at Cirencester Agricultural College, as an experiment to see if crossing domesticated strains with wild parsnips could improve them. The result was a phenomenal variety with long, slender roots, creamy flesh, smooth skin, and a narrow core – now considered the sweetest parsnip. It also boasts excellent resistance to disease. There has been confusion about whether this variety is the same as 'Hollow Crown' (left), but it is in fact a separate and even better-flavoured variety.

'**Tender and True**' Introduced in 1897, this variety has remained a popular choice among growers ever since. Its elegantly elongated root has tender flesh with a thin core that does not become woody. This veg-patch classic is known for its consistent production of long, straight roots, making it a common sight on show benches worldwide.

'**Viceroy**' An extremely rare heritage parsnip, of which little is known. Fortunately, the Irish Seed Savers Association, which works hard to preserve the heritage of food crops for future generations, has kept this variety alive. The seeds came from a heritage collection previously held by a now-defunct English seed company, Seeds by Size. 'Viceroy' has long, tapering roots and a delightfully sweet flavour, and is very hardy.

'**White Gem**' Selected in the 1970s from 'Offenham Market Parsnip', an esteemed early twentieth-century variety, this is now among the most popular and dependable options. Its short roots with their broad shoulders are tasty, winter-hardy, and easy to cultivate, even in poor, heavy, or shallow soil. It is known for its sweet taste, high productivity, and resistance to canker.

Potatoes

Solanum tuberosum

Also known as Papa, Prátaí, Riwai, Spuds, Tatties

There's nothing quite like a spud, the most comforting vegetable of all. Whether mashed, boiled, baked, or fried, tender tatties deliver a wholesome hit that's certain to satisfy even the pickiest eater. There are thousands of cultivars, from those in magnificent multicoloured jackets with vivid splashes of pink, purple, and gold, to others that appear unassuming until they are sliced open, unveiling eye-catching pigments from dark maroon to mauve to decorative black rings.

History

A cousin of the aubergine and tomato (see pages 125 and 160), these tuber-forming nightshades are native to the high altitudes of the South American Andes, centred on present-day Peru and Bolivia, and were first domesticated between 8,000 and 10,000 years ago on the shores of Lake Titicaca. The cultivation of the spud allowed the expansion of early civilizations in the region, and it formed an essential part of their diet as they moved from foraging to farming. They also discovered a genius potato preserving technique called *chuño*, a five-day freeze-drying method made possible by the fluctuating temperatures of these high settlements. Tubers would be left out to freeze in the bitter night and allowed to thaw in the sun the following day; the process was repeated for five days until the potatoes were perfectly dehydrated and ready for storage, where they would remain sound for several years. The Indigenous peoples' love for the spud went beyond just consuming it; they saw it as a cultural symbol, worshipping it, burying their dead with it, and even using its cooking duration as a basis for measuring time.

The potato spread to the wider world with the arrival of Spanish conquistadors in 1536. Seeking to ransack the region for precious metals, they instead unearthed the spud and its impressive taste, storage ability, and nutritional value. They hastily sailed this bounty home, and the tubers played a fundamental role in feeding the sharply expanding population of Europe. Not long afterwards, in 1589, the English colonialist Sir Walter Raleigh introduced potatoes to Ireland, although it took many decades for the spud to solidify itself within Irish culture. In the nineteenth century – by which time it was providing sustenance nationwide – the deadly arrival of late blight caused the Great Famine of 1845–52, in which an estimated 1 million people died. The most common variety being cultivated at the time (as much as 80 per cent of the crop across Ireland, it is thought) was 'Lumper', which, although not as tasty as others, was prized for its ability to thrive in poor soil, producing plentiful crops. However, it displayed little resistance to blight. It was grown in vast monocultures, so the horror quickly ripped through entire fields, decimating harvests and populations. Although almost lost from circulation now, this type is still available today and produces a bumper crop of large, bumpy tubers with the signature "golden potato" skin.

Culinary uses

Preparation

If boiling spuds, place them in a pan of cold water and bring them to a simmer, rather than adding them to already bubbling water. This prevents the starch in the potatoes from reacting too quickly with the hot water, which can cause uneven cooking and an unpleasant mealy texture.

Dishes

Potatoes possess the ability to present both creamy and crispy textures in a single bite. They are now such a mainstay in cuisine worldwide that it's hard to imagine life without them, from crisp-coated, fluffy-centred roasties with a Sunday lunch to the delicately smooth texture of gnocchi, crunchy hash browns, and thinly sliced and cream-baked dauphinoise. Whether simmered into a hearty stew or cut into matchsticks, deep-fried, and accompanying a burger, the versatility of the spud takes some beating.

In Peru, there are many dishes that shine the limelight on these tubers. One of the most famous is a popular Lima street food, *salchipapas*, the original loaded fries. Fried potatoes are doused in spicy *ají amarillo* (yellow pepper) sauce and loaded with beef sausage and other goodies, such as coriander leaves and coleslaw. A dish

that is equally messy and moreish is the much-loved *papa a la Huancaína*, tender boiled potatoes submerged in a spicy cheese sauce and garnished with hard-boiled egg and black olives. A much more elegant, refined Peruvian potato creation is *causa rellena*, a potato salad in the loosest of terms; it is a true work of culinary art with a blend of unique flavours and textures. Served cold, it features layers of seasoned mashed potato infused with tangy lime juice and spicy chilli with various delicious fillings, perhaps tender spiced chicken, succulent seafood, or creamy avocado. This wonderful dish is served on a bed of lettuce and garnished with brined black olives.

A multicoloured harvest of potatoes for a variety of uses. Some will be stored into the following year, while others (particularly the smaller ones, or any that are damaged) must be eaten more quickly.

Growing

Spuds can be divided into three categories (see table opposite). First and second earlies are also known as new potatoes. Ideal for small plots, these diminutive but fast-growing varieties are harvested in the summer, freeing up valuable space. Most have thin skin, waxy flesh, and a sweet flavour. All types of potato are frost-sensitive, but first and second earlies are more at risk of damage. First earlies should be planted no earlier than about three weeks before the last frost is likely. Protect their foliage with a double layer of horticultural fleece if frost is forecast.

Maincrop potatoes produce a heavy yield of big tubers with thick skins, making them well suited to winter storage. Most have an earthy flavour and floury flesh. Maincrops are planted once all risk of frost has passed, but they take a long time to mature and are at risk of the late onset of blight and soil-borne pests in the autumn.

Propagation

Although they can be grown from true seed, potatoes are generally cultivated from seed potatoes, small tubers kept from last year's crop that will produce a clone of the mother plant. Seed potatoes must first be chitted (allowed to sprout) in a bright spot four to six weeks before planting. This keeps the shoots short and stubby; if they are chitted in the dark, they will produce long, spindly shoots that break easily when planting.

There are many techniques and tricks involved in cultivating spuds, from growing through a membrane laid on the soil, to

Growing at a glance

Plant/harvest See table opposite

Spacing 30cm (12in) (first earlies); 40–45cm (16–18in) (other types)

digging deep trenches, to using pots or bags of compost. Yet the simplest and most effective way is to make an incision in the growing medium by pushing the whole length of a trowel in and levering the tool away, creating a neat opening for the tuber to slip into. Ensure the tubers are 5–10cm (2–4in) below the surface and that the eyes or chits (buds) are pointing upwards, before backfilling the soil or compost.

Aftercare

As the shoots emerge, earth them up by mounding the soil over the leaves, allowing the growing tips to poke through. This can be done twice or three times during the season. Tubers exposed to sun turn green and become inedible, so earth up plants with tubers visible on the surface immediately. Extra water is rarely needed, although first and second earlies may benefit from a deep drink several times during their final few

Saving seed potatoes

Keep back a selection of small spuds to grow the following year. Only save those from the healthiest plants, with no signs of blight or scab. The ideal size is that of a large chicken egg. Even tubers that have turned green from exposure to sunlight can be used as seed tatties. Store them in small paper bags until it's time for chitting in the spring.

Type	Plant	Growing time	Harvest
First Early	early spring (protected from frost)	10–12 weeks	early–midsummer
Second Early	mid-spring (protected from frost)	14–16 weeks	mid–late summer
Maincrop	mid–late spring	16–22 weeks	late summer–mid-autumn

A successfully chitted potato (opposite) with short, strong shoots that will not be damaged when the tuber is planted.

Check the tubers as you harvest them (below) and keep back any green ones for use as seed potatoes.

weeks if the weather is very dry. Water at the base of the plant and avoid wetting the leaves, to reduce the risk of blight.

Plant problems

Aphids, blackleg, blight, scab, slugs and snails, wireworm (see pages 49–51)

Harvesting

Pulling up spuds is exciting as you eagerly wait to discover what bounty lies below.

For early types, wait until the flowers bloom and the rich, dark green leaves fade. Before harvesting, rummage in the soil at the base of the plants and feel the size of the tubers; early varieties are at their best when harvested at about the size of a large chicken egg. Maincrops will continue to bulk up in the ground until mid-autumn; however, the longer they remain in the earth, the more they are at risk from pests lurking in the soil or the late onset of blight. Prise the plants carefully from the ground by pulling at the base of the stem. Most tubers will be attached to the roots of the stem or lurking just below the surface, but you might need a hand trowel to search out any that have developed deeper down. Sift through the soil carefully with your trowel or fingers to make sure no tiny taters are forgotten, or they will quickly sprout and produce unwanted plants. If the weather is dry, leave the tubers on the surface of the soil for a couple of hours after harvesting, to soak up the sun, dry off, and harden their skins.

Storage

Maincrop potatoes store best, although some second earlies will keep well if they are first allowed to grow large. Potatoes store best unwashed in large paper sacks; repurposed 25kg (50lb) flour sacks work a treat if you can get hold of them from a bakery. Keep potatoes in the dark in a cool but frost-free shed or other outbuilding, and check regularly for spoilt tubers, removing them before they have a chance to infect or rot their neighbours. If any potatoes start to sprout, remove the eyes and shoots.

First Early

'Beauty of Hebron' A rosy pink-skinned American heirloom developed from 'Garnet Chile' (see right) in New York State during the nineteenth century. This was one of the main varieties used to restock Ireland's farms and fields after the Great Famine, thanks to its early maturing and resilience to blight.

'Early Rose' A pink-skinned, early-maturing all-rounder with excellent flavour, developed in 1861 by Albert Bresee of Vermont, this is an offspring of the 'Garnet Chile' potato (see right).

'Home Guard' A Scottish-bred spud released during World War II, this was a mainstay in the gardens of wartime Britain thanks to its fast-growing and early-harvesting traits. It is a great-tasting potato that is well suited to salads.

'Red Duke of York' This delightful dry, fluffy potato – the perfect all-rounder – is wrapped in a royal red skin. It is said to have been found in Holland in 1942 among a crop of the renowned late nineteenth-century heirloom variety 'Duke of York', developed by William Sim of Fyvie in Aberdeenshire, Scotland.

Second Early

'Edzell Blue' A beautiful blueish-purple-skinned spud named after the village of Edzell in Angus, one of Scotland's most famous regions for potato cultivation. Although bred in the late nineteenth century, it wasn't made available until 1915. It has a mild flavour with a delicate sweetness, well suited to roasting.

'International Kidney' Born out of chance, this is the historical variety cultivated for the famous 'Jersey Royal', which has an EU Protected Designation of Origin (PDO) (see panel below). It is hands down the best salad potato thanks to its rich, nutty flavour and creamy texture, but it's also perfect for boiling, crushing, or baking into quiches and tarts.

'Ratte' This outstandingly well-flavoured heirloom potato is thought to have been developed around the city of Lyon in eastern France and has been grown since the mid-to-late nineteenth century, although some believe it has Danish heritage. The thin, oblong tubers have a delightful texture and have become a mainstay in the Michelin-starred kitchens of France.

'Shetland Black' These stunning creamy white-fleshed potatoes have a striking dark purple ring running through them. First documented growing on the Shetland Islands in 1923, they look exceptionally cool when cut into thin discs and fried, for an ornamental crisp.

Maincrop

'Fortyfold' A blueish-purple-skinned spud with off-white flesh, this is one of the oldest British-bred

'Edzell Blue'

tatties. It dates back to 1836, although it hasn't been grown commercially since the mid-twentieth century. It produces slight, knobbly, oval tubers with succulent, delectable flesh.

'Garnet Chile' The Anglican minister Rev. Chauncey Goodrich developed this heirloom in the 1850s, and it's the grandparent of many of the cultivars that are on offer today. Some see it as a holy grail for potato-breeders: resilient and productive, with exceptional flavour. It produces chunky, odd-shaped spheres with pinkish-red skin.

'Highland Burgundy Red' A striking deep red-fleshed potato bred in the Scottish highlands, this variety has a maroon centre with a yellow ring at the perimeter. Rare and difficult to come by, these richly flavoured sweet spuds were served to the Duke of Burgundy in 1936 at a dinner party at the Savoy hotel in London; it is said that their colour and taste went down a treat with the duke, so the variety was named in his honour.

'Makah Ozette' A truly delicious, earthy-tasting spud with a creamy texture. These caramel-coloured oblong, knobbly tubers have been grown for centuries by the Indigenous Makah of the Pacific Northwest of the United States. The potatoes found their way to the region during the eighteenth century with Spanish

A chance discovery: the 'Jersey Royal'

In the late nineteenth century Hugh de la Haye, who farmed on the steep slopes of the Bellozanne valley in Jersey, experimented with an absurdly large potato he had bought from the greengrocer, and which sprouted 15 shoots. He cut it up and planted the pieces. All but one of the resulting plants grew as large as the parent, and at harvest he miraculously unearthed the first ever bounty of small, thin-skinned, kidney-shaped tatties, which were initially christened 'Jersey Royal Fluke', but later abbreviated.

Māori potatoes

Taewa or Rīwai is the name given to a collection of potatoes cultivated by the Maori people of New Zealand before British colonialists proclaimed sovereignty over the land. The spuds are said to have arrived on the islands with early travellers hunting whales. Most of these types are irregularly shaped, with knobbles, grooves, and creases, and have terrifically marked jackets with contrasting colours and patterns. Over the years, some have been lost or made extinct; however, thankfully, owing to the ongoing work of Indigenous people, seed-savers, and research institutes, many of these terrific tubers are still available. Varieties to keep an eye out for are 'Huakaroro', 'Karuparera', 'Kowiniwini', 'MoeMoe', and 'Tūtae-Kurī'.

'Mr Little's Yetholm Gypsy'

conquistadors led by Salvador Fidalgo, who carried seeds and supplies from their travels in the South. The Makah soon chased the colonialists out and took control of the gardens and crops the Spanish left behind, and the spud became an essential source of carbohydrate in their diets. They stewarded this potato over the years, and it wasn't until the late 1980s that it was made more widely available.

'Mr Little's Yetholm Gypsy'
A striking purple potato that looks as though it has been splashed with beige and pink paint. It is thought to have been bred by Gypsies in the southern Scottish town of Yetholm, a stronghold for Romany people in the nineteenth century. One Mr Little acquired the tubers at a horse fair in the 1940s and stewarded the cultivar until the passionate potato preservationist Alan Romans received them from the Little family. The tubers are small to medium-sized, oval, and thick-skinned, with brilliant white flesh and an earthy, sweet flavour.

'Pink Fir Apple' An old French heirloom variety of long, haphazardly misshapen tubers with a dull, thin, antique pink skin, rich yellow flesh, a fantastic nutty flavour, and a buttery texture. It was introduced into the United Kingdom in the 1850s and has since won the RHS Award of Garden Merit.

'Red King Edward' This British-bred treasure stemmed from a naturally occurring genetic variation in 1916. The original 'King Edward', released in 1902, was believed to have been bred in Northumberland under the name 'Fellside Hero' before being developed by John Butler, who made it available at the time of King Edward VII's coronation and named it as a salute to His Royal Highness. It's believed that Butler had to write to Buckingham Palace to gain the king's consent to name the tattie in his honour. A decorative spud with a royal red-and-gold-marbled skin, it is a great all-rounder in the kitchen.

'Russet Burbank' This large, oblong, heavily russeted potato was developed in 1874 by the American horticulturist Luther Burbank and is now one of the most famous in the world. The top choice for French fries, it's one of the main varieties McDonald's requires its farmers to cultivate.

'Vitelotte' A vibrant purple-fleshed tattie with an elongated, knobbly appearance. Sometimes known as the truffle potato, thanks to its rich, earthy flavour, it was first listed in France during the nineteenth century but was in fact developed in Peru hundreds of years earlier than that. The dry, floury flesh has a distinctive nutty flavour with rich, earthy undertones.

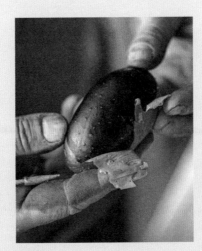

'Vitelotte'

'Pink Fir Apple'

Radish

Raphanus sativus

Also known as Daikon, Luóbo, Mooli

Radishes are renowned for providing quick harvests of tender, crunchy roots with a mildly sweet yet peppery flavour. They come in a rainbow of shades and shapes: golden globes and tapering, pointed purple types, long bicoloured roots in lime-green and creamy white, even some with fancy pink and purple jackets and vivid pigments running through their flesh.

History

A member of the brassica family, the radish is considered native to Asia, and wild forms still grow freely in China. Yet it was first documented in ancient Europe by the Greeks and Romans, and, over time, spread to become steeped in various cultures worldwide. The Greeks revered the radish, and carved its shape in solid gold to make lockets as offerings for the sun god Apollo at the temple of Delphi. In parts of India, it is believed that sleeping with a radish under the pillow will ward off nightmares and promote healthy rest. In Mexico, meanwhile, an annual celebration, Noche de Rábanos (Night of the Radishes), has been held since 1897 in honour of the root in the Christmas markets of Oaxaca. Artists and amateurs alike take to the streets to showcase their creations carved from radishes: everything from classic Nativity scenes to traditional Aztec and Mayan art, to nature and modern inventions.

Culinary uses

Preparation

Serve radishes as soon as possible after cutting them, since their punchy flavour dissipates quickly after harvesting. If they look limp, refresh them in a bowl of iced water for a few hours before serving.

Dishes

All too often, the radish is not given the limelight, and is used only for snacking on whole or chopped into salads. But it can play a fundamental role, providing a refreshing sweet-and-sour palate-cleanser for sushi when pickled, a delectable, wholesome side dish when roasted, a crunchy addition to slaws, or a delightful breakfast when pan-seared and served on toast with a poached egg. *Radis au beurre* is a simple Parisian springtime dish of just four humble ingredients served on a board, and is the perfect way to display their authentic flavour. 'French Breakfast', a group of red radishes with white tips, is traditionally used for it. The roots are cleaned and the tops removed, but a small section of the stem is left to act as a handle; the radishes are then dipped into soft room-temperature butter, sprinkled with sea salt, and eaten with crusty bread.

Takuan is a yellow pickle that is popular in Japan and one of the tastiest ways to preserve the country's daikon radish. The seventeenth-century Buddhist monk Takuan Sōhō is often credited with the recipe that is named after him. Whole daikon are harvested and hung outside to dry in the sun for two weeks on towering bamboo frames known as *daikon yagura*. This reduces the water content of the root and, in turn, increases the sweetness. The daikon are then fermented whole in a mixture of salt and rice vinegar and

Growing at a glance

Sow Late winter–late spring (spring types); midsummer–early autumn (winter types); late summer (spring types), 6–30°C (43–86°F)

Plant out Early spring–early summer (spring types); late summer–mid-autumn (winter types); early autumn (spring types)

Spacing 20–30cm (8–12in), depending on type

Harvest All year round

seasoned with yuzu, kombu, and sake lees (a white paste that's a by-product of the sake-brewing process), and the rich yellow colour – which becomes richer the longer they are left – is imparted by turmeric and the *benihana* flower. This pickle is also highly regarded in Korea, where it is known as *danmuji*. It is served with such foods as the noodle dish *jjajangmyeon*, where it cuts through the thick, rich, black bean-flavoured sauce perfectly.

Growing
Propagation
Radishes love cold weather, often bolting in the summer sun or producing roots that

The daikon radish
'Green Luobo'

some might find too pungently spicy. For optimal success, they should be grown in the cooler months of spring, autumn, and winter. These quick growers often provide the first bounty from new sowings early in the year, and can be divided roughly into two categories: spring and winter types. Spring types are often quick to mature and can still be sown in later months. Winter varieties are usually large and slow-growing, and do not perform well if planted early in the season. They also store well after harvest, and will last for months under the right conditions.

Spring radishes can be started in late winter if they are germinated indoors and transferred to an unheated polytunnel or greenhouse to grow on. The young seedlings are hardy and robust and will survive the low temperatures of late winter, but the initial warmth promotes faster germination. Sowing can continue every two weeks until late spring, when the roots become extremely hot and spicy. A second window for spring types opens in the late summer, providing sweet and mild harvests into autumn. Multi-sow all spring types in seed cells, in clumps of four, which can be planted out as a cluster. Straight after germination, they are resilient enough to grow on in an unheated polytunnel, greenhouse, or cold frame for two or three weeks before being planted out in the garden 20cm (8in) apart. Don't be afraid to bury their long stems if the seedlings have grown leggy.

Winter radishes can be sown in seed cells, two seeds per cell. Either plant them out as a pair or discard the weaker seedling if you want to grow larger roots. Allow the plants to grow for two or three weeks before planting them out in the patch 25–30cm (10–12in) apart.

Aftercare

Early plantings should be protected from the elements with horticultural fleece. Like all brassicas, radishes are at risk from

countless pests, so as the weather warms (and for later sowings), replace the fleece with mesh to protect the plants from birds and insects. Keep all radishes well watered until established; subsequently, for early types, a good drink every few days in dry spells will ensure crunchy, tender, mild roots, but later sowings should require little watering because of seasonal rain.

Plant problems

Birds, cabbage root fly, caterpillars, flea beetle, slugs and snails (see pages 49–51)

Harvesting

Spring types should be harvested as soon as they are plump and juicy; their tender flesh quickly becomes woody or sometimes

'Black Spanish Round' (left) and **'Red Meat'**

A bunch of mixed radishes is the starting point for a delicious and eye-catching dish.

airy as their centres hollow. Winter varieties are more robust and can be left in the ground until they are big and bulky, after which they can be lifted, manicured, and stored. For all types, twist the roots until they come loose so that you can harvest them easily without disturbing the soil; larger daikon types need more encouragement to release their extra-long roots from deep below the surface, and this can be done by rocking the roots gently or moving them in a circular motion.

Storage

Spring radishes are best eaten freshly picked, but they will stay tender and crunchy if you remove the foliage and store them in a bowl of water in the fridge. After harvesting winter types, trim the foliage and store the roots unwashed in a box in a frost-free shed or other outbuilding, where they should last for two or three months.

Winter

'China Rose' These long, thick rose-petal-pink roots have a delicate, sweet flavour and are delicious raw. The seeds were dispersed by Jesuit missionaries returning to Europe from China in the seventeenth century. Suitable for storing.

'Green Luobo' Stemming from northern China, where it is known as 'Qingluobo', this giant green-fleshed radish that fades to white towards the tip performs best in cool weather towards the end of the season. Sharp and spicy, with a sweet, almost fruity flavour.

'Mooli Minowase' An old Japanese daikon capable of reaching a length of 50cm (20in) if allowed. Mild, sweet flavour with very little heat, and a wonderfully crisp texture. Best sown later in the year for winter harvest.

'München Bier' A double-bounty radish that provides two harvests. This German heirloom can be left to produce an abundance of fleshy edible seed pods, which have a succulent texture similar to that of a sugar snap pea, combined with the signature smack of radish flavour. Unlike other radishes, the root doesn't become woody after the plant has run to seed, giving a second crop of tender roots. The tasty white flesh is traditionally sprinkled with salt and sugar and served as a bar snack washed down with a glass of beer in the pubs of Munich.

'Noir Gros Long d'Hiver' A thick, tapering black-skinned radish that has been grown across Europe since the sixteenth century. The creamy-white flesh has a sweet, spicy flavour and crisp, crunchy texture. It is very similar to 'Black Spanish Round', which dates from the same era. Black radishes are believed to have been developed much earlier than that, in what is now Syria. This is a choice variety for winter storage.

'Pusa Jamuni' It's not an old-timer – this type was released in 2013. It was developed by Dr Pritam Kalia at the Indian Agricultural Research Institute (popularly known as Pusa) in New Delhi, to demonstrate high levels of nutrients and antioxidants, which are present in the colourful pigments. The long, purple-fleshed roots are extremely decorative. A bright pink variety called 'Pusa Gulabi' was developed at the same time.

'Red Meat' Known as *shinrimei* in its native country of China, this is an eye-catching cultivar, sometimes called the "watermelon radish" because of its striking pinkish-red heart. The bulbous roots have a green-tinged skin, making a stark contrast when you slice the root to reveal the terrifically tinted flesh, which is crisp, sweet, and mildly spicy.

'Sakurajima' This spherical daikon holds the world record for being the most gigantic radish around. It has been cultivated for centuries in Sakurajima, an active volcanic peninsula that still plumes with smoke on the southern island of Kyushu, Japan. The humongous round radishes are capable of reaching 30kg (66lb) under the right conditions, but are usually harvested at about 6kg (13lb) in Japan. It has a delightful flavour and refined, buttery texture.

'Sichuan Red Beauty' A stunning red radish that is crimson to the core, traditionally used for pickling in Sichuan province, southwestern

'Red Meat'

Variety	Type	Time to maturity
'China Rose'	Winter	40–50 days
'Green Luobo'	Winter	60–70 days
'Mooli Minowase'	Winter	50–60 days
'München Bier'	Winter	65–75 days
'Noir Gros Long d'Hiver'	Winter	55–65 days
'Pusa Jamuni'	Winter	45–55 days
'Red Meat'	Winter	65–75 days
'Sakurajima'	Winter	90 days
'Sichuan Red Beauty'	Winter	65–75 days
'Violet de Gournay'	Winter	65–75 days
'De 18 Jours'	Spring	18–25 days
'Long Scarlet'	Spring	30–35 days
'Philadelphia White Box'	Spring	25–30 days
'White Icicle'	Spring	30 days
'Zlata'	Spring	35–40 days

China, owing to its spicy kick. The long roots with their bulbous, pointed tips are best sown for autumn and winter harvesting.

'Violet de Gournay' A vigorous French heirloom that has been cultivated at least since the nineteenth century. The long, irregularly shaped roots have thick, vivid purple skin and a crisp, creamy-white centre. Brilliant for storing.

Spring

'De 18 Jours' With its elongated, crunchy red roots with white tips, this is one of the fastest 'French Breakfast' types on the market, as its name suggests. Perfect for plugging short-term gaps in the garden.

'Long Scarlet' Once highly popular in America, this variety with its long, tentacle-like roots was developed in the nineteenth century in Cincinnati, Ohio. Very quick-maturing with tender, sweet, delicately spiced flesh.

'Philadelphia White Box' Quick-maturing, pure-white little globe-shaped roots that crop well in window boxes. Introduced in 1888 in Philadelphia, these radishes are pungent and have a peppery heat.

'White Icicle' With long, thin, tapering roots that look like white carrots, this is an old European heirloom that is also known as 'Ladies' Fingers'. It's fast-growing, stays sweet even when large, and boasts resistance to bolting in warm weather.

'Zlata' An old Eastern European type whose name means "gold" in Polish, thanks to the vibrant yellow skin of the roots. Globe-shaped with a crisp, crunchy texture, it is pleasantly mild with just a suggestion of spice.

'Wilhelmsburger' (left)
and 'Champion'

Rutabaga

Brassica napus

Also known as Kålrot, Moot, Nabo sueco, Neep, Snadger, Swede

This bulging, bowling ball-sized root vegetable is commonly farmed for animal fodder, or at best associated with being a watery accompaniment to a roast dinner. But the versatile rutabaga or swede is more than worthy of a spot on the most lavish dinner table. It has a delicate, bittersweet flavour finished by a peppery hit reminiscent of cabbage and turnip. Its bright yellow flesh is encased in a smooth skin in playful shades of green, purple, bronze, or burnt orange.

History

Rutabaga's exact origin remains unknown, but it is widely believed to have originated in Scandinavia, Russia, or Finland. Development and breeding are thought to have occurred independently and simultaneously across these regions. The name rutabaga comes from the Swedish *rotabagge*, meaning baggy root, and it was there that the vegetable was first recorded. In 1620 the botanist Gaspard Bauhin noted that these bulky roots grew wild throughout the country.

Over time, rutabagas have left their trace on local cultures in various parts of the world. Used in Celtic celebrations of Samhain, the end of harvest, they were among the first jack-o'-lanterns (or tumshies), pre-dating the use of the pumpkin. The custom is based on the myth of Stingy Jack, who tried to trick the devil and was condemned to roaming the Earth in darkness for eternity, with only a rutabaga lantern to light his way. This led people to carve demonic faces in swedes to ward off Jack's wandering soul and other ghosts and ghouls.

The winter of 1916–17, also known as the Rutabaga Winter or Kohlrübenwinter, was extremely challenging for the German population in the midst of World War I. As supplies dwindled, civilians were forced to subsist on rutabaga soup for breakfast, lunch, and dinner. The German government attempted to sway public opinion away from the association with cattle fodder by promoting the rutabaga as the "Prussian pineapple" through propaganda. This memory of difficult times, suffering, and misery meant that after the war, Germans held on to a deep aversion to rutabaga.

This vegetable is globally recognized as rutabaga, yet in the United Kingdom it is known as swede. It even has various names within the UK, depending on the region. In Scotland, swedes are famously known as neeps. In the northeast of England they are called snadgers, while on the Isle of Man they are traditionally referred to as moot or napin.

Today, the annual International Rutabaga Curling Championship is held in the pavilions of the Ithaca Farmers Market in New York state. The competition started spontaneously as a morale boost in 1997, when market traders rolled their goods down the aisles to stay warm during harsh winters. At first, the vendors showed no regard for the type of produce they tossed, and there are even stories of frozen chickens being hurled down the lane. However, the International Rutabaga Curling Championship High Commissioner has since established and enforced regulations. Contestants usually bring their own rutabagas, which may be modified as long as they can still roll in all directions.

Culinary uses
Preparation
Young rutabaga are remarkably tender and require no peeling; older ones must be peeled. Salt-baking the roots whole makes a delicious vegetarian centrepiece.

Dishes
Rutabagas can be fermented into sauerkraut, baked into pies, and braised into casseroles. *Steckrübeneintopf* is a classic German stew in which rutabaga is the star among a mixture of root vegetables; it is seasoned with nutmeg, herbs, and black pepper. Although it is often served as a vegetarian dish, some people like to add slices of Kochwurst sausage and chunks of Kassler ham to enhance the flavour.

Neeps and tatties is a cherished Scottish dish, popularly served on Burns Night, an annual event in honour of the life and work of the poet Robert Burns. This dish is made up of mashed rutabaga ("neeps") and potatoes ("tatties"), served separately, with haggis and a whisky-based gravy. Interestingly, a similar dish from North Wales is known as *ponchmipe*. It also consists of mashed swede and potatoes, but in this version the ingredients are mixed together with milk and butter.

Growing
Propagation
Rutabaga requires protection throughout its life. Sow seeds, germinate, and grow plants on in a greenhouse or potting shed or on a sunny windowsill to safeguard the tender seedlings from pests. For best results, broadcast-sow in trays and prick out the strongest plants into seed cells. Allow the plants to grow on for three or four weeks before planting them out. If the seedlings become leggy early on, transplant them into 9cm (4in) pots, burying the main stem as you do so. When planting out in the patch, bury the seedlings deeply so that their leaves are level with the soil, to support their fragile stems.

Aftercare
Water thoroughly after planting, then keep a close eye on the young plants and keep them moist until they are fully established.

Growing at a glance
Sow Late spring–early summer, 6–30°C (43–86°F)

Plant out Mid–late summer

Spacing 30cm (12in) for regular-sized rutabaga; 50cm (20in) for large rutabaga

Harvest Early autumn–early spring

'Ellen's'

Protect them with a mesh covering over supporting hoops immediately after transplanting. Young seedlings are vulnerable to flea beetle and cabbage root fly, which can stunt their growth. Mesh also prevents swede midge infestations, cabbage white butterflies from laying eggs, and pesky pecking pigeons from decimating the leaves.

Remove any dead or dying foliage weekly from the base of the plants. Decaying brassica leaves attract slugs and snails. Although rutabaga can tolerate dry periods during the summer, keep them watered, and monitor the weather in the autumn, when the plants begin to plump up. Water them well at this point to encourage swelling, particularly if the autumn has been dry.

Plant problems
Aphids, cabbage root fly, caterpillars, club root, flea beetle, pigeons, slugs and snails, swede midge (see pages 49–51)

Harvesting
Gently twist and pull the rutabaga with the assistance of a trowel so that you can get enough purchase to slice a knife through the roots. All plants should be harvested before the weather begins to warm in early spring, since at this point the roots will become tough and unpalatable.

Storage
Although they are often kitchen-ready from the early autumn, one of the beauties of growing rutabaga is that they can be left growing in the ground through the winter, bringing a much-needed burst of green to the garden and a hearty harvest during the bitter months. If heavy and prolonged frosts are prevalent in your area, however, harvest your rutabagas in early winter. Trim them and store them unwashed in a wooden crate or paper potato sack in a frost-free shed or other outbuilding, where they should keep until the following spring.

'Wilhelmsburger' and 'Champion'

Recommended varieties

'**Best of All**' Uniform globe-shaped roots with purple tops and creamy yellow flesh with a sweet, peppery taste. Easy to grow and known for its excellent resistance to cold, it certainly lives up to its name.

'**Cairns Family Heirloom**' Boasting tawny roots with a light red and green top, this variety is super sweet, especially after a frost. Evalynn Schnackenberg shared it with Seed Savers Exchange in 2013. It had been grown and passed down by her grandmother's cousin Leo Cairns, an enthusiastic gardener who had cultivated it since the 1950s in Washington state.

'**Champion**' A classic heirloom widely grown in Europe for centuries and renowned for its impressive hardiness. The root is creamy in colour with a bright purple-red top. Its rich flavour makes it perfect for braising in soups and stews.

'**Ellen's**' A hard-to-come-by landrace variety from the foothills of the Swabian Jura in southwestern Germany, preserved by a local family. It has a sweet, pleasant-tasting root of medium size.

'**Major Dunne**' A purple-topped golden rutabaga with long roots, less susceptible to soil-borne pests than other varieties. They are capable of reaching mammoth sizes without compromising flavour or texture. Once cultivated commercially in Northern Ireland, but no longer common, it is said to be named after Major John William Dunne, an early twentieth-century philosopher and pioneer of aeronautical engineering.

'**Westport Macomber**' The Macomber rutabagas, which can grow as large as a football, are white with green and purple shoulders. They are named after two brothers from Westport, Massachusetts, who developed them from Russian and Swedish varieties in the late nineteenth century. The white-fleshed roots are early to mature and store well.

'**Wilhelmsburger**' Bred in 1935, this German heirloom was developed explicitly for its culinary value, and is considered the most delicious rutabaga. Producing large roots with green shoulders and yellowish-white flesh, it is recognized for its hardiness, disease-resistance, and long storing abilities.

295

Turnip

Brassica rapa subsp. *rapa*

Also known as Kabu, Nabo, Navet, Nips, Wújīng

These quick-growing, easy-to-cultivate brassicas may divide opinion, but they are a unique-tasting winter ingredient with bitter, earthy, sugary notes. Although the classic image of a turnip is that of a snow-white, globe-shaped root with a purple or green top, these vegetables offer much greater variety. Some are long, black-skinned, and tapering, resembling a carrot, while others are rich maroon discs with groovy splashes of red running through brilliant white flesh.

History

The turnip's wild relatives grow in Europe and western Asia and are believed to have been domesticated for food for thousands of years. There are hints of turnip domestication in ancient Assyrian records from the first millennium BCE, and the mass cultivation of turnips occurred in the Hellenistic period (323–146 BCE), as the Greeks recognized their value. They saw turnips as a staple crop, providing nutritious food for soldiers and citizens and a secure food source during times of war and famine.

In ancient Rome, the turnip held a dual function. On one hand, it was a staple source of sustenance for the poorest citizens, while on the other, it was used as a weapon of sorts. When Vespasian (later emperor) was granted the position of proconsul, a high-ranking official, in Africa, he earned a reputation for strict financial management and budgetary control. As a protest against his policies, the local community pelted him with turnips and ran him out of town. The turnip's past also brings up personal slurs. The names "turnip-eater" and "turnip-head" were used from the fifteenth century onwards for simple-minded people living in rural areas, and it is believed that William Shakespeare often threw the word "turnip" around as an insult meaning "idiot". The term is used in a similar away in the novels of Charles Dickens.

After turnip plants arrived in North America, plantation owners, especially in the Southern states, commonly kept the roots for themselves, leaving only the top

'Hinona Kabu'

growth for their slaves. The enslaved people, many of whom were originally from the West Coast of Africa, had a diverse culinary heritage that included a variety of greens or *efo* – a requirement that turnip greens satisfied. Consequently, despite being eaten out of necessity, they proved a tasty and critical source of nutrition among enslaved communities.

Culinary uses

Preparation

Keep raw cut turnips in water or, better, peel and cut them moments before cooking or serving, since they quickly oxidize and discolour if exposed to air, in a process known as enzymatic browning. Don't throw away the greens; they're delicious when cooked in a hot frying pan with spices or tossed through pasta.

Dishes

Turnips possess a peculiar sweet and bitter flavour, giving them the unique ability to cut through yet simultaneously absorb rich flavours. They have recently transcended their position as an old-school vegetable considered suitable only for livestock fodder. Turnips are more versatile than they might seem. They can be roasted, mashed, or braised, cut into thin discs for salads, or even pickled, when their peppery flavour blends perfectly with the sweet-and-sour pickling liquor.

They are valuable as a complementary addition to hearty soups and stews, such as the classic French casserole *navarin d'agneau*. The hearty lamb stew, traditionally served in the spring, is famous for including *navets* (French for turnip). Their wonderful fleshy texture and earthy taste make them well suited to layering and baking in gratins. Whether you substitute them completely for potatoes or just slip a few turnip slices in among the spuds, the creamy cheese sauce elevates this vegetable to sumptuous new heights.

Growing at a glance

Sow Late winter–early spring; late summer–early autumn, 18–21°C (64–70°F)

Plant out Spring; autumn

Spacing 25cm (10in)

Harvest Late spring–early winter

Manicuring (see page 52) can be done easily as you harvest. Brush off extra soil and pull away any rotting or damaged leaves to give your precious produce the best chance of storing well.

The turnip, with its pungent and peppery taste, has gained popularity as an ingredient in India, particularly in the Punjab and other northern regions. During the cold months, people often enjoy *shalgam ki sabzi*, a semi-dry curry made by stir-frying turnips with spices, including turmeric, cumin, cinnamon, coriander, and chilli powder. Tomatoes are added to provide layers of sweetness and tartness that balance the flavour of the turnips, and the curry is typically served with *roti*.

Growing

Propagation

There are two windows of opportunity for sowing these cool-weather crops, since during the summer turnips naturally flower and will not swell or produce juicy roots. They respond well to being multi-sown and grown in clumps. Sow four or five seeds per cell and keep early sowings in a warm place to help them germinate; once sprouted, these hardy seedlings can be moved to an unheated potting shed or greenhouse to grow on. The seedling clusters are ready to be transplanted in as little as three or four weeks.

Aftercare

Even though they may still appear small, these plants are robust and will grow rapidly after being planted out in the garden. Protect early sowings with a covering of horticultural fleece, to shelter them from cold and bad weather as well as birds, flea beetles, and other insects. Later sowings will benefit from being covered with mesh or fine netting, to protect them from cabbage white butterflies and birds. Keep a close eye on newly planted turnips and water them until they become established. There may be enough seasonal rainfall that they have no need of extra water, but if the weather is dry, water them thoroughly as they begin to plump up.

Plant problems

Aphids, birds, cabbage root fly, caterpillars, club root, flea beetle, mice, mildew, slugs and snails (see pages 49–51)

Harvesting

These rapidly growing plants can be harvested at various stages of growth. However, all turnips must be picked before the first frost. Baby turnips have tender,

'Asuka Akane'

Hida beni kabu (red turnip)

'Nagasaki Akari Kabu'

succulent flesh bursting with sweetness, and tasty leaves. As they mature and grow to the size of a golf ball or larger, the sweetness mellows and the flesh becomes juicier and more crunchy. Whole clumps can be picked as one, or select the largest root from each cluster, allowing the smaller ones to continue plumping up. To harvest, gently push down and twist the turnip until it comes loose.

Storage

Baby turnips do not store well. If they begin to shrivel, they can be kept hydrated in a bowl of water. Large turnips, on the other hand, will keep for several months. Snap off any foliage and store them unwashed in a crate in a cool but frost-free shed or other outbuilding.

'Asuka Akane' A gorgeous, colourful Japanese turnip that has long roots with a sweet and mellow flavour that can be enjoyed raw, much like a radish, or pickled for a tangy twist. When sliced open, the flesh reveals a hypnotic array of magenta and creamy-white markings, almost too beautiful to eat.

'Boule d'Or' Golden, flattened globe-shaped roots with rich amber flesh and a robust, earthy flavour similar to that of rutabaga (see page 290). Tasting much sweeter and milder than white turnips, this variety is also known as 'Golden Ball' or 'Orange Jelly' and was initially listed in France in 1854. However, some people believe it was bred and developed in northern England and Scotland in the early nineteenth century.

Hida beni kabu In 1918 a handful of rogue red turnips were discovered growing among a crop of white 'Hakurei' turnips in the Nyukawa area of Takayama, Japan. Their creamy-white interior was marbled with red and slightly sweeter than 'Hakurei', making them an exciting and rare find. Recognizing their potential, local farmers saved and developed the new variety, which eventually became known as *Hida beni kabu* (the red turnip of Hida).

'Hinona Kabu' A fascinating, truly unique variety with a long, slender root and mild, peppery flavour. Its elegant roots are a rich, striking reddish-purple on top, creating a beautiful contrast with the snow-white beneath. Legend has it that these brassicas are native to

A special colour

The word *beni* in the name of the *Hida beni kabu* turnip signifies a specific shade of red extracted from the petals of the *benihana* flower, a plant cultivated in Japan since ancient times. *Beni* plays a significant role in traditional Japanese art, especially paintings, textiles, and pottery, and has become synonymous with Japanese craft.

Japan, having been discovered in the fifteenth century during the construction of Otowa Castle in Shiga Prefecture. However, recent studies suggest that it is in fact a hybrid of a popular old European turnip, 'Long Red Tankard', which may have been introduced to the region after the Meiji Restoration of 1868, which brought about the modernization and increasing Westernization of Japan. Because of their crisp texture and mild flavour, 'Hinona Kabu' turnips are traditionally used in Japanese cuisine for making *sakurazuke*, a pickle that derives its name from the beautiful pink colour the turnips acquire during the process.

'Nagasaki Akari Kabu' Perfect for pickling and delightful eaten raw, these breathtakingly beautiful and tremendously tasty turnips are traditionally cultivated in Nagasaki Prefecture, in the very south of Japan. A vivid violet skin conceals snow-white flesh dappled with purple.

'Noir Long de Caluire' Also known as *le navet du Pardailhan*, this long, tapered turnip was once famous in France, an ancient variety said to have featured regularly on the dinner tables at the Palace of Versailles. However, as a result of World War II, it was nearly driven to extinction as local agriculture suffered a significant decline. It became increasingly hard to come by and a real

"Turnip Townshend"

The eighteenth-century British agriculturist Charles Townshend, 2nd Viscount Townshend, had a great passion for turnips and devoted a significant portion of his life to experimenting with and advocating for this root vegetable. His efforts led to the development of new techniques of cultivation and crop rotation, initially raising eyebrows among farmers. Still, he revolutionized British agriculture and is often referred to as the "father of the British agricultural revolution". His innovative crop-rotation methods, including the use of turnips as a winter crop, helped to increase soil fertility, improve the health of livestock, and ultimately boost agricultural productivity. Thanks to his work, turnips became a staple crop in Britain and beyond, and he became known as "Turnip Townshend".

rarity, even in its home region. A late triumph for this turnip arose when a small group of dedicated growers formed the association Lou Nap dal Pardailha to preserve and restore it. Today, it is celebrated for its distinctive flavour and appearance. The carrot-shaped roots have thick black skin and sweet white flesh with a nutty flavour similar to that of chestnut, and have become a symbol of the region's rich agricultural heritage.

'Norfolk Green' Dating back to the late seventeenth century, this old-school turnip rose to massive popularity primarily thanks to the work of the 2nd Viscount Townshend (see panel above). This English heirloom variety from Norfolk produces big, bulbous roots

with vibrant green shoulders, and has a much more refined taste and texture than many modern types.

'Rond de Nancy' The "Round of Nancy" takes its name from its splendid spherical shape and the French town where it was first grown. With white flesh and plum-purple shoulders, it's deliciously sweet and mild. The locals, including market gardeners and home growers, raved about this turnip for its ability to adapt to different soil types and withstand the harsh climate of northeastern France. It was widely cultivated during the nineteenth century and so significant that it was mentioned in Vilmorin Andrieux's book *Les Plantes Potagères* (The Vegetable Garden) in 1885.

'Nagasaki Akari Kabu' (left) and *Hida beni kabu*

'Hinona Kabu' (left) and 'Asuka Akane'

'Boule d'Or'

Wasabi

Eutrema japonicum

Also known as Green mustard, Japanese horseradish

Real wasabi is one of the world's most expensive vegetable crops. It packs a sharp, pungent punch that will clear the sinuses, but also highlights the taste of the food with which it is served. Its value arises from the difficulty of growing it commercially, but it is relatively easy to grow on a home scale.

Wasabi is becoming more and more popular, and now appearing in all sorts of food, including wasabi ice cream and wasabi peas, but in an estimated 95 per cent of cases, imitation wasabi is used. There are two main reasons. First, the flavour and heat of real wasabi start to decline quickly from oxidation, usually within 10–15 minutes of grating the root. Second, commercial cultivation is tricky because of problems with access to seeds and cuttings, as well as pests and diseases and a long growing time.

The green paste (usually made from sweetened mustard, horseradish, and food colouring) that is commonly served alongside sushi is far removed from the real deal. Genuine wasabi is made by finely grating the rhizome (see panel overleaf) moments before serving. It has a herbal flavour and a sweet aftertaste that highlight the flavour of fish, rather than masking it.

History

According to Japanese legend, wasabi was discovered by samurai migrating into the mountains of the Kansai region of Honshū to live in peace after the Battle of Dan-no-ura in 1185. They stumbled upon the plant's large, heart-shaped leaves growing alongside rivers, and gathered the wasabi to season raw slices of cherry trout – a fish that returns to fresh water to spawn during cherry-blossom season.

This story has helped to establish wasabi as an iconic ingredient in Japanese food culture. However, modern archaeological evidence suggests that the ancient peoples of Japan were eating wasabi as early as 14,000 BCE, although it wasn't until the sixteenth century – with the rise in popularity of sushi – that the root became widely sought after. With its zingy flavour and an ability to counteract

"
Demand for genuine wasabi is continuing to increase worldwide.

food poisoning, it was prized as the perfect pairing for raw seafood. Today, much of Japan's wasabi is cultivated in Shizuoka, where commercial cultivation began about 400 years ago. Demand for genuine wasabi is continuing to increase worldwide, and the plant is now cultivated commercially in China, New Zealand, Canada, the USA, and the UK.

Culinary uses

Preparation

How you prepare wasabi depends on whether you use the leaves, stems, or rhizome. The leaves and stems should be washed and chopped if necessary; the root must be trimmed and washed (see panel overleaf).

Dishes

Wasabi leaves work well thrown into stir-fries or sauteed with noodles, and they're perfect deep-fried in tempura batter and served with a tangy ponzu dipping sauce. For a summery dish with a kick, try wasabi leaves in a salad with a *wafu* (Japanese-style) dressing of soy sauce, rice vinegar, and other flavourings.

Wasabi has an unprepossessing appearance that belies the delicate spiciness of its flesh.

303

Wasabi paste

To make wasabi paste, first remove any stems attached to the rhizome, wash the rhizome, and cut away any blemishes using a sharp knife. Don't peel the root, since the pungency and flavour are concentrated close to the skin.

When you're ready to eat, grate the rhizome extremely finely to release the intense flavour. You'll need a specially designed wasabi grater, as a regular cheese grater or microplane can't grate finely enough. The traditional implement (*oroshiki*) is made from shark skin, but today a stainless-steel wasabi grater (*oroshigane*) is more commonly used. Grate the rhizome slowly and gently in a clockwise circular motion. If you grate too forcefully, the texture will become coarse and grainy and the flavour and pungency won't be fully extracted. For an extra-fine paste, use a sharp knife to chop through the grated wasabi a few times in a rocking or circular motion.

It's worth noting that wasabi paste has a slightly different taste, texture, and colour depending on which end of the rhizome you use. The stem end is bright green with a fresh, herbal, aromatic flavour. The other end is greyish green and more pungent, providing a real kick. In Japan, gratings from both ends are combined to provide the perfect balance.

Because the flavour of wasabi comes from chemicals that are highly volatile and vaporize quickly after grating, its power diminishes rapidly. After 15–20 minutes, you'll be left with a green paste that tastes like cut grass and has little or no heat. For this reason, grate only what you're going to eat, moments before serving.

A simple but delicious way to enjoy wasabi paste is to incorporate it into homemade mayonnaise, which can be used as an alternative to regular mayonnaise in almost any dish. It works exceptionally well when slathered on a brioche bun topped with a beef patty to give a horseradish-like kick to your burger, or combined with garlic to make wasabi aioli for dipping crispy, herb-roasted potatoes.

New plants can be grown relatively easily from offshoots.

Wasabi stems have a crunchy texture and a peppery, radish-like flavour with hints of chive. They're traditionally steeped in sake lees (see page 286) to make the pickle *wasabi-zuke*. This delicious condiment has a pâté-like texture and a sweet, fruity yet savoury taste, and is spooned over rice or mixed with dried bonito flakes and soy sauce.

Growing

In my experience, this notoriously tricky plant is actually easy to grow provided you follow a few simple rules. It's a shade-loving brassica that's perfect for growing in a dark corner of the garden where everything else seems to fail, or as a fun edible houseplant.

Propagation

You can grow wasabi from seed, but I've had more success with buying a plant and taking cuttings to provide a constant supply of new plants. Wasabi plants create little offshoots towards the base of the stem, which can be snipped off and transplanted into small pots filled with a 50/50 mix of horticultural sand and compost. Spring and autumn are the best times to remove the side shoots, and I keep my potted-up seedlings in a shallow tray of water to ensure the soil remains moist and encourage rooting.

Wasabi seeds are trickier to obtain than plants, and much more challenging to grow. The seeds have a poor germination rate and must be stratified before sowing (see page 30). In early spring, sow them indoors in a similar way to brassicas, by multi-sowing in a tray and covering with a very fine layer of compost. Germination can be sporadic, so sow generously and be patient; it could take up to four weeks for seedlings to appear. Once the seedlings are large enough to handle, prick them out into individual seed cells to grow on. Keep them in a shaded area that never receives direct sunlight, since even a few hours of sun will kill them.

Aftercare

The best time to plant out wasabi is early autumn. Wait until the seedlings or plants have a well-established root system before transplanting. For plants purchased in 10cm (4in) pots, this is usually about four weeks after receiving them. If you have grown your plants from seed, wait until they reach 15cm (6in) tall and have several stems (roughly two months after germination).

Sunlight and dry soil are the biggest challenges when growing wasabi. It will wilt and die if exposed to direct sunlight, so plant it in a shady area. If you're lucky enough to have a stream in your garden, grow it on the banks or verge, where water will move through the soil.

When planting out in the garden, it's worth growing a few wasabi plants together. This will create a leaf canopy that provides a microclimate, as well as helping to retain moisture and shading the central stalk. Generally, the more wasabi plants that are growing together, the better they will perform. Root rot caused by compacted soil or poor drainage can affect wasabi plants, so you may have to try them in different parts of the garden until you find a spot where they are happy. Alternatively, grow them in pots and mix sand and gravel into the compost to improve drainage.

Plant wasabi so that its roots are buried in the soil, but ensure that the area where the roots meet the plant is just above soil level, making sure not to cover any part of the above-ground stem as this will cause rotting.

If you don't have much shade in your garden, use shade cloth to keep the plants out of direct sunlight, or grow wasabi in pots and move them around to avoid the sun. I grow three wasabi plants together in an extra-large container to create a leafy

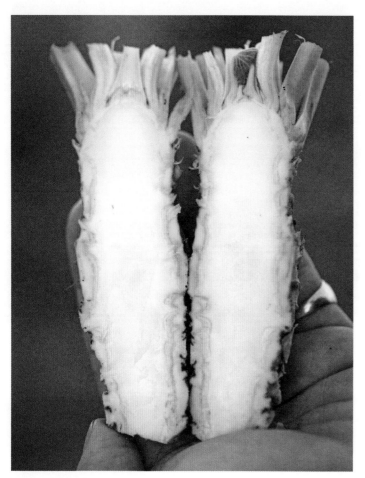

The pungent rhizome should be kept whole until just before eating.

> ## "
> ## This notoriously tricky plant is actually easy to grow provided you follow a few simple rules.

canopy, and mulch with compost topped with pebbles to help retain moisture.

Wasabi plants are pretty hardy and can withstand cold weather. Mine have even survived being submerged in snow for a few days and have battled through sub-zero temperatures for well over a week. Having said that, to be on the safe side it's advisable to protect your plants with fleece if freezing conditions are forecast, or move them inside if they're in pots. It takes around 18–24 months for the rhizome to reach full maturity, so it would be devastating to lose a plant halfway to achieving this. Always keep plants well watered, especially during hot periods.

Wasabi can also be grown as houseplants all year round, and the attractive leaves brighten up dark corners. As with potted plants in the garden, mulch them and water frequently.

Some people worry about wasabi spreading and becoming invasive. However, you can maintain control by removing the offshoots and replanting them elsewhere if wanted.

Plant problems
Aphids, blight, cabbage white caterpillars, root rot, slugs and snails (see pages 49–51)

Harvesting
The central rhizome will be ready for harvesting roughly two years after an offshoot is planted. It's advisable to wait until the rhizome has reached full maturity before digging it up, since the flavour will be at its sweetest and most aromatic. Luckily, you can feast on the leafy stems in the meantime.

Pick the leaves and stems regularly, ideally about every six weeks. Harvest the large, dark green leaves from the outer edges, leaving a ring of leaves around the central rhizome and the small leaves that have yet to unfurl. In the summer, I recommend harvesting fewer leafy stems to keep the canopy dense and protect the

Growing at a glance

Sow Late winter–early spring;
5–10°C (41–50°F)

Take cuttings Early–late spring,
mid-autumn–early winter

Plant out Early–late spring,
mid-autumn–early winter

Spacing 20–30cm (8–12in)

Harvest Early–late spring,
mid-autumn–early winter

precious central rhizome from the sun.
The flowers, which appear in February
and March, are edible and delicious when
fried in a tempura batter; the petals make
a good garnish and salad topper.

It's best to harvest the highly prized,
pungent rhizome in early spring or early
autumn, when it's 12–15cm (5–6in) long.
Lift the whole plant, being careful not to
break the rhizome. Using a sharp knife,
remove any offshoots and plant them in
pots, then take off the stems and leaves.
Clean up the rhizome by removing the
roots and brushing away any debris.

Storage

To prevent the rhizome from drying out,
cover it in a damp paper towel, pop it in
a plastic bag, and keep it in the fridge for
up to a month.

Recommended varieties

'Daruma' A beautiful bushy variety with
a zingy yet relatively mild flavour. The
dense foliage has thick leaves, which are
perfect for sautéing. It withstands hotter
temperatures than other wasabis and is
relatively resistant to root rot and other
fungal diseases. Tending to grow upright
rather than sprawl, it can reach 60cm
(24in) high. The knobbly rhizome,
10–30cm (4–12in) long and 2.5–5cm
(1–2in) thick, can reach full maturity in
under 16 months.

'Mazuma'
If you like your wasabi hot and spicy, this
is the variety for you. It's short and stocky,
with a height and spread of only 40cm
(16in), and is robust and resilient yet
slow-growing. The rhizome, 15–30cm
(6–12in) long and 3–5cm (1–2in) thick,
takes up to 36 months to reach full
maturity. 'Mazuma' produces an
abundance of beautiful, delicious white
flowers in the spring and tends to sprawl,
giving you lots of offshoots and tasty
foliage. The leaves have a distinctive
purple tinge towards the base.

Pods & Seeds

Bringing abundance and beauty to the garden, these crops are not just wholesome eaten fresh but also store for later feasting.

Peas

Pisum sativum

Also known as Petits pois, Pisello, Matar

Peas are a springtime treat that combine sugary and savoury notes with a deep green flavour. They're also an attractive addition to the garden, bringing structure and bursts of colour as their elegant winged flowers begin to bloom.

History

Peas are one of the oldest cultivated crops in the world. They have been farmed since the Neolithic Revolution (which brought the dawn of agriculture), and have been enjoyed as a food source by people across the Middle East, Asia, and southern Europe for thousands of years. The Middle East is considered the homeland of the pea plant, and carbonized pea remains have been discovered at numerous Neolithic sites in Syria, Turkey, Jordan, and Iraq. Centuries-old archaeological evidence of peas has also been unearthed in the Spirit Cave in northern Thailand, while the nineteenth-century archaeologist Heinrich Schliemann excavated jars of peas thought to be more than 3,000 years old in the ruins of Troy.

The ancient Romans were particularly fond of peas, and cultivated no fewer than 37 varieties. Dried peas, in particular, were a staple food for the legions of the Roman army, and were used on extended sea voyages, being easy to transport and storing for long periods. The Romans also believed that peas had medicinal properties beyond their nutritional benefits. Pliny the Elder recommended using podded peas to treat warts. The procedure involved touching each wart with a fresh pea, which was then wrapped in cloth and thrown over the shoulder. The rationale was that the pea would absorb the wart's negative energy and draw it out of the body.

During the Middle Ages, field peas were a reliable source of sustenance and crucial in keeping people from starving.

These older peas were smaller and more bitter than modern varieties, however, and it was not until the early Modern period in Europe that a new way of enjoying peas emerged. People started consuming the immature, green pods while they were still fresh, rather than drying them, and this provided a luxurious and innovative culinary experience. In England, this practice gained popularity in the sixteenth century, and the prized green peas became known as a delicacy by the wealthy.

In the eighteenth century Thomas Knight, a passionate plant-breeder living at Downton Castle in Herefordshire, achieved a breakthrough by developing the first variety to have a delicious sugary taste and succulent texture. Garden peas are thus famously known as English peas.

At this time in Britain, a pod containing nine peas was considered lucky. If a single woman found a pea pod containing exactly nine peas, she would hang it over the front door of her house, and it was said that the first man to walk through the door would be her soulmate.

Culinary uses

Preparation
If simmering, add just enough water to cover the peas, and consider adding

a pinch of sugar to bring out their natural sweetness. After roughly 60 seconds, the peas will begin to float, at which point they are perfectly cooked.

Dishes
These legumes lend themselves to far more in the kitchen than being overboiled and piled on one side of the plate in a sprawling mess. Home-grown peas freshly popped out of the pod have an elegant flavour that doesn't need overcomplicating. Thrown into risottos, blended into purées, or sautéed in butter, the possibilities are limitless. They can be paired with the most delicate fish or with the gamey taste of duck and lamb. The humble garden pea may be small, but it packs a full-flavoured punch.

If they make it as far as the kitchen before being eaten, the sweet and ever-so-moreish mangetout and sugar snap types can be used fresh in salads, but they come to life when cooked, especially in Asian stir-fries and broths. The sweet, crunchy edible pods present a refreshing balance to the bold flavours of Thai curries, Chinese hotpots, Vietnamese *pho*, and Japanese *sukiyaki*.

Soup and cooking peas bring a whole new level of flavour and culinary possibilities. The Italian *zuppa di roveja con pasta* is an exquisitely flavourful, comforting soup that warms the soul and satisfies the palate. Hearty, nourishing, downright delicious, and perfect for chilly days, this traditional dish hails from the central region of Umbria, where it has been enjoyed for centuries and is steeped in local tradition and culture. At its heart are 'Roveja' peas (see page 314), which

Delicately scented pea flowers – this one of 'Kent Blue' – are a charming addition to the patch.

> ❝
> **The humble garden pea may be small, but it packs a full-flavoured punch.**

have a distinctive taste and texture somewhere between that of a lentil and a pea. To add richness and depth, the legumes are cooked with other vegetables, such as carrots, onions and celery, and pancetta, and some people even like to use the soup as a sauce for pasta.

Another recipe that is steeped in tradition is the chip-shop classic mushy peas, a renowned accompaniment to that most British of meals, fish and chips. 'Marrowfat', a variety that dates back to the 1730s, is traditionally used for this thick, savoury side dish that began to crop up in chippies in the 1970s. To make it, the dried peas are soaked overnight before being simmered until dense and mushy. Mushy peas can also be served in fritters – the perfect vegetarian alternative to fish and chips. The key is to shape cooked, seasoned mushy peas into small, thin discs on baking paper and put them in the freezer 30–60 minutes before cooking. That will allow you to handle, batter, and fry them easily without the risk that they will fall apart.

Growing
Propagation

Peas perform best if they are sown early in the season, since later sowings are more susceptible to pests and diseases. Sowing them early also frees up essential space in the garden for succession planting after they finish cropping, during a busy period when most beds are brimming with plants.

Pea seeds are prone to being eaten by rodents, no matter whether they are sown directly into the soil or in pots or cells. Protect them by covering them with a cloche or keeping them in a rodent-free area. They're capable of germinating in low temperatures, and can be sown in an unheated greenhouse or potting shed. However, early sowings should be brought into the house to sprout if the temperature outside falls below freezing. Sow two peas per cell, to be planted out as a pair once the plants are about 7.5cm (3in) tall, roughly three weeks after germination. When transplanting, dib holes slightly deeper than required, to bury and support the fragile stems.

'Champion of England' is a prolific cropper in small spaces.

311

Aftercare

Cover newly transplanted seedlings with horticultural fleece until late spring to protect them from wind, cold weather, and birds, before starting to train the plants and erect support structures. Even the shortest varieties benefit from support to keep them upright when heavily laden with pods; bush and dwarf types can be staked with hazel sticks or short bamboo canes to provide the twining tendrils with something to cling to. Medium-sized and taller varieties can be grown up a trellis, hazel tepee, or strings. To make a simple support for these taller-growing types, knock two sturdy posts into the ground at either end of the bed and tie strings between them every 12–15cm (5–6in) to create a ladder frame for the peas to clutch on to. In gardens that suffer pressure from pigeons, it will probably be essential to cover pea crops with netting.

Water the newly planted seedlings until they have settled in and are growing strongly. They may not require additional water subsequently, except in particularly dry spells, since they grow during a wetter and cooler time of year. Do give them a good soaking once they begin to flower, however, to help the fruit set. To avoid mildew, water at the base of the plants and take care not to splash the leaves.

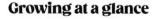

Growing at a glance

Sow Late winter–late spring, 4–24°C (40–75°F)

Plant out Early spring–early summer

Spacing 15cm (6in), in rows 30cm (12in) apart

Harvest Late spring–late summer

Plant problems
Birds, mice, mildew, pea moth, pea and bean weevil, pigeons, slugs and snails, voles (see pages 49–51)

Harvesting
The optimal time to harvest peas depends on the type. As they mature, they lose their sweetness as the sugar they contain is converted into starch. For shelling varieties that are to be consumed fresh, the pods can be harvested early – when they are thin and contain dainty but super-sweet petit pois-style peas – or allowed to plump up for a chunkier, more robust crop.

Mangetout should be picked when the pods are flat and tender, while sugar snaps should be harvested when their lush edible pods have swelled with tender, succulent peas. Pick sugar snaps and mangetout every three days to maintain sweetness and prevent the crop from over-maturing and becoming starchy.

Soup, regular shelling types being harvested for cooking, and any pea that is being saved for seed can be left to mature fully and even dry out partially on the plant. Once both plant and pods are brown and crunchy, harvest the whole plant, shell the peas immediately, and allow them to continue drying by spreading them out on a tray and leaving them in a warm, dry place for a few days before storing them.

Storage

No matter the type, peas quickly lose their sweet flavour, so if you are planning to use them fresh they are best eaten straight away. Check soup peas and dried peas carefully once they are thoroughly dry, and discard any that have holes or maggot damage; the crop is now ready for storage in airtight jars for a year or more.

Pea shoots

The tender, sweet shoots of pea plants are a tasty addition to salads and can be used as a garnish. The best part is that they can be grown indoors on a windowsill all year round, even in the winter. Instead of buying expensive sprouting or microgreen pea seeds, use regular dried organic peas from the supermarket. Plant them densely in a shallow tray (such as an old mushroom crate or punnet), using barely enough compost to cover them. While some people advise using paper towels, compost will allow you to get several harvests from one tray and, after all, it is the way nature intended. When the sprouts are at least 5cm (2in) tall, snip them off just above the soil surface.

The peas produced by 'Kent Blue' (left) are excellent for drying, and can be left to shrivel on the plant (below) before being harvested.

Garden peas

'American Wonder' A delicious, very short dwarf pea dating from 1878, this one grows to just 40cm (16in), perfect for containers or exposed sites. It is one of the first to mature, producing a large crop of long pods early in the year. It produces 8–10 wrinkled but sweet peas per pod.

'Champion of England' This wrinkled pea got its name for a reason. Bred by William Fairbeard in Kent in the early nineteenth century, it was one of Charles Darwin's favourites to grow, and in 1876 it was judged Best Pea by the *Journal of Horticulture*. Once a prevalent commercial variety, by the 1970s it was on its way to extinction because of its height, which made it impossible to harvest using machines. Thankfully, a few home gardeners kept the variety alive and passed the peas on to seed banks, and it is once again available to the public. The plants reach a massive 2.5–3m (8–10ft) in height. Laden with pods containing 8–10 peas each, they provide an excellent crop for a small amount of space, but this variety does mature later than others.

'Feltham Early' A hardy dwarf pea that's super early to mature, this variety was bred in the nineteenth century by one A. W. Smith of Feltham, southwest London, said to be one of his generation's most marvellous and prolific market gardeners. 'Feltham Early' reaches an average height of 45cm (18in) and is said to be hardy enough for overwintering if it is sown in November, for an extra-early harvest. It produces an abundance of long, pointed pods of 7–10 peas each.

'Glory of Devon' A truly delicious, rare heirloom pea that was awarded the prestigious RHS Award of Garden Merit in 1899. Once a popular choice among growers from Devon in southwestern England, it fell out of favour, and the seeds were unobtainable in the UK for decades, until the renowned seedsman William Woys Weaver sent a stock of peas to the Heritage Seed Library. It can reach 2m (6½ft) in height and requires support. It produces tons of bottle-green pods containing 8–10 small, succulent, extra-sweet petit pois-style peas over a long period.

'Suttons Phenomenon' A dwarf heirloom bred by Suttons and kept alive by the Heritage Seed Library, this variety produces extra-large pods containing 9–12 peas each – a phenomenal number for a dwarf type. The listing in Suttons' catalogue of 1933 describes it as "a splendid pea", "one of the finest varieties we have ever introduced".

'Thomas Laxton' This famous heirloom was introduced in the nineteenth century by Thomas Laxton, a legendary plant biologist and correspondent of Darwin. A tallish plant that reaches a height of about 1m (3ft), this productive variety produces enormous, sweet, tasty peas with large pods containing 6–8 peas each. It is highly resilient to pests and disease, cold-hardy, and relatively early to mature.

Soup and drying peas

'Carlin' Also known as "black badgers" or "maple peas", these brown peas have been grown in the UK for more than 500 years. Their firm, meaty texture, sweet, nutty flavour, and high protein content make them a perfect alternative to chickpeas. 'Carlin' is also used in the north of England to make "parched peas", a type of mushy pea cooked with vinegar and served on Bonfire Night. Plants can exceed 1.5m (5ft) in height and require support. They produce attractive purple-and-white flowers that suit both the ornamental garden and the vegetable patch.

'Kent Blue' This resilient aqua pea with blue and purple mottles is undeniably one of the most beautiful. It has been kept since the 1940s as a family heirloom in Sevenoaks, Kent. It is best used in soups, stews, and curries. It is a medium-sized plant that grows to about 75cm (30in) tall.

'King Tut' A strikingly beautiful purple-podded variety, this pea can be eaten as mangetout but tastes even better as a soup pea. It gets its name from the claim that its perfectly preserved seeds were found in the tomb of the Egyptian pharaoh Tutankhamun in 1922 by the archaeologist Howard Carter. He brought them back to England, where they were grown for the first time in 5,000 years. A contrary claim has it that the peas originated in the English country estate of Lord Carnarvon, who financed Carter's tomb-raiding expedition and named the pea in honour of the famous discovery. The deep purple pods stand out from the foliage, making picking easy. Inside, you are met with a stark contrast of big, bright green peas, 4–8 per pod. This tall, prolific plant reaches 1.8m (6ft) tall and will need support.

'Prussian Blue' Famous for the blue-green tint of its seeds, this pea was developed in Germany in the eighteenth century. Seed found its way to the USA and eventually came into the hands of Thomas Jefferson, who grew it in the gardens of Monticello, Virginia, after retiring from government in 1809. This variety needs support and will produce a large number of pods containing 7–9 peas each. It is particularly suited to making British chip shop-style mushy peas.

'Roveja' A long-forgotten ancient wild legume that originated in the Middle East. It was once widely cultivated in the Apennine Mountains of central Italy, where it made up the bulk of the diet of local farmers and shepherds. However, only a handful of Italian farmers still cultivate this wonderful heirloom. A stunning pea flecked with grey, brown, red, blue, and green, it has a distinctively earthy flavour and can be used in soups, sauces, and the Umbrian pasta dish *zuppa di roveja con pasta*. Most famously and deliciously, perhaps, it is turned into *farecchiata*, a type of polenta. The plants can reach 1.5m (5ft) tall and grow better with support.

Sugar snap peas

Calvin Lamborn Calvin Lamborn, the "father of sugar snaps", was a plant-breeder from the USA who developed the sugar snap we know today by crossing garden peas with a mutant pea with thicker-walled pods. The result is a unique plant that combines the sweet flavour of garden peas with the crunchy texture of mangetout. Having first become available to the public in 1979, sugar snaps are now popular among both gardeners and chefs. I recommend these varieties, all bred by Lamborn:

'Honey Snap' A rare golden-yellow sweet, sweet sugar snap variety that grows tall.
'Royal Snap II' A deep and delectable purple-podded snap, producing long and tall vines.
'Sugar Ann' A stocky dwarf type that is the earliest of all to mature.
'Sugar Daddy' A super-sweet semi-dwarf type, entirely stringless.

'King Tut'

'Amish Snap Pea' This variety was grown by the Amish community for generations before the modern sugar snaps entered the market in the late twentieth century. It is considered the only real heirloom sugar snap, although newer open-pollinated varieties have been around for a while and are grown and loved by many gardeners. Amish snap peas have a delicate flavour that is milder than that of their modern cousins, but they are just as tasty in a different way. The plants, which grow to 1.5m (5ft) tall, are covered in translucent light green pods that are perfect for snacking on straight from the vine, and very moreish.

Mangetout

'Bijou' This rare heirloom dates from the mid-nineteenth century and will produce the most enormous pods you've ever seen. These magnificent pods 15cm (6in) long or even longer are filled with tiny peas, making them the perfect snack straight off the vine. Once very popular, this giant mangetout almost became extinct but is now available again in small numbers, thanks to Real Seeds, which has been working to reintroduce the variety after acquiring seed found in a jar in someone's cellar.

'Carouby de Maussane' Originating in Maussane-les-Alpilles in southern France, this mauve mangetout was bred in the nineteenth century and has stood the test of time. Its succulent pods are 12cm (5in) long, full of flavour, and best harvested when the peas barely show. These vigorous vines can reach 1.5m (5ft) in height and produce attractive purple flowers that pop among the green foliage. Performs best when supported with trellis or netting.

'Jaune de Madras' A beautiful golden mangetout that adds a spectacular splash of yellow to both garden and dinner plate. It was bred in the nineteenth century by the French horticultural company Vilmorin Andrieux, using seeds that were said to have come from India. I acquired seed of 'Jaune de Madras' from the collector Adam Alexander, who mentions that the variety is synonymous with the later American heritage variety 'Golden Sweet', which is now commercially available. The plants are more than capable of reaching 1.8m (6ft) in height, and produce lots of crisp, sweet golden-yellow pods.

'Luz de Otono'

Broad Beans

Vicia faba

Also known as Fava beans

Broad beans explode with sweet, slightly nutty flavours when fresh, and develop a rich, earthy, umami taste when dried. They are more than a seasonal treat and should be a staple: high-yielding, easy to grow, and one of the earliest crops to mature.

History

One of the oldest cultivated crops in the world, broad beans played a major part in the Neolithic Revolution, when humans stopped foraging and settled down to farm. Until explorers first returned from the so-called New World in the late fifteenth century, bringing with them the American continents' bountiful varieties of bean, fava was the only bean consumed in Europe, most of the Mediterranean, and the Middle East. Archaeological evidence suggests that broad beans have been grown and consumed since Neolithic times in the Fertile Crescent (also known as the Cradle of Civilization), the moon-shaped region of the Middle East that was home to some of the earliest human civilizations and ancient agricultural advances. This vast area spans present-day Cyprus, Israel, Egypt, Iran, Iraq, Jordan, Lebanon, Palestine, Syria, and Turkey.

The Greek philosopher and mathematician Pythagoras prohibited his followers (the Pythagoreans) from consuming or even coming into contact with broad beans. His reason was the belief that the hollow stem of the plant allowed the souls of the dead to travel through the ground and into the beans, where they would lie in wait and possess the living. Pythagoras also famously warned that eating broad beans would cause one to expel a gas capable of taking away the "breath of life". By contrast, Egyptian pharaohs gave jars of broad beans as an offering to Hapi, the god of the River Nile, and the ancient Romans used dried broad beans to cast votes in the Senate. White beans were submitted to signal "yes", while darker ones denoted "no".

In the tenth century drought caused a dreadful famine in Sicily, and the population was forced to sustain itself on broad beans alone. The people prayed desperately to St Joseph for rain and promised to welcome the wet weather with a grand feast. Eventually, the rains came, and civilization recovered. Today, in honour of the great famine, many Sicilians begin their St Joseph's Day (19 March) celebration feasts with *maccu di San Giuseppe*, a delicious soupy stew of broad beans.

In the Middle Ages broad beans were looked down on by the upper echelons of European society as being food for the poor. They were an essential source of protein for most people, commonly used in pottage, a thick, well-flavoured soup typically eaten by peasants.

Culinary uses

Preparation
For the best eating experience, double-pod broad beans. Remove the beans from the outermost shell and blanch them in boiling water for 60 seconds before refreshing in a bowl of ice-cold water. Now make a nick in the shell of each, allowing the bright green beans to be easily freed from their tough, leathery skin.

Dishes
Cooking with fresh broad beans adds a lively burst of colour and sunshine to any plate, while dried broad beans offer a deep, rich, starchy, savoury flavour that is distinctly different. Fresh beans, with their creamy texture and delicate, sweet flavour, are a delightful seasonal addition to many meals. They are particularly delicious when paired with summer fish dishes, and their meaty texture makes them a hearty addition to salads. They can be tossed whole into frittatas and omelettes, blitzed with ricotta and other ingredients to stuff tortellini, or blended into a dip or spread. One of the most famous uses (dried or fresh) is in authentic falafel, for a delectably moist, soft result.

Doubanjiang, the life and soul of Sichuan cuisine, is a beloved, age-old fermented hot and spicy broad-bean paste that is a staple in every Chinese kitchen. Ancient legend has it that during a time of war in Chengdu, fleeing residents accidentally stored cooked broad beans in a bag of chilli flakes. Upon reaching their destination, they discovered that the beans had fermented into a deliciously spicy paste, which they began to enjoy. As a result, locals began fermenting their own paste, spreading its popularity across the Sichuan region.

Scafata di fave is a traditional Umbrian peasant dish that signifies the arrival of spring in Italy. The soup is typically made with fresh broad beans, often with the skin still on, combined with other seasonal vegetables. It is flavoured with cured meat, such as guanciale or pancetta, making it a hearty and substantial meal, especially when served with crusty bread and butter.

The fully dried pods conceal a delicious crop of fava beans.

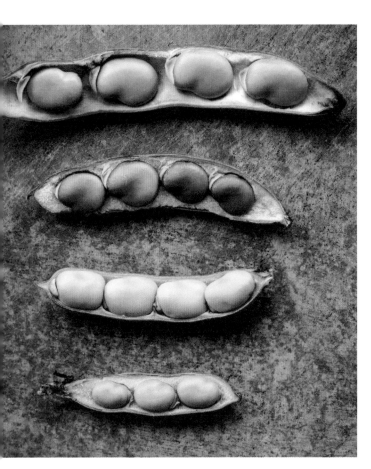

A selection of broad beans (top to bottom) 'Crimson Flowered', 'Karmazyn', 'White Windsor', and 'Syrian Small'

The ancient Egyptian vegetarian dish *ful medames* is now a staple across the Middle East. Traditionally eaten at breakfast, it derives its name from the Arabic for "beans" and (probably) a Coptic word for "buried", referring to the original method of plunging a pot of dried beans and water into the cinders of a fire. The beans were left to simmer gently overnight, ready for breakfast the following morning. This fabulously rich dish is traditionally seasoned with cumin and garlic, finished with lemon juice, olive oil, parsley, and fresh tomatoes, and served with freshly baked flatbreads to scoop it all up with.

Growing

Propagation

There are three windows of opportunity for sowing broad beans (see panel above).

If you live in a region with mild winters, broad beans can be sown in late autumn. Unlike other varieties of bean, they are tolerant of some frost (down to about -5°C/23°F) and can be overwintered for an extra-early harvest the following spring. They can also be sown in late winter or, for a late harvest, in spring.

Direct-sowing broad beans can be a challenge. Rodents dig up and feast on the seeds, while birds peck and pull emerging shoots, often killing them or at least stunting their growth. For this reason, I sow broad beans in large seed cells and keep them in the potting shed, where it's easier to protect them from pests. While some people may soak bean seeds before sowing, or propagate them in deep root-trainers, I find that germinating them dry directly in seed cells works perfectly and doesn't affect the development of the plant.

After germination, allow the seedlings to grow for about five weeks before transplanting them, and be sure to plant them slightly deeper than the length of the plug's root ball, to support the fragile stems. Water generously; the water hitting the compost will naturally backfill the holes. Cover newly planted broad beans with a protective layer of mesh or horticultural fleece, to reduce wind damage and keep the leaves safe from pesky pigeons.

'Aquadulce Claudia'

Aftercare

Being a cool-season crop, broad beans rarely need additional moisture, except during unusually dry spells. However, when they begin to send out masses of flowers, water them generously to help the fruit set and promote well-developed pods. A trick to mitigate aphid damage is to pinch out the growing tips of the plants once the stems have become full of flowers; this also encourages the plant to focus on producing pods.

As the plants become tall and heavily laden with pods, they're susceptible to being blown over by strong winds. Although it is not critical, it may be beneficial to provide support on exposed sites. Stake single plants with a bamboo cane, or tie together a whole row by encircling the crop with strong string wrapped around two fence posts, one at each end of the bed.

Plant problems

Birds, blackfly, chocolate spot, mice, pea and bean weevil, rust (see pages 49–51)

Harvesting

Snap the pods downwards at the point where they meet the main stem. You can start picking broad beans while they are small, when they can be eaten like sugar snap peas or mangetout. Alternatively, leave them to grow bigger and become soft and buttery – delicious when podded and eaten fresh or cooked. Finally, if you let the pods mature fully, they will turn dark brown and can be harvested as fava beans. Don't allow them to get too gnarly before harvesting, however. When clearing the plants away at the end of the season, snip the stem at soil level, leaving the roots and their valuable nitrogen nodules in the ground.

Storage

Broad beans are best eaten freshly picked; they have a short shelf life and will keep for a week if left inside their pods. When storing fava, shell the beans immediately after harvesting and keep them on a sunny windowsill to continue drying until they become completely hard. Only then can they be transferred to an airtight jar. The dried beans can be used as seeds the following year, although they may not grow true to type if other varieties are grown nearby, because of cross-pollination.

'Aquadulce Claudia' A Spanish heirloom bred specifically for autumn sowing. One of the hardiest varieties, it produces an enormous number of extra-long lime-green pods early in the season. It was released in 1885, selected by the French seed company Vilmorin from the older variety 'Haba de Sevilla'. These white-skinned broad beans are best consumed fresh rather than dried, and perform just as well when sown in the spring as in the autumn.

'Crimson Flowered' This variety was first documented in 1778, and is said to have been grown by the convicts of Norfolk Island in the Pacific Ocean, east of Australia. These short, stocky plants have flowers with beautiful maroon petals that stand out when compared to the standard black-and-white blooms of other broad beans. The variety was once believed to be lost forever, but it clawed its way back from extinction in 1978, when an elderly woman from Kent, Rhoda Cutbush, donated her remaining four seeds to the Henry Doubleday Research Association (now the Heritage Seed Library). The association grew the seeds and successfully reintroduced them to the trade. Miss Cutbush, who had received the seeds in 1912, had maintained the variety single-handedly for more than 60 years.

'Grano Violetto' This Italian heirloom is named after the striking violet-purple colour of its beans when they are left to mature and dry out thoroughly. It's super-tasty and well suited to autumn sowing, being resistant to cold and very early to mature.

'Horse Bean' This is a fascinating heirloom variety that has been cultivated for centuries. It resembles the beans that would have been farmed during Roman times, for feeding both people and livestock. The plants tend not to branch and bush out, making them low-yielding, but as a result they can be planted more densely. The wonderfully rich, robust flavour of the beans makes them perfect for dips and spreads.

'Karmazyn' A long-pod bean of Eastern European origin, with a dusty-pink skin. *Karmazyn* is Polish for "crimson", referring to the varying reddish-pink hues on the shell of the beans. These short, compact plants are great for exposed sites, and the beans have a rich flavour that is suited to both fresh and dry eating.

'Maris Bead' Despite being commonly used for green manures (see page 47), these small, round, beady beans are perfect for drying for use in soups and stews, thanks to their irresistibly tender texture and rich, meaty flavour. They were developed at the Plant Breeding Institute in Cambridge, eastern England. Despite their small size, they pack a lot of flavour in every bite.

'Reina Mora' An outstanding Catalan heirloom variety that's now exceptionally rare and hard to come by, this compact, cold-hardy plant produces extra-early, heavy yields in the spring if sown in the autumn. Its name means "purple queen", since, once the pods ripen fully, the beans' skin transitions from lime-green to a distinctive deep purple.

'Syrian Small' The seed collector Adam Alexander discovered these beans in 2011 while exploring the city of Damascus at the beginning of the Syrian civil war, and named the variety. According to Alexander, local teenagers used to sell these broad beans from giant wheelbarrows brimming with produce. The beans are usually harvested while young and underdeveloped, because the residents of Damascus typically cook and eat them whole, much like mangetout. The small, compact plants produce short but tightly packed pods. I've found that, when left to mature and dry, the beans are incredibly robust and well suited to cooking into soups and stews.

'Crimson Flowered'

Beans

The realm of beans is an enchanting one, where towering vines of runners are adorned with vibrant blossoms and the leafy bushes of soy embrace the earth below, offering both ornamental delight and culinary abundance. Harvested when green for a crisp, sweet treat, or carefully dried, shelled, and stored for a hearty feast, beans are a powerhouse in both veg patch and kitchen.

Growing

Beans come in two basic types according to their growth habit: bush (which include soybeans) or climbing (which come in fine, shelling, and runner varieties). Bush types are compact and easy to grow in gardens with limited space, or on gusty exposed sites where taller plants would blow over. Climbing beans bring height and contrast to the patch as well as a delightful display of insect-friendly flowers, a sense of privacy, and a calming charm as a naturally attractive backdrop. All the beans listed in this section are lovers of warm weather and will quickly be killed by frost, so, no matter the type, the same sowing and germination techniques apply.

Propagation

I don't pre-soak my bean seeds, but I do start them off in cells, rather than sowing them directly in the vegetable patch. Many people say that beans must be propagated in deep root trainers, but I've found that they grow perfectly well when germinated in cells; although their long roots curl around inside the cell, they quickly spread once planted out, so there is no impact on their growth and I save a small fortune in potting compost.

There's no need to rush into sowing beans – they are best left until the weather has warmed up. Sow one seed per cell (you may need to use a larger-celled tray for the bigger runner-bean seeds) and keep them in a warm place. A clear cloche helps to lock in warmth and moisture while deterring rodents from pilfering the freshly

'Merveille de
Piemonte' (top),
'Greasy Grits'
(middle), and
'Blauhilde'

Growing at a glance

Sow Late spring–early summer, 16–32°C (60–90°F)

Plant out Spring–summer

Spacing 35cm (14in) (bush types); 15–20cm (6–8in) (climbers for shelling/fine types); 30cm (12in) (runners)

Harvest Summer–autumn

sown seed. Once sprouted, allow the seedlings to grow on in their cells for about three weeks. Only once the risk of frost has passed completely should they be planted out in the garden to soak up the sun. It's common for the foliage to yellow if the ground temperature is cold; it's easy to mistake this for lack of nitrogen, but in fact it is simply that lower temperatures inhibit the beans' rate of photosynthesis. Don't be alarmed – they will bounce back and return to their natural colour once the temperature increases.

Aftercare

Bush types require no support and crop well in containers and pots. Bury them deeply when planting out. Early plantings may benefit from a protective covering of horticultural fleece to shelter the seedlings from wind. Provide adequate moisture while the plants establish if the weather is dry. As the flowers appear, give the plants a generous drink every few days to encourage the fruit to set; if they are too dry at this stage the yield will be reduced.

Climbing beans require support for their long vines, whether obelisks, trellising, bamboo structures or twine; all work well, yet I've found tepees to be the most efficient, sturdy, and aesthetically pleasing. Mine are constructed using 6–8 hazel poles spaced 30–40cm (12–16in) apart, in a circle with a base diameter of 1.2–1.4m (4–5ft). It can also be beneficial to wrap twine around the outside of the tepee to give the tendrils something else to clutch on to.

Climbing beans can be planted out in the patch before the supports are erected, giving easy access to cover the tender seedlings if a late cold snap is forecast. Just be sure to mark out the perimeter of the tepee first so that you plant the seedlings in the right place. Keep a close eye on the seedlings during the early stages, in case they need help getting established on the support; simply twist the vines around the structure, taking care not to snap the stems. These ferociously vigorous plants are water-guzzlers, requiring plenty of moisture, especially as the flowers begin to emerge. A thorough soaking every few days during dry weather should suffice and encourage proper pod development.

Plant problems

Aphids, rodents, rust, slugs and snails (see pages 49–51)

'Gambero Verde' flowers (above) and the climbing bean 'Blauhilde' (opposite)

Harvesting

All fresh pods can be snapped off by hand or snipped for a cleaner cut. With all types, constant picking encourages the plants to continue developing new pods.

Fine beans

Can be picked at any stage, yet boast a tender texture and sweeter flavour when harvested on the smaller size, and will become stringy if allowed to swell too much. Ideally, pick when the pods reach roughly 10cm (4in) in length.

Runner beans

Best harvested while young and tender, roughly 15cm (6in) long, the pods should snap open with ease and the beans within should be small and pale. If left too long they become tough and fibrous.

Soybeans

The pods should be a vivid green and the beans will be visible inside the pod, slightly immature but well rounded.

Beans for drying

No matter the type, allow the pods to mature fully on the plant and begin to dry out, at which point they will shrivel, turn brown, and become brittle. It's essential to avoid harvesting the pods after rain, to ensure the beans are as dry as possible.

Storage

Fresh beans can be kept for a few days in the fridge, but are best used as soon as possible after picking. To dry beans, shell them from their pods on the day of harvest, discard any rotten or damaged beans, then spread them out in a single layer on trays and leave them in the warmth of the house until they are fully dry and hard. They can be stored in airtight jars for feasting on later.

'Cannellino Montalbano', 'Merveille de Piemonte' (also the plant seen right), and 'Borlotto Lamon' (top row, from left), and 'Hannah Freeman', 'Aztec Cave Bean', and 'Coco Sophie' (bottom row, from left)

Common bean

(Phaseolus vulgaris)
Böna, Fagiolo, Feijão, Frijoles, Tarhapapu

Whether you are relishing the crisp, crunchy texture of slender fine beans straight from the patch or indulging in the robust richness of drying varieties in the winter months, these beans are a universal ingredient with a multitude of uses. Some have hulls of beige, brown, and black, while others don mesmerizing marbled jackets. The pods can be simple yet elegant in monotones of green, yellow, and purple, or extravagantly striped and dappled with bursts of bright magenta, mauve, and maroon.

History

Beans' roots are firmly planted in the Americas. The fascinating story of their domestication was once thought to have unfolded in both Meso-America and the southern Andes around 8,000 years ago, leading to the creation of two distinct gene pools. Yet genetic studies have now unravelled a twist in the tale, revealing that domestication first took place in Mexico. Beans were highly regarded by many early civilizations and became an integral ingredient for Indigenous communities across North, Central, and South America, providing a wholesome crop that could be dried and stored as a reliable source of protein throughout the winter.

66
Beans are a powerhouse in both veg patch and kitchen.

Culinary uses

Preparation

There are many myths about rehydrating beans for cooking: whether to soak them or not, when to salt the pot, and so on. The tastiest and best way is to soak the beans overnight in plenty of cold water, then cook them in their soaking water (which may need topping up). Lightly season the pot after soaking and before cooking. When eating these beans fresh, choose younger, stringless pods. They can be added raw to salads for a crunchy bite.

Dishes

In their tender fresh form, the best way to flaunt the fantastic flavour and texture of common beans is to sauté them with caramelized shallots and finish with a squeeze of lemon and a crack of black pepper. But these fresh beans can do far more. They make a tasty alternative to cauliflower when baked in a creamy cheese sauce, and can hold their own as the star of vegetable curries and casseroles, such as the delectable Greek dish *fasolakia yiahni*. This traditional braised delicacy is prepared by slowly cooking the fresh pods with olive oil in a rich, savoury tomato sauce, perfumed with a blend of herbs and spices.

When dried, common beans are completely different, a wholesome, hearty, creamy treat capable of absorbing flavours and spices, leaving the belly full and the soul comforted. From aromatic, fiery barbecue baked beans to the sweet, herby hits of a Tuscan stew, there is no shortage of hearty and delicious recipes. *Frijoles refritos* (refried beans) from northern Mexico is a simple yet superior way to

"Beans, beans, the musical fruit"

This notorious rhyme, sung in various versions in school playgrounds, refers to the fact that eating beans makes you toot like a flute. The effect is brought about by the complex carbohydrates the beans contain, which the gut has difficulty digesting – hence the flatulence. In Mexico and Central America, a herb called *epazote* has for millennia been incorporated into beany dishes to help solve this problem. As well as providing a pungent oregano-like hit, the natural chemical compounds in the plant counteract the gassy by-product.

cook up a bounty of dried beans, often served as a side dish or used as a filling for tacos. It is made by simmering the beans until soft, then mashing them with flavourful aromatics, such as chilli, garlic, and cumin. The creamed beans are then cooked in a pan with a touch of oil until crispy and golden-brown at the edges. Refried beans work well with any type, but especially black beans. Mashed beans aren't just a winter-warming meal, either; cannellini types (see overleaf) are the perfect alternative to chickpeas when blended with lemon, tahini, and garlic into hummus.

In American cuisine, beans are famous for their part in the nourishing trio known as the "Three Sisters", alongside squash and corn (see pages 154, 174, and 338). For Three Sisters stew, the three are simmered with spices into a thick and savoury soup that's a testament to Indigenous peoples and the bountiful harvests of the passing season.

Beans are famous for their part in the nourishing trio known to Indigenous Americans as the "Three Sisters".

'Triomphe de Farcy' (opposite) and 'Cherokee Trail of Tears'

Drying: bush types

'Arikara Yellow' This delicious, creamy-textured variety is named after the Arikara people of the Dakotas, who first cultivated it. The other part of the name is deceptive, however, since the beans are not yellow but rather a muted pink or brown. The Arikara people developed this variety specifically for short-season growing. It is said that they shared their stock freely with William Clark and Meriwether Lewis on the Corps of Discovery Expedition in 1804–6, and the two men relied on the beans for sustenance during their journey across the continent.

'Cannellino Montalbano' A premium cannellini, beloved in Tuscany for its robust flavour and meaty, tender texture, which holds up well when cooked. Slow to mature, it produces an abundance of pods.

'Great Northern' This old American heirloom grown by the Mandan people of the Great Plains, North Dakota, is perhaps the best-textured white bean available, with an incredible ability to soak up sauces and flavours. Early to mature and resistant to drought.

'Hutterite' A pukka soup pea that cooks quickly and has a nutty, buttery taste. The off-white beans are said to have been introduced to the USA by European Hutterian Brethren during the nineteenth century.

'Jacob's Cattle' First stewarded by the Indigenous Passamaquoddy people, who occupied land in Maine and New Brunswick. These beautiful beans are charmingly splotched and dotted, reminiscent of cattle. They are reliable, known for their heavy yield and their ability to thrive in cool climates. With a creamy texture when cooked, they are often baked or stewed.

'Santa Maria Pinquito' An essential part of the barbecue cuisine of Santa Maria Valley, California, this small pink bean is prized for maintaining its firm, plump texture when cooked. Its origin has been a topic of debate among ranchers and historians, some of whom believe that it was brought to the area by Spanish vaqueros, while others argue that migrant citrus workers from Mexico introduced it to the region. A third story tells of a European immigrant who grew a garden full of these beans before sharing them with her neighbours. Perfect for making *frijoles borrachos* (drunken beans), an aptly named dish of legumes in beer.

'Soldier' A delicious New England heirloom that takes its name from the distinctive maroon patterning over the bean's "eye" (the scar where it was attached to the pod), which resembles a toy soldier. Perfect for baked beans, since it holds its shape after cooking.

Drying: climbing types

'Aztec Cave Bean' Speckled like the hide of a cow, this bean is said to have been found sealed in ceramic vessels in caves of New Mexico. Analysis demonstrated that the beans were more than 1,500 years old. Runs rampant and is highly productive.

'Blue Shackamaxon' These big, bold purple pods are easy to spot and harvest. The origins of the variety can be traced to the Lenape people of the Northeastern Woodlands of Delaware. When dried it takes on a stunning blue-black hue. The beans are smooth and silky, with a rich, nutty flavour.

'Borlotto Lamon' Hands down the best-tasting of all borlotti beans, this stems from the valleys of Lamon in northern Italy, an area famous since the sixteenth century for the production of beans. Variegated red and yellow pods contain beans that are delightfully mottled and marbled.

'Cherokee Trail of Tears' This jet-black bean has played a significant role in the history and culture of the Cherokee people. Its name derives from the arduous journey undertaken by many Indigenous people during the forced relocation known as the Trail of Tears in the mid-nineteenth century, during which they smuggled seeds in order to continue cultivating their ancestral foods. The Cherokee treasured the crop for its cultural significance and rich history, and the beans became a symbol of hope and perseverance in the face of genocide and ethnic cleansing. Traditionally ground into flour, the beans are also delicious in soups and stews.

'Coco Sophie' Highly productive and early to mature, this rare, old-school French heirloom dates back to the eighteenth century. The pods are bursting with brilliant white oval beans perfect for the stewing pot.

'Lazy Housewife' This variety (claimed to be the first to require no stringing) was given its misogynistic name in the nineteenth century. It is traditionally eaten fresh, but can be left to mature into creamy-white beans that are perfect for casseroles.

'Mostoller Wild Goose' What started as a wild-goose chase ended with the fascinating discovery of an heirloom bean. According to the Mostoller family, the discovery of this bean dates back to 1865, when the family were out shooting birds on their land in Somerset County, Pennsylvania. On butchering one, they were astonished to come across a handful of undigested beans in its stomach. The family grew, stewarded, and christened the bean in honour of the waterfowl. This variety is a vigorous producer of pods containing ornate white beans with a brown-speckled saddle over the eye.

Fresh: bush types

'Beurre de Rocquencourt' Pale yellow, delicately flavoured, and early to mature, this historic variety was developed in a small town on the outskirts of Versailles, in north-central France, in the nineteenth century. It is great in climates with shorter seasons, producing an abundant bounty of buttery beans.

'Black Valentine' A dual-purpose producer of succulent light green pods when young and hearty black-shelled soup beans when left to mature. It is almost legendary in the USA thanks to its ability to withstand cool temperatures while still producing enormous yields.

'Comtesse de Chambord' Now somewhat rare and hard to find, this delightful variety is very productive, producing a heavy bounty of skinny, crunchy pods. It was developed in the Loire Valley, central France, during the nineteenth century.

'Fin de Bagnols' One of the thinnest fine beans available, as slender as a shoelace, this is a culinary treasure from the heart of the Beaujolais countryside in east-central France. Boasting some of the best-flavoured pods on the market, it is very productive and incredibly succulent.

'Merveille de Piemonte' An outstanding type for looks, taste, production, and adaptability. Intricately marbled in purple and gold, the pods of this bean from the Italian Alps stay soft, sweet, and tender even when large.

'Pencil Pod Black Wax' This luminous-yellow slim bean with black seeds is considered by legume aficionados to be the most flavoursome of all the yellow fresh eating types. Developed in the USA in 1900 by Calvin Keeney, "Father of the Stringless Bean", it is productive, resilient, and outrageously tasty.

'Triomphe de Farcy' An amazingly flavoured nineteenth-century French heirloom that crops extra early and in profuse

amounts. The long, thin pods are crunchy and crisp in texture with a rich, nutty taste, making them a chef's delight.

Fresh: climbing types

'Anellino Verde' An Italian heirloom variety with green, curly, crescent-shaped pods that have a meaty bite. It is stringless, an abundant producer, and highly sought-after by chefs owing to its fantastic flavour and unusual twisted shape. It is sometimes known as the shrimp bean because of its tightly curled configuration. A golden-yellow type is also available, 'Anellino Giallo'.

'Blauhilde' A German heirloom variety dating back to the nineteenth century, highly prolific, ornate, and resistant to pests and diseases. It has delightful violet flowers followed by a heavy crop of very dark pods.

'Greasy Grits' A treasured variety of delicate, tender snap beans that originated in the Appalachian region centuries ago. This stand-out variety produces beans with a rich, nutty flavour that is truly exceptional, and

a smooth, slightly shiny skin – hence the name.

'Kentucky Wonder' A tried-and-tested American favourite dating back to the mid-nineteenth century. This superabundant, vigorous, tender green bean was first listed as 'Texas Pole' in 1864, but underwent a name change in 1877.

'Meraviglia di Venezia' A prolific producer of big, bulky banana-yellow pods that stay tender even when large. This culinary gem from Venice is now a rare and endangered variety.

'Red Noodle' (*Vigna unguiculata* ssp. *sesquipedalis*) Also known as the yard-long bean because of the incredible length of its pods, this variety is a popular ingredient in Asia for stir-fries and hotpots. Sweet, stringless, and very tender, it produces scarlet beans that excel in flavour and texture.

'Trionfo Violetto' This triumphantly abundant stringless purple snap bean produces very long, slender pods with a deliciously crisp texture and refined sweetness. A heritage Italian variety, it is considered by many to be the best-tasting purple type.

'Red Noodle'

Runner beans
(*Phaseolus coccineus*)
Ayocote, Ayocotl, Botil, Fagiolo Rampicante

Aptly named for their rambling, quick-growing nature, this is the type of bean that most closely resembles Jack's magical, fairy-tale beanstalk. They ascend rapidly, their twining vines constantly in pursuit of higher ground, and their lush, vibrant green foliage provides a beautiful backdrop. With elegant flowers in shades from ethereal white through pastel pink to striking scarlet, as well as bicoloured beauties, runner beans are a botanical spectacle.

History

Originating from the tropical and humid upland regions of Mexico and Central America, the runner bean is perennial in its native home, producing tuberous roots that are considered to be poisonous owing to the presence of the protein lectin, yet are eaten by Indigenous Central American people, who employ various techniques to remove the toxins before consumption. The fascinating story of runner beans in Britain dates back to the seventeenth century with their introduction by John Tradescant the Elder, a renowned gardener to the royal family. For close to 100 years, they were grown solely for their aesthetic appeal. It was the eighteenth-century botanist Philip Miller of the Chelsea Physic Garden in London who found that runners were also delicious. They have since become a staple in the country's allotments and gardens, and are enjoyed for their rich flavour.

Culinary uses
Preparation

Young beans can be eaten in their pods and are delicious in stir-fries. String runner beans by cutting off the top and tail of the pod with a knife, then using a vegetable peeler to remove the strings from both sides.

Dishes

Simply shredded and stir-fried with garlic or incorporated into complexly spiced tamarind and tomato curries, young, fresh, and tender runner beans gracefully find their place in the summer larder. Left whole, they can be blistered over an open flame until charred and smoky, a sensation when paired with a fiery salsa or a pungent *bagna cauda*. Once dried, they transform into an endlessly versatile ingredient that can be used in an array of dishes, from savoury bakes to hearty stews or comforting casseroles, such as the delectable and wholesome Greek classic *gigantes plaki*, enormous white buttery beans of the variety 'Gigante' (see opposite) in an indulgent, herby tomato sauce that sings with the flavours of the Mediterranean.

The dark pods of 'Black Knight' with long 'Crusader', wide 'Gigante', 'Sunset', and 'Rhondda Black'

'Aztec White' This ancient variety is thought to be of Aztec origin and is said to have been discovered perfectly preserved in sealed pottery unearthed among the remains of an ancient civilization in New Mexico (separately from 'Aztec Cave Bean'; see page 330). It is very short-growing for a runner. The chunky white beans it produces are delicious and the plants are exceptionally resistant to drought.

'Black Coat' This old-school runner was first documented in the mid-seventeenth century by the German botanist Michael Titus. A short-growing type with dainty pods, yet the delicious black beans are chunky.

'Black Knight' A stunning dark purple-podded runner with striking florescent-purple beans when fresh. The dark pods contrast with the green foliage, for easier picking. It's believed that Edmund Knight, Bishop of Shrewsbury 1882–95, stewarded these beans and dispersed them among the members of his congregation.

'Crusader' An old black-beaned exhibition type that produces remarkably long pods. Vigorous, robust, and tasty, it is perfect for competitions.

'Czar' This reliable, well-flavoured runner has stood the test of time. It is a brilliant choice for drying, producing long pods filled with chunky, creamy-white butter beans.

Variety	Flower colour	Pod length
'Aztec White'	White	10–15cm (4–6in)
'Black Coat'	Crimson	15cm (6in)
'Black Knight'	Crimson	20–30cm (8–12in)
'Crusader'	Crimson	40–45cm (16–18in)
'Czar'	White	25–30cm (10–12in)
'Gigante'	White	15–20cm (6–8in)
'Painted Lady'	Crimson and white	15–20cm (6–8in)
'Rhondda Black'	Crimson	35–40cm (14–16in)
'Scarlet Emperor'	Crimson/ orange	30–35cm (12–14in)
'Sunset'	Pink	20–25cm (8–10in)

'Gigante' This is the Greek variety traditionally grown to produce soft, fantastically flavoured, creamy-white butter beans for making the classic dish *gigantes plaki* (see opposite). It performs well in cooler and wetter regions, too, and produces short pods containing between two and four massive beans. It is an absolute culinary delight and a must-grow.

'Painted Lady' She is a natural beauty with her bicoloured rich red and ivory-white blooms. The name was a nod towards Queen Elizabeth I, who famously adorned a powdered white face with light red hair, and the variety was first documented by the Royal Horticultural Society in 1633; however, it's thought to have been grown in the UK since the mid-sixteenth century. This delicious heritage bean is robust and resilient, producing an enormous quantity of short pods containing dark beans mottled with peachy pink.

'Rhondda Black' This variety was bred on an allotment in the Welsh valley of Rhondda by Alan Picton in the early 1960s, after he discovered a naturally occurring black variation among a crop of purple-beaned 'Enorma' runners he was cultivating for a competition. Picton developed and stewarded the variety over the subsequent decades as a showcase black bean capable of reaching mammoth lengths. Real Seeds has since built up a seed stock from a small handful of beans, and has made the variety available to the public.

'Scarlet Emperor' This old-timer has been one of the most popular runner varieties in the UK since its introduction in 1633. The long vines are profusely adorned with large, fiery orange flowers. This boisterous grower is one of the most reliable and resilient, producing a mass of long pods containing beans dappled black and purple.

'Sunset' A stunning pink-blossomed heritage variety with black, mauve-splashed beans. This shorter-growing type is worth a place in the garden for its excellent display of peachy-pink blooms alone.

'Crusader'

'Gigante' (overleaf, left) and 'Czar' (overleaf, right)

Soybean

(*Glycine max*)
Daizu, Dàdòu, Edamame, Mejukong, Soja

Soybeans produce a profusion of leafy branches that creates a lush, bushy presence in the patch. The fuzzy green pods look like velvet cocoons concealing the riches inside. Once unlocked, the beans reveal hues ranging from the glow of lime-green and lemon-yellow to pristine white, earthy buff tones, and rich, deep browns.

History

The soybean was native to China before seeding its way through Asia, and the ancient Chinese held it in the highest regard, considering it one of the five sacred grains indispensable for their civilization. In the early nineteenth century it was brought by American traders to the USA, where it was fermented into the first American-grown soy sauce.

In the USA it was also a coffee substitute and a potential car-making material. Amid the ravages of the American Civil War in the late nineteenth century, the Southern states faced a severe shortage of coffee. In this desperate situation – and despite the fact that it contains no caffeine – the soybean emerged as a saviour, offering an alternative to a morning brew when roasted and ground. Local seed dealers caught on and as a lucrative marketing campaign promoted their soybeans as "coffee berries" and "coffee beans".

The soybean car was dreamed up by Henry Ford, to combine the fruits of the automobile industry with the resourcefulness of agriculture. He claimed he would "grow automobiles from the soil", envisioning a car constructed entirely from soybean-derived plastics. This revolutionary idea never made it past the concept, however; Ford had to postpone his beany plan because of World War II.

Sprouting soybeans

Soybeans are not commonly used dried, owing to their long cooking time and indigestible hulls, but they can be sprouted into the most delicious authentic Korean *kongnamul* beansprouts, which are traditionally used in stir-fries, soups, and other dishes. Rinse the dried beans, pop them into a glass jar, add water to submerge them, and leave them unsealed overnight at room temperature. Drain and replace the water, then cover the container with muslin to allow air circulation and retain moisture. Keep the jar in a dark, warm place, refreshing the water a few times daily. The beans should all have sprouted in three or four days. Drain thoroughly, discard any unsprouted beans, and store the sprouts in the fridge for up to five days.

Culinary uses

Preparation

Boil fresh soybeans in their pods for a minute or two, to retain their texture. The dried beans should be soaked overnight and simmered until soft.

Dishes

Thanks to their versatility, soybeans are a staple ingredient in Asian cuisine, from the velvety richness and subtle sweetness of tofu, made by curdling soymilk, to tangy and meaty tempeh, a centuries-old Indonesian cake of fermented soybeans with a nutty, earthy flavour and a firm texture that makes it perfect for grilling or pan-frying. Miso paste and soy sauce are known for unleashing a tsunami of umami flavours on the palate, and both are made by fermenting these beans. Yet the most delightful way to snack on soybeans is when they are young and green, briefly boiled, when they have a succulent texture and fresh, sweet taste that can be enhanced with lashings of garlic and chilli salt.

Plants and pods of 'Tankuro'

Recommended varieties

'Agate' This fast-maturing edamame bean is a Japanese heirloom variety that is highly productive and boasts fancy green-and-brown seeds when left to mature.

'Gaia' A modern open-pollinated cultivar, this one has gorgeous lime-green beans dappled with black. It is a fantastic short-seasoned type.

'Lammer's Black' A wonderful short-season heirloom variety and an abundant producer of black, thin-hulled beans that cook quickly, this is the ideal choice for tofu and tempeh.

'Midori Giant' This is considered one of the best edamame types, highly adaptable and robust. The plants produce heavy yields of pods bursting with big, juicy green beans.

'Shinonome' A delightful old-school yellow bean ideal for making soymilk, tofu, and miso, and doubling as a splendid sprouting type.

'Tankuro' A premium variety from Japan, highly regarded for its delectable rich and nutty flavour, which is unlike that of any other type. The beans are encased within a chestnut-brown hull.

Corn

Zea mays

Also known as Choclo, Maize, Mazorca

The brief joy of harvesting freshly picked corn is one of the most satisfying and anticipated of the year. This versatile crop comes in a rainbow of colours and various types – sweet, dent, pop, flint, flour, and pod corn – and can be enjoyed fresh, popped, or ground into flour.

History

The domestication of corn is believed to have begun about 9,000 years ago in the Central Balsas River Valley, Mexico, marking the beginning of a long and complex process that led to one of the most important food crops in human history. Indigenous farmers selectively bred *teosinte*, a wild grass native to the area, to develop a crop of palatable, productive, and nutritious seeds. Genetic and archaeological studies suggest that these early seeds were dispersed throughout North, Central, and South America as people migrated before corn was fully domesticated. The spreading of partially domesticated seeds played a crucial role in shaping the diversity of corn. Over thousands of years, ancient farmers across the continents developed the crop independently and simultaneously until it was fully domesticated and adapted to each region. The result is a vast array of varieties, each suited to the specific needs and conditions of its local environment.

The cultivation of corn was pivotal in the development of Meso-American civilizations, providing a dependable food source for nomadic peoples. It supported the growth of settlements, facilitating the emergence of massive city-states and empires, such as those of the Olmec, Maya, Aztec, and Inca. These civilizations relied heavily on the production of corn, not only for sustenance but also for its religious and cultural significance, as it became a symbol of life and fertility and was deeply intertwined with social and political structures.

The continuous need to improve the corn harvest led to remarkable agricultural innovations. In the Peruvian Andes, farmers developed terraced mountainside gardens to cultivate corn, to prevent soil erosion and retain water on the steep slopes. Similarly, in shallow lake Texcoco, the Aztec created floating island gardens known as *chinampas* to grow crops,

> **The continuous need to improve the corn harvest led to remarkable agricultural innovations.**

'Stowell's Evergreen'

including corn. These artificial gardens were constructed by layering mud and reeds on to the lake bed, creating a fertile area for farming.

The cultivation of corn also had a significant impact on the development and expansion of Native American societies. It allowed the creation of more substantial and permanent settlements, which led to the development of complex political and social structures. The Pueblo, a group of peoples in the southwestern United States, are believed to be the first to have cultivated corn, and it transformed their way of life to a remarkable extent. Swiftly

becoming a staple food crop, corn also developed into a holy plant with a deeply entrenched cultural significance. The Hopi people held sacred corn dances to honour their deity of fertility and growth. These dances were performed with great reverence and were believed to bring good fortune to the community. Cornmeal-based paint was used to create intricate designs on the body, and musical instruments were fashioned from corn husks. Rattles made by filling dried corn husks with small stones or beads were used for rhythmic sounds during the ceremonies. Similarly, the Zuni people – another Pueblo community – incorporated corn in their traditional healing practices, believing it to possess medicinal properties capable of curing ailments and promoting well-being.

The Lakota Sioux of Dakota and many other Indigenous American peoples carved pipes from dried corn cobs for smoking tobacco and other sacred herbs during ceremonial rituals. Plaited corn-silk hair ornaments were worn by the Apache and Navajo, among others, and while many peoples made cornhusk dolls as toys for children, the Iroquois and Oneida peoples integrated them into their religious practices. The Iroquois also traditionally wove corn husks into sandals.

Corn was being cultivated extensively across the Americas, from Chile to Canada, by the time Christopher Columbus brought the seeds back to Spain after his maiden voyage to the Caribbean in 1493. This marked the beginning of a global swap of crops, animals, practices, metals, diseases, and so on, known as the Columbian Exchange. Most corn was milled and cooked into polenta-type dishes by poor people in Europe, and used by European colonialists as a form of payment for African slaves. It also made up a large part of the enslaved people's diet during the notoriously squalid transatlantic voyages.

The various kernels contain different amounts of starch, and each is suitable for a different purpose. Below are (from left) 'Dakota Black Popcorn', 'King Philip', 'Puhwem', 'Hopi Purple', and 'Golden Bantam'.

Culinary uses
Preparation
The tastiest way to cook simple corn on the cob is to simmer the cobs in a half-and-half mixture of seasoned water and milk with a generous knob of butter for roughly 6 minutes. The cooked cobs can be flashed over a barbecue for a smoky finish, if you wish, but they're incredibly creamy and succulent straight out of the pot. The rich, buttery cooking liquor can be kept for use as a base for corn soups or chowders.

Dishes
The culinary world of corn extends beyond a mere collection of recipes. This is an almost holy crop with deep historical roots, and a food staple that dominates the diets of entire civilizations, old and new. In Mexico and South American countries, cornflour tortillas are widely consumed daily as tacos, a small hand-sized tortilla topped with meat, beans, salsas, and other fillings. The tortilla was invented thousands of years ago, and Mayan legend has it that it began when a local peasant prepared one as a present for a ravenously hungry king. Its popularity spread and the tortilla became an essential food source for the Maya and Aztec people.

In present-day Mexico, street-food vendors commonly serve a popular dish called *elotes*. Although the recipe varies by region, it typically consists of a whole grilled sweetcorn smothered in a thick sauce made from mayonnaise and sour cream. The corn is topped with a generous amount of *cotija* cheese, ancho chilli powder, and fresh lime juice.

Cachapas is a beautiful sweet and savoury corn pancake served at roadside stalls in Venezuela. It is traditionally cooked on a *budare*, a flat, round metal skillet without any rim or raised edges. *Cachapas* are typically stuffed with *queso de mano*, a soft white local cheese, then folded in half and grilled until crisp and crunchy on the outside yet moist and tender inside.

Be sure to harvest corn when it is still young and tender.

Pollination

Corn is wind-pollinated, and the male tassels at the top of the plant release pollen, which must fall and drift on to the female silks if proper cobs are to develop. Planting in blocks encircles the emerging cobs with male pollen. Ideally, avoid cross-pollination between sweetcorn and other varieties of corn, since it can lead to starchy, poorly flavoured kernels. One way to prevent this is by staggering sowings of different types by three weeks, or growing each variety in a separate part of the garden. The problem may occur if your garden is near commercial agricultural maize fields, and in that case it is much more challenging to prevent.

The sweet, creamy flavour of corn lends itself to soup-like beverages, such as *atol de elote*, a popular hot drink served in a clay cup called a *jarrito*. It consists of blended sweetcorn, milk, and water, sweetened with brown sugar, seasoned with cinnamon, and thickened with cornflour. The brew is often served for breakfast in Mexico and South American countries with *tamales*, a traditional Meso-American dish of corn-based dough stuffed with meat, cheese, fruit, vegetables, and chilli. The parcels are steamed inside corn husks, which are then opened and used as a plate.

Corn-silk tea, prepared using the dried brown silks of ripened corn steeped in hot water, is believed to be an ancient concoction that dates back 6,000 years to the Indigenous peoples of Central America. The herbal infusion was said to have healing properties and was used to treat a wide range of ailments. It tastes slightly sweet and mildly earthy, and is perfect for enjoying before going to sleep.

Growing

Propagation

Sow early to give these sun-loving crops a head start, but it is crucial to protect the seeds and seedlings from cold. Germinate them indoors on a windowsill or other warm spot about three weeks before the last frost is likely. Alternatively, wait until the risk of frost has passed completely before sowing. Direct-sown corn is vulnerable to attack from birds, slugs, and rabbits when the sprouts emerge, so I sow mine in seed cells, either singly or two seeds per cell so that the weaker seedling from each pair can be discarded after germination. To protect the newly sown seed from rodents, cover with a cloche.

Allow the seedlings to grow for at least three weeks, then – only once the risk of frost has passed completely – plant them out in the garden. To improve pollination, plant corn in blocks rather than rows (see

341

Growing at a glance

Sow Early–mid-spring, 16–34°C (60–93°F)

Plant out Late spring–early summer

Spacing 25cm (10in)

Harvest Late summer–early autumn

panel on previous page). Water generously after transplanting, and if the weather is still chilly or a late cold snap is forecast, protect your newly planted-out seedlings with a layer of horticultural fleece.

Aftercare

As they grow, the seedlings require additional watering only if the weather is particularly dry. Once the cobs begin to appear, water the plants thoroughly twice a week.

Plant problems

Badgers, birds, corn smut (see panel, right), rodents, slugs and snails (see pages 49–51)

Harvesting

The corn harvest is a fleeting moment that should be embraced and cherished. Harvest the cobs as soon as the silks turn a rich, dark brown and dry out. A quick test of the crop's maturity can be performed by gently peeling back a small section of the husk or making a small vertical incision with a knife to observe the kernels' progress. Another way is to make a small nick in one of the kernels. If the liquid released is watery, the corn is underripe. When the liquid is creamy and milky, it is perfectly ripe and ready for harvesting. However, if a thick, opaque liquid is discharged, the corn is overripe and the sugars have turned into starch, resulting in a loss of the delicious sweetness and soft, buttery texture. To harvest, snap the cobs from the main stem by pushing them downwards. Other types of corn, such as dent, flour, and popcorn, cannot be harvested early and should be left on the stalks for as long as possible, to allow them to mature and dry naturally. However, it is crucial to harvest them before the first frost, to prevent damage.

As the cobs mature, they become very susceptible to animal attack. Entire crops can be decimated overnight, the whole cobs stripped to the core like something from a cartoon. Some people suggest cutting the tops and bottoms off plastic bottles and wrapping the resulting tubes around developing cobs, but it's best to try to beat the little blighters to the bounty by harvesting the cobs as soon as they begin to mature. In gardens with high pest pressure, it may even be necessary to harvest corn prematurely to avoid a total crop failure.

Storage

Sweetcorn should be eaten as fresh as possible, but other types are best hung to continue drying in a warm, airy spot with their husks pulled back to expose the cobs. As the kernels become fully dry, they will start falling from the cobs, at which point it is easy to remove the kernels by rubbing the cobs in a downwards motion. Store dried kernels in airtight jars.

A blessing or a curse?

Corn smut (*Ustilago maydis*), also known as *huitlacoche* or Mexican corn truffle, is a fungal disease that engulfs corn cobs in a blue-grey pebble-like fungus. Considered a delicacy in Mexico, the edible fungus has a sweet, smoky, earthy, corn-like flavour with delicate hints of truffle, and is used in many recipes. However, outside Mexico, it is usually seen as a threat by large-scale farmers, who use toxic fungicides to prevent it from growing, or even destroy entire crops of infected plants.

'Burro Mountain Popcorn' One of the oldest heirloom popcorns. The seeds were discovered by Frank Tatsch, preserved inside pottery thought to be 600–1,000 years old in caves in New Mexico. Set in dainty, pointed white cobs, the kernels have a sweet, nutty flavour when popped.

'Country Gentleman' This variety – named after a famous nineteenth-century agricultural magazine – was introduced by the New York seed firm Peter Henderson & Co. in 1891. It is a cross between 'Stowell's Evergreen' (see right) and 'Ne Plus Ultra' (1882). 'Country Gentleman' has a sweet, rich, milky flavour, and its cobs are larger than those of both its parents, but it retained 'Ne Plus Ultra's haphazard, zigzagging pattern of tightly packed, misshapen white kernels, known as shoe pegs.

'Dakota Black Popcorn' Although smaller when popped than shop-bought popcorn, the fantastic flavour and crispy crunch keep you dipping into the bowl for more. This pre-colonial indigenous popping variety matures early and produces glossy, dark, pointed kernels that puff a brilliant white.

'Double Red' A spectacular variety with stems, foliage, husk, cob, tassels, and kernels a vivid burgundy-red, bred by the founder of Peace Seeds

in Corvallis, Oregon, Dr Alan "Mushroom" Kapuler. Kapuler developed it at his small organic farm in the late twentieth century using Indigenous American methods and principles. Can be harvested as sweetcorn or left to mature and used to make flour.

'Double Standard' This modern but open-pollinated bicoloured sweetcorn was developed by the US seed company Johnny's Selected Seeds as a robust corn for cool climates. It is a cross of an early white heirloom and the popular yellow 'Burnell'. Tasty, early, and the first open-pollinated yellow-and-white-kernelled corn.

'Golden Bantam' This sugary yellow corn swept across America, swiftly putting white, orange, and black varieties out of fashion after its release in 1902. After visiting family in Greenfield, Massachusetts, E. L. Coy, a keen seed-saver, was served the corn. Amazed by its sugary flavour, he acquired seed and sent it to his friend Washington Atlee Burpee, the founder of Burpee Seeds. Burpee grew it, agreed that it was one of the best-tasting corns available, and hastily listed it in his catalogue. This robust variety performs well even in cool summers.

'Hopi Purple' Traditionally grown by the Hopi people of Arizona, these beautiful purple cobs thrive in arid conditions. They were cultivated for making into *piki*, a colourful bread cooked over a fire on an enormous baking stone. The Hopi used the corn (and its relative 'Hopi Blue') as a body paint and textile dye.

'King Philip' This charming copper-coloured cob is a cherished flint corn from the Wampanoag Native Americans. It was named after the seventeenth-century leader of the confederation of Indigenous people, Metacom, called King Philip by English settlers. It is not clear whether the Wampanoag shared the seeds freely or if colonists stole them during King Philip's War (1675–76), a brutal conflict that occurred when Indigenous people desperately attempted to protect their

land from colonial control. After their defeat, Metacom was captured, beheaded, and quartered; his head was mounted on a spike and displayed at Plymouth Colony for 25 years. Traditionally, this corn was ground into meal for making cakes, bread, and fritters; it is now listed as an endangered and culturally significant variety on the Slow Food Ark of Taste.

'Puhwem' Considered a sacred "mother corn", this holds special significance for Native Americans. It was carefully preserved by Nora Thomson Dean of the Lenape/Delaware community in Indian Territory, Oklahoma. Dean, who was born in 1907, dedicated the latter part of her life to preserving, celebrating, and spreading the knowledge and traditions of her people. This is one of the tallest indigenous American corns, capable of exceeding 3m (10ft). The creamy-white kernels are traditionally ground into flour but can also be eaten at their milky stage, if cooked. The thick stalks are often dried and used similarly to bamboo for building, and the leaves are used for roofs and walls and sometimes woven into shoes.

'Stowell's Evergreen' Bred in 1848 by the farmer Nathaniel Newman Stowell of Burlington, New Jersey, who crossed 'Menomony Soft Corn' with 'Northern Sugar Corn', this was later referred to as the "king of all white sweetcorn". In 1855 Stowell sold a bag of seeds to a friend for $4, for cultivation only in his own patch. Unfortunately, Stowell's crafty friend sold the kernels to the seed company Grant Thorburn & Co. for $20,000. Thorburn made the seeds commercially available the following year. These long white cobs were named "evergreen" because they remain sweet and milky for longer than other sweetcorns.

'Strawberry Popcorn' This short variety produces small, squat, tightly packed dark burgundy cobs resembling giant strawberries. Its history remains a mystery, but its petite, rich red kernels are considered among the best for popping.

'Double Standard'

Index

Page numbers in **bold** refer to main entries

Seed Suppliers

https://go.dk.com/uk-seed-hunter-suppliers

To help in your search for heirloom seeds, I've compiled a comprehensive list of seed-growers, farms, companies, and outlets worldwide. I've also included organizations, research centres, and other resources for those interested in learning about heirloom seeds and preserving precious heritage crops. To access the downloadable list, scan the QR code above or follow the link.

One of my favourite gardening tasks is searching for new seed varieties. In preparation for this book, I spent six months connecting with seed companies, seed-savers, and growers across the world. I visited organizations, including the Heritage Seed Library seed bank in Coventry and the seed company Real Seeds in western Wales, and I was in regular contact with Baker Creek Heirloom Seeds in Mansfield, Missouri. Jere Gettle, the owner and master seedsperson of Baker Creek, was very supportive of my project and has given me great advice. Countless other seed-lovers and organizations throughout the world have supported me by sending seeds to grow and feature in this book.

Winter is a great time to restock the seed collection, and in the cold months I enjoy browsing catalogues to discover new crops to grow. When buying seeds, it's a good idea to check if any local seed farms offer the specific varieties you're looking for. Local farms often have better-adapted seeds, producing plants more resilient to your climate.

I also encourage you to carry out your own research and unearth outlets I may have missed. Check out the many independent growers and seed farmers on eBay, Etsy, and other online marketplaces; attend local seed swaps; and trade seeds with fellow growers.

If seed swaps are not prevalent in your area, why not set one up? Through the power of plants and seeds, we can begin to forge resilient communities that work together. A dramatic shift in globalized food and seed production is needed, and it's at this grassroots level that we as growers can unite and play our part in the fight for heirloom and heritage seeds!

Acknowledgements

Firstly I'd like to give a very special mention to Kate Forrester and Mollie Taylor of Four Acre Farm, Ringwood, for their continued support and for enabling me to grow my garden on site.

A tremendous shout-out to Charles Dowding and his momentous effort at promoting no-dig growing and soil health. Without your inspiration I would never have written this book.

I'd like to send a massive thanks to all the seed companies and organizations that supported me on this project, and an extra BIG up to Jere Gettle and the Baker Creek Heirloom Seeds family over in Missouri for their substantial contribution to my debut book.

Huge appreciation and love to the whole DK crew, my number-one choice of publisher. From start to finish it has been a dream to work alongside such a creative and elite team of designers and editors, and I believe together we have created an exciting, insightful book that will stand the test of time.

Hats off to sharpshooter Rachel Warne, who was behind the lens and captured the stunning snaps throughout the book.

A heroic mention to Stuart Cooper, who played a fundamental role in germinating the idea of a book on heirloom and heritage food crops and developing my idea of The Seed Hunter.

Green thumbs up to all the heirloom seed-savers, enthusiasts, and growers who make this community so inclusive and welcoming. May we all continue to spread the word so that future generations get to taste the delicious flavours from our past.

Lastly, a sassy little number goes out to my nearest, dearest, and grooviest friends: Joe, Matty, Tereza, and Anna. <3

Publisher's acknowledgements

Dorling Kindersley would like to thank Vanessa Bird for indexing, Kathy Steer for proofreading, and Adam Brackenbury for colour repro work.

Editorial Manager Ruth O'Rourke
Senior Editor Alastair Laing
Senior Designer Barbara Zuniga
DTP & Design Coordinator Heather Blagden
Production Editor David Almond
Senior Production Controller Stephanie McConnell
Jacket Co-ordinator Emily Cannings
Art Director Maxine Pedliham
Publishing Director Katie Cowan

Editorial Rosanna Fairhead
Design Vicky Read
Photography Rachel Warne
Illustration Jessica Ip

First published in Great Britain in 2024 by
Dorling Kindersley Limited
DK, One Embassy Gardens, 8 Viaduct Gardens,
London, SW11 7BW

The authorised representative in the EEA is
Dorling Kindersley Verlag GmbH. Arnulfstr. 124,
80636 Munich, Germany

A CIP catalogue record for this book
is available from the British Library.
ISBN: 978-0-2416-6711-8

Printed and bound in China

www.dk.com

This book was made with Forest Stewardship Council™ certified paper – one small step in DK's commitment to a sustainable future. Learn more at **www.dk.com/uk/information/sustainability**

About the Author

Mitch McCulloch, The Seed Hunter, is a London-born former chef who now collects, cultivates, and champions some of the world's rarest heirloom food crops.

After years of service to the stove, Mitch hung up his apron in pursuit of a more natural lifestyle, and on discovering the world of heritage crops, he developed a passion for their preservation and promotion. He began documenting his collection online and engaging with vegetable growers, seed-savers, and farmers across the globe.

As part of his seed-hunting quest, Mitch enjoys travelling to new destinations around the world to visit small-scale farmers and seed-savers. He has been working with Baker Creek Heirloom Seeds in Missouri to ensure that his seed discoveries are banked and the supply increased.

Mitch is an avid no-dig grower and has appeared on BBC *Gardeners' World*, showcasing his diverse garden. He has written articles for the Royal Society for the Protection of Birds and the Bumblebee Conservation Trust, and is a course leader for the charity and nature skills platform Earthed.

@mitch_grows